THE BRECKER B
Funky Sea, Funky Blue

Ken Trethewey

Jazz-Fusion Books

First published 15 January 2014 by:

*Jazz-Fusion Books
Gravesend Cottage
Torpoint
Cornwall PL11 2LX
United Kingdom
ISBN: 978-0-9560083-4-3
©2014 Ken Trethewey*

For Chris, Joe and Helen, my musical family,
who love music as much as I do;
and
For session musicians everywhere,
who make the stars shine more brightly.

Other publications by Ken Trethewey in the Jazz-Fusion Series:
John McLaughlin: The Emerald Beyond (2008, 2013)
Pat Metheny: The Way Up is White (2008, 2012)
Jazz-Fusion: Blue Notes and Purple Haze (2009)
Herbie Hancock: Blue Chip Keyboardist (2010)
Miles Davis: Dark Prince (2011)
Weather Report: Electric Red (2012)

Contents

THE BRECKER BROTHERS: 1
Funky Sea, Funky Blue 1
Contents 5
Foreword 11
Randy and Michael Brecker: The Brecker Brothers 15
To Where It's At: NYC 16
Blood Sweat & Tears 21
In His Brother's Footsteps 23
Randy Brecker: *Score* – 1969 (****) 24
Dreams: *Dreams* – 1970 (***) 28
Dreams: *Imagine My Surprise* – 1971 (***) 30
White Elephant: *White Elephant* – 1972; Re-released as Mike Mainieri & Friends:
White Elephant Vol. 1 and *Vol. 2* – 1994 (***) 32
Electrickery 34
Hal Galper: *Wild Bird* – 1971 (***) 35
Hal Galper: *The Guerrilla Band* – 1972 (****) 37
Horace Silver: *The Pursuit of the 27th Man* – 1972 (***) 38
Larry Coryell: Introducing the Eleventh House – 1974 (***) 39
Billy Cobham 41
Billy Cobham: *Spectrum* – 1973 (***) 42
Billy Cobham: *Crosswinds* – 1974 (****) 43
Billy Cobham: *Total Eclipse* – 1974 (****) 44
Billy Cobham: *A Funky Thide of Sings* – 1975 (***) 45
Billy Cobham: *Shabazz* – 1975 (***) 47
Other Projects In The Early 1970s 48
George Clinton's Parliament 49
Clive Davis, Steve Backer and Arista Records 51
The Brecker Brothers: *The Brecker Brothers* – 1975 (****) 54
7th Avenue South 60
The Brecker Brothers Band: *Back To Back* – 1976 (***) 62
The Brecker Brothers: *Don't Stop the Music* – 1977 (***) 64

The Brecker Brothers: *Heavy Metal Bebop* – 1978 (****) 67
The Brecker Brothers: *Détente* – 1980 (****) 68
The Brecker Brothers: *Straphangin'* – 1981 (*****) 71
Warren Bernhardt, Michael Brecker, Randy Brecker, Mike Mainieri: *Blue Montreux* and *Blue Montreux II* – 1978 (****) 75
Jaco Pastorius: *Jaco Pastorius* – 1976 (*****) 78
Joni Mitchell: *Shadows And Light* – 1980 (*****) 79
Jaco Pastorius: *Word Of Mouth* – 1981 (****) 80
Jaco Pastorius: *The Birthday Concert* – rec. 1981, rel. 1996 (****) 82
Jaco Pastorius: *Invitation* – 1983 (****); 85
Jaco Pastorius Big Band: *Twins I & II* - rel. 1999 (****) 85
Decline and Fall 85
Steps: *Smokin' in the Pit* – 1999 (rec. 1980) (*****) 86
Steps: *Step by Step* – 2000, rec. 1980 (***) 90
Steps: *Paradox* – 2000, rec. 1981 (**) 91
Steps Ahead: *Steps Ahead* – 1983 (***) 92
The Electronic Wind Instrument (EWI) 94
Steps Ahead: *Modern Times* - 1984 (***) 95
Steps Ahead: *Magnetic* – 1986 (****) 98
Steps Ahead: *Live in Tokyo* – 1986 (**) 100
Randy Brecker: *Amanda* – 1985 (***) 101
Randy Brecker: *In The Idiom* – 1987 (***) 103
Michael Brecker: *Michael Brecker* - 1987 (*****) 104
Michael Brecker: *Don't Try This at Home* – 1988 (****) 110
Randy Brecker: *Live At Sweet Basil* – 1989 (****) 114
Paul Simon: *The Rhythm Of The Saints* – 1990 (****) 116
Randy Brecker: *Toe To Toe* – 1990 (****) 117
Michael Brecker: *Now You See It...(Now You Don't)* – 1992 (****) 119
The Brecker Brothers: *Return of the Brecker Brothers* - 1992 (*****) 123
The Brecker Brothers: The Return of the Brecker Brothers Live in Spain 1992 [DVD] – 1994 (*****) 128
The Brecker Brothers: *Out of the Loop* – 1994 (*****) 130
Don Grolnick Group: *The London Concert* – rec. 1995; rel 2000 (***) 134

Brecker Brothers: *Live in Tokyo U-Port Hall*, 1995 [DVD] – rec. 1995; rel. 2010 (***) 135
Randy Brecker: *Into the Sun* – 1995 (***) 136
Michael Brecker: *Tales From the Hudson* – 1996 (****) 139
Michael Brecker: *Two Blocks From the Edge* – 1998 (****) 141
Michael Brecker: *Time is Of the Essence* – 1999 (****) 144
Bob Berg, Randy Brecker, Dennis Chambers, Joey DeFrancesco: *The JazzTimes Superband* – 2000 (****) 149
Randy Brecker: *Hangin' In The City* – 2001 (****) 151
Michael Brecker: *Nearness of You* – The Ballad Book – 2001 (***) 154
Herbie Hancock / Michael Brecker / Roy Hargrove: *Directions in Music* – 2002 (*****) 155
Charlie Haden with Michael Brecker: *American Dreams* – 2002 (*****) 158
Michael Brecker Quindectet: *Wide Angles* – 2003 (*****) 160
Randy Brecker: *34th N Lex* – 2003 (****) 164
Bill Evans / Randy Brecker: *Soulbop Band Live* – 2004 (****) 167
Randy Brecker with Michael Brecker: *Some Skunk Funk* – 2005 (****) 170
Michael Brecker: *Pilgrimage* – 2007 (****) 173
Randy Brecker: *Randy in Brasil* – 2008 (*****) 177
Randy Brecker: Nostalgic Journey: Tykocin Jazz Suite – 2009 (****) 180
Randy Brecker: Jamey Abersold's Play Along Jazz, Volume 126 – 2009 (****) 181
Randy Brecker With DR Big Band: *The Jazz Ballad Song Book* – 2011 (****) 181
Randy Brecker: The Brecker Brothers Band Reunion – 2013 (****) 181
Summaries and Analysis 186
1. The Brecker Brothers Band 186
2. Albums As Leaders 188
3. Albums As Sidemen 189
4. Work As Session Musicians 190
Concluding Remarks 193
Appendix: George Whitty Discusses Working With The Brecker Brothers 201
References 207
Acknowledgements 210
Grammy Awards 211
Discography 212
CDs by The Brecker Brothers: Randy and Michael Brecker as leaders 212

DVDs by The Brecker Brothers 216
Compilations of Previously Released Material (prm) by The Brecker Brothers 216
Unofficial Releases of Brecker Brothers Material 217
CDs by Randy Brecker as leader 218
DVDs by Randy Brecker 222
CDs by Michael Brecker as leader 223
DVDs by Michael Brecker 225
Unofficial Releases of Michael Brecker Material 226
CDs and DVDs with Randy and/or Michael Brecker as sidemen (in approximate order of recording). 226
Randy Brecker Discography (excluding albums of previously released material) 247
Michael Brecker Discography (excluding albums of previously released material) 259
Albums on which both Randy and Michael Brecker appear (excluding albums of previously released material) 269
Single Releases by The Brecker Brothers 274
Index 276

The Brecker Brothers, at the North Sea Jazz Festival, 10 July 1992. (Photo: Louis Gerrits)

Foreword

Michael Brecker was the kind of guy many men of my age would have loved to be. Tall, lean and rangy, he was shockingly handsome and awesomely talented. Like him, I too played the saxophone. I had chosen the instrument well before I had heard Michael's name, and before I really knew what jazz-fusion was. Once I had seen Mike play, I thought he was the coolest dude on the planet. An example of what I mean is available in the Steps Ahead DVD, *Copenhagen Live* (2007). [1] In December 1979, Michael joined a band called Steps, formed by Mike Mainieri. Alongside him were Don Grolnick, Eddie Gomez and Steve Gadd. By 1983, the band had evolved into Steps Ahead that made a film and an album. This was the band's first disc in this incarnation, having evolved out of the original 1980 group, Steps. Leader Mainieri was joined by Peter Erskine (drums, fresh out of Weather Report), Eddie Gomez (bass and long-time sideman with Chick Corea), Eliane Elias (piano, Brazilian 23-year-old making her debut, and displaying on her left hand the rock given her by fiancée, Randy Brecker). Lastly, of course, there was *the man*. Here is an hour-long performance of continuous delights, not least of which is the sheer pleasure of watching Michael Brecker at work.

I have never been interested in the wildly exaggerated stage antics of rock stars. I once watched alto saxophone player Charles MacPherson in the Mingus Band when I was 21. He barely moved on stage, but oh boy, did he play! Watching Michael Brecker play in *Copenhagen Live* is similar. One of the world's greatest blowers moves around the stage with minimum impact. When he is watching, he sits quietly, soaking up the atmosphere and context of his friends' work. When he plays, he stands at the microphone and simply blows and blows, his dark eyes mostly closed, his fingers working effortlessly to find the countless permutations of key presses he needs to keep his brain satisfied. No annoying mannerisms are on display from this stylishly dressed guy as he creates majestic music with no other *aide-mémoire* than the live cues of his fellow players. Incredibly, within twenty-five years this dark-haired, lithe, undemonstrative superhuman would have passed away, an irreplaceable loss to the world of music.

There must be many saxophone players, who, like me, adored Michael's music, but had arrived at it through hearing his wonderful contributions as invited guest and session musician on many of the most famous releases during the period of the 1980s when the Brecker Brothers band was in hiatus. The fact that Michael had a brother who was equally talented on trumpet passed me by for a while. But to study only what Mike was playing was like playing our saxophones with one hand, and it led to a serious misapprehension of what our hero was really about. The truth is that Randy and Michael Brecker are two of the most talented musicians we have been fortunate to hear. Many would argue that Randy Brecker is a better trumpeter than Miles Davis. Randy's ability with trumpet and flugelhorn is on a par with the great virtuosos of the instrument such as Dizzy Gillespie and Clifford Brown. Large numbers of people have always loved Miles's fragile sound, but his ability to touch hearts and influence younger musicians was about far more than simply playing the trumpet. When you listen carefully to Randy Brecker's music, you realise how astonishingly good he is. His purity of tone, his smoothness at speed, his occasional incandescent delivery, his capacity for invention, not to mention a capacity for some of the most refreshingly different musical compositions and harmonies: all these are probably unparalleled across a broader spectrum of music than any musician has ever achieved. As if that were not enough, more than any other musician, he has extended the use of electronics in trumpet playing. If proof were needed of Randy Brecker's unique achievements, readers should inspect his discography at the end of this book where it is clear that he has a presence on at least 1,200 albums from most of the stars of many genres. It would be easy to argue that Randy's immense contributions to jazz outshine even those of his brother. A trumpeter of immense stature who supports other musicians, Randy has pursued a remarkably busy career in bands of his own too, so this book will outline as much of his work as space allows. Randy has been not just the world's most demanded session musician on trumpet, but is one of the megastars of jazz too.

In the context of my assertion that Randy is certainly the greatest trumpeter of his generation, the following words attract a sense of impossibility, of me suffering from an infection of hyperbole. Nevertheless, it is largely irrefutable that Michael Brecker was the greatest tenor saxophone player of his generation. Much of what I have said about Randy is applicable to Michael too. From an early age, influenced by John Coltrane, he developed the deep-seated desire to play the saxophone as well as anyone possibly could. He set about achieving his goal with a single-minded approach and dedication that was clear to everyone who knew him. Just over three years younger than Randy, and with the same insatiable desire to become a top musician, it was natural that their musical paths would be closely matched. And so it was that the phrase, 'The Brecker Brothers,' would make a bigger impact on public awareness than the names of the brothers themselves.

There is a perception in the world of art and to some extent music, that to be a truly great artist you must sacrifice everything on the altar of purity. No compromise is allowed. You must live in poverty, suffer physical and emotional damage, and die at an early age, to become a candidate for true greatness. Curiously, it is OK to fail in all other aspects of life, but you must not prostitute yourself in any way to commercial interests. In music, Charlie Parker and John Coltrane at once come to mind.

During this large work, which necessarily encompasses the enormous careers of not one but two of the greatest jazz men in history, I wanted also to focus on the role of session musicians, to make sure that, in the future, musicians receive the recognition they deserve. I have therefore placed a stronger emphasis on those musicians who have stood alongside Michael and Randy than I might normally have done. It is a backhanded compliment to describe someone as a great session musician because it implies that the person is not quite good enough to be a star. The truth is that stars would not be what they are without session musicians. It is an inconvenient truth that, in all areas of life, some team members frequently eclipse the team leader.

My own favourite example of arrival on the public stage is when, during the recording of his last studio album, *LA Is My Lady* (1984), Frank Sinatra changed the lyrics of the classic tune, *Mack The Knife*, to assert that he was being excellently backed by "The Brecker Brothers." As an act of career recognition, that would do for me! No session musician could ask for more.

This book is the seventh in my series of books about jazz-fusion. The description of Randy and Michael's work in that genre alone would have been lengthy. However, it is impossible to ignore the interwoven strands of straightahead jazz. Along with musicians like Pat Metheny, Herbie Hancock, Wayne Shorter, and others, Randy and Michael have refused to be pigeonholed. They became children of mother jazz, but were lucky enough to be allowed to experiment in the developing world of fusion.

There have been other examples of successful brother-partnerships in jazz, most notably Nat and Julian (Cannonball) Adderley, Percy, Jimmy and Tootie Heath, and the three Jones brothers – Thad, Hank and Elvin. However, my judgement is that Randy and Michael Brecker were the most successful brother-partnership in the history of jazz. This book will explain why.

For those readers unfamiliar with the form of my books, I should explain that they are not autobiographies, but commentaries about recorded works. My aim is to describe the careers of my subjects, using material that is readily available to all readers. I would hope that my readers will be sufficiently interested to buy at least some of the recordings described, and to read this as they listen. I am keen to promote jazz, a subject that I believe is quite mysterious to many people these days, so this book should not only inform, but also educate readers about the mysteries, as well as the wonders of this music and the incredibly talented people who create it.

I understand that mere expression of opinions is anathema to some readers, but, besides being a musician myself, I have a lifetime of analytical experience through my work as a scientist and engineer. Therefore, I include a certain amount of analysis and explanation to support my opinions. Although that is primarily concerned with CDs, I also include some discussion of DVDs. The sequence is not always strictly chronological, because of occasional large discrepancies in the dates of recording and publication. I have tried to make the sequence logical, rather than follow some immutable rule.

As to content, well, there is so much I could have included, but did not. I have considered two complex careers in this way:

- Core albums in which either Randy or Michael or both have acted as leaders;
- Albums in which either Randy or Michael have performed as members of an identifiable band, i.e. as sidemen;
- Albums in which either Randy or Michael have made a guest appearance in one or more tracks, i.e. as session musicians.

I have included commentary about all of the core albums, but only a selection of the sidemen albums. With a few exceptions, I have not written about albums in which they were session musicians. I made exceptions in the cases of Billy Cobham and Jaco Pastorius, for I felt that these parts of the story were both significant and interesting.

I have made every effort to compile a complete discography for Randy and Michael, but I have omitted so-called "compilation" albums in which material has been previously released. I would strongly encourage readers to use this book as a guide to the magnificent careers of these two men and to study the discography to widen their appreciation of just how extensive have been the careers of Randy and Michael Brecker.

In the early stages of my project I was fortunate enough to obtain Randy's support, and I want to express my sincere gratitude to him for his positive and friendly response.

Randy and Michael Brecker: The Brecker Brothers

If you grew up watching American movies, as most of us did, you will know what I mean. Imagine an affluent, leafy suburb of Middle America. A variety of detached dwellings, some wooden, some brick-built, many shapes and designs. Chimneys that extract the smoke from cosy fires in winter. Expansive green lawns that, according to Joni Mitchell, hiss in summer; a comfortably-off middle class white family – mom's a great cook, dad wears a suit to the office, three kids, junior proms, high school, college - you know what I mean.

The family I'm thinking of, however, is not exactly run-of-the-mill. Dad is a lawyer, but he's a serious musician too. According to his youngest son, he sues by day and swings by night. The musical muse is strong throughout the whole family. When he's not at work, Dad plays lots of jazz records - many by trumpeters like Miles Davis, Dizzy Gillespie, and especially Clifford Brown. In particular, Brown has a strong presence in the Philadelphia area, and is gigging there in 1956 when, to everyone's horror, he is killed in a car accident as he leaves the gig. Robert's eldest son hears trumpet players that impress him, and, aged about eight or nine, the kid borrows a trumpet from school. Soon he is good enough for Mom and Dad to pay for him to take lessons from a professional trumpeter in the Philadelphia Orchestra. In his mid-teens he is working with local saxophone player, Billy Root. Later, at Indiana University, he plays with Booker T. Jones, who soon becomes famous with his band, the MGs. [2]

Now it is 1966. Bob and Ticky (from Tecosky) Brecker's eldest son, Randal Edward (born on 27 November 1945), is due to graduate from Indiana University. The University Jazz Ensemble in which he plays has just won a competition at the *Notre Dame Jazz Festival*, judged by bandleader, Clark Terry. Part of the prize is the opportunity to go to Asia and the Middle East on a State Department sponsored tour. Randal doesn't return.

While in Beirut, he sees an advertisement in *Down Beat* magazine promoting the *First International Jazz Competition* in Vienna, with judges such as Cannonball Adderley, and Joe Zawinul. Several of Randy's fellow band members choose to go too. They are all kids aged 17-20: George Mraz, Jan Hammer, Miroslav Vitous, Eddie Daniels - all become close friends. In the final of the trumpet competition, Franco Ambrosetti edges Randy into second place by the merest tenth of a mark.

While his colleagues at home are graduating, Randy experiences a stream of musical adventures, of which one, in particular, impresses him. Mel Lewis had just recorded his first record with Thad Jones, and wants to take advantage of the opportunity to play the music to Cannonball Adderley in a hotel room in Vienna. So Randy finds himself in that hotel room with Lewis and Cannonball. At last, they persuade him to return to New York City. He is just one semester short of finishing his music degree and he registers at New York University, but inevitably, the demands of the busy music scene and its unusual working hours are incompatible with student life. He is now, *de facto*, a professional musician, and, thanks to a meeting with the judge of the school music competition, he gets a job with the Clark Terry Big Band.

Meanwhile, Robert and Ticky's younger son, Michael (born on 29 March 1949), has become extremely good on the saxophone. One night over dinner in the summer of 1966, Robert Brecker tells a house guest, a young guitarist called Larry Coryell, that Michael would eventually play tenor better than just about anybody. "And he was right …" wrote Coryell, many years later. [3] Michael graduates from Cheltenham High School in 1967. A great admirer of his older brother, he too chooses to attend Indiana University the following year. He lives for a year at Wilkie Quad, a part of the Indiana University campus in Bloomington, two states away to the west. Spanish is his chosen subject, but it seems to hold little attraction compared to the optional music classes he has chosen. Indeed, Mike is so extravagantly talented that the discipline of learning to read music eludes him at first. He becomes friends with a young trumpet player called Randy Sandke, who remembers that Mike was not too good at sight-reading music. [4] Curiously, this perceived deficiency in his musical ability means that he is selected only for the University's second band, a decision the University will surely never live down!

He makes up for this deficiency by obsessive, extensive practice. To assist in their practice sessions, Mike and another friend, Steve Grossman, compete to transcribe the latest records by John Coltrane. Predictably, Spanish studies get in the way, so in 1968 he leaves the University to play full-time in bands. After a spell in Chicago, where Mike's encounters with drugs and law enforcement are in danger of getting him into serious trouble, he moves to New York to join his brother in late 1968 / early 1969.

To Where It's At: NYC

The Beatles tune, *I Want To Hold Your Hand,* shot to #1 in the US Charts in January 1964 as Randy was returning to the second semester of his first year at the University of Indiana. It heralded the British Invasion of the American music scene. Then, in August 1964, during the Beatles' second visit to the USA, Bob Dylan, who had built a career as a new-age folk singer, was influenced enough by the Beatles to meet them in a New York hotel. Thereafter, possibly due to the marijuana that Dylan had introduced them to, the Beatles' song writing seemed to take on a new creativity. Dylan's style began to change too. He was now influenced by experiments with folk-rock conducted by his friend, blues singer, John Hammond, and soon he hired Robbie Robertson, Levon Helm and Garth Hudson who were in a band called The Hawks, plus Rick Danko and Richard Manuel, for a new electric backing group later called The Band.

Dylan's album *Bringing It All Back Home* (March 1965) announced to the world that he had 'gone electric'. Many of the fans that had previously enjoyed his freestyle acoustic folk ballads were upset.

Some big cities are all about cars. Los Angeles is about cars. You drive everywhere. You need to. In New York, however, you can walk most places. You want to. I once spent a whole week walking the streets of Manhattan. The minute I arrived there I belonged. Thanks to TV and movies, I'd seen it all before; the signage, the cops' uniforms, the big yellow taxis, and the subway trains. Everything was so familiar that I felt I owned it. I felt like I was related to the Kennedys and the Rockefellers. I constantly looked up, and felt small. Native New Yorkers don't look up. They've learnt. You can be whatever you want to be. No one cares. In New York, there are no surprises, yet everything is marvellous. Anything can and does happen on the streets of New York. Nothing is extraordinary. Nothing is right, nothing wrong. It's not a capital, not a state capital, not a national capital, yet in many ways it's the capital of the world. In the jazz way, that is.

Music is a pathway, a short cut through the established system. Musicians are dreamers. They dream of becoming stars, of making music that will change the world. Whichever part of the world a jazz musician comes from, he soon knows he must leave home to make his fortune. As Dorothy discovered, the yellow brick road leads only to one place – the muso's version of the Emerald City. The jazz musician's dream can be fulfilled only in New York. Through music you really can change the world.

New York is full of people who have run away from home, musical émigrés. They wouldn't be anywhere else. They need the place more than their next fix. They need to be in the company of other musicians of similar mind. They need to be seen, not by those who will buy their records (for such people exist everywhere), but by those who will hire them, and above all, by those who will allow them to make records. Musicians need to be seen by other musicians who will help them to make reputations. Your reputation precedes you. The stars will call you by virtue of your reputation. You need to become a hot property so that when a regular band member falls sick or is double booked, you are there to receive the phone call, ready to fill his place. There is no personal life, only the next gig.

First things first. Find a place to crash. Who do you know? Walk the streets to investigate anything that looks like a possible venue. Go to a club every night and take your instrument. Try to get into the club for free. Don't drink too much, it's too expensive. Stay up late. Forget sleep; sleep only when you can no longer stand. Prolong your wakefulness by whatever means possible: junk food, another cigarette, just one more drink. And if you have to indulge in *that* kind of activity, make sure you know where the next one is coming from.

Talk to the musicians when they have stopped playing. Try to befriend them. Ask to sit in. Try to find out where gigs are happening, where the best muso-haunts are located. Network. During the waking hours, join friends, woodshed, try stuff. Then more clubs, more bars, shady men, false promises, dishonesty, strippers, gays. Barely legal, sometimes you're on the thin edge of the law.

At last you get a gig. Turn up on time, every time. Or else...

Randy arrived in New York sometime in late 1966. The city was on fire with musical experimentation. Rock bands were already starting to use horns as well as electric guitars. Now was the time for musicians with jazz backgrounds to start experimenting with rock techniques. Randy visited as many clubs as he could, sitting-in wherever he was allowed. This, of course, was a feature of the way jazz musicians worked. Their facility with improvisation allowed them - with no rehearsal - to join in spontaneously with bands. Such opportunities were the way they could show off their skills, and get invitations to join other bands. Musicians in rock bands, because of their generally lower levels of musical abilities, needed more pre-planning and rehearsals before new musicians could be admitted into their bands.

Randy's immense natural talent complemented his already impressive technical ability, and quickly got him work in the conventional jazz environment. To earn a living he played in strip clubs, and other dubious establishments, such as the *Metropole* on Broadway, which he thought was fine because he learned a lot of R&B tunes there.

One of his first employers was Clark Terry. He had worked in Duke Ellington's band during the 1950s and was a big influence on the young musician. It was a big band environment that Randy knew well. "... big bands were very prevalent in New York, not only working bands but rehearsal bands. It was a good way to read new music and meet a lot of musicians." [5]

At the end of 1967, Randy was playing regularly with Duke Pearson's Big Band. Pearson was already making records in smaller group settings and was now ready to try a large band format. Recordings with Randy Brecker in the band were made in December 1967 and December 1968, and are preserved on a Blue Note release called *Introducing Duke Pearson's Big Band* (1968). It is Randy's earliest appearance on record. (A 1998 edition CD contains these tracks plus other bonus tracks.)

So that was his bread and butter; the jam came elsewhere. In his off-duty networking around the New York clubs, Randy was soon mixing with musicians like Warren Bernhardt (piano / keyboard), Mike Mainieri (vibes), Donald MacDonald (drums), Joe Beck (guitar), Bob Moses (drums) and an old friend, Larry Coryell (guitar). Typically the music involved rock rhythms, blends of electric guitars with wind instruments, and vocals, unlike jazz music, which was mostly instrumental. Sometimes, the music included spontaneous improvisations with no pre-planning. In the jazz of the mid-1960s, it was extremely fashionable to play such music, inspired by the likes of Ornette Coleman and John Coltrane. At first, these kinds of sessions were usually experimental and unpaid. But something big could always come out of it.

Baritone sax player, Ronnie Cuber (b1941, Brooklyn NY) was on the scene at this time. He didn't much want to join the experimentalists, but was still excited by what was going on. "Well, my vision was always straight-ahead jazz. And to be included in what was going on, and potential money-making projects, I didn't have too much of a resentment. [laughs] It was like, hey, this could turn into something. I mean, guys like Randy, Michael, Barry Rogers..." [6]

Ronnie described the first time he saw Randy playing. "I was walking by the *Metropole* Cafe, the *Metropole* used to be on 49th St and 7th Ave and the doors were wide open. You could hear bands while you were standing on the sidewalk and you could actually see them from the sidewalk and not have to walk in and buy a drink. But you know how things go when clubs are starting to move to strip bars and topless, so in the afternoon, one matinee, I saw this trumpet player, and he was playing for some kind of a... it was like a... it turned into a bar where you could have a live band and see girls dancing to the music, and I said Wow! this trumpet player sounds pretty damn good, and slowly but surely we met somewhere on the scene. [6]

Larry Coryell (b1943, Galveston TX) arrived in New York in September 1965, only a few months in advance of Randy Brecker. A 22-year old electric guitarist, he represented the new generation of musicians born into the heart of cultural change. Larry and Randy were already friends. Randy told me, "I met him before I came to New York because he was such a big influence on me. In 1964, I spent the summer in Seattle. I had a girlfriend there from College and I took some courses from the University of Washington, creative writing courses, and Larry was living there and I played with him on a regular basis. He was just a great guitarist. He had a great organ trio, and I'd go play all the time, and it was a great, really wonderful, musical summer. He moved to New York shortly before I did, so we re-met there and he had a wonderful band." [5]

Larry's recollection is told in his autobiography. "In 1964 or 65, Randy Brecker came out to the University of Washington for a summer program. We met and hung out, and one afternoon at the *Penthouse* jam session he walked on stage with his trumpet. They called *Nardis* and my mind was blown - somebody my age playing that well. Randy later told me he'd never played that tune before." [7]

Larry Coryell made his recording debut on Chico Hamilton's album *The Dealer* (1966), recorded in September of that year, but record companies were restrictive in what kinds of music they would allow, and this appearance is rather academic compared to other live goings-on. Anything and everything was possible, and an important catalyst was the availability of drugs – not just alcohol, but marijuana and LSD. Musicians were just as interested in John Coltrane as they were in the Beatles or Dylan, but their adventures with hallucinatory drugs made the extraordinary and the imaginary into possibilities, if not realities. So the combination of rock and jazz was an obvious thing to do. And besides, the music was the image: it became important to dispense with smartly cut suits and short hair that represented the establishment. The new uniform was casual dress and long hair.

All this became common in early 1967 when Coryell joined Gary Burton's band for a season of quartet gigs around the New York area. From these nights came the album *Duster* (1967), often touted as an indicator of the progress of jazz-rock fusion. Steve Swallow's *General Mojo's Well Laid Plan* shows only a slight indication thanks to Coryell's lead on electric guitar, but apart form a gentle backbeat, it is hardly rock music. But the evidence from records is often misleading. Under direction from their sponsors, bands were often unable to present music on record that was representative of what they did live.

Larry Coryell's band, The Free Spirits, recorded a collection of songs that was reportedly trying "to imagine how George Harrison would have played Coltrane." Sales of the record, *Out of Sight and Sound* (1967), were poor, so its existence could not have influenced the wider world of music. However, it does record some of the changes occurring in New York at the time. The tracks were limited to around three minutes because of the demands of the music company who were looking for saleable material in the popular format. They also included the kind of dreadful vocals that characterised early jazz-rock fusion.

For Randy, Larry Coryell was the real creator of jazz-fusion. "He really was - for want of a better word - the 'Godfather of Fusion'. He was really the first guy. I don't think he gets enough credit either. When he moved to New York he set the whole town on fire... He had the blues thing from growing up in Texas, he was real familiar with the idiom, and he changed the direction of a lot of the music that was happening in New York, singlehandedly. He had a group called The Free Spirits with Bob Moses, Jim Pepper, and they were probably, literally the first jazz-rock band. It was a really exciting time because jazz musicians were listening closely to the rock musicians. The Beatles, I think, had a big influence because the tunes were so musical. Really, you couldn't deny the fact that this was real music. Even the greatest jazz connoisseur had to admit that there was something happening to rock and pop music. It was really exciting so you found really great musicians trying to add new things to the lexicon." [5]

I wanted to know if Randy thought free jazz had biased the output. "Well not quite, but that was in there too. There was a free element in Larry's first band in fact, a lot of the guys embraced the *avant-garde*, and anyway, when you look at Hendrix, he was in there too, obviously, playing, and all the sound effects, so there was a deep connection there too. A lot of that didn't sell though, I mean you had to weed it out, but it was part of the process. All the stuff was going on at the same time." [5]

Larry described his jazz-rock technique in his book. "My challenge back in 1966-67 was... to find a concept that would infuse the fresh, contemporary sounds of rock and pop with the jazz tradition. The partial answer for this would come from the *avant-garde* – players like Albert Ayler, and Coltrane's disciples Pharoah Sanders and Archie Shepp. ...I wasn't going to settle for simple variations on the pentatonic. Rather, I would play over a rock beat, lines that sounded more or less like jazz guitar and implied a more chromatic sound to the phrases." [8]

Many observers agree with Randy and believe that Coryell has not had the recognition he deserves in the formulation of jazz-rock. This is undoubtedly because of the discrepancy between what he was doing live in New York between 1965 and 1970, and what appears on record. (It is also an opinion often expressed by those who were unfamiliar with what was going on in the UK.)

Ginell explains it thus: "Unfortunately, a lot of his [Coryell's] most crucial electric work from the '60s and '70s is missing on CD, tied up by the erratic reissue schemes ... and by jazz-rock's myopically low level of status in the CD era." [9]

Blood Sweat & Tears

Randy and Larry would play intermittently over the next few years, but not formally join forces until 1973 in Larry's band, Eleventh House. However, there was much more to happen yet. In between the bread-winning conventional jazz gigs, they would hang out wherever the latest 'happenings' showed up. Their constant networking and immediately recognisable potential as brilliant instrumentalists paid off. Randy got a job with Al Kooper's new band, Blood Sweat & Tears, formed in 1967. Incredibly, in 1965, Kooper had gatecrashed a Dylan recording session, and then been invited to play a Hammond organ solo! That turned out to be apocryphal for Dylan fans at the start of his electric period. Kooper soon afterwards joined the band, Blues Project, before creating BS&T. Kooper himself said that a source of inspiration for the BS&T project was the #1 hit, *Kind Of A Drag* by The Buckinghams. This was music identified as brass-rock, in which the traditional format of rock bands (electric guitars, bass and drums) was supplemented by a section of trumpets, trombones, and saxophones. [10]

The first BS&T sessions took place in September 1967. A band consisting of Kooper (keyboards), Steve Katz (guitar), Bobby Colomby (drums) and Jim

Fielder (bass) opened the show for Moby Grape at the *Café Au Go-Go* in NYC. However, the band only took on its full-formed fusion style when joined soon afterwards by horn players Fred Lipsius (saxophone), Randy Brecker, Jerry Weiss (trumpet) and Dick Halligan (trombone). The final line-up debuted at the *Café Au Go Go* on 17–19 November, 1967, and then moved to *The Scene* the following week. Recording sessions for tracks that would become *Child Is The Father To The Man* (1968) took place from 11 November to 20 December 1967. The album was released by Columbia on 21 February 1968. It was a minor hit in the Billboard pop album charts where it reach #47. The album did also benefit from a significant transition that took place amongst the record-buying public in 1968, when a change of emphasis from singles to albums took place. Nevertheless, because of its wide distribution, the record's influence was great in the world beyond NYC, and is the reason why many observers incorrectly attribute the creation of jazz-rock fusion to BS&T. Its impact was almost entirely due to Kooper's creativity, a factor that was largely lost on succeeding albums because Kooper departed from the band after just one album; most opinions concur that the band's best album was the first one.

Coincidentally, Randy left BS&T at the same time to play with Horace Silver, but there was no correlation with the split that drove Kooper out. Kooper had been unhappy about the band's desire to hire David Clayton-Thomas, who would potentially compete with Al for the lead vocals. Meanwhile, Randy was already negotiating with Horace Silver. The jazzer's musical reasoning prevailed. Brecker: "Well that [BS&T] was a great band but I didn't get to solo much. I played on one tune. That was sad I think. A lot of the guys in the band were really jazz musicians first, too, and they were really great players, Freddy Lipsius, Bobby Colomby… But when Horace called, I really wanted to take that gig. It was a quintet and I could play to my heart's content. So I left Blood Sweat & Tears in early '68 to join Horace." [5]

The experience had shown Randy a clear difference between jazz and rock: "As a jazz musician, you feel like yourself; as a rock musician, you feel like a star." [11] He was clearly happier with his own company. At the final band meeting, his last words to BS&T as he left the room were, "You'll never make it without Al!" [12]

There was a downside too. Interviewed by Michael Davis, Randy told how he was earning $100 per week with BS&T, but was offered $250 per week with Horace. It seemed like a good deal. However, with Horace, he only worked on average two weeks a month, and had to pay tax and hotel bills from the proceeds. The final sting in the tail was that, at the time of the split, BS&T were offering equal shares for band members, and the band's second record went on to sell eleven million copies. "Everything is for a reason," Randy said philosophically. [12]

In His Brother's Footsteps

Michael Brecker was consigned to love jazz from birth. How could he not? His dad was an active jazz musician and his house bore a close resemblance to a music venue, with jazz being constantly played live or on record. Mike's brother had decided to follow his father's interest in the trumpet by borrowing an instrument from school when in the third grade; his older sister was also learning to play the piano. By the time it was Michael's turn, there were only clarinets left at school, so his choice was made for him. Soon there was a family band. Randy: "Both Mike and I tripled on vibes and drums - Mike was really a great drummer all his life. Our sister, Emmy, played bass; Dad played piano."

Once Michael had started playing clarinet, he was soon taking lessons from Leon Lester, principal clarinettist in the Philadelphia Orchestra. But something was not quite as satisfying about the clarinet as he felt it should be; clarinet was not a prominent instrument in jazz groups. So, while at Cheltenham High, he switched to sax after hearing Cannonball Adderley's album *Jazz Workshop Revisited*. "When I heard Cannonball, that was it!" he told interviewer John Robert Brown. "I started trying to learn his solos from records. Those were some hard solos to learn. But it was a good way for me to begin to learn the language of jazz."

"I got into King Curtis and Junior Walker, those schools, at the same time I was listening to Trane and other jazz. So I feel like I really grew up with both. More and more these days, you hear people borrowing from all sorts of areas. I've always wanted to somehow come up with a style where everything sounded integrated, without sounding like jumping from one thing to another, or just throwing things in haphazardly. But it takes time, it takes a lot of playing." [13]

His life changed the day he heard John Coltrane. "If it wasn't for John Coltrane there would be no me. He literally catapulted me into music." [14]

Whilst they lived under the same roof, Michael and Randy used to jam together a lot in the bathroom. They loved the acoustics, the reverb was exciting, and the hours they spent together gave them a special knowledge of each other's playing that can only be achieved by such a close relationship. Curiously, nursery rhymes were often the choice of material. They worked as step-off points, and it was from these simple lines that they learned to improvise together, driving the music further and further away from the original starting point. Randy said that *Pop Goes the Weasel* on his album *Score* (1969) was included with these happy and extremely beneficial hours in mind.

At last, Michael went a step farther than his brother when he won the award for best tenor sax player at the 1968 *Notre Dame Jazz Festival*. [11] Then he and his mates threw a spanner in the works. "In the finals at Notre Dame we upset things without really meaning to, by playing rock 'n' roll after we played jazz in the preliminaries. They didn't want to set a precedent by awarding the prize to a group that played rock, so they didn't award a [group] prize. They gave us all individual prizes and that was it.

"I came to New York and the first group I played in was Birdsong, an R&B band led by Edwin Birdsong." [13]

Edwin L. Birdsong (b1951, Los Angeles CA) is a keyboard / organ player who was known for his experimental funk / disco music. He never achieved chart success. Birdsong was the son of a minister and grew up in LA in a strict fundamentalist environment. He joined a gospel choir, and served in Viet Nam before arriving in New York to study music. It was now that he formed his band, Birdsong, and recruited the young Michael Brecker, alongside drummer Billy Cobham. In 1971 Edwin signed a record deal with Polydor. Under Polydor, he issued his first two full-length albums, *What It Is* (1972) and *Supernatural* (1973). Michael said, "That was the first real R&B experience I had, and I really enjoyed it. The first time I heard R&B drumming, it knocked me out. In fact, Billy Cobham was in that band briefly." [13]

Randy Brecker: *Score* – 1969 (****)

Palaeontologists spend a lot of their time chipping away at stone surfaces, and hope that one day they will find a missing link in the fossil record. Well, in May 2008, I finally found mine when Randy Brecker's album *Score* (1969) fell onto my doormat. At the time this music was recorded, Jan / Feb 1969, Randy is a recently turned 23 year-old. Let's take nothing away from him - this is his album and he gets the focus he deserves, but his nineteen-year-old brother Mike plays on all of the tracks, so this is very much the first Brecker Brothers album. It's a coup for Randy, earned from his three years of hard work gigging around the New York area. He was a friend and employee of pianist and composer, Duke Pearson. As luck would have it, Pearson was also in a powerful position as A&R man for Blue Note Records, one of the biggest names in jazz. He arranged a contract for a one-off record for jazz's favourite label. The business lineage of the record industry is often hideously complex. The album copyright for *Score* (1969) belongs, not to Blue Note, but to Capitol Records, which had been bought out by Liberty Records, and which also owned Blue Note. In the late 1960s, straight-ahead jazz labels – of which Blue Note was surely the straightest – were feeling the cold winds of change from the rock revolution. With Blue Note founder Alfred Lion now dead, and his partner, Francis Wolff, in physical decline, Pearson was carefully attempting to re-orientate a declining business towards a more profitable format, the newly emerging sound of jazz-fusion, even though the formula that might unlock huge record sales was very unclear. Only through experiments with records like this could the complementary ingredients of success be identified. Pearson was convinced that Randy Brecker could be one of those new, young musicians to discover the correct formula.

A true Blue Note album of this vintage would normally have had a straight, simple and factual cover design, but an album targeted at a new audience should be found in the front of the record stores among the racks of rock, not the jumbles of jazz in the back. Both Capitol and Liberty were, of course, labels for popular musicians and here is an album with a picture of a cool male hunk on the front and some psychedelic art on the back, a fashionable product with a clear market. The flaw in the design intent, if there was one, was Randy's pose with a trumpet instead of a guitar.

Thus it was that, on 21 January, 1969, Randy and Mike travelled to Rudy Van Gelder's studio in Hackensack New Jersey for the first of two sessions to record an important album in the history of jazz-fusion music. This album is a fine example of how some jazz musicians were thinking at the start of 1969, immediately before Miles Davis had burst onto the scene with his influential *In A Silent Way* (1969) – that disc was recorded a matter of days after this. Randy's album is a varied mix of many styles – not just jazz-rock – and it exemplifies his broad approach to music. In the notes, he says, "There isn't any type of music that I don't dig at one time or another. All music is an expression of some segment of society. As long as it is sincere, it's valid. There are different levels of intellectuality, but that doesn't make it better or worse." [11]

However, Randy's experiment with jazz-rock was done very much with the help of the brothers' friend, pianist Hal Galper, a man far more noted for his post-bop and free jazz work than his music in the fusion arena. Hal Galper (b1938, Salem MA) studied piano at Berklee Music College during the period 1955-58, and then played the local circuit around Boston before going on tour with Chet Baker in 1967. Afterwards, he settled in New York, where he met Randy Brecker.

Randy recalled, " I first met him [Galper] at a gig he was playing with Phil Woods at the top [floor] of the *Gate*, the *Village Gate* [Jazz Club] it was an afternoon concert and I'd met Phil previously, before I came to New York. I sat in with the band and Hal and I got talking, and we played together several sessions, and eventually I had a gig at the club called *L'Intrigue*, it was a several months gig ... and I used Hal as the piano player, so we got very familiar with each other's work." [5]

Unexpectedly, it is Galper who contributes the two jazz-rock numbers on the album, not Randy. On this date, at least two years after leaving BS&T, Randy has still not come up with a composition that is a jazz-rock fusion piece. His year with Blood Sweat & Tears must have influenced him enormously, yet when Nat Hentoff asked who his main influences were, he lists all the usual jazz greats and quotes no rock musicians. There is, however, little doubt about where his interests lie. Randy: "I like both rock and jazz, and although the two forms are pretty separate, the cross influences are growing. More jazz guys are getting with rock feeling and are listening to more of rock. At the same time, rock bands are becoming looser in their improvising. But rock improvising is still essentially of a different kind; it's on a lesser level of complexity than that of jazz." [15] We note that Randy says that "rock and jazz are pretty separate". He clearly does not yet see the jazz-rock fusion as having truly occurred. To him, a new jazzer should have a much broader horizon, and this view is perfectly clear from listening to this album. There is a clear acoustic-electric divide. The two 'rock' tracks, *Score* and *The Vamp*, are both written by Halper and there's no doubting their rock intent. Larry Coryell's electric guitar and Chuck Rainey's electric bass tend to dominate Galper's electric piano, and Bernard Purdie's drums are in a different vein from Mickey Roker's jazz sticking. Randy's selection of Coryell, Rainey and Purdie – three men who were the hottest fusion men in town at this time - for his record is a clear indication of the intention to present jazz-rock music.

Score comes across today as the most interesting track because with its tight, cute horn phrases, it is closer to the style of jazz that the Brecker Brothers will develop later. Michael's soloing is also interesting, the creation of an immature, yet very capable musician. Randy benefits from his extra years and demonstrates some of the chops that must have impressed Duke Pearson. Of course, Coryell has a natural advantage by playing an electric guitar, and doing so in the style of a rocker, rather than a jazzer.

In comparison, *The Vamp* is as primitive as that fossil I talked about earlier. It forms the basis for much of what Miles Davis later played through the period from 1970 until his retirement. Vamps, based on improvisation over single chords to rock rhythms, were Davis's modal model for the way ahead, a road that I have suggested elsewhere [16] was unpopular and not the route to riches that Davis hoped it would be. Influenced by Davis, others used vamps too during these years. Joe Zawinul even continued to use jazz-fusion vamps in his bands long after Weather Report disbanded, despite vamps not being common in Weather Report's repertoire. The adoption of vamps by Davis and others did indeed represent a new form of jazz-fusion that was taking place at a lower intellectual level, in line with Davis's wish to appeal to poor black kids. Randy agreed when he said the improvising was "…on a lesser level of complexity than that of jazz" and seemed to imply that this was what jazz-rock might evolve into. However, it is evident that Michael, Randy and Larry found it somewhat taxing to continually find new ideas to play over that monotone chord. For at least some of the time, first Michael, then Randy are reduced to a kind of scrabbling around for a diamond dropped in the musical dirt, finally resorting to a desperate scream to keep the momentum going. As a result the music is weak and repetitive, but still exploratory. Fortunately, the Brecker Brothers were later able to identify a form of jazz-fusion that retained the intellectual integrity of jazz, yet also excited listeners with the rock-based elements too. It wasn't until

Miles was in retirement in 1976 that their own brand of jazz-fusion was able to take off in parallel with David Sanborn, Pat Metheny and others, almost always without using vamps.

The remaining six tracks are a pleasant mix of other jazz styles, including some that are strong fusions with folk music. *Bangalore* is the opener, a tight, modern straight-ahead piece that combines come unexpected changes of tempo with some of the freer harmonies that Randy had probably been playing in the clubs with Hal's bands. *Name Game* is another Halper tune that changes constantly throughout, but is firmly in the jazz mainstream. *The Weasel Goes Out to Lunch* is a simple duet based on the nursery rhyme, *Pop Goes the Weasel*, in which the brothers experiment with some novel jazz harmonies. It was an example of what the two brothers regularly worked out on. "We've done a lot of playing together, working out variations and improvisations on old folk tunes and standards like *You Are My Sunshine*. The empathy and telepathy we share is really uncanny and we get into some fresh and exciting things." [11]

Pipe Dream, is a jazz waltz with significant folk harmonies. *Morning Song* and the *Marble Sea* are fusions of jazz with Latin-based rhythms. Fusion is, indeed, a big element throughout the tracks, but it's not all jazz-rock.

Randy himself comes across as a young musician who sees his role as a jazz musician who must not be pigeonholed. That's very much a philosophy that came about as a result of the '60s music revolution and we have heard it promulgated by most of the musicians in this series of books. "I didn't think about it with regard to categories. Sure, there are elements not only of rock and jazz, but also of what I'd call folk. In *Morning Song* and *Pipe Dream*, for instance, I was thinking of what it's like listening to Donovan – soft, pretty melodies." [17] *The Vamp* is such a simple format that anyone could have written the song, but it was written by Galper, not Randy. And Galper did not propel himself into jazz-fusion in the way that others (such as the Brecker Brothers) chose to. Randy told me, "They [Hal's compositions] were great tunes. Well he's an expert musician and anything he sets his mind to do he can do. I think even back then he was a jazz musician first, but he wrote some really good tunes for that record. I think he was somewhat unfamiliar with the genre but he just soaked it up." [5]

In 1969, record producer and writer, Michael Cuscuna, talked to Randy in detail about the possibilities for jazz-rock synthesis. He reported that Randy did not see himself as a strong arbiter for the way forward in jazz-rock. Though he liked rock music, his experience with BS&T had led him to be sanguine about joining the serried ranks of rock musicians and he didn't see it as a particularly strong attraction for him. [11]

So *Score* was really just a one-off at this point – a rare, vital find in the fossil record of jazz-fusion, that offered a menu of Randy's versatility of styles, as well as great jazz. Randy had not intended it to be a formula for the way ahead for jazz-fusion; that remained unclear. More experimentation was necessary.

Dreams: *Dreams* **– 1970 (***)**

In the late 1960s, players of brass and woodwind instruments had been less than enthusiastic about their exclusion from the money-printing machine of pop music, which had been largely built to the blueprints of guitar-based bands. Saxophone players who had practised long and hard to learn the kinds of skills demonstrated by the likes of John Coltrane, were miffed to find that guitarists who could barely play their instruments, and singers with even less talent, could make millions at a stroke. Since Randy had left the band, however, Blood Sweat & Tears had been making truckloads of money from a style of pop music tattooed with colourful jazzy designs. Of course, not everyone approved of the inclusion of brass and woodwind jazz instruments into rock band music. Stump, for example, refers to "the brusque shoe-horning of these elements into otherwise straightforward rock numbers" as a "cheap gimmick." [18] The stupidity of such comments is underlined by the extraordinary successes achieved later by bands like Maurice White's Earth Wind and Fire, a group formed in 1970 that was producing multi-platinum albums of great sophistication and musicianship from 1975-79. By 1980, the model was sufficiently well honed for Huey Lewis and The News to become one of the best-selling bands of the 1980s, earning seven platinum albums with *Sports* (1983) and three with *Fore!* (1986). It is, of course, always difficult to put music like this into clear classifications, but there is no doubt that these bands occupied real estate in the commercial zone of popular music – not jazz. Yet the music would not have been possible without much of the ground-breaking work by jazzers exerting their influence on pop and rock music, and, when necessary, taking session jobs for the stars. For proof, we need look no further than the great jazz sax player Stan Getz guesting on Huey's album *Small World* (1988).

A band called Dreams laid some of the first turfs on the new lawn. Inspired by a brief stint with BS&T, and an appearance on their first album *Child is Father to the Man* (1967), Randy Brecker certainly felt that their formula for success could work for him too. In 1969, while working with Horace Silver, he got an excited call from his brother, Michael (then aged 20) that a new band was in the offing. Randy was soon at the centre of a new grouping made up of Michael, Barry Rogers (trombone), Doug Lubahn (bass) and Jeff Kent (keyboards). John Abercrombie was chosen for the necessary presence of electric guitar, whilst Eddie Vernon was chosen as lead vocalist. They invited Billy Cobham, a drummer already known and admired by all of the musicians, to fill the drum seat.

Randy told Steve Bloom, "The idea [of Dreams] was to improvise and stretch out, which we did in concert. We didn't write charts, which was probably a naïve way to do it. We used to spend hours jamming up horn parts." Mike added, "It was a band ahead of its time. We incorporated a lot of R&B, which was something BS&T didn't do. It was a crazy concept. There were no overdubs – we just went in and played our sort of out-funk. Unfortunately, the two albums never lived up to the live performance." [19]

Randy told Michael Davis that the band was very different from BS&T, and much better because the plan was *not* to have arrangements, which would normally be necessary for a horn band. "We obviously needed horn parts, but we rehearsed every day, we would just jam up the tunes every day, playing stuff over and over." [12] The spirit with which the horns played in Dreams was really special. It was the first time that Randy and Michael really got to play together in their professional careers.

The demonstrably successful BS&T format required the music to be almost entirely vocal, with room for only short instrumental solos. It was not the context to make jazzers feel comfortable. However, this recipe resulted in the placement of the band's albums in the record shop racks labelled 'pop music'. Jazzers, disgruntled by having to play 'below themselves' in such bands, could thus be pacified by thoughts of pecuniary advantage. Another approach, however, was to counterbalance a subset of pop-targeted content with another of chunky instrumentals. This was the Dreams formula. Most of us already know the outcome: from a commercial point of view, the BS&T formula was enormously successful; the Dreams formula wasn't.

From the start, the music was almost all written by Kent or Lubahn. The first four songs, *Devil Lady*, *15 Miles to Provo*, *The Maryanne* and *Holli Be Home* are clearly targeted at airplay with their short, simple song formats. But the album is seriously back-loaded and metamorphosises into jazz-fusion from then on. Thus, *Try Me* adopts a funky jazz stance based on Kent's lively bass line and vocals, although an improvised centre section breaks into a free-for-all. At last Cobham's playing comes to the fore, and the band really sounds like a cut above the average pop-rock group. Then a long, uninterrupted section fills the whole of the second side of the vinyl disc. *Dream Suite: Asset Stop / Jane / Crunchy Grenola* begins with a great sax solo by Michael that lasts for 1.15 minutes, and develops into an undisciplined funky rave. After six minutes it shifts into a sixty-second waltz-time instrumental. A minute later, *Jane* commences at 7.00, a rather poor composition disguised with some colourful ensemble playing that fades at 9.35 into the final part of the trilogy, an instrumental led by a storming tenor sax solo. By twelve minutes a funky groove is established. At 13.30, Cobham cues in a much slower tempo and some random instrumental noodlings before he takes his own chance to shine in a short solo that leads straight into the funky *New York* with no break, despite indications to the contrary on the album cover. Vocals now take a back seat as, once more, it is Mike Brecker's platform. Somehow, Randy's subsequent attempt to take the music forward is a slight anti-climax, but the piece stomps out in a blaze of glory with a quite different feeling to the one established at the start of the record. At last we begin to see the real way to blend jazz with rock.

Dreams: *Imagine My Surprise* – 1971 (***)

After the first album, there was a feeling that the band had not reached its full potential with the first line-up. The jazzers in the band could not contain their disappointment with the perceived lack of improvisation ability of the rockers. A certain amount of disagreement ensued in the leaderless ranks of Dreams. Two of the band's founding members, Jeff Kent and Doug Lubahn (both rockers), became history after just one record, "fired by the band", according to Billy Cobham. [20] Randy Brecker said, "No, there was kind of a... we usurped his [Doug Lubahn's] position. There was kind of a mutiny that started with the trombone player [Barry Rogers], and Billy [Cobham] the drummer, and Mike and I went along with it, and also a musical thing. Both Doug and Jeff [Kent] - and in hindsight we made a big mistake, although we were caught in a bind - Doug and Jeff were the instigators of putting the band together, it was all their own material. There were some great songs, harmony, they were rock players they weren't really improvisers in that sense, so month after month we found ourselves - how can I put it - limited in what we could do in the band because they weren't quite able to keep up as improvisers. So it was a tough decision but we wanted to keep the band together because the other part [performing rather than writing] was so strong, as players, so we auditioned other pianists and bass players and we came up with Don Grolnick and Will Lee." [5]

Randy was especially pleased with finding Lee. "Yeah, I still have the audition tape. We auditioned, and about 20 seconds later he had the gig, he played so well. He came sight unseen. A friend of mine in Florida said, well, there's this kid here, he plays really good, his father is Dean of the Music School at the University of Florida in Miami. Why don't you try him? So I called him up and that's true, he never went home. Well, he went home to pack his bags, but he's been here ever since." [5]

Don Grolnick (piano) and Will Lee (bass) were to become close friends and core band members. John Abercrombie also left, to be replaced by jazz guitarist Bob Mann. Most members of the band contributed to the vocals, again led by Eddie Vernon. With a regular gig at the *Village Gate*, Dreams became well known as a horn band and it was very much this unit that eventually evolved into the Brecker Brothers Band.

The new band recorded the album, *Imagine My Surprise* (1971). It contained a further collection of vocal tracks with a strong brassy-jazz backing, but because of the significant personnel changes, the music is very different from the band's previous album. The opener, *Calico Baby*, ironically penned by the band's newly 'retired' members, formed a kind of sentimental bridge between the old and the new. It was typical of the band's new trademark and clearly influenced by songs like *Spinning Wheel* (1968) by Blood, Sweat & Tears, but it was set in the format that was proving successful for other musicians trying to navigate the same course - Jessie Colin Young, for example. Jazz-inflected solos were part of this format (within well-defined limits) and Michael Brecker's tenor saxophone sound provided the mould into which hundreds of other tenor sax players doing solo breaks in pop music would pour their juices. Michael's own career would develop far beyond that of a role model. He used his consummate musicianship to develop a successful mix with another much purer recipe of straight-ahead jazz formulated according to the calculations of Coltrane and Davis. With such an equation, the result put him at the epicentre of late 20th century jazz saxophone, a spot really only contested by Wayne Shorter, who was a very different kind of player.

The tracks to *Imagine My Surprise* constituted a broad range of styles, and a proportion of them were covers. Goffin and King's *I Can't Hear You* was clearly derived from popular music, although Carole King was by now starting to write and perform in her own style of crossover music. The band's arrangement is a good example of how a pop song could be given a jazz gloss, especially in the capable hands of the Brecker Brothers. Stevie Winwood's *Medicated Goo* had been a big hit for Traffic, underpinned by its funk-rock tarmac. The collection also included *Don't Cry My Lady* and *Child of Wisdom* both written by Jerry Friedman, a guitarist whose possible claim to fame was to play on Paul Simon's *Still Crazy After All These Years* (1976). *Child of Wisdom* was a good piece of early blues-funk that featured a particularly raunchy solo from Mike Brecker, who also added some Sanborn-like moments to *Don't Cry My Lady*. There were self-penned numbers too. Written by trombonist Barry Rogers, *Here She Comes Now* is a soulful funky trip blended with a softer more melodic chorus. Compared to the rest, Don Grolnick seemed to be a different class of composer, and his song *Just Be Ourselves* at track four is clearly in a higher league, despite some moments of uncertainty in the vocals that were more to do with the lack of recording and rehearsal time than poor concept. The horn arrangement is superb, with Mike Brecker once again surfing the wave-crests.

There are two contributions from Randy– *Why Can't I Find a Home* and *Imagine My Surprise*. This second piece was placed last on the album, the slot often used for experimental recordings that don't necessarily conform to the artistic direction of the rest of the album. Here was a track that was superficially rather silly, and well suited to the slot that record companies know gets played least. On first hearing, it is little more than a novelty track thanks largely to the exaggerated vocals that, in some places, were similar to Donald Fagen's output with Steely Dan, and in others to Bobby McFerrin's singing on his beautiful eponymous album of 1982. However, beneath the clownish exterior, Randy's deep-seated jazz background is ever-present. Just like the surprise when Jack pops out of his box to reveal that he is, in fact, Jill, arranged differently, this jazziest track on the album could have been majestic, even allowing for its extraordinary avant-garde finale.

After two modestly successful albums aimed at the pop market, the strained strands that struggled to keep the band together finally parted. The jazzers may have become frustrated with the lack of commercial impact and the constant need to suborn themselves to singers with small talents and large egos. The Brecker Brothers were destined to make their own mark with another configuration by successfully developing the funky style of jazz-fusion.

Meanwhile, by 1971, Billy Cobham had started sitting in with Miles Davis and was a friend of John McLaughlin. The two men began to hang out and practice together and Billy was John's obvious choice for his new band, the Mahavishnu Orchestra. Billy had been a major draw for Dreams and once he was gone, much of the band's cohesion went with him. Michael admitted that Billy's wonderful drumming had been the main focus for Dreams. "We naturally gravitated to building the music around Billy. We couldn't find someone to replace him so we gave up." [19] So, early in 1972 the dreaming stopped when the sleepers awoke to a somewhat harsh reality: despite making an impact that is talked about in hushed tones to this day, the band was considered to have failed to meet its commercial objectives. There's no justice in this world...

White Elephant: *White Elephant* **– 1972; Re-released as Mike Mainieri & Friends:** *White Elephant Vol. 1* **and** *Vol. 2* **– 1994 (***)**

For many years, the name White Elephant (even more so than Dreams) was the stuff of jazz folklore. The moniker came to the fore thanks to an eponymous double vinyl album simply labelled *White Elephant*. It contained a collection of recordings covering a wide range of styles of music, but was seen at the time as a presentation of jazz-rock fusion to be heard alongside, and on a par with, other recognised releases in the new genre. Presented as a band of some twenty musicians, for those in the know, the people involved were at the centre of the New York whirlwind that was sucking in top jazz musicians and spewing out music that was exciting and new.

The leader of the band was Mike Mainieri (b1938, New York), a vibraphone player probably best known for his work in the band Steps Ahead that I shall review later. In his early years, he became a leading vibraphone player in the jazz mainstream, where he played with such artists as Billy Holiday, Dizzy Gillespie, Coleman Hawkins, Wes Montgomery and Buddy Rich. At 20 years old, he won the *Down Beat* "International Jazz Critics Award." The trouble was that he found himself in competition with another vibes man, Gary Burton, who was nearly five years younger and awarded the more prestigious title of "Jazzman of the Year" from the same magazine – the youngest ever to do so. Fortunately, the thought of working in the shadow of Burton for the rest of his life did not in the least faze Mainieri, who went from strength to strength. At the age of 24, he recorded his first straight-ahead jazz album as leader of his own quartet called *Blues On The Other Side* (1962).

By the mid 1960s, it was becoming difficult for players of certain instruments to compete with amplified guitars. Mainieri is regarded as being the first to develop electrification for his vibraphone from 1965 onwards. Even though the vibraphone was an instrument mostly unknown to rock music, it did not prevent Mainieri from taking a leading role in the jazz-rock fusion revolution. He had become a close friend of flute player, Jeremy Steig, who is widely regarded as one of the foremost experimentalists in jazz-rock fusion. Mainieri and Steig played together a great deal from 1965 onwards, although the two men's paths did not seem to cross on dates when recordings were made. Nicholson gives a strongly favourable review to the album *Jeremy & The Satyrs* (1968) [21] Led by Steig, the band also contained Warren Bernhardt (piano), Donald MacDonald (drums), Eddie Gomez (bass), and a much praised but unknown guitarist called Adrian Guillery. Unfortunately, the recording did not feature Mainieri who was absent for some reason. Although the record, like Coryell's *Out of Sight and Sound* (1967), was driven, for commercial reasons, to be untypical of the band's much more experimental character, nevertheless, it was still applauded by Nicholson as being a strong early member of the first tranche of jazz-rock fusion albums. Mike's own album *Journey Thru An Electric Tube* (1968) was also made with Steig, Bernhardt and MacDonald, and was very much influenced by the psychedelic space that most twenty-something musicians were occupying.

In 1969, Blood Sweat & Tears were exploiting great success without Randy Brecker, who was working with Michael in Dreams. At about the same time, Mike Mainieri, began to lead a long series of experimental sessions at a number of recording studios around New York. What began as a small group of players, soon expanded into a bigger, loose collective. Although they were 'after hours' sessions, they were not really jam sessions. Mainieri prepared charts for the attendees to play, but the sessions were intended to be opportunities to try new things. Played by jazzers, there was a strong rock vibe and, as was being done with the Dreams catalogue, there were vocal numbers. Significantly, the band was never fixed in size, and by the time Mainieri decided to record some of the works that had been played, it had grown to around twenty.

Ronnie Cuber remembered, "That [White Elephant] was just a band put together by Mike Mainieri, and it started out with five horns, bass, drums, guitar, keyboards and Michael on vibes and I started inviting people to come and listen to the band. People had charts and vocals, but if I invited say, George Young, the alto player, he would stop by to hear the band and then he would get his horn out and start playing with the band and then like in a week or two he was considered a member of the band. So the band kinda grew." [6]

Asked if he remembered much about the sessions, Randy laughed. "Well not too much because they were always late at night and we were half asleep and stoned out of our brains. He [Mainieri] also picked up on that thing that Dreams had been together for a while, and Mike and I had been in town together for a little while, and he had the nucleus of a band, a small band, and one by one, new people came to town, among them John Faddis, and he added John on trumpet, Steve Gadd moved to town, he added Steve Gadd. Well, we already had a drummer, Don McDonald, but Gadd was great, so all of a sudden we had two drummers. Tony Levin came to town, so we had a new bass player, and we kept adding horns and it became quite a large ensemble. Then we recorded that record only after midnight, after we were done with all the sessions. He wrote all the music, organised the whole thing, and eventually years later, it finally came out. I think we only did one White Elephant gig all in all." [5]

After sessions of recording that took place in the A&R Recording Studios and the Record Plant in New York, a double vinyl album was released on the Just Sunshine label by executive producer Mike Lang under the band name of White Elephant. It was the collective's only release and garnered a deserved place in jazz-fusion history that, because of the scarcity of the albums in the days before Internet sales, became the stuff of legend. However, in 1994, Mike Mainieri was able to use his own NYC Records label (formed 1991) to release two CDs, *White Elephant Vol. 1 and 2*, under the band name, Mike Mainieri & Friends.

All of the music was original, written mostly by Mike, but with some by guitarist Nick Holmes. Perhaps sadly for Mike, it was one of Holmes's compositions, *Battle Royal* (1972) that, with two minutes cut from its original format, was selected for release as a single, possibly because of its resemblance to the style that was so successful for BS&T. There were a few occasions when the band made public performances with as many as 23 musicians on stage, but apart from the recordings and a large dollop of nostalgia for White Elephant, there is little left of the band's existence apart from a very large footprint of influence over musicians lucky enough to hear the animal play.

Electrickery

Randy's experience of playing with BS&T had shown him that, even playing a naturally loud instrument such as a trumpet, he needed to boost his decibels to compete with amplified guitars. It was obvious he could start using microphones as part of the band's PA, but it wasn't as easy as it appeared and problems soon became apparent. Bespoke trumpet amplifiers were needed.

I suggested to Randy that by 1971, the 'electric trumpet' had moved on from being experimental to just another musical instrument. Randy replied, "Well by then I was [using electrical amplification]. I think we first explored electricity through the horns and it was strictly because we were having difficulty hearing ourselves just using a mike. The Hammond Organ Company came out with a thing called a Condor, which had kind of organ stops, and both myself, my brother and Barry Rogers were in a band called Dreams, and we decided to try to use these Condors. We had Barcus Berry pickups on our horns. So that was the start of it." [5]

Randy then offered a great insight into Miles's use of the wah-wah pedal to modify the sound of his trumpet during the early 1970s. "We hired John Abercrombie to join Dreams at one point because we thought we needed a guitar player. He, like many others of us in the band, thought of himself as a jazz musician first. So he always brought along a wah-wah pedal because he thought that made him sound more like a rock player, and he used it on every solo, if you notice, on the first Dreams record. One rehearsal he didn't show up, and he'd left his pedal there, and I will never forget this, so I plugged my quarter-inch guitar jack into it and said, I wonder what it will sound like on trumpet? And it sounded great, so that was the beginning of wah-wah trumpet in '71. And Miles used to come and hear us at the *Village Gate*, all the time, and I don't know if that's what gave him the idea, but shortly after that he started using that [wah-wah sound] too. Years later he came up to me and said, [RB imitates Miles's husky voice] 'You know, I love my wah-wah. Do you love your wah-wah?' That's the only thing he ever said to me in his life." [Laughter] [5]

Hal Galper: *Wild Bird* – 1971 (***)

During the lifetime of Dreams, Michael and Randy were also involved with Hal Galper, a post-bop pianist who had spent a lot of time with tenor saxophone player Sam Rivers. Sam had briefly held down the sax position in Miles's band, but Sam's freer style of playing didn't suit Miles and, after a year, Rivers was replaced by Wayne Shorter. In his own band, however, Rivers was free to play how he liked, and his loose style suited Galper. Indeed, Galper says that Rivers was experimenting with free jazz at the same time that Ornette Coleman was releasing *The Sound of Jazz to Come* (1959). [22]

As we have seen, Galper had worked closely on Randy's first album, *Score* (1969). Then, in 1971, Hal decided that he wanted to include Michael and Randy in his band and hired them for his own first album as leader, *Wild Bird* (1971). The music is clearly experimental, with Hal playing electric piano and Randy playing electric trumpet in places. The music is free-wheeling, and at times furiously improvised, with all of the musicians given license to stretch out in compositions. Inevitably, perhaps, the music seems to be influenced by the style adopted by Miles Davis's band at this time.

The Breckers' first appearance on Hal Galper's debut album accords with an experimental agenda. Electrically modified sounds paint abstract ideas over simple, repeated themes of chords or other harmonic motifs. *Wild Bird* (1971) was made with both brothers, Billy Hart (drums), Don Alias (percussion), Victor Gaskin (bass) and Bob Mann on guitar. The leader had, for the time being at least, chosen to forsake the acoustic piano and operate on electronic keyboards only, whilst allowing his musicians scope to mutate their own sounds with electricity.

The opening track is *Convocation*, which starts and ends with an evocative *a tempo* theme that moves smoothly between Bm and G. Then, at 1.20, into a slow four-beat rhythm led by Billy Hart and dominated by the electric piano, with effects applied so that it sounds even more atmospheric. The theme is comprised of three cycling chords of B, D and E, over which the soloists add their own interpretations, Hal going first, followed by Michael and then Randy who uses some wild trumpet effects. It's a very effective plan that succeeds, thanks to a combination of the haunting minor-key setting and the creative collaboration of the musicians.

The title track, *Wild Bird*, is laid down by an alternating harmony that juxtaposes the triad G# / C / F with G / B / F#, with Bob Mann's guitar now prominent to hold the chords in place. Randy and Michael play the theme in unison on trumpet and soprano sax until Randy solos using electronics as well as extremely fluid excursions to add novelty to his work. Michael then follows in the same vein on tenor saxophone, leaving Hal's electric piano for last. The two drum kits of Hart and Bill Goodwin create complicated layers of rhythm towards the end before the theme is repeated.

Change Up begins with a heavy rock sound, complete with fuzz bass and guitar. Michael tears up the foreground with a loose solo right from the start, his ranting mostly disguising the peculiar cycle of five four-beat bars.

Track 4 is *This Moment*, a long piece that offers much scope for development of the gentle theme, whilst retaining the electric fingerprint that keeps the album honest.

Listeners expecting an album of straight ahead sounds may have been shocked by this menu of advanced ingredients, and maybe they didn't get as far as the final track, *Whatever*, where there is at last something for them to associate with. Randy's solo is played in the traditional trumpet style with clear tones and athletic delivery. Michael sits this one out as Bob Mann gets a solid solo, which he plays in conventional jazz guitar tones. Meanwhile, those listeners who switched off early will have missed some great sounds on this rare album.

Hal Galper: *The Guerrilla Band* – 1972 (****)

The *Wild Bird* album was followed a year later by *The Guerilla Band* (1972). The title suggests that Galper now felt he was in a stable relationship in these turbulent times. His musicians were much the same: Randy and Michael were once again playing horns, Don Alias and Steve Haas played percussion, with Gaskin and Mann appearing again on bass and guitar respectively.

The Call is the opening track, music that balances a slow melody on top of a fast moving monochordal background, or drone, in C major throughout. Once the brief statement of the theme is over, Michael takes off with an improvisation on soprano saxophone. This is a very clear echo of the kind of format Miles Davis had adopted at this time, especially evident when Randy solos, although there are significant electronic trumpet effects included at the end of his solo. Hal plays Hammond organ for his own solo while the bass, guitar and drums keep the vibe rolling.

Figure Eight opens with a pseudo-rock theme played in unison on bass, guitar and organ to a complicated sequence of syncopated phrases that needs careful counting. It's a clear attempt to create something novel. Played twice over 20 seconds for each cycle of sixteen bars, the music proceeds with an ensemble B-section that again has a slow melody placed over the rhythmic background. Each soloist plays in loose harmony over the syncopated A-section theme and the smoother B-theme. This creates a very original effect, especially when transitioning between the A and B themes.

Black Night also opens with an *a tempo* theme expressed by the horns before breaking loose into a fast, four-in-a-bar mainstream tune with Hal leading on electric piano. By 2.30 the band is entering total freedom, but by three minutes it has returned to its original slow form. The brevity of this track seems to leave the listener wanting more.

Welcome to My Dream is another shorter track of four minutes in which the horns play a haunting tune over a rippling backdrop that moves through some pleasant, unexpected chord changes. Once Galper has taken up the reins of his song, he drives his dream into energetic, warm zones. The horns draw the music back to the original theme for a faded ending.

Rise And Fall is a chunky, hypnotic offering with a similar strategy of slow, unison melodies over deliberate rhythms, but new tones. The title clearly refers to the cycle of changes chosen, which oscillates periodically in tone and semi-tone steps that make me feel like I am watching some speeded-up video of flowers opening and closing each day.

Finally comes *Point Of View*, another member of the current style of songs, this one based in E that cycles constantly through a set of changes that move through three chords closely related to the E root, and with the bass holding to it tightly. It's a far more interesting variation on a simple drone that gives plenty of scope for the soloists to build upon the mood set up by the composer's tonal landscape.

In summary, this is a very good album that is not dated and that deserves exposure to a wider audience. Sadly, in view of its great rarity, that is unlikely. Clearly, Hal Galpin had his own interpretation of what was expected from cutting-edge jazz in the early 1970s, a view that does not coincide with what others, including the Breckers, were envisaging. Maybe they still were not sure. Nevertheless, Galpin's contributions with this album especially, much assisted by the Breckers' inventions, have freshness and vitality even today. Randy told me, "Well that was mostly his brainstorm. We did four or five excellent records with Hal, but by then he had really formed a thinking process as far as his fusion writing, and he had his own conception really, kind of utilising electricity but keeping it as open as possible, even more than we did in Dreams because there was no singing, it was all instrumental music. I actually think some of his music was really way ahead of its time. They were done really early on and they were quite exceptional records and they didn't get really enough recognition." [5]

With regard to the monochord vamps, Randy said, "Miles started the modal thing, which is the same thing, vamping on one chord, and jazz-rock fitted to that perfectly. If you had players that could just kind of listen to each other, so it just wasn't strictly, that was a problem. If you had a real rock guy, who just knew kind of Cm7, for instance, and he'd just stay on the chord, but the jazz guys could kinda shape the chord and go up a half step or down a minor third, and keep the tonal centre happening. So they could experiment harmonically a lot more, and I think that's what Miles showed with his records, that we could take the elements of rock but expand the boundaries." [5]

Horace Silver: *The Pursuit of the 27th Man* – 1972 (***)

After Dreams, the brothers worked together for the best part of a year in the Horace Silver Quintet. Silver (b1928) had started out as a saxophonist, but changed to piano. Later, in 1950, he was 'discovered' by Stan Getz when Silver's trio accompanied the great sax player. Silver made a reputation as a major recording artist on the Blue Note label during which time he became one of the creators of the 'hard bop' style of jazz. In 1955 Horace became a founder member of the Jazz Messengers, but allowed the name to be taken up (and made much more famous) by Art Blakey at his own expense. His career as a premier league pianist was already well cemented when the two Brecker Brothers agreed to play in his band for the album *The Pursuit of the 27th Man* (1972). Silver was a giant of a previous jazz generation, and it was never on the cards that he would become a significant proponent of jazz-fusion. Nevertheless, the first of the three tracks on which the Breckers play is *Liberated Brother*, a traditional number that does have an element of funk. Bob Cranshaw's electric bass is another concession to the new music, but more than half of the album is devoted to a quartet formation with Dave Friedman on vibes, in place of the Breckers. This good Blue Note album is therefore better placed on a mainstream discography than it is in a jazz-fusion catalogue. Life in Silver's band was good, but soon, it was time to move on. After touring on the club circuit for some time, the boys grew tired. Randy: "We would go back to the same clubs all the time and there's only so many jazz clubs in the country." [19]

Larry Coryell: Introducing the Eleventh House – 1974 (***)

By 1973, Larry Coryell was still searching for the elusive unit that would set him amongst the still small set of successful jazz-rock fusion bands. It was during a conversation with the very talented percussionist, Alphonze Mouzon early that year, that the two of them planned a new band. "We wanted to head towards combining the integrity of jazz with some of the glitz and excitement of rock and funk. We felt it was a combination of styles whose time had come." [23] The band was called The Eleventh House, and consisted of Larry and Alphonze with Randy Brecker, Mike Mandel (keyboards) and Danny Trifan (bass). The band name was provided by Larry's wife; taken from astrology, it was used to represent the positive sense of friends, hopes and aspirations.

Speaking at the time, Randy told Jim Schaffer that it was a difficult decision to commit himself to Larry, but the decision was made easier when he heard about Alphonze. "When I found out that he was going to play I really wanted to do it, because I've got a thing for really good drummers and he's a real bitch man... He's really fun to play with ... everybody is. I mean, musically, it's really been working out. The bass player, Danny [Trifan] is really good and Mike [Mandel] really does original shit on the synthesiser. And Larry's playing great, he's been real cool, taking care of business. Things definitely are looking good." [24]

The first album was *Introducing the Eleventh House* (1974). The album begins with a track by Larry called *Birdfingers*, an energetic assembly of upward and downward chromatic runs, appropriately set in a metre of eleven beats. Randy is notably playing electric trumpet for his nimble arpeggios. Track 2, *The Funky Waltz*, is Alphonze's creation and, even though it is formatted in 3/4 time, it certainly sounds like a kind of funk-rock music. Larry's fuzzy wah-wah sound adds welcome colour to the feel of the music. *Low-Lee-Tah* is a Larry composition. It has a clear flavour of the middle-east and has a heavier, rock aspect to its mix. Mandel's tune, *Adam Smasher*, is the first of two consecutive tunes he contributed. A straightforward piece with nothing that would sound out-of-place today, the music must have been exciting in the early days of fusion. Mandel's second tune is *Joy Ride*, a relaxing, melodic presentation with some smooth chord sequences and colourful harmonies. The band winds itself up for some explosive electric passages, and Coryell continues nis role as rock guitarist with gusto.

The second half of the album continues with the altogether more serious *Yin*. An extended thrash in C, there's much energy and distorted electronic chicanery on display, together with a certain element of Mahavishnu Orchestra. Larry's title, *Theme For A Dream*, is sufficiently explicit to convey its message. Carefully orchestrated for the recording, it still leaves Larry with a little room to explore his ideas over the rest of the band. His next contribution is *Gratitude "A So Low,"* a clumsily titled, unaccompanied solo track. The album continues with a prog-rock composition by Larry and the unintelligible title *ISM-Ejercicio*. After a long, random introductory section, at 1.30 it turns into a heavy-metallish, Hendrix vibe with Randy blowing hard. The album closes with Mouzon's *Right On Y'All*, a much more straightforward party of organised rock frolics.

Talking about his equipment, Randy said, "What I was using on the concerts was a Condor, and an echoplex and a wah-wah pedal. Condor, it's made by Hammond – it's like a multivider. I'm also going to start using a Mutron. It's just incorporating it into the music, because you can always have the effects. You can't let it get the best of you because sometimes the shit can just go out of control. It's hard though because you've got so many things to think of at once. You have to really use your feet and both hands at the same time. It's a challenge to get it together." [24]

As soon as the album was finished, the band was able to leave for an extensive European tour that lasted a couple of months. It was an important opportunity for the band, and also for Coryell's future career, since it was his name that was most associated with the new venture. A self-admitted victim to serious misuse of drugs and alcohol, he took the difficult decision to give up substance abuse to help it succeed. [25] It was only after the band returned to the USA and began to tour there that Coryell went back to his old habits, an action that contributed to a fracture on the band's structure. The excitement that the players had at the start of this new project was dissipated by the end of the touring period. In his autobiography, he wrote, "My behaviour as bandleader changed drastically when I drank; I started scolding the musicians onstage, and acting bossy and unpleasant. It was the beginning of my slide back into the bottle and the joint." He follows that in the next paragraph with, "Around that time, Danny left the band. I'm not sure why." [26] Perhaps the reason was clear to everyone else.

Trifan decided to leave, followed by Randy, who had decided to work with his old friend from Dreams, Billy Cobham. Trifan would famously soon join Blood Sweat & Tears, and appear on the albums *More Than Ever* (1976) and *Brand New Day* (1977). Of losing Randy, Larry wrote, "I was so upset about Randy leaving that I went to his place – a spacious loft in the Bowery –

and stood outside the door and tried to talk him into staying in the band. It was nothing more or less than alcoholic dramatic-bullshit behaviour ... I got over it – by getting more loaded." [26] Superficial inspection of the album's content quickly announces that Randy's role was restricted. None of his compositions were included, and there is no question that the album showcases Coryell as the band's star performer, just as John McLaughlin had been identifiable as the main man on the early Mahavishnu Orchestra albums, another successful band that couldn't hold together for too long. Maybe, after the extensive series of tour gigs, Randy was given more to do, but we might speculate that, once his commitment to Eleventh House was complete, he was easily lured to Billy Cobham's new outfit.

Billy Cobham

Drummer Billy Cobham Jr. (b1944, Panama) moved to Brooklyn with his family when he was three years old and then to Queens when he was thirteen. Drumming was a big part of his early life as he listened to conga players in Robert Fulton Park at weekends. These immigrants from the Latin communities of countries like Puerto Rico, Columbia, and Cuba sought to keep their traditions alive by regularly practising their fierce Latin rhythms. As a consequence, Billy's early life was infused with rhythm. Cobham Sr. was a pianist so Billy's early listening was to Count Basie, Erroll Garner, George Shearing, and Dave Brubeck. The popular music of his time was by singers like Frank Sinatra, Billy Holiday, Dinah Washington, Ella Fitzgerald and Nat King Cole, but Billy loved drumming best of all. He listened to as many drummers as he could and was impressed at how Count Basie's drummer, Sonny Payne, could raise the performance of the band with such a small drum kit.

His first gig was playing drums for his dad when he was eight. Later he attended the School of Performing Arts and the High School of Music and Art in New York City. He joined a marching band and this naturally led him to join the US Army in 1965 where he became a percussionist with the Band. He left the Army in 1968, turned professional, and began playing with Shirley Scott and Stanley Turrentine. He recorded with George Benson (guitar), but his first high point was reached when he joined Horace Silver's band with Randy Brecker, Bennie Maupin and others. In March 1968, he recorded some tracks for Silver at Rudy van Gelder's studio, and in January 1969 recorded the Blue Note album *You Gotta Take A Little Love* (1969). However, it seems that he was dissatisfied with Silver's pay, and left before the year was out.

When John McLaughlin decided to form his new jazz-rock fusion band Billy was his first choice drummer. The two men had met during their sessions working with Miles Davis, and they got on very well together. John also hired Jan Hammer, an amazing keyboard player and Rick Laird on bass, but his masterstroke was to choose an electric violinist, Jerry Goodman, for the line-up.

This gave the band a slight edge in sound that resonated with popular audiences. The band, Mahavishnu Orchestra, became very successful thanks to three excellent albums: *The Inner Mounting Flame* (1971), *Birds of Fire* (1973) and *Between Nothingness and Eternity* (1973). *Rolling Stone* magazine labelled 1974 as the *Year of Jazz-Rock*, a title due in no small part to the success of the Mahavishnu Orchestra. Not only did the Mahavishnu Orchestra come top of *Down Beat* magazine readers' polls, but *Birds Of Fire* was voted best album, John McLaughlin was voted best guitarist, and Billy Cobham was consistently voted best drummer from 1973 to 1977. (I should emphasise that this acclaim was only ever given by ordinary listeners; jazz critics consistently refused to acknowledge that jazz-rock fusion was anything other than a carbuncle on the jazz organism from which they all claimed a living.)

However, at the very moment they reached the big time, Mahavishnu disintegrated because of dissatisfaction amongst the musicians. At some point, very creative minds need to showcase their work in packages of their own design. Success alone was not sufficient to hold a band together, and with so much going on, there was the ever-present optimism that the next grouping of musicians would press all the right buttons. Billy had lots of ideas, and was ready to capitalise on his success and go it alone. Both Michael and Randy would appear with Cobham's band over the next three years, even whilst they were involved with their own projects. Now, as jazz-rock fusion waxes rapidly towards its popular zenith, the storyline becomes ever more complex, with musicians appearing in, and disappearing from, many different combinations.

Billy Cobham: *Spectrum* – 1973 (***)

Billy Cobham decided to capitalise on his new status as a major star of drumming (many said he was the world's best), as well as to build on the success of the Mahavishnu Orchestra, and to learn lessons from its catastrophic split. In his new outfit, sponsored by Atlantic Records, he assembled an explosive group that included the brilliant Jan Hammer – also now ex-Mahavishnu. On bass he got Leland Sklar (b1947, Milwaukee WI), who, having been 'discovered' by James Taylor, couldn't settle down with any single band, but took his unique 'fuck-off' beard to countless recording sessions where he both dazzled and scared stars in equal measure.

Everything on Billy's debut album, *Spectrum* (1973), came from his own pen. Apart from being a startling demonstration of power drumming, the album is noted for introducing the astonishingly talented guitarist, Tommy Bolin (b1951, Sioux City, IA). Bolin was beginning to make a big impact on the rock scene, and, following a spell with Deep Purple, would probably have gone on to true greatness had it not been for a heroin overdose whilst promoting his second solo album, *Private Eyes* (1976) in December 1976. Listeners need look no further than this album's opener, *Quadrant 4*, to see what I mean. Surely, this is one of the best examples of early jazz-rock fusion on record?

Billy's album consisted mostly of music for his new quartet, supplemented by guest appearances from Joe Farrell (flute, sax), Jimmy Owens (flugelhorn), John Tropea (guitar) and Ron Carter (acoustic bass). There are several substantive tracks – *Quadrant 4*, *Spectrum*, *Taurian Matador*, *Stratus* and *Red Baron*, with some short interludes as introductions. There are also a number of drum solos on this record, which is absolutely fine if the contract holder is a drummer who needs to demonstrate his talents. *Searching for the Right Door* is one such solo and lasts but a short time. The title track, *Spectrum* is next up. It is a full band sound with horns and flutes as well as the keyboard quartet. *Anxiety* is another of the Cobham drum solos, played impeccably, as would be expected. Then comes a quartet piece, *Taurian Matador*, a somewhat tautologous title since matadors work with bulls! It begins with a real contest between the two contestants, though I'm not sure who is the matador or who wins. Both Hammer and Bolin give as good as they get, with Cobham and Sklar taking the roles of picadors. The album is an interesting mix of music ranging from funky groove-based *Red Baron*, the gentle Brazilian lilt of *Le Lis*, to the curious electronica of *Snoopy's Search*. It stayed on Billboard's jazz charts for five months, and that was a big success by any standards.

Billy Cobham: *Crosswinds* – 1974 (****)

For Randy Brecker, the switch from Coryell to Cobham, besides being a useful exit from a deteriorating situation, was important for career reasons too. Randy: "The Coryell gig was one of my best experiences musically, because I was the only horn, we were playing good tunes, everybody was writing. The only thing that wasn't happening was that he was tied up to a really lame record deal, and at the time it looked like it was going to be years before he could get out of it. Billy called during that time, he was leaving Mahavishnu and wanted first of all to make a record...There was talk about getting a band together. That was a hard decision from me, it was good music on both sides. I got to play more with Larry, but Billy's band seemed to offer more exposure and better gigs." [13]

So Randy was playing with Eleventh House at this time, and Michael was earning good money doing studio sessions. However, immediately following the release of *Spectrum*, Cobham went on tour, and extended the line-up to include the Brecker Brothers, with Garnett Brown (trombone), George Duke (keyboards), John Williams (bass) and John Abercrombie (guitar). With this larger group, new ideas were quick to emerge and a second album, *Crosswinds* (1974) was recorded featuring these musicians. In many ways, this was a potentially formidable combination, a kind of Dreams II.

Crosswinds (1974) has rather more substance and rather less gimmickry than its predecessor. With its Earthy themes gathered up under the umbrella of jazzy tone poems, there is artistry in the album that purveys more of the sense of a soundtrack than of a coherent band operating in jazz-rock fusion. There is some excellent ensemble playing, numerous thoughtful passages throughout Billy's compositions, and breathtaking drumming. Randy and Michael are allowed solos: Randy for the tumbling *Flash Flood*, Michael for the plucky *Pleasant Pheasant* and also for the luscious *Heather*. John Abercrombie is also a major contributor, with solos on *Flash Flood* and a spotlight slot on the final track *Crosswind*, which closes the album on a strong flavour of 1970s jazz-rock fusion. It's a masterful album through and through.

Billy Cobham: *Total Eclipse* – 1974 (****)

Cobham's personal jazz-rock journey continued apace with what was now looking like a biannual event, the release of another album, this one called *Total Eclipse* (1974). Clearly influenced by the significant coverage of the moon landings, Billy's latest set of compositions removed himself from the protection of the Earth's atmosphere and headed for lunar orbit. Listeners are first threatened by the awesome power of the Sun for *Solarization*, and then subjected to the incomprehensible physics underlying its *Second Phase*. The gentler aspects of the Sun come to the fore with *Crescent Sun*, another of Cobham's home-spun Latin-based cocktails. Our *Voyage* in space proceeds at great speed, assisted by Randy's rocket power and, of course, Billy's extraordinary energy. Abercrombie's electro-magnetic thrusters drive the ship off into the distance. In contrast to the power of the Sun and the coldness of space, the Moon is a fun place, as are the people who Cobham finds there; the *Lunarputians* are a funky lot, for sure. The title track, *Total Eclipse*, demonstrates clear light and shade. Mike plays a strong solo on soprano sax, as well as some flute in the ensemble passages, before the music moves into a final phase of rock guitar heat. *Bandits* is an interesting distraction slotted into the running order that disturbs the theme, although the next titles achieve little more. Forget the titles. *Moon Germs* is unrelated to the Joe Farrell composition of the same name, but is a strong piece of big-band-sounding jazz-rock in which Cornell Dupree joins Abercrombie on guitar. At last, Michael is given a tenor saxophone solo, although it is simply too short, and the track suffers from pre-CD-not-enough-space-on-the-vinyl syndrome. A very pleasant interlude ensues in which Randy plays a superb, bluesy duet with Billy – now on piano – entitled *The Moon Ain't Made Of Green Cheese*.

Randy's soliloquy leads perfectly into the substantial track called *Sea Of Tranquillity*. There's clearly much to explore here as Billy leads his men through what is hardly a bare monochrome lunar landscape, but rather a colourful and complex panorama of uncharted, dusty landscapes. Mike now gets the solo he deserved in *Moon Germs* and the solar wind is such that, at times, we can't see these musicians for moon-dust. Milcho Leviev secures his position with some solid work on keyboard around the middle of the track before the main themes are repeated. The final passages emphasise the rock credentials of the guitar once again; at 8.35, the dust settles and tranquillity returns. With *Last Frontier*, Billy pays homage to the astronauts' endeavours with a solo drum and piano piece. It is a very good end to a very good jazz-fusion album that, unfortunately, was still not sufficiently appealing to the wider record-buying public.

With the album in the can, Billy substituted Milcho Leviev for George Duke, Alex Blake for John Williams, and Glenn Ferris for Garnett Brown, and the band hit the road at the end of March 1974 as a warm-up act for the Doobie Brothers.

Milcho Leviev (b1937, Plovdiv, Bulgaria) was a Bulgarian émigré who had excelled in his country's State Academy of Music. With a thorough grounding in conventional classical music, he developed a reputation for exploratory performance and composition in jazz, and fitted straight into Don Ellis's big band soon after his arrival in the USA from 1970 until his presence in the Cobham band solidified. Glenn Ferris (b1950, Los Angeles) became a musician at a very early age, studying classical music first, and then jazz trombone with Don Ellis where he will have befriended Milcho. Alex Blake (b1951, Panama) was a close friend of Billy's with the same central-American birthright, and the same Brooklyn upbringing. His career began with Sun Ra's Arkestra in 1970, before joining Cobham's band for *Total Eclipse*. Adept on both acoustic and electric bass, he became a devotee of jazz-rock fusion and moved on to play with most of the top New York-based jazzers.

In the summer of 1974, the band toured Europe, but it was still proving hard to hold the band together. The new genre had reached such a point of development that everyone - encouraged by the massive success of the Mahavishnu Orchestra - could see the potential in going out on his own. No-one wanted to play second fiddle in somebody else's band. Good though Cobham was, he was a drummer. In particular, the Brecker Brothers, as lead instrumentalists and composers, rightly anticipated stardom for themselves, but they wouldn't find it playing on other peoples' records. They wanted to scribe their own mark on the musical monument, and Cobham was still not cutting it commercially, despite the considerable promise of these albums.

Billy Cobham: *A Funky Thide of Sings* **– 1975 (***)**

The Brecker Brothers continued to appear on Billy's Cobham's albums. Next came the clumsily titled *A Funky Thide of Sings* (1975), along with Glenn Ferris (trombone), Alex Blake (bass) and John Scofield (guitar), who began to settle in post for a while. Others, like guitarists Cornell Dupree and John

Abercrombie, would flit in and out like one of Cobham's trade winds. This album is one of those frustratingly misleading packages that undoubtedly caused many potential customers to look at other albums in the rack. Not only is there no singing on the album, but it is neither about orang-utans, nor is it funny in any way. This is serious funk, played with much energy and verve. Billy likes to sprinkle his albums with his own solos, and here he does so as an introduction to three of the tracks.

The opening track, *Panhandler*, is fiery funk, with an insistent foreground bass riff, regular tight brass licks, and Sco's electric guitar sounding as much like a rocker's as you will hear. Add in Billy's heavy-duty stick-work, and the result is an exciting introduction to this album. *Sorcery* is an opportunity to break out the electric gizmos, and, using much the same formula as on the previous track, plus Billy's crash cymbals, the short second track is an extension to the first. Track 3, *A Funky Thide Of Sings*, allows Michael the first horn solo, and is another similar Cobham composition with good horn writing, lively bass and a memorable funky theme. Blake's tune, *Thinking Of You* is funky in a different way, with some good chord changes missing from the earlier tracks. Michael and Sco take turns to solo and by the time the tune fades at 4.15, the memory of a good tune is strong.

Most notable from our present point of view is the first appearance of Randy's composition, *Some Skunk Funk*. Here recorded in 1974 and it is one his latest tunes, and one of which he is very pleased, since it features on the eponymous debut album from the new, yet-to-be-formed (1975) band, The Brecker Brothers. This will be discussed in depth below. For now, this is a virgin version. Unambiguously intended to be a rabble-rouser, this interpretation is dominated by Cobham's hyperactive percussion, especially when he resorts to crash cymbals that sometimes eclipse the other musicians. Nevertheless, it follows the BB version quite closely, played at an identical 132 bpm, and allows Michael plenty of room to unzip his holdall. Randy, however, chooses not to solo on his own tune, but the track is five minutes of sizzling funk.

Next is *Light At The End Of The Tunnel*, a classic example of the kind of 1970s music that was used in classic cop movies and TV series. Track 7 is a drum solo lasting almost ten minutes, called *A Funky Kind Of Thing* that makes use of some electronic effects that were probably novel at the time. Even without the effects, it is a good example of Billy's mastery of his kit, but is not especially funky. Presumably, it was this kind of music that helped get Billy voted "Best Drummer" in the Christmas *Down Beat* poll. The final track is *Moody Modes*, a substantial composition of twelve minutes, written by Milcho Leviev, who starts it off, and sets the scene for a combination of thoughtful improvisations on acoustic piano, coupled to some ensemble sections in which Randy's trumpet at last finds a place in the foreground. For those listeners beginning to tire of the other, more popular offerings, this is a fine piece of modern jazz, properly developed and adventurously performed.

Probably Billy Cobham's most commercial record to date, this album (excluding the final two tracks) is filled with short pieces that have instant appeal and must have received a lot of airplay. It still has much to offer in 2013, but remains a curious package.

Billy Cobham: *Shabazz*– 1975 (***)

Tom Barlow writing the sleeve notes for *Spectrum* (1973) described fusion musicians who "believed that the way forward was to continue playing jazz, plug-in, incorporate rock beats and crank the volume up to 11." [27] Cobham apparently also saw fusion as "a natural transition to a heavier feel, set in motion by 1960s boogaloo." Hmm. The listener's anticipation for the album was whetted by sentences like "Some of the electronica sounds primal but is more fun than techno." On the sleeve notes for Cobham's next release, *Crosswinds* (1974), Barlow continued the same sickly vein of writing: "Here is an album inspired by his [Cobham's] obsession with capturing nature through the eye of a lens, which he viewed in terms of 'sound portraits'. Cobham even took the photograph for the album cover. 'From the sonic to the visual, this was the whole concept, and the album was a snapshot of who I was at the time... I was looking for the real Billy Cobham by exploring and representing the things that moved me.' This is the piece that Billy would have written for the Mahavishnu Orchestra had he been given the chance." [27] Barlow had suggested that Cobham had not felt that his own compositions had been given the respect they deserved with Mahavishnu, but the split was about far more than that. Apparently, the shadow of McLaughlin's band still loomed large over Billy.

The Brecker Brothers went on tour with Billy Cobham in the middle of 1974 and *Shabazz* was assembled as a collection of four live recordings, three from the *Rainbow Theatre*, London on 13 July, and with one track taken from the band's earlier performance at the *Montreux Jazz Festival* on America's Independence Day. The band was the same one that had recorded *A Funky Thide of Sings*, except that John Abercrombie was back instead of John Scofield.

The title track has much to offer the listener. First, it's another fine example of Cobham's amazing power drumming technique in which, as a left-handed musician, he plays a right-handed kit. Randy plays a substantial, blistering solo using a muted wah-wah electric sound until 9.00 when it is Milcho's turn to mesmerise the audience with a synthesiser improvisation to Billy's relentless driving pulse. Finally, at 12.13, the players are mustered for a final run through the long-forgotten theme.

The five-minute recording of *Taurian Matador* is another focus for Leviev's creativity, as well as more intricate, amazing drumming from the boss. The short passages of ensemble playing are tight, despite some phrases that are so fast that individual notes are lost in the frenzy.

Red Baron gives time for breath, with a slower funkier rendition of this popular piece from Billy's repertoire, but it's not long before the need to expend energy bursts through. This time, Glenn Ferris gets a solo spot, followed by a jazz-rock improvisation by John Abercrombie. The Breckers play only in support for this track.

The fourth and last track is entitled *Tenth Pinn*, which begins with seventy seconds of drums and then enters an extensive series of demanding improvisations at speeds sometimes in excess of 185 beats per minute. The final third of the track is also taken up with another of Billy's exceptional drum solos.

Listening to this group of Billy's albums is well worth the exercise, for, even as the Brecker Brothers are not spotlighted except for a few solo spots, their main contribution is in providing masterful horn colourings to Billy's powerful music. It is Billy Cobham who, rightly, resides firmly in the spotlight throughout the albums, leading from the front with astonishing tirades of drumming, whilst his sidemen purvey his mostly tuneful, imaginative compositions in very demanding situations. Billy's approach to drumming was described by one contemporary observer as audacious, over-the-top, unmatched and very different. [28] Without question, these albums (along with his work for Mahavishnu Orchestra) contributed substantially to Billy's reputation as being the strongest drummer of the 1970s.

In 2001 Billy Cobham was named one of the "25 Most Influential Drummers" by *Modern Drummer* magazine. Griffith summarised Cobham's career thus, "Although there are many all-time greats, Billy Cobham is one of the very few who can truly be called a pivotal drummer in music history. He changed the way we set up our drums and cymbals, he changed the way we play them, and he changed the way we play music." [28]

As Billy Cobham continued into the future with a long series of solo-led projects, and a joint enterprise in further fusion with George Duke, the Brecker Brothers' plans were at last beginning to crystallise, and they left his band at this point.

Other Projects In The Early 1970s

During the early 1970s, lots of other projects had opened up for the two brothers. One of the more curious was their involvement with John Lennon and Yoko Ono in the Plastic Ono Band, showing that both men were entirely content to get involved in the wider world of music. Having made his mark, Michael went on to appear on Lennon's *Mind Games* (1973), and Ono's *Feeling the Space* (1973), and *A Story* (1974).

Michael and Randy also played on the milestone recording of Average White Band's *AWB* (1974), with its notable track, *Pick Up the Pieces*. The Average White Band is a funk and R&B band formed in 1971 by Alan Gorrie (vocals / bass) and Malcolm Duncan (tenor saxophone), with Onnie McIntyre, Hamish Stuart, Roger Ball, and Robbie McIntosh joining them in the original line-up. The band had a series of soul and disco hits between 1974 and 1980 and continue to perform in 2013. Emanating from Glasgow, Scotland, the band didn't find success until the musicians went to the USA. A support slot at Eric Clapton's comeback concert in 1973 was a good start, and MCA Records released their debut LP, *Show Your Hand* (1973). The record sold poorly. Then, hearing a demo tape at a party in 1973, Atlantic Records' Vice President, Jerry Wexler, signed them on first hearing. The band relocated to New York where producer Arif Mardin took charge of the band's second album, *AWB* (1974). Mardin drafted in a number of session players to boost the sound of the material. Besides the Brecker Brothers, there were Marvin Stamm and Mel Davis (trumpets), Glenn Ferris (trombone) and Ralph MacDonald (percussion). The single *Pick Up The Pieces* was released in the United Kingdom in July 1974 but failed to chart. When the album was released in the United States in October 1974, radio stations there started to play the song, and on 22 February 1975, it went to the top of the US singles chart and peaked at number five on the soul charts. After its US success, the song charted in the UK and climbed to number six. *Pick Up the Pieces* also made it to number eleven on the US disco chart. The record is probably their best-known tune today. Meanwhile, the album *AWB* (1974) reached #1 in the US charts the following year.

George Clinton's Parliament

The full story of George Clinton's musical career is long, complicated, amazing and unique. Needless to say, there is no room here to do more than describe it in outline, but I must include this material because of connections to the Brecker Brothers.

George Clinton (b1941, Kannapolis NC) began his musical career with a doo-wop band called The Parliaments, named after a cigarette brand. In the early 1960s he worked in Detroit as a staff songwriter for the Motown label, and began to specialise in songs with strong funk content. He formed a wide group of friends with whom he performed in a number of groups. Many of these talented friends went on to have notable careers of their own. For example, Maceo Parker (b1943, Kinston NC) was a brilliant alto saxophone player with a readily identifiable sound. William (Bootsy) Collins (b1951, Cincinnati OH) was a very successful singer-songwriter who was a leading exponent of the slap bass style of electric bass. With his band, the Pacemakers, he was hired to back

James Brown in 1970, when they became known as the J.B.s. Collins joined Parliament in 1972. Bernie Worrell (b1944, Long Branch NJ) was a keyboard player who joined Clinton's first group, The Parliaments in 1970. A fully trained musician, he made a speciality of playing the Minimoog, as well as the Hammond organ and Fender Rhodes electric piano. Worrell contributed a great deal to the band's catalogue of songs and arrangements. Fred Wesley (b1943, Columbus GA) was a trombone player who joined Clinton's collective in 1975 along with Maceo Parker after leaving James Brown's J.B. band, in which he both led the band, and orchestrated much of the music. Later, he would break away from Clinton too with his own band, The Horny Horns.

The flightpath of these musicians begins in 1970 with the formation of two parallel bands. The first was Parliament, which released an album called *Osmium* (1970) on the Invictus label. It featured Clinton and Worrell, with Raymond Davis (vocals), Ramon (Tiki) Fulwood (drums), Clarence (Fuzzy Haskins (vocals), Eddie Hazel (guitar), Tyrone Lampkin (drums), Billy (Bass) Nelson (bass), Lucius (Tawl) Ross, (guitar), Garry Shider (guitar), Calvin Simon (vocals), and Grady Thomas (vocals). The album had little success, and it was not until the band signed for the Casablanca record label as a group of five musicians and five singers, that it made an impact in the charts. Those records released over the period starting with *Up For The down Stroke* (1974) and ending with *Trombipulation* (1980) saw an ever-changing line-up of players and singers.

To make matters more complicated, in parallel, in 1970, Clinton started up a second band called Funkadelic. The band was contracted to a different label called Westbound Records and released eight albums from 1970-76, and then a further four albums under different labels, before disbanding in 1981. Therefore, many writers describe Clinton's work under the umbrella name Parliament-Funkadelic and the membership of both bands is best described as a 'collective.' In the 1980s, the bands evolved again, this time into a unit called P-Funk, a name obviously derived from its progenitors. By this time, the collective had developed a powerful sub-genre of music that some call P-Funk, perhaps best described as psychedelic funk, but based upon a distillation of funk music with provocative lyrics, wildly extravagant costumes, and themes based on strange, fictional, extra-terrestrial characters. Not surprisingly, the bands were very popular in live performances where the show-biz elements gave rise to high entertainment value. This live performance style was transmitted to the records, which became renowned for purveying fun, party atmospheres. However, external observers could easily conclude that the bands' performances, both live and on records, were more about expressions of an over-arching Clinton 'culture' than they were about performance of the music, which had become a small part of the overall P-Funk circus.

It was into this remarkable mix that the Brecker Brothers found themselves invited. As Parliament began its upward trajectory in the mid 1970s, Randy and Michael appeared as guest musicians on the most successful albums, *Mothership Connection* (1974) and *The Clones of Dr Funkenstein* (1975). After a hiatus, they also appeared on the band's last album, *Trombipulation* (1980). There followed just two other guest appearances, as both men played for the P-Funk Allstars on the track *I Really Envy The Sunshine* from the band's *Plush Funk* (1980) album; Michael also played on *Oh I* from Funkadelic's *The Electric Spanking Of War Babies* (1981).

When I asked Randy about these times he replied, "Yeah, George and all those guys, Bernie Worrell and the guys that wrote for him and played in the horn section, but Bernie comes to mind first. He was a wonderful arranger. You couldn't really classify any of those guys. They loved music, they were funksters first, but they knew all about fusion, and Bernie and Fred [Wesley] wrote a lot of those charts, and those guys are expert arrangers, Fred especially, a jazz musician first, but had a great feeling for funk and fusion and the whole thing, and any situation you could put him in. He would write great arrangements, and we would just follow, you know. He was a big influence on my own writing as a matter of fact, those sessions were valuable learning experiences for me and my brother." [5]

Clive Davis, Steve Backer and Arista Records

Clive Davis (b1932) was born into a Jewish family in Brooklyn, New York. After qualifying with excellence from the Harvard Law School, in his thirties he found himself appointed as General Counsel of Columbia Records, for which company he became Vice President and General Manager in 1966. As holder of probably the most powerful position in the music industry, he soon made his mark by recognising the value of rock music to the business. He hired Janis Joplin's Big Brother and the Holding Company in 1967. Then, in 1968, he was responsible for hiring Blood Sweat & Tears, of which Randy was a member. Davis followed up on these decisions with acquisition of many groups and artists who would become top names: Chicago, Santana, Boz Scaggs, Billy Joel, Bruce Springsteen, Aerosmith and Earth, Wind and Fire, are some examples. In addition, he signed such artists as Neil Diamond, Pink Floyd, Herbie Hancock and The Isley Brothers. [29]

Clive Davis soon came into personal contact with his unrelated namesake, Miles Davis, who had been Columbia's biggest-selling jazz artist since 1956. However, jazz music, which had been the dominant music form for several decades, fell way behind when the sales of pop and rock music exploded exponentially in the 1960s; jazz was not the lucrative market it had once been. At first, Clive was not alone in finding it hard to bridge the gap between his angle for business and Miles's unique angle on music. At first, the two men had what might be called a 'difficult' business relationship, but, once Miles had sussed Clive out, Miles wrote that, "He and I got along well, because he thinks like an artist instead of a straight businessman. He had a good sense for what was happening; I thought he was a great man." [30] Clive was generously supportive to Miles during the next critical phase in his musical career, and encouraged Miles in his drive to extend jazz into the world of rock and pop music. (Despite all that, Miles still fell out with Columbia, and eventually signed a contract with Warner Bros.)

Clive Davis continued to secure his position within CBS Records until 1973 when he was fired for alleged misconduct. The event turned out to be a small deviation in the course of music history, for Clive Davis soon reappeared working for Columbia Pictures. In 1974, Clive Davis took over as President of Bell Records, and by 1975, had merged the various Columbia Pictures legacy labels such as Colpix Records, Colgems Records, and Bell into a new company called Arista Records, of which he was president. From this time, the music executive increased his influence with signings such as Barry Manilow, Melissa Manchester, Dionne Warwick, Aretha Franklin, and perhaps his greatest success, Whitney Houston.

I asked Randy how the Brecker Brothers Band had come into being. "Yeah, well we [Randy and Michael] were really busy together. We were playing with Billy Cobham, who was in Dreams. He left to join Mahavishnu, Mike and I rejoined Horace Silver, with Will Lee from Dreams and we played with Horace for about a year. I played with Larry Coryell and the Eleventh House - quite a lot of different people. I played with Stevie Wonder for around nine months. Mike was just getting his chops together playing with a lot of people. By 1974 or so, I had the idea or the urge to write my own music because I'd been playing so much of other people's music and also another great musician came to New York, Dave Sanborn, who I'd gone to camp with. We went to a music camp when we were fifteen together, and stayed in touch. He was playing with the Paul Butterfield Blues Band while I was playing with Blood Sweat & Tears. We were pretty close friends, and when he moved to town, and Mike was in town, they both came relatively around the same time - 1969 into 1970 - I had the idea to write with them in mind as the horn section. The intent was to do a solo record. I hadn't really thought of the name.

"You remember I mentioned the rehearsal big bands that used to exist in the 1960s? Well by now bands didn't exist that much because rock had taken over, but essentially we had a rehearsal fusion band. I would go to Don Grolnick's loft apartment, a lot of the guys, Will, Don, Chris Parker who played drums, lived in the same place, and once a week we'd all go and try stuff we had been writing. You see I was writing a lot; Grolnick was writing a lot. I was writing specifically a lot for Mike and Sanborn, as a horn section, so we'd go there every week and just try this stuff. At one point I had about nine or ten tunes of my own stuff, and I was just getting ready to go around and do a demo and try to sell it as a Randy Brecker solo record.

"I got a call from a man named Steve Backer who had just signed a production deal with Arista records and Clive Davis. It was a new record company, and I had worked with Clive when he was the president of Columbia, so I knew his ex-routines, and this was a nice opportunity. The catch was, and this is kinda funny, Steve Backer said, you know, if you call your band the Brecker Brothers, I'll sign you guys right now. You don't have to a demo. I heard about this music you're writing. And my first reaction was no, no, this is supposed to be a Randy Brecker solo record. It's my record. I've spent a lot of time writing all this stuff. Mike and Dave hadn't thought about a career yet, they were still in the shed practising. And I held my ground for a couple of days when Steve kept calling and saying, you call it Brecker Brothers, and I started thinking, Well this is really a nice opportunity, he's not going to bend, and of course my brother and Sanborn played great, and I thought it's going to sound kinda funny if Sanborn's going to be in the front line and we're going to call it Brecker Brothers, but OK Steve, call it Brecker Brothers.

"And that's how it started, but you know it was a good idea. And Steve liked the fact that people respond to brother bands, and it was a little funny that Sanborn was kinda the invisible guy, he was with the band for a couple years, he played on the first two or three records, until he started his own career, but that's how it started.

"The first record was propelled - let me say this, too - so I recorded my nine tunes, I think I had ten, but I recorded nine. I played them for Clive, *Some Skunk Funk*, *Sponge*, all these tunes that later became kinda classics. He said, well I love what you're writing but you have to go back and do a single or basically I'm not going to release this. I protested once again. I said, no this is supposed to be... I already... we called it Brecker Brothers, this is supposed to be my solo record. Now you want us to go and do a single, I don't know about that, and he said, well either you do it, or I won't put it out, so he made us go back. We went back to our rehearsal studio and we were very lucky, in a way, because inside of three hours we had jammed up with two of them, and it became *Sneaking Up Behind You*. I still have the cassette, and we stuck it on the record. And that's what really sold the thing. It became an R&B hit. We rose up the charts, it became number 2 or 3 on the urban R&B charts and that's what really sold the record, *Some Skunk Funk*, in the beginning. *Skunk Funk* was a longer sell, and the next thing we knew we were way more popular than we had ever envisioned. This was supposed to be a hobby, because we were all doing studio work. So that is it in a nutshell." [5]

Steve Backer (b1944) started working in the pop music industry in 1969 at MGM / Verve and Elektra. From there he moved on to become general manager of Impulse! Records. He started with Clive Davis's Arista label in 1974 as Director of Jazz A&R. Later, he would go on to become another well respected powerful music industry mogul working for such labels as Wyndham Hill, RCA and Novus.

Interviewed in the late 1990s about the declining jazz record sales, Backer said, "To beat a situation like you have today, you can't think that a record is just ten songs. You have to think in terms of meaningful producers, alternative marketing possibilities. You have to figure out how you help to create a new trend without being manipulative of the music or musicians. Whatever the new movement is, whether it's fusion, or New Age, or instrumental pop music, or the young lions, or the *avant-garde*, if you can be part of the movement you have a great chance of being successful. It's not even about the quality of the recordings, really. It's about a complex coalition of things, and when the mainstream press, for example, has tired of the young lion idea, it has to find something else to write about. Television shows, or fashion magazines, don't care about quality, they care about the package, and to break a jazz artist out you need that outside support. The music has to be sold as a pop product, where the artists signify something extra-musical." [31]

Randy was well aware of the musical realities of hitting the big time. "It's weird. I went to a discotheque the other night and I heard myself on five tunes in a row, all by different artists. 'Somebody's cleaning up man,' people are probably saying. Unfortunately, it's not us. You have to have an amazing hit of your own before you see one cent after the sessions and even then, if it's your record, it's going to take you years to recoup the royalties. That's the way it's set up." [13]

Arista would be the Brecker Brothers' label for no less than eight albums. The legacy of the Brecker Brothers Band music spanning 1975 to 1982 is today carefully managed as part of the Sony BMG Group. Recently, this material was re-released under Randy's supervision as *The Complete Arista Albums Collection* (2012). The albums are a priceless part of the history of music, and I shall now describe their contents in detail.

The Brecker Brothers: *The Brecker Brothers* – 1975 (****)

By 1975, fusion was so well established across the spectrum of pop-rock-jazz-soul that we need only look superficially at the broader music environment to find Tower of Power, a band that had been specialising in horn-driven soul-based music since tenor sax player Emilio Castillo formed the band in 1970. Originally based in the West Coast Bay area of San Francisco, the music was very much influenced by James Brown. Thus, for example, by the time of the album *In the Slot* (1975), featuring mostly vocal tracks but with the instrumental gem *Ebony Jam* (1975) played by Castillo, with Steve Kupka and Lenny Pickett (saxes), Mic Gillette and Greg Adams (trumpets), Chester Thompson (organ),

Francis Rocco Prestia (bass) and David Garibaldi (drums), the template for a similar kind of sound in jazz was already crossing over from the popular arena. Tower of Power worked with many artists including the Monkees, Santana, Elton John, Linda Lewis, John Lee Hooker, Rod Stewart, Jefferson Starship, Heart, Spyro Gyra, Lyle Lovett, Poison, Phish, Toto and Aerosmith. They would also be one of the forces behind the immense success of Huey Lewis and the News in the mid 1980s. In covering such a wide range of the music of the 1970s and 80s, their influence has been immeasurable.

The very fact that fusion was now so popular was, of course, the reason why Michael was in such demand from musicians across the full spectrum of the music business. Everyone wanted a tenor saxophone solo on their album tracks and Michael, at 26, was already regarded as the best in the business. He didn't need to lead his own band when there was so much work playing sessions. Nevertheless, The Brecker Brothers did come into existence at the beginning of 1975 and became one of the best-known names in jazz-fusion and indisputably, the best 'brothers band'. In January 1975, Michael and Randy went into Todd Rundgren's studio called *Secret Sound* on 24th St. NYC to record an album that was to play a major part in the history of music, the first in a series of six by The Brecker Brothers. It was called *The Brecker Brothers* (1975). By this time, there was significant experience amongst session musicians to make it a strong idea. Harvey Mason, their first choice drummer for the recording, had appeared on *Head Hunters* (1974), a massive fusion hit for Herbie Hancock. And there was, of course, Dreams. Fortunately, ex-Dreamers Don Grolnick and Will Lee were available to join. They stayed for several years, whilst Mason's place on the record was taken by Chris Parker in the band.

Although the band did not break any records for album sales, or weeks ranked highly in the charts, it was sufficiently influential to bring about a change in the sound and style of music itself. Their colourful, brassy, funky sound brought jazz-fusion down a couple of notches from its cerebral, virtuosic decibel-driven heights and made it more accessible to the wider public without sacrificing quality in the process. To say that it went so far as to change the form of popular music, even to re-invent easy listening music would offend some people, but the trademark sound of the Brecker Brothers was absorbed by many thousands of other musicians and regurgitated in movie and TV scores throughout the eighties.

It was really from this point that the sound of a tight horn section playing short, syncopated, often very staccato, phrases emerged. A number of specialist, dedicated small groups of musicians sub-contracted their services on literally thousands of albums. Jerry Hey is one such very successful trumpet player who contributed greatly to the development of this element of jazz-fusion. His career began in 1976 and has so far won him seven Grammy awards. Some of the many artists Jerry has worked for are Michael Jackson, Quincy Jones, Earth

Wind & Fire, Al Jarreau, Toto, Barbra Streisand, Whitney Houston and Elton John. Along with his playing partner, trombonist Bill Reichenbach, Jerry is to be found on many records that were much enhanced by their colourful, tight jazz inflections, such as *I Am* (1979) by Earth Wind and Fire, Michael Jackson's *Off the Wall* (1979), *Thriller* (1982) and *Bad* (1987), Al Jarreau's *Jarreau* (1983) and *High Crime* (1984).

So, whilst the Brecker Brothers Band was not the trailblazing outfit of the time, Randy and Michael had already spent years of close involvement in the process that led to tight jazz-fusion outfits. When the band finally emerged in 1975, it was their very unusual harmonies that set them apart. Perhaps the most famous piece on which they played as hirelings was *Pick Up the Pieces* from *AWB* (1974). Everyone who lived through this period would have heard this tune by the Average White Band, a piece that feels like it must have massively impacted on the music scene. Yet it was entirely untypical of that Band's music – AWB did vocals, not instrumentals. The fog starts to dissipate when inspection of the *AWB* sleeve notes reveals that not only Michael and Randy, but Ralph McDonald, Marvin Stamm and Glen Ferris were also in support. Few people, on the other hand, were as familiar with the Breckers' equally excellent *Sneakin' Up Behind You*, recorded a few months later in January 1975. It's tempting to conclude that the funky rhythm and even the harmony in the melody shared a common starting point, but, whilst Average White Band did not repeat the success of their first serious instrumental jazz-fusion piece, the Breckers took the guts of their own piece and developed it strongly over the coming years. Both pieces are credited to the entire set of musicians in the respective bands that played them. It would make an interesting subject for debate as to who was influenced by whom.

One of the most obvious ways the Breckers developed their style was in their use of harmony, which at that time was very experimental. Without turning this discussion into a difficult essay on music theory, I would sum up by describing the music as two keys working against (or, perhaps, in resonance with) each other. We might call this, parallel harmonies. It is exemplified in the first two tracks of their debut album.

Some Skunk Funk opens the album, and, as on Cobham's *A Funky Thide Of Sings*, is played at its intended pace of 132 bpm. Already there is a feeling that the melody doesn't quite match the accompaniment. Imagine a pair of ballroom dancers. The two partners perform carefully choreographed steps in close harmony that is characteristic of the given dance form. Sometimes, as in a tango, the dancer's legs become closely intertwined in exotic intercourse. They don't normally step on each other's toes, but it's close. I think the harmonies played by Michael and Randy were comparable to a new style of funky tango. As with many things that are new, it takes a while to catch on. Dance purists might be offended at the way their carefully defined styles are being extended.

It's a seriously funky track, though, and it doesn't seem to matter: there's a lot of other stuff to take your mind off the details of the harmonies being used.

It's difficult not to notice the mismatch of harmony in the next track, *Sponge*, where the two keys (I ought really to say modes) are more obviously set against each other. Setting two players to play lines that are only a semi-tone apart was forbidden in most traditional methods of composition. Not so here. Both of these tracks are less jazzy in the sense that they concentrate on getting across the composer's ideas, rather than those of the performers. Therefore, improvisation takes a back seat, to ensemble playing.

Track 3 is *A Creature of Many Faces*, a thoroughly rock-based piece in which, during almost eight minutes, there is more scope to develop several ideas, as well as to feature both lead instruments in solos, Michael from 2.40 and Randy from 4.05. The beautiful, clean solo sounds, placed well into the album, are in contrast to all that has gone before, and they come as a welcome change. Unlike the prickly sponge, this is a sea creature you could allow to play with your kids.

With *Twilight*, it's back to the formula of the first two tracks – lots of ensemble, changes of tempo and rock rhythms in the roots. Then, unexpectedly, everything changes into a fast samba with Don Grolnick playing organ! Later, Steve Khan's solid electric guitar work takes the melody through. The boys squeeze a huge amount of ideas into seven minutes and forty seconds, and there's a lot of orchestration behind the energetic delivery.

Track 5 is *Sneakin' Up Behind You*, discussed above. Again, there are no solos on show, and it's all about horn tone that sounds almost as if a single new instrument has been invented. As I listen, however, the trumpet naturally seems to catch my ear above the sound of the two saxophones, and sometimes I get the incorrect impression that Michael is not contributing much to the album.

The next track, *Rocks*, is perhaps the most remarkable on the album. This piece pops up occasionally on albums by other jazzers looking for something that seriously challenges them. After a slower, written intro, it bursts into a fast rock rhythm with drums and bass working superbly together, wah-wah guitar, and, over-riding it all, a stunningly difficult melody. At last, from 2.32, there is a wonderful duel between the two saxophones. This track is a highlight of the album.

Levitate is a composition that broadens the scope of the album, adding variety in the form of a quiet, contemplative and beautifully executed modern jazz piece. It floats, suspended in mid-air, as its title decrees that it must, and Randy's solo swirls in a mist of emotion. It's all about feel, and less about rhythm, in this gentle four-beat ballad. Then, in total contrast, *Oh My Stars* is a number in which Randy exercises his vocal chords instead of his lips. Throughout his career, Randy shows a desire to sing his music and this is an early example. His slightly husky, weak style is quite self-effacing as he tries to hide behind his humour and his broad Bronx dialect mimicking English West Country 'r's. Sanborn plays an excellent solo, and this could have made a good instrumental, but I shouldn't complain about the vocals in this case.

D.B.B. is an enigmatic title for a final funky flourish that, with Mason's excellent assistance, and another driving tenor sax solo, brings this very good, innovative album to an exciting and rewarding close.

Most observers would conclude that it was the Brecker Brothers who set the pace for this style of jazz-fusion that was so different from what was happening with the likes of Weather Report, Chick Corea, Mahavishnu Orchestra, and, to some extent, Herbie Hancock. The Breckers' brand of jazz-fusion was very different from these other contemporary fusion bands. Even without the unusual harmonic structures, the sound was different. Guitarist Steve Khan remembers it especially: "Of the great jazz-fusion groups from the early '70s (Weather Report, Mahavishnu Orchestra, and Return to Forever), the Brecker Brothers Band was the only group to feature a 'mini' horn section, and what a horn section it was." [32]

Steve Khan (b1947, LA) was the son of famous songwriter Sammy Cahn. He was a late arrival as a guitarist, first choosing drums as his preferred instrument. When he made no progress on drums, he made a determined switch to guitar in 1966, whereupon he made rapid progress until he moved to New York in 1969, having graduated from UCLA. His first big gig was for Larry Coryell's Eleventh House band (for whom Randy played too), and from there he played in a 1973 version of BS&T. By the time he was chosen to play with the Brecker Brothers, he was a close friend of Larry Coryell and was making his own albums, which started with *Two For The Road* (1976), *Tightrope* (1977), *The Blue Man* (1978), and *Arrows* (1979). So would begin a long series of albums with Steve as leader of small jazz groups, and the same strong song-writing skills that his father had used so successfully would be evident throughout Steve's career.

The presence of David Sanborn (b1945, Tampa FL), in the band for the album, was a major coup. Fortunately, Randy and David had been good friends since 1961 when they had both attended a Stan Kenton band camp at Indiana University. (It also firmed up Randy's plans to go to IU to study music.) Randy made friends with Don Grolnick, Keith Jarrett, Lou Marini, and Mitch Farber, but it was their common love of R&B that brought Randy close to David Sanborn, a relationship that lasts to this day, despite the divergence of careers. Sanborn was special even then, winning many prizes with each passing year. He had gained much experience playing on the road with the Paul Butterfield Blues Band from 1967 to 1972, during which time he played at the famous *Woodstock* festival. Next he became sax player of choice for the likes of Paul Simon and

Stevie Wonder, for whom he played on *Talking Book* (1972). His tone and soulful style had become unique, and was highly sought after. The album *Taking Off* (1975) was the start of his own major solo recording career, and propelled him to stardom. He quickly became too busy to go out on the road with the Brecker Brothers.

Let's not forget the other musicians in the band who were as essential as the three horn players: Don Grolnick (1948-1996, Brooklyn, NY), a friend since Michael's earliest days in New York, was a brilliant keyboardist with a real flair for composition. His own tunes were to pop up everywhere over the next two decades and he would be in constant demand with the other jazzers of the New York circuit. Grolnick also played keyboards for David Sanborn's band from 1980-84, as well as with Mike Mainieri and Mike Brecker in Steps and Steps Ahead, and on many other albums with the likes of George Benson, Mike Stern, Bob Mintzer and Peter Erskine. For over twenty years, he was James Taylor's musical director.

Will Lee (b1952, San Antonio TX) was inspired to learn the drums after watching the Beatles on the Ed Sullivan show. Growing up in Miami, he had a band at 12 and quickly changed to bass, an instrument that he felt offered more opportunities to play in bands. Later, specialising in bass, he graduated in music from the University of Miami. It was Randy Brecker who spotted his talent and invited him to audition for Dreams, his first big break. Lee was to become a 'regular' in Brecker line-ups, his outstandingly rhythmic and funky style becoming a major part of the Brecker brand.

Despite the band's name, it was ostensibly Randy's gig. Big Bruv's imprint is stamped all over the early albums. On #1, he contributed almost all of the music and acted as producer, with or without help on occasions. He even demonstrated more than a passing interest in singing, presumably with the object of applying a commercial gloss to the product. Fortunately, there were plenty of instrumental recordings that tend to be of more interest to us today. Randy's work in the vocal arena was not really bad, although the timbre of his voice and the New York drawl may be annoying to some ears. These flaws are compensated by more than a dash of humour in his lyrics, the strong tunes and, of course, that magical Brecker sound. The evidence is that Michael was content to take a back seat in these early days of the band. Whilst he contributed a growing proportion of songs, and solos as time went by, there were occasions on the albums when his presence is very little in evidence.

Michael told *Crescendo* magazine in 1980 that he had not really wanted to form the band. "As for the Brecker Brothers band, to be honest, neither of us wanted to do it. He [Randy] had been writing, and he was originally approached by Arista to do a record, that I was going to play on, and it turns out they wanted to use both of us. I didn't want to get involved, because I wanted to stay free but

I said okay, what the heck, there wasn't anything commercial on there anyway. So I did the record, and then it ended up that we had a little minor hit on there, and it turned into this monster that I hadn't foreseen. Then I just started getting used to it, and eventually I started contributing with the music and everything. The way it is now, we're going to branch off and start doing our own projects and it's really a welcome relief. However the Brecker Brothers band is a very musical setup. I think we have a unique thing to say. I'm certainly not going to give it up. I like playing with Randy, I like his writing, and all that, but the time has come when we just have to pursue some of our own avenues for a minute. It's all constructive." [33]

A *Down Beat* reviewer found a good description of the new Brecker Band jazz-funk style. "[Randy] Brecker has done an exceptional job in capturing a tight yet unencumbered large group sound. The Breckers' success stems from their ability to make complex and difficult arrangements appear simple and clear. The ensemble playing is magnificently scored with the rich orchestration, and yet the overall effect is of a single melodic voice." [34]

Around March 1975, in a 'Debut Feature' article for *Blues & Soul* Magazine, Randy told the interviewer that their hit record, "*Sneakin' Up Behind You*, is influenced from three sides - the AWB, Herbie Hancock, and Stevie Wonder." [35] The magazine was especially interested in the fact that, along with AWB, two or three white British and American bands had finally broken through into charts usually dominated by black musicians. The magazine reviewed the album thus: "Brass stars, Mike and Randy Brecker, are currently disco scoring via their funky instrumental, *Sneakin' Up Behind You*, which has a definite *Pick Up The Pieces* flavour to it. But that hit is slightly misleading if you're thinking of following up by buying the LP because *Sneakin'* is the only directly commercial cut on display. The brothers lean far more towards jazz, although their rhythms are at all times infectious and frequently funky." [36]

It's hard not to conclude that *Sneakin' Up Behind You* was influenced by working with the Average White Band. To some extent, Randy agreed. In the same interview he said, "We've become tight friends with the Average White Band guys. I wouldn't say that they had actually physically influenced us, but our single does owe something to *Pick Up The Pieces*, which we played on. But where they used five or six horns on their first album, we only used three. That album was the first time that we have met the guys and of course they used only themselves for their new *Cut The Cake* (1975) album. But for their sessions they wrote all of the parts and we only played what they wanted, so we don't take any credit for creating their sound." [36]

7th Avenue South

In the mid 1970s, as the jazz-rock fusion craze was at its height, work as a session musician was lucrative and plentiful for both brothers. Even so, it is both surprising and curious that they should agree to a sojourn in arguably the most outrageous band of the time. In December 1976, they briefly joined Frank Zappa and the Mothers of Invention. Zappa's contribution to music history is describable in many ways, most of which would be controversial and take a book to complete. Since this book is about jazz-fusion, I am not even going to attempt that. Some would argue that Zappa was using ideas based in jazz-fusion at this point in his career, but that is hardly surprising since there wasn't a lot he didn't try. Perhaps this is indicative of just how deeply jazz-fusion was penetrating the entire music business. Certainly, if Zappa had decided to do jazz-fusion, he could not have hired two more appropriate practitioners. During this short tour with Zappa for about a week, the Brothers contributed to the recording, *Live in New York* (1978). It was here that they met drummer Terry Bozzio, whom they hired to play in the band for *Heavy Metal Bebop* (1978) and the ten-day tour that went with it. What is perhaps more surprising is that Mike and Randy could find the necessary time away from their own projects. In particular, there was one very big project in the wind. Playing on the road with Zappa was one thing, but playing in small, constantly changing jazz groups with musicians such as Hal Galper, Chet Baker or Mike Mainieri, to name but a few, in their own New York jazz club, would surely be something else entirely!

Around 1977, Michael and Randy decided to capitalise on their position at the hub of New York's jazz-fusion community by taking the unusual step of opening their own jazz club. It was called 7th Avenue South and it probably had the broadest remit of any jazz club in existence at that time. As a result, some projects came to fruition that might never otherwise have occurred. Michael: "We had a very open booking policy. We weren't strictly, you know, an acoustic jazz club; there was a lot of electric music there as well. And we changed up a lot, and tried to, you know - our niche was that we sort of presented interesting music in many genres - a lot of R&B groups - and a lot of groups had their start there as well. And we attracted a New York audience that wanted to come out and enjoy themselves and hear some music. Steps Ahead had its beginning there. Jaco's Word of Mouth band actually began as a gig at 7th Avenue, and he wasn't allowed to advertise it because of his record company, but it was standing room only - and it was purely from word of mouth - so that's where that came from." There were many advantages, of course, but there were also less obvious downsides and it is interesting to note that Michael told Jason West he would never do it again! [37]

Ronnie Cuber remembered the club as one of his favourite haunts. "Well they opened a club called 7th Avenue South and it was a great venue because, being friends with Michael and Randy, I was able to book a few gigs on my own in the club and it became a real hotbed of young musicians, great musicians coming up, and having showcases. It was a great scene. It stayed open for about three or four years and then they sold it to another party. It just wasn't the same.

They changed the bandstand around to the other side of the room. It was a double level club. When you walked in there was the bar and the lounge, and then there was a staircase going up to where the music was. It was a nice club." [6]

The Brecker Brothers Band: *Back To Back* – 1976 (***)

It is sometimes the case that a band's second album really defines its identity. As far as the audience was concerned, The Brecker Brothers *Band* was promoted as just that, but with *Back To Back*, released a year later, The Brecker Brothers Band was celebrated in pop music style with a gatefold album spread showing its happy, smiling members photographed sitting in a line on the banks of the Hudson River, and wearing denims and uniform shirts emblazoned with the band logo. (In 1976, no British band would have done that!) Not for these guys, any suggestion of moody, pouting egos; instead, the message is one of a group of youthful musicians having a great time, and working together as a team. Besides Randy and Michael, there are Will Lee, Chris Parker, Don Grolnick, David Sanborn and Steve Khan. The rhythm section of keyboard, guitar, bass and drums is fronted by trumpet, tenor and alto saxophones, a formula that had become established as probably the most popular and versatile in the new jazz-rock-funk era.

Compared to their first album, *Back to Back* (1976) at first seems schizophrenic and inferior, as if Randy had used all his best ideas on the first album and needed help from his friends for the second. As he did for album #1, Randy continues to act as producer for promoter Steve Backer, but, unlike #1, nothing on this album is Randy's work alone, and there is quite a lot of co-written material, especially vocal pieces. Randy didn't get a lot from his brother! Michael contributed one of his own compositions, *Night Flight*, and helped with a couple of others. The interpretation, once again, is that this album was being pushed hard into the arena of crossover music – a strong move by jazz musicians to push open the door to popular music culture.

Keep It Steady (Brecker Bump) is a strong, commercial opening track. Will Lee's bass is in the foreground, and besides providing a powerful funk rhythm he is the main contributor to the 'Bump' element of the title. Co-writer Steve Khan plays the first solo, followed at three minutes by a set of what we might today call, 'classic Sanborn licks'. The sound has the feel of Sly and the Family Stone, with good use of backing vocals that don't dominate the music. Released as the B-side of the band's second single, there is a strong sense that the record company was aiming for the same customers that were buying Average White Band's *Pick Up The Pieces*.

The A-side of the single was *If You Wanna Boogie... Forget It*. In this number, the front line is supplemented with Lew Del Gatto's baritone sax. The piece has a stronger vocal line, with Will Lee now the nominated vocalist for the album. Fortunately, Lee never forgets his primary duties as funk electric bassist *par excellence*, whilst Grolnick's boogie is evident on acoustic piano.

Track three is *Lovely Lady*, a self-descriptive title that accurately indicates a soft ballad, not all of it sung, but enough to call it a vocal track. Rarely, we hear Michael on flute during this piece, and from 2.30, a romantic solo from Randy on flugelhorn is a highlight.

Night Flight is a heavy-duty instrumental piece from Mike's pen. Steve Gadd replaces Parker for this track, whilst the addition of lots of Brazilian-flavoured percussion from guests, Sammy Figueroa, and Rafael Cruz, pumps it up significantly. Steve Khan plays rock riffs on electric guitar as the horns make light work of their tightly written, fast phrases. The great excitement of this multi-layered music is capped off with a far-out electronic trumpet solo from Randy from 1.45, and Mike solos hard from 3.20 to 4.45. The difficult chord sequences over complex constructions place this piece in a higher echelon compared to the rest of the album. It's the liveliest night flight I've ever taken – definitely red eyes only here!

The vibrant, instrumental jazz-fusion mood continues with Randy's composition, *Slick Stuff*, which has more flute playing from Michael – listen well, for you'll struggle to find this anywhere else. Once again, the flavours are mostly funk, with close-harmony horns mixed with flighty flute phrases. Randy fleshes out the slick, melodic theme as he solos over two cycles from 1.50; Mike follows the pattern from 2.52. Chris Parker's drumming supported by Ralph MacDonald's rhythmic support is very impressive throughout and Will Lee's funk bass is extraordinary.

Dig A Little Deeper is Will's take on a funky party. With the background filled out by tight horns and dynamic backing vocals, this is a good example of the popular formula for 1970s jazz-funk.

Grease Piece is a very strong blues-funk instrumental number. After a 15-second, tight, funk intro, the horns play the theme up to 1.20 in a style that was created by the band, and which became a monogram for David Sanborn's early career. As Michael takes a substantial gutsy solo, commencing low and winding itself up tight, Sanborn is strong in the background. It cannot be overemphasised just how much this track defines large sections of blues-funk that crossed over into popular music. It could easily have been selected for the single release.

What Can A Miracle Do is an appealing ballad, written by Don Grolnick and Luther Vandross, but sung by Will Lee, who demonstrates a fine voice, more in the spotlight than he was for the third track. The track is the kind of music that is perhaps too sugary for listeners who prefer macho-funk-rock sounds. However, this is another part of the formula that was strongly promoted as commercial boundary-crossing material, designed to sell in greater quantities than jazz musicians were used to.

I Love Wastin' Time With You is another vocal number, but is richer in funk and jazz, especially with lively contributions in the first half from Don Grolnick on acoustic piano, as he did also on the previous track. The second half of the track is dominated by repeated choruses in which the tension is continuously increased by rampant horns and punchy rhythms. It's a good way to end a good album.

The problem for jazzers is that any kind of move into the prevailing pop music culture is assessed, not as steps ahead, but as steps down or back. So, after the fireworks of album #1, this could come as a disappointment to some listeners who disapprove of the commercial elements inserted into this otherwise creative, original new jazz form. This was the essence of the bad feelings many writers had about jazz-fusion.

The Brecker Brothers: *Don't Stop the Music* – 1977 (***)

Album #3 of the sequence of releases by the Brecker Brothers at once dispels any thoughts that the band was a discrete unit. Maybe on tour it was, but a quick look at the personnel alone shows that a change in the production objectives had been made. David Sanborn had decided to build a solo career – very successfully, as it turned out. The sound of the second saxophone was lost from now on. Instead of simply replacing him, the horns had been expanded and a string section brought in, presumably to make a bigger footprint in the commercial market. Executive producer Steve Backer had now hired Jack Richardson to be in charge of production. Richardson, a Canadian, had achieved great commercial success for the Canadian Coca Cola Co. through a record featuring a band called The Guess Who. His production of the successful album *Wheatfield Soul* (1968) led to a big international hit called *These Eyes*, and on to further success with rock outfits such as Alice Cooper and Badfinger.

Sometimes, when you pick up an album that you haven't heard for a while, your memory of it plays tricks on you. When I pick up the third Brecker Brothers album, *Don't Stop the Music* (1977), my memories are depressed by the lowlights instead of being excited by the highlights. The worst example is the opening track, *Finger Lickin' Good*, and its inevitable associations with advertisements for fried chicken. Straightaway, Richardson's footprint is noticeable. Not surprising, then, that this was chosen for the B-side of the band's latest single. A composition by Randy, this music might just have passed the test of good taste had he not asked his mom to write some words (I hesitate to call them lyrics!) for it. Let's move on...

The album might also have had a better residence in my memory with some different sequencing for - unlike the previous disc, which is an album of two halves - this is a collection of alternates. There are some very good pieces here, and track two, Michael's *Funky Sea, Funky Dew* is one of them. Not only is there a strong melody that works across genres, but Michael's delivery is of the kind that attracted the attention of thousands of musicians who wanted this sound on their records. The same style was what contributed to David Sanborn's commercial success, except that here Michael employs the smoother side of the tenor saxophone, rather than Sanborn's rougher textures of his alto instrument. At 1.45 the piece moves up a gear into a funky mode, whilst retaining a big band sound with horns and modern percussion comfortably placed alongside strings. By the time the music enters the fade-out ending, the mood has evolved with subtlety from gentle ballad to lively funk.

Next is the crossover production, *As Long As I've Got Your Love*, primarily an instrumental but with a substantive vocal track as Doug and Beverly Billard perform their own composition. Randy kicks it off with a beautiful smooth intro that leads into the gentle funk of the theme. With the vocal track placed back in the mix, the music retains its instrumental identity, and this formula is one that became standardised across the genre at this time. Randy's solo is exemplary. Although it undoubtedly met production criteria at the time, it is a rather disposable piece of what would become known as 'elevator music'. Such recipes proved very controversial for they were successful in bridging the divide that separated what the general public perceived as indigestible jazz. This music was the catalyst for the development of twenty years of a popular genre of music known as smooth jazz – hated by jazz connoisseurs, but providing many ordinary people with comfort and ease from stress in their increasingly busy lives.

Squids comes next, in complete contrast to the previous music, and one of Randy's good jazz compositions that goes back to the odd harmonies I've discussed earlier. One notable component in the underwater toolbox is the white-hot thermic lance of Hiram Bullock's guitar. The metaphor of the squid is a perfect image for this music, as the imaginary divers go in search of these somewhat alien undersea life-forms. Randy's electric wah-wah trumpet is like a harpoon gun, threatening the creatures with razor-sharp spears, whilst the effective chordal vamp of the rhythm section continues behind. At 2.56 the A and B themes return, up to 3.25 where a quiet bridge section breaks the tension and sets up an impressive solo from Michael. The wonderful rhythm section very gradually winds the tension and encourages Michael to take more and more risks amongst the rocks until, from 5.30, he is generating blistering phrases for a further 30 seconds when the cycles complete the return to the theme. Most listeners to this album would probably agree that this fried food tastes better than the stuff marketed at the start of the record.

Don't Stop the Music seems to be a filler because, supplied by guitarist Jerry Friedman, it is awful, though for different reasons than with track one. This is designed to fill the slot marked 'disco music' that was so popular at the time and that had seduced Herbie Hancock away from his usual haunts. You really need to be out of your mind on drugs to appreciate this piece, which endlessly regurgitates one or two simple ideas, yet uses excessive human resources to do it. Crazy though it seems, the Fabulous Brecker Boys have almost been relegated to the back row of their own record. The justification of this track is that it became the Brecker Brothers' third single release, with *Finger Lickin' Good* on the B-side.

In *Petals*, Randy turns yet again, this time towards one of his more harmonically advanced ballads. The music is given a commercial treatment with horns and strings, nicely arranged by Doug Riley, and sounding like a full orchestra. However, it's still a child of jazz, and, once the theme is delivered, there is just enough room for some solo work from Randy's law-abiding trumpet. Michael sits back on this one, and even Steve Gadd, sitting in for Chris Parker, sounds underemployed. The track succeeds by providing variety to the album, as well as being very pleasant on the ear.

Surprisingly, the worst position on the album is reserved for the best track, a piece called *Tabula Rasa* that tries to emulate the remarkable composition *Rocks* from the first album. For this track, the boys import heavyweight drummer Lenny White and the result is that Michael is encouraged to perform one of his most stunning solos on record. Randy must have been seriously tested when, having agreed that Michael would take the first solo, White's power-drumming inspired Mike to perform to his limit for three explosive minutes. How could Randy follow that? Well, he gave it a good shot, and the result really doesn't matter because, with a final detonation from White, the track takes this album out on an unexpected high. Those who purchased this album because they liked the 45-rpm single may well have been entirely bemused by the jazz tracks they didn't know. I'd like to think they were blown away.

I alluded briefly to the number of musicians that appear on this record. Well, in response to the loss of Sanborn the brothers expanded the horn section to seven! Besides Mike and Randy, there are Lou Marini (alto sax), Lew Del Gatto (baritone sax), Alan Rubin (trumpet), David Taylor and Barry Rogers (trombones). My conclusion is that David still bettered this Goliath! As if that were not enough, there was a string section of thirteen, arranged by Doug Riley and led by Gene Orloff, not to mention the usual BB suspects: Parker, Lee, Grolnick, Khan and MacDonald. Finally, there was a generous supply of other guests moving fluidly between the tracks: Steve Gadd and Lenny White (drums), Doug Riley (keyboards), Jerry Friedman, Sandy Torano and Hiram Bullock (guitars), Sammy Figueroa (percussion) and a team of vocalists. Given the very generous finance that must have been expended on this record, it is a great shame that the album does not sit well in the memory banks when viewed from 2013. Perhaps it's just one of those albums that seemed so much better in 1977. Yet it acts as a perfect bridge that works both ways, encouraging those ears schooled only in popular sounds to venture a little further into serious jazz, whilst also giving jazzers an opportunity for some light relief from harder styles.

In any case, it is an example of music that combines the direction of immensely talented musicians – Randy and Mike – with an innovative creative alignment by a producer who relates mostly with pop music.

The Brecker Brothers: *Heavy Metal Bebop* – 1978 (****)

If there was ever an album with the stated intention to fulfil the requirements of jazz-rock, this it: the title alone is testament to that. Heavy metal rock music is "traditionally characterized by loud distorted guitars, emphatic rhythms, dense bass-and-drum sound, and vigorous vocals." [38] All these elements are present on this album, except for the "vigorous vocals", but with the added jazz components of 'electric' trumpet and saxophone, something that was not common, even at this time. The album was recorded live at *My Father's Place* on Long Island, New York, except for the first track, which sounds as if it might have been. By 1978, the Brecker Brothers had become one of the hottest jazz-fusion bands in North America. So, by selecting the best tracks from their albums, BB were able to put on one of the best shows in town and this is a record of one such event.

Track one is *East River*, which is constructed in the Brecker equivalent of Phil Spector: a jazz-fusion 'wall of sound', with an infectious funky virus, a masculine bass smokescreen, and the band supported by a 'cast of thousands', singing and clapping and having a party - in the studio!

The live tracks of the album were performed by a quintet with Neil Jason (bass), Barry Finnerty (guitar) and Terry Bozzio (drums) in the line-up. The first live track is *Inside Out*, a new composition by Randy, based on a 12-bar blues format. All the instruments except drums are electric, and this takes the music as far into rock music as the Brecker Brothers ever went. With substantial solos from Randy, Michael and Barry, who shows the kind of capacity that persuaded Miles to hire him in the early 1980s, this nine-minute extended number is seriously hot.

Of the four remaining tracks on this 42-minute vinyl format collection, two are from album #1 – *Some Skunk Funk* and *Sponge*, and two from album #3 – *Funky Sea, Funky Dew* and *Squids*. Played live, of course, everything is turned up several notches. With more pace and a greater tension to please the crowds, live albums always have an edge that is missing from studio records. This is no exception. *Skunk Funk* is almost indecently fast – now up from 132 bpm to speeds in the range 145-150 bpm. It makes me wonder if the term 'funk' can be applied to music played this fast. However, in the history of the band, it will be played many times more, sometimes at even greater speeds than this.

Michael's sound is very odd, like a cross between sax and electric guitar in overdrive, with which he seriously competes on several occasions. Live tracks are always different because of the absence of overdubbing and they do sound a lot different here from their studio-recorded counterparts, the more so for the effect of the electrification of the sax and trumpet. Adoption of 'electric trumpet' and 'electric saxophone' was a bold move for fusioneers like the Breckers. When the decision led to them picking up things called EWIs (pronounced *ee-wees*), it alienated many jazz fans, but it worked perfectly for this type of material.

Sponge, with its strange harmonies coupled to electrified sounds, is quite extra-terrestrial and makes a very strong presence on this album. Fans of live music will very much appreciate this CD for Michael, in particular, plays far out of his skin. At the end of *Funky Sea, Funky Dew*, a large dose of theatricality is provided by a long saxophone cadenza in which Mike makes sounds the like of which had not been heard before by most observers; it's a real crowd pleaser.

The final track, *Squids*, gives scope to Neil Jason's great slap bass and Terry Bozzio's excellent drumming, both of which greatly add to the album's vitality. I nominate it as one of my candidates for the title, 'Best Live Jazz-Rock album.'

In June 1979, the brothers were reported in a *Down Beat* interview where they were both (dare I say it?) down beat. They were now halfway through their fifth year in the Brecker Brothers, with four excellent albums to their name, but they were unhappy with the way the music business was working for them – or not, as the case may be. It was time to complain. As far as the Arista contract was concerned, the band had never made any money and they were in debt to Arista because of advances on royalties. They said that with sales of only 100,000 per album, Arista was not prepared to pay the costs of a tour up front. [19]

The down side of working in countless studio sessions was that they were over so fast, you didn't get to make any real professional input. It often turned out that they were asked to add an overdub to one track of an album without the star of the album ever being present. To add insult to injury, they could often be musically criticised for the overdub when the critic had no idea of the circumstances in which it was made. Another aspect was that they were doing so many sessions that they couldn't remember which ones they had done even last week. For two musicians who were jazzers at heart, they told their interviewer that there was no point in going back to straight-ahead jazz at this point. They had put their eggs in the jazz-fusion basket and they had to make it work – with or without Arista. They sure seemed tee'd-off.

The Brecker Brothers: *Détente* **– 1980 (****)**

The album *Détente* (1980) was clearly intended for the pop market. Randy reined in his own vocal talent and hired established singers to purvey his music to a more lucrative market. We should remember that there was already a strong precedent for jazzers to indulge themselves in pop-jazz vocal albums. Herbie Hancock is the most notable example with such albums as *Sunlight* (1978), *Feets Don't Fail Me Now* (1979), *Monster* (1980) and *Magic Windows* (1981). Herbie had hidden his vocal prowess behind the electronic distortion of the vocoder, a decision that did not help his cause. As a result, there was a significant price to be paid in terms of adverse criticism, and for a time Hancock's reputation was seriously dented by what was generally seen as his 'pop misadventure'.

The cast list for *Détente* is a précis from a *Who's Who* of jazz: fusion stars such as Don Grolnick, Marcus Miller, Steve Gadd, Hiram Bullock, Paulinho da Costa, Ralph McDonald and Airto Moreira were well supported with the likes of Neil Jason (bass), Mark Gray (keys) and Steve Jordan (drums). Last, and by no means least, came George Duke who not only made some excellent synthesiser contributions, but also produced the album. That was a logical decision given that George was a jazz musician with success in the world of popular music too.

It's interesting to note that, unlike John Lennon and Paul McCartney, who attached their names to anything that either man composed (*Yesterday* was a Lennon-McCartney number, even though McCartney composed it exclusively; *Strawberry Fields Forever* was Lennon's), the Brecker Brothers mostly kept their own compositions separate from each other, yet often gave joint credit to other musicians. These were brothers who were close, but not in each others' pockets! On this album, five tracks were written by Randy, four by Michael.

The first three tracks, *You Ga (Ta Give It)*, *Not Tonight* and *Don't Get Funny With My Money*, are pop-vocal numbers with not much jazz soloing. The opener is a soul-funk fest that is musically tight and as good a disco track as you could find. Following on is *Not Tonight*, a slightly less tensioned piece that is nevertheless well written, arranged and performed. Again, no soloing, except for a brief 15-second burst from Michael, which is allowable since he composed it!

Randy is the one who, it would appear, was the frustrated vocalist, but he also added specialist singers such as Carl Carlwell, D. J. Rogers and Luther Vandross.

Randy gets his way with the third track, *Don't Get Funny With My Money*, which is a fine example of his style of humorous composition, which he will use regularly over the years. His skill at writing amusing lyrics is enhanced by a comic, slightly edgy voice and a perfectly selected blend of rhythmic and melodic lines that come together in a song that will make most dour characters smile. Unlike some instances where humorous songs might demean the artistic value, Randy's compositions in this style are part of the entertainment value of a performance. This one has a slick, funky bass, tight horn motifs, and a great deal of rhythmic energy that Randy draws out with a strong solo.

Track four is *Tee'd Off*, a Michael number that is a genuine piece of instrumental jazz-funk of the quality and style that had already become a BB trademark. At track five comes the instrumental piece, *You Left Something Behind*, which begins with some more rarefied flute and then continues into another very accessible tune, written by Randy, which could easily have been played by Sanborn. Towards the end, there is a background vocal that is another style-defining feature of Randy's commercial formula. Although the listener can hear lyrics, the singing is not presented in the way of a foreground vocal and the piece retains its instrumental character.

The album has a curious shape to it by changing midway through. Side 1 (on the vinyl) is all about commercial sound with four of the five numbers being vocal pieces. On Side 2, however, (the final four tracks, 6 to 9), it steps up several musical gears and delivers superb jazz-funk-fusion instrumentals.

Track six is *Squish*, a real highlight, as a result of which, it is the track of choice for the later compilation album *Sneakin' Up Behind You* (2006). The memorable melody has the searing hot guitar sound of Hiram Bullock, supported by synth-based funky wah-wah rhythms from the rest of the band. This progresses for two minutes before it falls into a crack of meditative backwash behind a gentle trumpet solo. Mark Gray is on Rhodes – always a warm sound – Jason is on bass and Jordan on drums. By 3.00 it has moved up a gear with the help of Airto's percussion, the trumpet has gradually heated to a temperature that would cut steel, and by 3.35 the tune has re-orientated itself towards the chorus. Then it's back around the loop once more for a tenor sax solo until 5.00 when the piece takes a final pass through the theme and goes out on a final squirt from Bullock.

The next track is *Dream Theme*, a soulful ballad that could have come straight off a contemporary David Sanborn album such as *Carly's Song* or *If You Would Be Mine* from *Hideaway* (1980), or *Rain on Christmas* from *As We Speak* (1982). It's not surprising that there are such strong similarities in style and sound, in view of the closeness of the Breckers' relationship with David, and the presence of Grolnick, Miller and Bullock, all musicians from Sanborn's wonderful 1980s band. Clearly there is a cross-fertilisation of ideas going on between these musicians. Michael's solo on tenor saxophone is on a par with much of Sanborn's work on alto – both of the highest order - and from 3. 20, Randy comes in with a beautiful muted trumpet solo that sounds like Miles Davis. Michael returns at 4.20 for a final pass through.

Baffled was written by Randy. It has a strong, full-band theme with long choreographed sections of drums and percussion linked to ensemble passages. Bullock's electric guitar sound is in the lower register and adds a rather menacing element to the mix. Then, from 3.05 there is a long, open section for solo trumpet which adds a real depth to the piece, aided by a thumping Brazilian rhythm. Throughout, Duke's work on synthesiser adds greatly to the atmosphere, and, altogether, this is a very good piece.

The last track is *I Don't Know Either*, which has a main theme written with the kind of angular harmonies and pithy melodies we heard on *Back To Back*. It's a very funky piece that truly seals the classification of this album in the jazz-fusion-funk category. It went a long way towards establishing the reputation of the Brecker Brothers' recordings.

The Brecker Brothers: *Straphangin'* – 1981 (*****)

The Brecker Brothers seem to have (partially, at least) resolved some of their differences with Arista, for in 1980 they were touring Europe again. One report in France's *Jazz Hot* magazine, summed up their July gig in Nice thus: "Another appearance, more sustainable in the skies over Nice, was that of the Brecker Brothers UFO, deafening in the roar of its reactors, brilliant as a thousand fires with its sophisticated instruments. Entangled in the development of their autopilot, poorly served by the quite amateurish festival sound system, these studio sharks here felt like fish out of water. Yet their music, with the legacy of seventies Miles Davis, brought the festival what it lacked until then: namely the echoes of music turned resolutely towards the future. Careless of historical references, they played an original repertoire with conviction, in a band that comes across as a perfect unit with sometimes uncontrollable virtuosity." [39]

Perhaps the finest example of this vintage of funk-jazz-fusion is the title track of this magnificent album, helped in no small part by the presence of Marcus Miller on bass. It's no coincidence that Marcus had also just recorded on the Crusaders album *Standing Tall* (1981) and the rhythms from that album are clear on this record. Barry Finnerty had been a member of the Crusaders' touring band from the time of their hit album *Street Life* (1978) and it may have been he who recommended Marcus to the boys from Texas. To have worked with the Crusaders was to have been immersed in one of the most soulful, funky environments you could find anywhere. Marcus had had to travel from New York to Nashville to record the album by this LA-based band. Although he didn't join the band or play with them on any other albums, it is very likely that both Marcus and Barry acted as a conduit, bringing a lot of what they had learned from the Crusaders back to the New York scene. At the time of the *Straphangin'* recordings, Marcus had recently come to the fore of New York jazz by his remarkable virtuosity and ability to sound like Jaco Pastorius. He was also expert in the slap bass technique that was at the root of the best funk jazz, but as this album testifies in places, he could also play mainstream fours and bebop lines. Miller is an extraordinary all-round musician who could play almost any instrument he laid his hands on. He had a wide appreciation of exactly what was necessary in most situations and was already interested in production. It is hardly surprising that he was hired for Miles's comeback band.

Straphangin' is a composition by Michael. The intro is a little off-putting, its very traditional, straight theme sounding like a fanfare at a feminist fête. But there follows a beautiful contrast as the boys arrive on the scene with their hot rods. The main theme is one of Michael's best and it set the standard for everyone else to match. It sounds very much like some of the Crusaders' music of this period. The repeated lines have everything you could want to find – syncopation and funk with jagged melodies and frizzy harmonies in colours that can only be found on BB albums. Once the solos begin at 1.58, the format is to take the piece right down to a relaxed, almost pastoral sound (you can even hear birdsong in places!) and then to slowly change gears upwards, a popular formula that works particularly well in this case. Mike's solo is superb. His fluid lines simply pour from the groove like perfectly heated engine lubricant from a revving camshaft. Randy's solo too, from 4.24, is in top gear. At 6.48, the theme returns for a simple repeat of first time around and the girls turn out in their bling for the symmetrical ending. Let's not forget the excellent support of the rhythm section. Richie Morales is a less well-known drummer who did a fine job on the album. Mark Gray's keyboards are as good as any of the delightful Fender Rhodes chord sequences by that man from the Crusaders, Joe Sample.

Track two is *Threesome*, a piece by Randy that is a slow, soul anthem written in 3/4 metre and folded, origami-like, into a curious new harmonic structure. A cartoonist takes recognisable features of his subjects and exaggerates them or moulds them into new forms, whilst retaining the link to the original. Here too, the music in this piece is a caricature of other musical forms you cannot fail to recognise. Yet this is Brecker jazz at its most imaginative. Never middle-of-the road, this innovative creation is music you may either love or hate.

Bathsheba has a stunning introduction with big horns playing ensemble and deceptively cool. Suddenly the piece launches into a fast samba-type tune that reverts periodically to a slower, half-tempo bridge. This time the solos are by Michael (1.50) and Mark Gray (3.50), who takes an excellent solo on synthesiser. It's a tightly played piece, which is necessary for tunes played this fast. The sound of the synth is very modern and cutting edge with lots of note bending; this is the kind of sound that prevailed throughout the 1980s (especially, for example, Chick Corea in his Elektric Band performances of the mid 1980s) yet this is only 1981. Gray's fluidity and energy are remarkable. As you'd expect from Latin music, there's excellent percussive support from Sammy Figueroa and Manolo Badrena.

Jacknife once again demonstrates Randy's penchant for melodies that tease and surprise. Fast, and tightly played with his brother in their now trademarked counter-harmony, the piece moves along at a pace that challenges the listener but doesn't leave him breathless. Randy's solo begins at 1.50, and is played with strength and clarity. Miller's bass is notable, especially when at 2.40 he breaks into swing time and his walking style is briefly on display, supported by the crisp, straight-ahead beats of Morales. After the bridge at 3.45, it's Mike's turn to develop a solo, which he does with style up to 5.25 when the piece is brought to a speedy end with one more repeat of the head bars.

Why Can't I Be There is extracted from Randy's alternative catalogue of luscious, but not over-sentimental tunes that delights for his beautiful tone on flugelhorn. The purity of sound and the closeness of musical thought from the players is a joy to hear.

At the time of this recording, *Not Ethopia* had already been debuted on the Steps album *Smokin' in the Pit* (1980), so Michael must have had a good plan for how he wanted to produce it. The theme of the piece is so challenging that only the very best musicians could possibly attempt this. It appears in other places when musicians want to seriously impress. For example, Frank Gambale and Allan Holdsworth used it as a duelling piece for an album of some of the most stunning guitar-technics on record, *Truth in Shredding* (1990). It is played at the frantic pace of 155 bpm, and is a *tour de force* for Michael who solos from 1.15. In fact, the solo is easier to play than the impossible melody line, for Michael uses many of his usual devices as part of his interpretation. Then at 3.08, the young, fearless Miller takes a solo that is played on a fretless Fender Jazz instrument in the style of Pastorius. Morales is expert, playing behind Miller. Randy comes in at 4.10 with a solo that negotiates the chord changes brilliantly until 5.12 when a final short coda takes the piece out to a uniquely breathless ending.

Spreadeagle is perfectly named, representing one of the most clumsy, unnatural human positions, for this gangly melody and lawless harmony are as gawky as a ballet in a bordello. From 1.38, Barry Finnerty gets free reign for the kind of blow Jeff Beck would have enjoyed, but other less accomplished rockers might have struggled to cope with the chord sequences, and Finnerty deserves much credit for his showpiece. After that, it's more of the barmy theme, which is now starting to feel more like a straightjacket than an uncomfortable stance.

Straphangin' was the final album of the sequence of Brecker Brothers recordings and it is only now that the listener gets the feeling that Michael is on an equal footing with his brother. Both men are contributing songs, and share the production.

If this series of records had been started in 1971, the band might have hit the same heights as Weather Report or Mahavishnu Orchestra. Return To Forever was also making waves before the Brecker Brothers band arrived. The band was certainly a latecomer to the jazz-fusion ball, even though its members had written the recipe for the punch. Nevertheless, the catalogue of music presented to the world was unique, and as valuable as any of the other contributions by famous jazzers. It carried off the crossover elements with more success than, perhaps, Herbie did, but Herbie's circumstances were different. He had already cast himself into Miles's stratospheric world and could not change direction without offending a large number of stalwart fans. The Brecker Brothers, being slightly younger, had no such baggage and were accepted for what they were – fusioneers of the first order. It didn't matter that they had taken a few years to polish their tools; when the time was right, their bands hit the scene with panache and every bit of street cred that New York could offer.

Although I have reported some similarities to Miles's style in the early 1970s, by the time of the formation of the BB band the music had become pointed in a diametrically opposite direction to what Miles Davis was doing from 1970-76. This music is the exact opposite of his minimally directed monochordal free improvisations. Though Miles had expressed his desire to create black peoples' music, the Brecker Brothers were more successful with soul and funk rhythms. The musicians work to an agreed design; the structures are firm and fixed according to the current building regulations, but the point is that there is a seemingly endless resource of new colour and texture as the composer creates melody lines, harmonies and chord sequences that were all completely new at the time, like a bricklayer setting fresh clean bricks into a mortar of constantly changing consistency and colour. The resulting walls were angular and unpredictable in direction, but they stood strong to this day – buildings that served also as works of art. It was the same formula that had been adopted by many other major New York jazz-fusion musicians, especially David Sanborn, who, of course, had been a founder member of the Brecker Brothers Band.

In their position as torchbearers at the head of this sub-genre of jazz-fusion, the Brecker Brothers reached the very pinnacle of their achievement with *Straphangin'*. Then, as happens so often in music, circumstances conspired to change the terms on which they could operate. They decided to head off down different alleyways of their own. Michael admitted that they both needed to take a break from each other and do separate projects. Their blazing jazz-fusion torch was handed to Marcus Miller who might well have stayed with the band had they chosen to carry on. However, the Brecker Brothers metaphorically licensed Marcus to carry their work forward with David Sanborn and their other friends from early BB times. The termination of this strand of music history caused Miller to turn all his energies towards the Sanborn creative line with a brilliant degree of success. Michael turned to Mike Mainieri's band Steps, which we shall investigate shortly, and the electronics would take a back seat for a short time.

It would be sad to think that it was Michael's death early in 2007 that resulted in a series of new editions of these early Brecker Brothers albums, but it is a simple commercial fact of life that the death of a well-known musician is good for his sales figures – John Lennon, Buddy Holly, Elvis Presley are well-known examples. In the jazz part of the Universe, Michael was as big a star when he died, as the other three were in theirs. However, it is a fact that the editions of these Brecker Brothers CDs available today all date from 2007. Later, Randy was invited to produce a box set of this music called *The Complete Arista Albums Collection* (2012), which includes two additional, rare albums under a different band name that I shall describe shortly. With its detailed notes, the eight-album box set is an excellent, essential acquisition for all fans of this formative period of music history.

Warren Bernhardt, Michael Brecker, Randy Brecker, Mike Mainieri: *Blue Montreux* **and** *Blue Montreux II* **– 1978 (****)**

On 21 / 22 July 1978 (the same year that the BB had recorded *Heavy Metal Bebop*), the Brecker brothers played two sets at the *Montreux Jazz Festival* in Switzerland under the name of the Arista All Stars. It was a great band, but it was a *different* band, formed of Michael, Randy, Mike Mainieri, Warren Bernhardt (keyboards), Steve Jordan (drums), Steve Khan (guitar) and Tony Levin (bass). The presence of Bernhardt and the pervasive tones of Mainieri's vibes were far more identifiable with jazz than with rock, and it created a different identity from that of the Brecker Brothers Band. Larry Coryell made a guest appearance, as did Eddie Gomez. Both sets were recorded, but for the purposes of release, the music from the two concerts was not presented in the same order of recording. The tracks were issued on two vinyl records as *Blue Montreux* and *Blue Montreux II* that are scarce today. Fortunately, the two *Blue Montreux* discs were included in the recently released Brecker Brothers box set, *The Complete Arista Albums Collection* (2012).

Characterised by four cool guys in crisp shiny blue bomber jackets, the album photographs indicated that this 'All-Star' band was a quartet of Arista artists, with 'guest' appearances by Levin, Jordan and Coryell, presumably for the usual contractual reasons. Tony Levin (b. 1946, Boston) had made an indelible impression as a session musician on the New York circuit throughout the 1970s, and had yet to find his most notable home with the unique prog-rock band King Crimson, which he did from 1981 onwards. Steve Jordan (b1957, NYC) was still in his teens when he played in Stevie Wonder's Band. His work in NYC was secured when he got a place in TV's *Saturday Night Live* band in the late 1970s, and the Brecker Brothers were happy to use him as a sit-in for the increasingly busy Steve Gadd. Steve Khan was already a favourite choice in Michael and Randy's circle of friends.

The title track adopts a slow, funky pace of around 92 bpm, and a form that consists of a slowly revolving cycle of sections. The first main section (A) is heard from 0.30 to 0.50 without horns, and from 0.50 to 1.10 with horns. Each 20 seconds contains eight bars, and the theme is a memorable melody played over a slowly oscillating pair of chords based on G and F. Next comes a section (B) that seems straightforward at first from 1.30 to 1.58, but is made much more interesting by a syncopated, concluding cadence from 1.58 to 2.04. Next, Randy improvises over section A, and we would normally expect section B to follow. However, a new section of eight bars is introduced, consisting of what I call four 'Armageddon' chords, because they are both exciting and threatening in equal measure, in contrast to the lightness of feel that precedes them. Once they are done, at 3.08, it's back to theme A, but with a funkier feel, until sixteen bars later, at 3.48, theme B returns, and the concluding cadence leads through to 4.24 and Mike Mainieri's improvisation. The entire sequence proceeds, as expected, to 6.40 whereupon the improvisations conclude and the original composition is repeated. The concluding cadence is modified into a superb ending, and the piece ends at 8.30 to the great enjoyment of the live audience. It is a wonderful example of a jazz-fusion composition of the period: crafted, melodic, funky, interesting.

The second track is Randy's number, *Rocks*, which appeared on the first BB album, *The Brecker Brothers* (1975). As I indicated previously, this is a much more hardcore fusion piece, with a fiendishly difficult melody, and a fast, aggressive rhythm that suits heavy electric guitar. Many would not consider vibraphone to be quite the most suitable instrument for this macho environment, but Mike Mainieri does a great job convincing us otherwise.

I'm Sorry is an opportunity for Mike B to take centre stage and to play a beautiful ballad composed by Mike M. This is a perfect example of the kind of playing that made him such a popular guy to call up for session work. The presentation is neither kitsch nor oversentimental, but instead is played with feeling and great funk. Besides a stunning performance from Michael, Mike Mainieri's interpretation is remarkable for showing just what a creative and funky player he can be. Levin and Jordan contribute greatly to the funkiness and Warren Bernhardt's playing is supportive. Randy appears not to play on this one.

Magic Carpet is another of Mike Mainieri's compositions, which begins with some heavy descending chords, and scorching electric guitar sounds from Steve Khan, but then settles down into a fast jazz-rock rhythm. Led by Steve's searching improvised solo, and supported by Jordan's solid rock drumming, it is not until 3.22 when Warren Bernhardt mimics the guitarist's energy with his keyboard playing. The same descending chords are used to end the piece at 5.18. There's no evidence of either brother on this one.

Randy returns on his own composition, *Buds*, a piece that appears on no other record. The song has a Latin rhythm and a widely appealing melody. After Randy's great delivery, Bernhardt takes over to make a solid improvisation. Then it's back to the head, and this seemingly short piece is over before you can say beer.

Warren Bernhardt is represented as the composer of track 6, entitled *Floating*. It's a dreamlike, rather surreal feeling that is expressed in the theme. Michael is called upon for some impressionistic playing from 2.16, for about two minutes, before Warren brings everyone down to earth with some more straightahead playing. At last, it is possible to hear Levin's conventional bass work. Finally, Mike Mainieri takes the last improvisation slot, and plays in his more ethereal style of vibes. It's a good composition, but pieces like this have as much shelf life as last night's dream.

The album ends with a trio consisting of Randy, Warren and Mainieri playing Mike's piece, *The Virgin And The Gypsy*. This is a tale of dangerous love in the dusty Spanish countryside. Each soloist is able to show some beautiful jazz casts in this dramatic tone poem.

The music on the first album is a great mix of material ranging from the more acoustic style that would form Steps early repertoire, to the seriously electric sounds that would come later with Steps Ahead. If there is any disappointment to be identified, it is the very low profile of Tony Levin in the mix. In view of the extraordinary reputation he later acquired, his presence on this record is very muted. My conclusion is that he suffered from the difficulties associated with recording live bass in the 1970s. By today's standards, it is poor.

The second album, *Blue Montreux II*, begins with a heavy funk rock piece called *A Funky Waltz*, written by Alphonze Mouzon, in which guest Larry Coryell plays an intense improvised solo. The track was a strong feature for Coryell's band Eleventh House on its 1974 eponymous album. There is not a lot of structure or content to describe here, but the piece was delivered with high energy, and, in the live environment, the audience clearly enjoyed it.

Steve Khan's piece, *Candles*, is an entirely different sound, the more so because Michael Brecker chooses to play the melody on soprano saxophone. There are strong echoes of the Orient here, with slow, intense themes depicting forested Japanese hillsides or thick Vietnamese jungle, where candles are probably a vital necessity for the inhabitants, as long as they are indoors.

Michael Brecker's single contribution to the album is *Uptown Ed*, a barnstorming straightahead number that is played with Mike M, Warren, Steve Jordan, and guest bassist, Eddie Gomez, who would become the first choice for Steps. The brute physicality of music played at such breathtaking pace is always a source of wonderment to me, but the scale of difficulty of the main theme is as great as anything Michael has put on record. I can't imagine how it is possible to play this on a vibraphone. Like Michael, Mainieri is amazing.

The mood is sweetened for the next track, Mainieri's *Love Play*, a fascinating, developing piece that omits the brothers. Fusion seems to be taking a back seat as Mike and Warren have fun with this very melodic and likeable piece. Then Steve Khan steps forward, and he blows more than a few socks off with a funky, electric guitar thrash that occupies a memorable centrepiece of this eleven-minute rendition. When you think it's all done, from 8.25 there is an exceptional ending that outshines all that has gone before, and generates the kind of ecstatic climax we might expect. The audience cried for more. I just cried.

A second Khan contribution, *Cloud Motion*, feels like the encore. It's supposedly a full-band piece, and here, placed last on the album, it is in a good position to close. Randy plays the first improvisation and is extremely impressive. Steve Khan comes next, his slick, rock-guitar sound is the polish on his substantial creative veneer. Mike Mainieri reminds us just what a fine, all-round musician he is, the more so since he is performing on an instrument not best suited to the fusion environment. Even Tony Levin is at last heard poking his solid bass notes through the tapestry of jazz-rock sounds, although he still doesn't solo. We don't hear much from Mike B on this track.

Overall, the tracks contained on these two albums are extremely varied, partly because of the choice of material and partly because of the variable combinations of musicians and instruments. The album is never dull, and has not dated in any way. These two albums make an excellent pair of recordings from the apex of the jazz-rock fusion period, and, thanks to their inclusion on the excellent Arista box set of Brecker Brothers' recordings, they can now be heard properly, and in context, on CD.

Jaco Pastorius: *Jaco Pastorius* – 1976 (*****)

It was probably just another session gig when Randy and Michael were called up by Bobby Colomby to play on a funky jazz-fusion piece called *Come On, Come Over* for the phenomenal bass player, Jaco Pastorius's debut album, *Jaco Pastorius* (1976). It is a piece that was absolutely right for its time. It enabled Jaco to demonstrate how his style could be used to make a funky composition, ideal for live disco, into a throbbing, exciting experience for both band and audience. It set the scene for many others to copy. The band overflowed with talent. Besides Mike and Randy in support, David Sanborn gives one of the blistering solos he would become famous for in the years immediately afterwards. Herbie Hancock is also featured on electric piano. Peter Graves played bass trombone, and soul singers, Sam and Dave, provided the vocals. Jaco also arranged the horns, another early indication that there was more to this musician than just playing bass. It was the beginning of another notable relationship in the career of the Brecker Brothers.

The album was a great success, not just because it contained some excellent and very varied music, but also because the audience was astonished at the bass playing it contained. Word that there was a new star on the scene quickly reached the ear of Joe Zawinul, and soon after the album's release, Jaco was a member of the chart-topping jazz-fusion band, Weather Report.

Joni Mitchell: *Shadows And Light* – 1980 (*****)

For Mike Brecker, the summer of 1979 was allocated to a project that was to give him some of the greatest visibility yet, outside of the jazz community. He had been hired by Joni Mitchell to take part in her project *Shadows and Light* (1980). Jaco was not only Joni's bass player, but also her Musical Director. Joni had recently been working with Jaco Pastorius, chosen because of his uniquely lyrical style. The last thing she wanted was a plodding four-in-a-bar beat and she knew that Jaco would deliver something far more than that. Another friend of Joni's, Don Alias, was hired for drums and percussion. Don was also to have one of the most prolific careers as a sideman, and contributed to many of the Brecker Brothers' albums. Finally, Joni had also hired Pat Metheny and Lyle Mays from the Pat Metheny Group. Pat asked Mike to play on his up-coming album *80 / 81* (1980) and the two men were to form a close personal and professional relationship from now on.

Shadows and Light (1980) became one of Joni's most successful musical projects. Her music had begun in the purest of folksy singer-songwriter fashion, but driven by Joni's immensely creative skills, had ventured into jazz-folk fusion. Jaco's presence was strong on the albums *Hejira* (1976), and *Don Juan's Reckless Daughter* (1979). Then came an album with Charlie Mingus. By 1978 he was a sick man and unable to play, but he was still able to work with Joni for her album *Mingus* (1979), on which Jaco played. Although she continued to love jazz, and chose to work with tenor sax-man Wayne Shorter for the rest of her career, after this, Joni's style evolved into new areas divergent from jazz-fusion. In Joni's career, *Shadows and Light* remains the final chapter in a brief, but intense and beautiful collection of vocal jazz-fusion music in which (rarely, in my opinion) lyrics achieve a value that is equal to the music.

Jaco had been clean when he had originally met Michael and Randy in 1975, but when Michael met Jaco again for the *Shadows And Light* tour, it was a different Jaco. Michael told Bill Milkowski, "He was definitely drugging a lot. There was a lot of partying going on. It was just a symptom of the times – everybody was doing cocaine then." [40]

Jaco Pastorius: *Word Of Mouth* – 1981 (****)

In 1980 Jaco signed a solo deal with Warner Bros. For the next few years, Mike and Randy would become a part of several projects with Jaco's travelling circus. Work on Jaco's *Word of Mouth* album began in 1980, and consisted of much laying-down of tracks. Jaco managed it in a unique (most would say haphazard) way, with some of the music being developed as it went along. The opening track *Crisis* is the best example, a new take on the idea of collective improvisation. Entirely disorganised, this is a piece of music that is essentially the work of one man, for although many musicians play on it, they were not allowed to hear each other or to interact with anything other than the bass line. He controlled the recording, the mixing, and the selection of all musicians. Michael was asked to join Jaco for a session in which he had to lay down an overdub track, whilst being allowed to hear only the bass line. It is said that Jaco would randomly inject a brief snatch from another overdub track to inspire the solitary musician as he played.

Jaco's method of touring around, getting various musicians to record a track, was very expensive. The record company was displeased, but Jaco simply became more and more obstinate. He would engage in major rows with them, and turn up for meetings both late and drunk. His behaviour was frequently obnoxious; he sometimes wrecked offices and frequently offended staff. The recorded montage Pastorius creates is thus exactly what you might expect – an incoherent assembly of frantic lines mimicking Jaco's frantic bass. It is not a horrible piece – just disappointing. However, it succeeds in one very good way and that is as a wonderful lead into the second track, which is in total contrast to the first and much sweeter for it.

Three Views of a Secret is a timeless piece of music that is in every way what *Crisis* is not. Bursting with melodies, rich harmonies, organised yet unpredictable, it is cleverly orchestrated, jazzy, classy, intriguing and very, very lush. Many people believe this is Jaco's finest piece.

Liberty City is a long, well-developed composition in a lively tempo that sounds at first as if it is going to be a kind of New Orleans-style rag piece. Then, a groove is started up with bass, percussion, harmonica and steel pans improvising together – a very unusual combination of musicians. Next is the main theme that consists of a series of smoothly joined chords. It blends into a slick big-band sound that circles a series of changes. After another burst of the bass groove, Herbie Hancock comes in to solo over Jaco's bass lick. The ever-present theme continually changes its fix. Just before the half-way point, a new middle section arrives with a rather harsher edge that gives the brass scope to briefly open their bags before the bass groove returns, possibly a touch too soon, with the chirruping harmonica adding its two-pennyworth. From this point on, it's more of the same combination of themes, with a host of great harmonies and variations. Some might say the piece is too long, but I do not agree, for the musical listener (rather than the musical grazer) always finds something new. At the end we find some very sonorous bass synth lines that stomp around like some drunken ogre, before the steel pans provide a gentle landing into the next track.

Chromatic Fantasy is a typical piece of Jaco extravaganza. Just in case we had forgotten how good a player he actually is, he plays a stunning solo that almost no other bass player at the time could have played. Without a break, we suddenly find ourselves in the undergrowth of a Japanese water garden. Interesting, but you have to ask, "What is going on here?" The answer is soon revealed in the most delightful way, for the piece turns out to be a lead directly into *Blackbird*, played on bass, harmonica and percussion. Short and very sweet, the whole triage is brilliant. Jaco is clearly able to play the entire piece solo, as well as providing his own accompaniment and rhythm, but he treats us to the wonderful sound of Thielemans who delivers the well-known theme in a lyrical jazz style. The jazz variations continue throughout, as also does the Japanese texture. It's all a strange, yet wonderful, combination. Then, yet another surprise, as *Blackbird* takes on a heavy rock presence, complete with fuzz guitar, simulated by Jaco on bass, of course. Surely not? No, Jaco-in-the-Box has fooled us again with a seamless entry into his title track, *Word of Mouth*. This is fusion from the side of rock.

Punctuated with the distant sound of children's voices that appear from time to time throughout the final track, another seamless join leads into *John and Mary*, which has strong Weather Report flavourings. Wayne Shorter is evident on soprano saxophone, doing what he does best. A complete break in the middle brings in an orchestral section that caused great consternation to the project's financiers because, having hired and recorded an entire orchestra, he was dissatisfied with the result, erased the tape and did the entire thing again with new musicians.

The album is, without doubt, not what the record company wanted. At the time, Jaco gave them a lot of problems and he paid the price for it later. From our distant perspective, it is a good, but not a great album. It could have done without the poorly conceived and unoriginal first track. The compositions are excellent, at times, and the slick joining of tracks in the second half is a joy. It certainly did not require the presence of all 95 people listed in the credits to achieve its aims, and it is obvious that Jaco's project management was crazy. Far worse was to come.

While the WoM recording shenanigans continued, Jaco organised a quintet in August 1980 with Michael Brecker, Bob Mintzer, Don Alias and Peter Erskine to play some gigs at *Seventh Avenue South*. For contractual reasons they were not allowed to advertise, but the gigs were a sell-out and Jaco said that the publicity had occurred by word of mouth. The name of his new band had been found.

The Weather Report Tour of Japan in 1981 began very badly. Jaco destroyed the stage performance by playing badly and at maximum volume. He was often drunk on stage and Zawinul almost fired him on the spot several times. Eventually, matters came to a head and Jaco was made to realise that he couldn't carry on like it. He respected Joe enough to play well for the later gigs on the tour and the band then returned to the US in triumph where he helped them record the music for the next album Weather Report (1982). The *Word of Mouth* album came out in the summer of 1981 and became Japan's best-selling jazz album of that year. The growing interest in his new band, coupled with his growing disinterest in Weather Report was assisted by Zawinul's attempts to drive his band in new directions, mixing Jaco's bass to lower levels on the albums and allowing less solo time.

Jaco Pastorius: *The Birthday Concert* – rec. 1981, rel. 1996 (****)

An excellent posthumous album was released on the Warner label in 1996 and compiled by Jaco's friend, Peter Erskine. Entitled, *The Birthday Concert* it is a collection of material from two gigs recorded in Florida on the evening of Jaco's thirtieth birthday, 1 December 1981. It was a great occasion. A couple of concerts were organised in a Fort Lauderdale club and, fortunately for us, the gigs were recorded. Some of the musicians had already been playing together and others were drafted in to make up a 23-piece big band. Michael and Randy were present, as also were Bob Mintzer, Peter Erskine, Peter Gordon and Dave Bargeron.

By this time, Jaco's behaviour had become almost permanently unstable. On stage, a typical characteristic was his trick of suddenly turning up his amp to full volume and then playing something that was entirely unrelated to what the rest of the band was playing. This was, of course, very destructive and his fellow musicians simply could not work with it. Their only option was to walk off the stage and leave him to make out with just the drummer. Of course, this would provoke an adverse crowd reaction that would simply make matters worse.

Invitation is a seventeen-minute showstopper and this track was used to open the second show of the evening. Erskine himself calls it a 'tour de force'. Besides Jaco, the players are Mike Brecker and Bob Mintzer, both on tenor saxophones and Don Alias on congas. Erskine: "The saxophone playing of Brecker and Mintzer is astounding, as is Alias' conga drumming. Of course, nobody could ever, or will ever, play the bass like Jaco does on this. Michael plays the first solo and Bob follows. Michael plays the cadenza at the end. There's a lot of high level cat and mouse here." [41]

Erskine is referring to a common practice of musical on-stage competition that takes place when two of the same instruments take part in the same piece. The piece is played in the spirit of the saxophone duels fought out by some of the old-time players. The reality is that, good though Mintzer is, Brecker (now in his early 30s) is in a class of his own. He turns up the wick to full, launching most of the tricks in the saxophone-player's bag onto his approving audience. His playing is little short of astonishing, and breathing takes a very poor second place to the stream of notes that emanate from his punished reed. Poor Bob Mintzer must have been rather shell-shocked to have to follow behind him, though he excelled himself. Jaco, on the other hand, is enveloped by Brecker's broadside and rises fully to the occasion. As a result, I agree entirely with Erskine: the bass playing on this track had probably never been equalled up to this point, and like Bob Beamon's world record in the long jump, was considered unsurpassable for years. Surprisingly, it is not for the bass solo, imaginative though it is, but rather for the unbelievable way he fills the vortices that swirl around both saxophones. The final Brecker cadenza alone is a valuable collectible. Being freed from the chivvying, supportive comfort of the rhythm section is extremely scary for all but the most expert player. Then to unleash such a stream of creativity, at such a ridiculous pace, whilst remaining entirely in tempo, is a source of wonderment to us mere mortals. This album should be in all jazz collections, if only for this track alone. I believe it is one of the milestones of recorded jazz.

The track that follows, *Three Views of a Secret*, could be an anti-climax after that. However, this piece, composed by Jaco and recorded on his first *Word of Mouth* album, has always been highly rated. Milkowski loves the piece. It is composed and orchestrated and the version that appears here is not very far removed from the original, showing that Jaco himself was very happy with it.

For a live piece, *Liberty City* is also similar in format to the studio version on the *Word of Mouth* album but is shorter than might be expected and two-thirds shorter than the studio version. The delights are a great new set of textures to absorb. Jaco's licks are embellished in places, and Brecker's saxophone takes on a new prominence instead of harmonica, also substituting for Hancock's solo. The short brassy middle does not disappoint, with a lively bunch of well-lubricated horn players anxious to boost the atmosphere of the gig. Jaco enters for a surprisingly brief solo before the piece starts its final phase, a neat diminuendo providing a lull that leads to the climax. The audience sounds truly pleased with this.

The classic Pastorius composition, *Punk Jazz*, begins with a wonderful flourish from both Brecker and then Jaco, to the sweet backdrop of those syrup-laden chords, and then the gutsy punk rhythm kicks in to take the piece along. Everything that follows has a raw beauty, like the metal safety pin piercing the beautiful woman's navel. Harmonies are edgy, but smooth chords provide the gloss. Jaco's punchy bass is clear, as always, but minimal, for a change, and tugs the tune along beneath Michael's inquisitive saxophone. Great!

Happy Birthday appears in a big band version written specially for Jaco. It features some luscious jazz chords, the kind of thing that has always attracted me to jazz. I'd be delirious if someone played this for me! Jaco certainly seemed to enjoy it: "You dig?"

Reza begins with a percussive interlude. There's lots of fun here as a high-pitched whistle from nowhere spells out the first theme. Then, from the opposite end of the pitch spectrum, comes the same tune in the form of a blast from the brassy bass end. Suddenly, an animated second theme in fast triplets begins that contrasts completely with the first. Everyone takes turns to have a go with the first theme as others improvise on top. Then, the pied piper returns, this time to a more sophisticated rendition of theme two in chord form. A herd of African elephants appears from nowhere. (What?) Then comes Jaco for a burst of bass to the accompaniment of African percussion. The brass instruments admire the elephant calls, and the piece returns to its two themes once more for a final flourish. This is certainly an odd, but entertaining piece.

Domingo is a very fast big-band piece designed to set pulses racing. After the initial statements of theme, we enter a wonderful Brecker / Pastorius / Alias trio that surely flies along, attracting more and more musicians as it does so. Jaco momentarily engages overdrive, making his bass sound just like a racing engine. Then the full band enters to provide the competition for the race to the finish that kicks up dirt onto the chequered flag and screams over the finishing line.

The album is completed with *Amerika*, a performance of the American national song on solo bass in the style that perfectly summarises Jaco's methods. Though it is included almost as a novelty number, it is certainly not trivial.

Jaco's introductions that precede it give the impression that he is fully in control of his senses at this point, in contrast to his outrageous conduct at many subsequent gigs. He seems to be on his best behaviour - it's his birthday, after all. Milkowski's book, however, paints a picture of cocaine-fuelled performances by almost every musician at this point in history. It took a very strong will to resist, night after night, the temptation to join the higher level of being. We cannot make judgements based on our own circumstances. Should we be grateful to the stimulant that enriches creative genius and gives us such breathtaking entertainment, or should we curse the evil chemical that has been so destructive in other ways?

Erskine has done a great job in editing and presenting this material, and the result is an album that ought to be present in all jazz collections. For a live album, the record has more than the usual rough edges and occasional glitches. However, it must be remembered that this was a band put together especially for the occasion, and, on some tracks, consisted of twenty-one musicians. There could not have been much time, if any, for rehearsal, so it is a remarkable piece of professionalism.

Jaco Pastorius: *Invitation* – **1983 (****);**

Jaco Pastorius Big Band: *Twins I & II* **- rel. 1999 (****)**

The Word of Mouth band that hit the road early in 1982 consisted of around twenty musicians. Now Randy was a full member of the band, as were a number of his session musician friends, such as Don Alias, Wayne Andre, Dave Bargeron, Elmer Brown, Randy Emerick, Peter Erskine, John Faddis, and Bob Mintzer. The starting point was the Savoy Theater in New York on 15 January. Milkowski, who was in the audience, remembers that the venue was not properly heated and that Randy had to play trumpet whilst wearing gloves. [42] On 2 and 3 July 1982, the band's sets at the *Montreal Jazz Festival* were filmed, and a number of DVDs of the two gigs are available today.

In September 1982, Jaco took his WoM Big Band on tour to Japan. The stories of Jaco's crazy exploits on this tour are legion, and interested readers are strongly recommended to read Milkowski's fascinating book. Amongst the madness, there was, however, some very good music, and recordings made at three of the gigs on 1, 4 and 5 September later appeared in several forms. An official release by Warner Bros. is *Invitation* (1983). Sixteen years later, to capitalise on Jaco's posthumous popularity, and to recoup some of their enormous outlay on *Word Of Mouth*, Warner Bros. produced a longer version of the recordings as *Twins I & II* (1999).

Decline and Fall

In December 1982, a year after the *Birthday Concert*, WoM made a tour to Italy. There were no rehearsals and Jaco's behaviour was at its most extreme. They began with a concert in Milan to 20,000 people, whereupon Jaco was so misbehaved that there was a huge riot that involved the police, tear gas and water cannon. The band was lucky to escape alive. It is a testament to the loyalty of a band of musicians that they even considered staying together after such a debacle, and it was not the only time he threw such a fit. However, he did pull himself together for some of the later gigs and the band played well.

Off-stage, Pastorius took to playing bizarre pranks on the band members, such as pretending to fall out of the back of the bus. After a while they grew to expect anything. Then, one night when he fell from a balcony whilst performing a ridiculous balancing act, no-one took any notice that he had seriously injured himself. He received a badly broken arm and other minor fractures, the tour was terminated and they all returned to the USA.

Oddly enough, despite all the antics, his reputation survived at first, purely on the basis of his perceived genius and ability. The accolades continued to flow. In 1982 he was voted "Best Jazz Musician" at a time when some of those who knew him would have described him as plainly mad.

In 1983 Mike Stern, another bad boy of jazz, was fired by Miles Davis because of his behaviour. Jaco had wanted to hire Mike for some time, so Stern joined the band for the Word of Mouth European Tour, followed by a long six-week tour of the USA. By the end of 1983, Warner Bros. had fired Jaco. The *Word of Mouth* album had run greatly over budget, the second album had turned into a fiasco, and, although they did release *Twins*, the record was not what Warner wanted.

Jaco's association with Mike Stern was not good for him. Throughout 1984 and 1985 they both indulged on massive drugs and booze binges to such an extent that Stern finally broke and went into a rehabilitation clinic. Jaco somehow never gave way under the strain, yet his life totally disintegrated. His friends and fellow musicians began to shun him because he was not only bad for their careers but he was so unpleasant to be with. Finally, after another catastrophic gig at the Hollywood Bowl in 1984, during which Jaco played his usual trick, his musicians deserted him on stage. Word of Mouth was disbanded.

During 1985 Jaco continued to play using the name of Word of Mouth but the band was not really extant because he would use any musician who would play with him on a night-by-night basis. There was no continuity and both his behaviour and his performances were now beyond the pale. He had been banned from playing in all New York nightclubs except for two that billed him as 'The Bad Boy of Jazz'. From time to time, he was able to blag studio time and to persuade musicians to come to sessions. Randy was one of them. However, Jaco was never able to pay for the work he asked people to do, or for the studio hire. Tapes were made, but left in boxes without further work. Some of these have appeared as 'unofficial' recordings, notably the Jazz Door release, *Jaco Pastorius in New York*, recorded in November 1985 with Kenwood Dennard, Hiram Bullock, Alex Foster and others. That December, on his 34th birthday he is quoted as saying, "I can't believe I'm still alive." When asked why, his reply was, "Because I wanted to be like Jesus. I expected that at 33 I'd be off the planet." [43] It wasn't long before Jaco was beaten to death by a bouncer he'd offended outside a nightclub. A large hole was left in the music world following Jaco's death on 21 September 1987, aged only 35.

Steps: *Smokin' in the Pit* **– 1999 (rec. 1980) (*****)**

Even from the time of Miles Davis's retirement in 1976, jazz-fusion had evolved into a genre of its own with real commercial potential, thanks to the likes of Weather Report, Return to Forever and Mahavishnu Orchestra. The result, according to Baird, was a music that tended to be "long on accessibility and usually short on actual jazz chops," a comment that is hard to disagree with. [44] However, he carried on to say that "Whilst it's melodic, easy to like and more than a little influenced by lighter pop styles like folk rock and show tunes, the Steps Ahead vibe has always meant *serious fusion* [my italics]; no Spyro Gyra horn histrionics or Yellowjackets grooving here!"

It is an insult to say that Spyro Gyra and Yellowjackets were not intended to be serious fusion. Baird is, however, right to say that the music of Steps Ahead is accessible, that it is serious jazz music, and that both are excellent qualities. However, the music of both Spyro Gyra and the Yellowjackets is in the same rich musical vein, and to distinguish between them in such a fashion shows bias, to say the least. All three bands were part of a movement that helped to provide a very healthy living for jazz musicians, up to the turn of the century. This was achieved by presenting an attractive vitality to modern music that maintained bridges from popular cultures into the jazz mainstream. Without these bridges, pure jazz, in the shape it had evolved into in the mid 1960s, could have passed out of existence very quickly indeed. Sadly, it could be argued that this is actually occurring now, in the early 21st century, for the same kinds of reasons. From the 1980s, jazz has been eclipsed by hip hop, rap and other forms of popular culture that have no natural bridges to jazz, other than perhaps a certain native sense of rhythm. As that young generation today moves into its 40s and 50s, today's parents do not expose their children to jazz and, as a result, there is little affinity for jazz in modern culture. In my experience, many people have no understanding of what the word 'jazz' stands for.

Amongst the many talented musicians who came to play at the diminutive club on the corner of 7th Avenue South and Leroy Street (now redeveloped) was Mike Mainieri. After years of sitting at the focus of New York jazz-fusion bands – large and small - Mainieri was ready to create a new, small, tight outfit that would, with the help of Michael Brecker in particular, some ten years his junior, become one of the most respected jazz-fusion bands. It would be achieved initially by means of a unique cool sound that was a world away from the louder rock elements of fusion. This was a form of jazz-fusion played by such a band of jazz heavyweights that even the purists found it hard to be rude about it. Later, the band would go as far into electric jazz as it was possible to go, with spectacular results.

Again, you could ask the question, "How did Michael find the time?" He had many projects on the go in 1980. For example, he played with Randy in Chaka Khan's backing group for *Live at the Roxy* (1980) along with Hamish Stuart (from the Average White Band) brilliant funk bassist Anthony Jackson and keyboardist Steve Ferrone; the album *Naughty* (1980) followed. He also played on the Steely Dan album, *Gaucho* (1980). He was doing session work on albums for the jazz-fusion band Spyro Gyra, which had had a smash crossover hit with *Morning Dance* (1979) and their follow-up album *Carnaval* (1980). He played for Bee Gee Andy Gibb's *After Dark* (1980) and *About Love* (1980) by Gladys Knight and The Pips; the list of artists he worked with is both broad and long. Michael had also been invited to appear alongside saxophonist Dewey Redman on Pat Metheny's *80 / 81* (1980). This was to prove an important encounter because it marked the start of a long-standing relationship with Pat. And, of course, the Brecker Brothers band was still busy until the band suspended activities after the *Straphangin'* album. Despite all this, in the autumn of 1979 he joined the outfit called Steps that Mike Mainieri had for some time been working up informally at 7th Avenue South.

The five-piece grouping consisted of the two Mikes with Don Grolnick, Eddie Gomez and Steve Gadd; it was immediately popular, and played to sell-out audiences. The band was just a 'jammin'' outfit with which to have fun at Seventh Avenue South. All the guys were so busy that there seemed no incentive to plan a formal band. Mainieri said, "We had no big idea, or plans to record an album or go on the road, as we never knew when everyone was available to play at the club. I don't recall ever rehearsing. When we did perform, we would arrive to a sold-out club..." [45]

It was fortuitous that, one night, a freelance Japanese journalist made some informal recordings that later received airtime on the radio in Japan. As a result, Mainieri was offered a contract from Nippon Columbia for three albums, all of which would be released initially only in Japan.

Thus, in December 1979, the band travelled to Tokyo. On 15th and 16th, two performances were recorded live at *The Pitt Inn*, and just one day later, on 17th, the band recorded in the studio. The live performances were released on *Smokin' In The Pit* and the studio tapes became the album *Step by Step*. Almost two years later, the third album of the contract, *Paradox*, was recorded live at Seventh Avenue South, by which time, Peter Erskine had replaced Gadd.

It was not until the end of the century that these albums became available to listeners in the west. To our great delight, in 1999, Mainieri later released an expanded 2-CD version of *Smokin' In The Pit* on his own NYC Records label. It runs to almost two and a half hours of thrilling music, and is as good value as can be found anywhere. It contains some of the most outstanding virtuosity from all of the musicians, but Brecker and Gadd fans should buy this album for it contains some of the best examples of their astonishing live playing. The music is mostly acoustic jazz, but some of the music points to the jazz-fusion style in terms of rhythm, if not electrics.

The usual play on words is present in the titles. *Tee Bag* was written by Mike Mainieri and the title is probably a reference to keyboardist, Richard Tee, a friend and much respected studio musician who recorded prolifically until his untimely death in 1993. At that time Tee was leading the band, Stuff, of which

Steve was a member. This piece is a lively straight-ahead tune that swings through a simple heads-solos-heads format with a bluesy vibe.

Next is the Grolnick tune, *Uncle Bob*, a slightly more complex melody at a slightly more complex pace, but still mainstream swing, and good live material. This piece was not present on the original edition, but is a bonus track on this CD, which is also enhanced with some alternate takes of the main tracks.

Grolnick's intricate melodies are always popular, even when he isn't in a band's line-up, so his work is on show again at #3 with *Fawlty Tenors*. There are two versions of this piece, which is a good study for those who want to see how jazz is performed in a live setting. After a thirty-second intro on bass, the ensemble plays the theme twice, slightly differently on each occasion. The solos commence from around the one-minute mark. The basic structure is a repeated 16-bar fast rhumba rhythm followed by eight bars of swing fours. The soloists take turns, and the sequence is different with Mike M and Don swapping positions on the two tracks; Michael B takes the last spot. Each musician plays through the twenty-second cycle for as long as his inspiration lasts. Across the two tracks, each extended improvisation is of great interest in terms of the development of the theme and the interaction with the rhythm section. In particular, Gadd's reactions to the solos are wonderful; points to listen out for are his play with Don on the alternate take (track 5) at around 5.28 and with Michael B throughout both his solos. Similarly, Michael B's playing is as good as you will hear anywhere, notably as he winds things up from 9.19 on the alternate take, and from 8.45 on the original.

Mainieri leads off at track four with a good version of the classic tune, *Lover Man*, perhaps best known for its version by Charlie Parker. *Song to Seth*, track six, is a low-key ballad by Mainieri without saxophone, whilst *Momento* is a short cameo piano solo by Don.

The second disc begins with *Young and Fine*, a piece by Joe Zawinul from the Weather Report fusion album *Mr Gone* (1978), which was an album played heavily throughout 1979. *Not Ethiopia* was a new piece by Mike Brecker that would appear on the Brecker Brothers album *Straphangin'* (1981) in the following year. The remarkable feature of this piece is the combination of pace with the extraordinary melody, which is rather like taking a garden hosepipe and putting your thumb over the nozzle with the water turned on. The notes spray everywhere but are constantly pulled downwards under the force of gravity. Even Mike B, the composer, exhibits a little hesitance in places as he copes with the sequence of dots. A nice example of musical sadism was to invite Japanese guitarist Kazumi Watanabe to join the band for this number; he copes remarkably well. In fairness, the solo section is more straightforward because the chord sequence is not nearly as challenging as the main theme. In this 1999

CD edition, there is an alternate track added for extra value, with Watanabe absent.

Soul Eyes is a gentle counterbalance to the muscle power of *Not Ethiopia*. A cover of the popular number by Mal Waldron, it's a focus for Don and Mike M, with the saxophone appearing only during the later stages. Again in contrast, the bonus track, *Recordame*, is a technical showpiece for Brecker and Gadd. Brecker is like a gymnast performing a floorshow – just when you think he has reached the edge of the mat, he finds not one, but two extra somersaults! Gadd, on the other hand, is like a finely tuned racing engine. This is not a solo for those expecting stunts and grunts, but it's got the lines of a Ferrari and its class is obvious to those who study such things.

Sara's Touch is the first appearance of a piece by Mainieri that starts out as a beautiful ballad, but transforms into a highly charged workout to bring this collection to a superb close. As a demonstration of the incredible virtuosity of Michael Brecker, this album is a must for jazz-sax aficionados. In the live setting, he is looser and becomes even more creative. His chops are mind-boggling; in particular, he demonstrates a new sound on his horn by which he makes it honk almost in parallel with his licks.

This is one of the best live jazz albums and fully deserves to be awarded five stars.

Steps: *Step by Step* – 2000, rec. 1980 (***)

On 17 December 1979, the day after completion of the recording of *Smokin' in the Pit*, the boys entered the Japanese studio, as agreed, to record *Step by Step* (1980), an album that was published in Japan only and remained for many years beyond the reach of Western ears.

Mainieri described the band perfectly: "In retrospect, what fired the imagination of this combination of musicians and their audiences, was that this acoustic group…had the ability to swerve in and out of various musical forms with the attitude and abandonment of a New York taxi driver." [45] In the context of a live band that was casually formed, besides playing whenever they liked, they could also play whatever they liked.

Step by Step is a concise but beautifully proportioned collection of what could best be described as contemporary modern jazz. The opening track, *Uncle Bob*, was written by Grolnick and is a perfect example of a lively acoustic mainstream piece in swing time and with a classic format. The theme is short and straightforward, and the eleven-minutes of content are filled with excellent straight-ahead blowing by the entire band. All of the musicians play well, but this is a magnificent demonstration of drumming from Steve Gadd, especially during the first solo by Mike Brecker who develops a special intensity that Gadd follows with brilliance. Before the theme returns at the end, Steve plays a very good sequence of 'fours' in which he alternates with each of the other musicians in turn. Although all of the five tracks are good, this is out on its own.

The second track is *Kyoto*, first in a series of three compositions by Mainieri. It's a nice piece of cool, instrumental jazz that is typical of the early 1980s and the new generation of jazz-fusion music that uses back-beat rhythms, yet remains acoustic. Written in the song format, it has a headline melody and solos that follow the chord sequence. After a gentle start, it winds the tension up slightly before a gentle bridge brings the listener back to the original theme.

In *Belle*, Mainieri is rather less formulaic with an extended composed theme in waltz time that includes Gomez on bowed bass, orchestral style. Once into his solo, Mainieri swirls around the ballroom, interjecting some good blues touches, but this is an environment in which Grolnick thrives, and his thoroughly modern piano style is luscious, intense and, like Lyle Mays in Pat Metheny Group, concentrates on soulful invention not technical wizardry. This is a triumph for Grolnick, although Mainieri's composition is full of playful melody and execution, as perfect as the finest ball gown.

Bullet Train is another Mainieri piece written with respect for his Japanese hosts. An up-tempo piece with a snaking melody, it has a Latin rhythm that, strangely, successfully communicates the feel of the famous high-tech mode of transport as it carves its way across the beautiful Japanese landscape.

Finally, *Six Persimmons* is by Grolnick, a ballad written inside a churning chord sequence. Grolnick leads by example and coaxes his accompanying bass and drums into a gentle swing time whilst sticking closely to his changes. Gomez plays a well-articulated solo and Brecker takes the song out with a sensual flourish that is a low key ending to this very good album.

Steps: *Paradox* – 2000, rec. 1981 (**)

In September 1981, more than eighteen months after the initial Japan trip, further performances were recorded at the band's home base in 7th Avenue South. These were edited to become the album *Paradox*, again, not available outside of Japan until 2000 when Mainieri combined the record with *Step by Step* to form a double CD edition that he released under the name, *A Collection*, for NYC Records.

This album is a significant step deeper into straight-ahead jazz and ventures into free improvisation – something not found on other albums by this group. Typically, each track has a theme (though it is not something that you'll be singing on the way to work) and a more extensive improvisation section. The intent behind the music seems to be aptly described by the abstract title of the opening track, *NL 4*. It's left to the listener to figure out what, if any, meaning is present in the composer's mind. Further curiosity is engendered by the titling of the next track, *The Aleph*, named after a symbol used in ancient alphabets. There are two versions – one being almost ten minutes in length, and the alternate bonus track just over nineteen minutes. Written by Mainieri, the music is dominated by long, free improvisations. *Patch of Blue*, also by Mainieri, seems inspired by the band's Japanese experiences, and *Four Chords* is, as they say, exactly what it says on the tin. Almost eleven minutes of jazz are built around a minimal theme and variations. *Take a Walk* is a swinging piece by Mike B that seems inclined towards a style of bass playing, and offers Gomez a chance to take the limelight. After a statement of the theme, it lapses into a twelve-bar blues wearing a heavy disguise. In *Nichka*, Gomez uses a couple of minutes to show off with a solo that incorporates some exotic harmonics not much used on double bass.

Steps Ahead: *Steps Ahead* – **1983 (***)**

With Peter Erskine replacing Steve Gadd in the drums seat, Mainieri, Brecker Grolnick and Gomez began to tour – something that had not been attempted outside of Japan. Without the benefit of promotion through album sales, audiences had to discover Steps by way of their live performances. As they toured, a wider audience began to appreciate the band's qualities, and it was only a matter of time before Steps would become linked to a major recording company, with everything that that entailed.

In 1982, the part-time band that had begun its existence three years earlier at Mike and Randy's New York club signed a deal with Elektra Records, an act that expressed every intention of making Steps an internationally recognised band. Soon it was discovered that another US band had been using the same name and, as a result, legal issues forced a change of name to Steps Ahead. The band's new scope, however, also precipitated a change of personnel. Besides Gadd's departure, Don Grolnick moved on to spend more time playing with David Sanborn; he was replaced by Eliane Elias, a young and very capable jazz pianist from Brazil whom Eddie Gomez had met and persuaded to go to the USA. She seemed to have all the credentials for becoming a star. Randy Brecker, for one, was quickly smitten.

The band's first album, as so often, was given the band's name to maximise the marketing potential, and – unusually at this time – a film was also commissioned. The film, now available on DVD [1], was made for Titania, a Danish TV company, in the beautiful grounds of the Ny Carlsberg Glyptotek sculpture museum. I have already described the band's demeanour, which is cool and artistic in the extreme. The music itself is well fitted to the visual imagery and many non-jazz-oriented listeners might find this a great bridge into jazz.

The album begins with *Pools*, another fascinating piece by Don Grolnick with a delicate, mysterious melody and a tenuous improvisational base that, with its two chords drifting about in the breeze, seemed to hang in the air on gossamer threads. As the two Mikes blow out their solos, I wonder what exactly holds this piece together as they play off the two root notes against each other. This is one of those tunes that professionals make sound so easy, yet tantalises with its craft, and thrills with its originality. Each soloist in turn presents a thesis on what the piece means, before the original, rather hypnotic, theme returns. The playing on this piece is advanced jazz, yet in a style that would not offend any jazz fan, and it is even possible to hum the tune of this Grolnick special. Well! Whatever next?

The mood created in *Pools* is maintained in the second track, *Islands*. It's as if the two titles were deliberately chosen to complement each other. Full of delightful, catchy phrases and unexpected changes of direction, it is an immediate success. Eliane takes the first solo, and unsurprisingly develops a Latin rhythm that bounces along undemonstratively until Mainieri takes over, again with a two-chord base for some of the time. Then, as composer, he takes full command, and shifts the piece in new directions until Brecker comes in with just a minute to go to play out the theme. Although this is a simple composition, it is the clever variations during the main solo that are the highlight of this track.

Loxodrome is by Eddie Gomez. It's a quite different style of composition that sounds modal yet clings to the wreckage of traditional harmony like a frog to a leaf in a whirlpool. Erskine is magnificent throughout this fast, swing-time number, as he teases and toys with each soloist, sometimes leading, sometimes following. Without the joy of listening to this demonstration of brilliance, *Loxodrome* is a tough test for many ears. It's followed by Mike Brecker's *Both Sides of the Coin*, an extended work-out for Brecker that many listeners will love for its audacious and extrovert display. This is Brecker's stage and he takes full advantage.

Once again, the mood changes entirely for *Skyward Bound*, written by Mainieri. It opens as a very gentle ballad with Brecker's doleful saxophone leading the mourners. At 2.00, Mainieri sweeps in with a superb entry that is simply spine-tingling. After a brief solo, the two Mikes share the last exposition of the melody like two drunks in a bar at closing time with no homes to go to.

Erskine has always been equal to jazz composition, and *Northern Cross* is his contribution on this disc. It's a fast, swing piece with just sax, bass and drums at first and no chordal fix. After some clever interplay between sax and drums, Mainieri joins in, and by 2.10 you get the feeling that there's a tune in there somewhere. By now, it's a monochordal base with piano, bass and drums supporting the vibes with some good single-note rhythmic punctuation. A change occurs at 4.12 as the band take up a bridge with four descending notes, and then for the final minute it's everyone backed up behind Erskine's solo as the piece fades out.

The last track is an abstract piece entitled *Trio – An Improvisation*. Needless to say, this is an abstract piece that defies description. Played by bass, sax and vibes alone it avoids taking the path of random noise in favour of some clearly responsive interactions between the players.

Steps Ahead is a solid member of the class of acoustic jazz mainstream albums that any self-respecting jazz enthusiast would be happy to play. Sadly, however, Eliane's contribution to the album is minimal, apart from a brief solo on track 2. It would be good to think that the album cover art, with its image of four men carrying a woman, was not intended to relate to the album contents. However, it is undeniable that Elias is a "lightweight" [46] compared to Grolnick, whose presence in the previous line-up would have intimidated anyone. Perhaps comparative inexperience and unfamiliarity with the material was to blame for her lack of profile on the disc. In the same review, jazz critic Richard Cook is kind to Elias and says that her later solo albums were occasionally "captivating", located "between soft Brazilian pop-jazz and a tougher New York sound." [46] Clearly, to participate in an improvisation such as the one on the last track was simply outside of her musical experiences in Brazil, but she could hardly be blamed for that. Nevertheless, despite making a good account of herself in the film, she was absent from the next album, replaced by Warren Bernhardt as the band – like the frog alluded to above – abandoned the swirling leaf and plunged deep into the colourful, turbulent waters of jazz-fusion.

The Electronic Wind Instrument (EWI)

At this point, it is necessary to discuss an important development that took place in the late '70s to early '80s regarding the development of a new electronic saxophone. Actually, it is inaccurate to describe it as such, but that was probably what was in Michael's mind on the day when he first came into contact with one. In fact, it was an entirely new kind of musical instrument, an electromechanical device operated by the breath and fingers of the player. Its main difference was that it could create an electronic signal that could be fed via MIDI to a synthesiser. In fact, the instrument had started out as a new kind of trumpet, called an electronic valve instrument (EVI) by its inventor, Nyle Steiner.

Steiner was an experienced trumpet player who had worked with the Utah Symphony Orchestra in the 1960s. He first had the idea of an electronic trumpet in the 1960s, and used his manufacturing skills to build a prototype in his own workshop in the early '70s. His first playable EVI was completed in 1975, which he called the Steiner Horn. At an early stage, Randy had examined the EVI to see how it might fit with his own playing, but he found it to be too different from the traditional trumpet. He felt that playing it would have been like learning an entirely new instrument.

Shortly afterwards, Steiner developed a woodwind version of his device that he called, the Electronic Wind Instrument (EWI), known to most people as the 'ee-wee'. Michael found the EWI entirely to his liking. Steiner: "I developed my own transducer using whatever - I tried a lot of things out. A lot of the main parts I had to build myself. The first one was just a switch. You blew, and it turned on and off - just like pressing a key. Later, I built a proportional transducer." [47]

The early models consisted of two parts: a wind controller to convert the player's actions into an electronic signal, and a synthesizer to create whatever sound was desired through suitable programming. Steiner built everything himself. Recent models, such as the Akai EWI4000S or Yamaha WX7, are self-contained with the synthesiser in the lower part of the controller. The instrument has the same fingering system as a soprano saxophone, and is similar in size and shape.

The wind controller part of the EWI has a mouthpiece with sensors for both air pressure (to control volume) and lip pressure (to control vibrato). It can be played fast, because there is no movement of the keys; the positions of the musician's fingers are sensed by changes in the electrical conductivity beneath his fingertips; a set of rollers under the left thumb is used to change octaves. A particular advantage is the span of eight (!) octaves offered by most instruments, compared to the maximum of three on regular saxophones.

A recording exists of Michael playing an early version of the EWI during a gig with a Don Grolnick band called Idiot Savant at the Breckers' club, *Seventh Ave South*, on 18-20 August, 1984. [48] It is likely that he got the instrument directly from Nyle Steiner in 1983, studied a lot, and tried it a lot during gigs in the club. The early model Michael used can be seen in videos posted on the Internet. [49]

In 1986, Steiner met representatives of the instrument manufacturers, Akai, to discuss the commercial production of EWIs. It was agreed that Akai would adopt up the project. "Soon they had a model ready for production, it was very buggy at first, but soon it was all worked out. This first model was the EWI 2000, and EVI 2000". [50]

Steps Ahead: *Modern Times* **- 1984 (***)**

There is a remarkable transition into the next album by Steps Ahead, for the music becomes very strongly electronic and synthesiser-based. It is such a powerful change that, even though Eddie Gomez is listed as playing bass, his role as an acoustic bass player in the band has almost been extinguished. Indeed, this is the last Steps Ahead album on which he appears. (Miroslav Vitous, a founding member of Weather Report, suffered a similar fate after *Mysterious Traveller* (1974) was recorded.) Even Peter Erskine's position seems threatened by the introduction of electronic drums on some tracks. However, Erskine had joined the band after leaving Weather Report and, as a leading exponent of jazz-fusion drumming, could not be intimidated by electronics. Michael Brecker, although electrified to some extent on *Radio-Active*, had just acquired his EWI, but chose not to use it on this album. The big change in sound is achieved by a number of means. Firstly, Mainieri is himself a keyboardist, and he contributes quite a number of synthesiser parts to the tracks, but his main keyboard player is now Warren Bernhardt, a brilliant musician who went on to be musical director for Steely Dan in the 1990s. Additionally, a third synthesiser specialist, Craig Peyton, is added to several of the tracks, especially *Radio-Active*, which he co-wrote with Mainieri.

Modern Times is aptly named for a recording in the age of the synthesiser. The record begins on such a high that it seems destined to be awarded five stars. Michael's composition *Safari* is of a typical high standard. It begins with an infectious and very African-sounding motif played repeatedly on synth to sound like a simple Panpipe. At 2.15, the piece becomes altogether odder as the synthesiser bass takes a prominent, almost elephantine role. After this, there's an improvised section over the same motif that now starts to shift around amongst the keys. It's all very cleverly thought out, as we have come to expect from Michael. From 5.25, Mainieri's vibes take over, and in the background Brecker duets with himself on soprano and tenor until the faded ending.

Oops is by Mike M and it's a piece of powerful (if slightly schizophrenic) jazz-fusion played on his synth vibes. Again, there's a strong hook in the melody that makes my feet move irresistibly, but unlike a pop music context, this theme moves through some subtle – and unsubtle – changes. At 2.28, for example, there's a sudden shift to a second chorus that leads at 2.48 into a much freer improvisation for Mike B's tenor. At 3.30 it breaks into swing fours until 4.38 when it shifts into a new bridging section. Then at 5.08 the main melody returns, with Erskine contributing greatly to the rhythmic feel. His playing is especially strong and imaginative at this point.

Self Portrait is a superb ballad from Mike Mainieri. If it's really intended to be a portrait of himself, then it's a picture of a king of melody. The two Mikes play the luscious theme in sync over a pulsing synthesiser sound that is present throughout much of the track. At last, Gomez can be heard on this track, although his bass line is quite simple, reduced to a slow ascending pulse behind Mainieri's beautiful vibes. Mike M's solo is short and sweet, and tries to build to a gentle climax as the saxophone comes in behind him for a couple of passes that end with the delightful bridge section. Then it's over to the tenor man, who raises the hairs on the back of my neck with his gorgeous phrasing. His crescendo, slowly built to a stunning climax, is the real highlight of this album and one of the great moments on record, spoiled only by another faded ending.

By the time I get to track four and the title track, *Modern Times*, with the afterglow of the previous track still in my head, it's looking like this record could merit a rare five star award, but it's not long before I realise the album has peaked. The mood for the opening is unsettling and at 1.50 there's a break into a short Gomez acoustic bass solo. From 2.40, Mike M takes the solo on vibes. Brecker's role on this one is somewhat secondary as, strong with synthesiser backing, the lead keyboard is Warren Bernhardt's acoustic piano, which leads from 3.58 and then takes the piece out to its end at 6.17. This is an interesting piece that just loses the edge developed by the first three tracks.

Radio-Active is an electronic extravaganza with a big input from synth specialist Craig Peyton who demonstrates the amazing power of the Oberheim synthesiser, an instrument that was to have a major impact on the music world. The opening is dominated by a style of play similar to what we now call the '*Miami Vice* sound' from the famous mid-1980s Jan Hammer TV film theme. Peyton is, according to the sleeve notes, responsible for the bass sound on a Pro 1 synthesiser, and for the electronic DMX drums that Peter Erskine plays. Even Mike B is playing electronically distorted sax, overdubbed with himself. Specialist Roddy Hui was employed to mix this very electronic track. As for the actual music, well, it's very much a drone that occasionally breaks into a new key to avoid the monotony, but by 5.30 the piece doesn't have much more to say, yet goes on for another three minutes. There's a Chinese-sounding motif that merely comes across as a musical cliché and even Mike M's vibes solo adds nothing more to the piece, which by six minutes has clearly stalled. It's a disappointment on a track that was clearly intended to be a centrepiece of the album. The music shows some prescience of what is still to come in the 1980s, but misses its mark.

Now You Know is a pleasant, happy tune that, helped by Brecker's soprano sax, reminds me of Spyro Gyra. Bernhardt plays a nice acoustic piano solo, but the music is still synth-focussed. There's a short synth bass solo instead of an acoustic one from 3.50, and Chuck Loeb is reported to be guesting on guitar, though it is to little effect. Overall, this comes across as a rather trivial piece.

Old Town begins, once again, with the sound of the Oberheim, which has clearly played a big part in the planning of this record, much to the detriment of Eddie Gomez, who has all but disappeared. Again, the sound is very much like that of Weather Report, with the use of a drone and wordless vocal samples. From 2.10 there's a second theme to the rhythm of a military drumbeat and a somewhat ineffectual tenor solo from 3.05. There's a disappointing, unsatisfying feel about the melodies, which are simple, and sometimes simplistic.

When the record ends, it's impossible not to feel a sense of disappointment for what it might have been. At the start, there was so much to deliver, but it did not materialise. The album is so different from what has gone before under the 'Steps' banner; it's a clear statement of an exciting jazz-fusion identity with the new addition of electronics, synthesiser effects, drones and faded endings. In the end, the melodies and constructions in the last four tracks are rather too facile after the sophistication of the earlier compositions. Furthermore, there are no solo performances of special note. Thus, if you are not so partial to the sound of synthesisers, this album is not for you.

Steps Ahead: *Magnetic* **– 1986 (****)**

The boys were back on track for *Trains*, a major league jazz-fusion track from Steps Ahead, with all the qualities we could wish for. It is a majestic construction with fine, lush harmonies and chord sequences, and superb melodies that penetrate your soul for days after you have listened to the music. Right from the start, the main theme is presented for thirty seconds as an introduction, and there are echoes of many TV themes in these few bars. Then, at 0.30, there is a beautiful suspended chord, before the main theme commences at 0.38, focussed on a single chord. As it repeats a second time at 1.07, there is a withering chordal transition that lasts until 1.22. At 1.38, the main theme returns. 4.48 and 5.03 From 2.20 Brecker's sax comes in, but he's using a double-tracked sound from a synthesiser. This is not especially technical playing, but it's especially juicy. At 4.20 the majesty returns with even more pomp than before. At 4.48, there's that change again, through until 5.02. As the theme repeats to the ending, Hiram Bullock comes in with a screaming guitar solo that ends at 6.46 leaving Chuck Loeb's acoustic guitar engine rumbling down the tracks like Metheny's *Last Train Home*. Every player is perfect on this track. Bailey's great bass lines are simple, but so effective, and audible from the very start. Erskine's playing is so creative and forceful, but not overpowering. Chuck Loeb's strummed backwash is steady and undemonstrative, but very effective to the overall sound.

Beirut is a number by Michael Brecker that is based around a theme having distinct middle-eastern tones. It captures magnificently the tension and drama of life in the war-torn Lebanese capital. This is music to put fear in the hearts of imaginations, for the portrayal is of a beautiful city and its people, rich in history and culture, completely enveloped in hatred and destruction. There's enough to contemplate in the first three minutes alone with themes, bridges and choruses. It is not until 3.20 that the piece starts to quieten down, except for Erskine's thudding beat. Mike B comes in quite gradually on his EWI, and proceeds to improvise over a chord sequence that again is from the top drawer. He cuts out at 5.25, and it's a return to the back alleys of Beirut for a moment as Mainieri comes in with his vibes synthesiser, and then circles through that great chord sequence yet again. This is music that must be played loud to achieve its full stunning effect. Soloing is over at 7.24, and the Beirut theme comes straight back in until the end, which is orchestrated rather more than other recent tracks.

From the Middle East we cross at once to the Louisianan wetlands with *Cajun*. The sound of a banjo is heard in the in the background as Michael Brecker outlines his theme on EWI. From 1.48, the music changes up from a rustic to a cooler, more rounded, sophisticated style. Then the tenor saxophone becomes the focus as it takes us through a comfortable sequence of smooth chords. At 3.20, Peter Erskine sets up quite a rock feel to introduce the sax synth from 3.30. But it's brief, before Mainieri enters with his vibes synth sound From 5.20, there's a final flourish from EWI as the Cajun dance is executed to the monochord rustic rhythm. There's a nice harmonic chord at the end from Bailey's bass as the banjo doodles the piece out.

Many would argue that the electrification of *In a Sentimental Mood* by Steps Ahead partners Brecker and Mainieri is a step too far. Perhaps I am biased on this track, for I am especially sentimental about this, one of Duke Ellington's finest melodies, because it was one of the first jazz pieces I really liked. To play it entirely electronically is quite radical, even for jazzers. Just two musicians play the music on this track, with Mainieri on keyboards and Brecker on EWI. It's hard for the untrained ear even to recognise Michael Brecker on this track, but as you listen to the luscious melody, you can become aware of all the little inflections and embellishments that Michael usually employs on his saxophone coming through. More than that is the demonstration of the great range of his EWI, from the highest altissimo pitch to the lowest rumble in the bass. I regard this as an excellent demonstration of the scope of the EWI, for our wind maestro employs a recently invented musical wind instrument to maximum effect. It's utterly beautiful, but I feel many listeners may not agree. Over many years, Michael developed solo demonstrations of virtuoso EWI playing during his live performances. This is a good example, rare on CD.

Magnetic Love is related to the title of the album, but the line-up is slightly different, and the skills of George Duke have been enlisted to add a new feel to the piece. In essence, it is a vocal track with Diane Reeves singing the lyrics, but she has been put back a little in the mix so that the strong electronic effects remain the dominant force throughout. It's even a little robotic with some computerised vocal lines added in places. But it's also an excellent commercial piece, as you might expect with George Duke in charge. From 3.08, Mike B plays a tenor sax solo. Reeves returns at 4.13. Her last note is frozen in space as the music circles around and around, right to the end.

Sumo conjures up the right mental image of this music. The theme is harmonically clumsy, its body-shape unnatural, and there's no place to hide any modesty it might have. It's all electric and synthesised. A burst of contorted saxophone from 3.05, a scream of physical strain at 4.55, it all makes for a unique combination of ballet steps.

Peter Erskine writes both of the final tracks. On *All the Tea in China*, Bailey appears to be playing fretless bass, and the Oberheim is in evidence with its constant *cha-ka-cha-ka-cha-ka* sound in the background. Erskine has made a pretty good job of writing a tune suitable for this album, but it falls short of the quality of the rest. There is a clear Chinese feel to the melody in places, even though electronic synthesisers would seem inappropriate. At four minutes there is the sound of running water, and some free improvisation takes the piece out to a conclusion with Erskine adding percussion to the pastoral effects.

Next, *Something I Said* begins with what suggests is going to be a more conventional tenor sax ballad. Piano, guitar, and vibes all work to create a lovely ending to the album, but it's just too feathery to make a substantive contribution to what is still a very good album.

The CD ends with *Reprise (Magnetic Love)*, a very brief restatement of the title track. It's interesting to speculate why it was thought necessary to add it. Was it to make up for the drop off in impact from the last half of the album?

Yet again, we have a Steps Ahead album that could have been a stunner - worth five stars. However, there is just not enough exceptional material to keep the album consistently high in quality throughout. Nevertheless, there are enough superlatives on this album to make it well worth the purchase. The first five tracks are excellent for different reasons.

Steps Ahead: *Live in Tokyo* – 1986 (**)

After the 1985 studio recording of *Magnetic*, the band went on the road the following year, but with a brand new rhythm section of Mike Stern (guitar), Darryl Jones (bass) and Steve Smith (drums). One of the gigs, in *Kan-I Hall*, Tokyo was recorded and issued later on a laser disc, but it was not until 1994 that Mainieri released the CD version on his NYC label.

The music on *Live in Tokyo* (1986) features tracks from the band's previous two albums, *Modern Times* (1984) and *Magnetic* (1986). It reminds me of the reasons why I prefer studio recordings. Although it is undeniable that playing live can bring out the best in jazz musicians, you can also have unsuccessful gigs transcribed to disc, especially when, years later, it's the only gig you have in the vault and there is a good commercial reason for publishing it. Music that was intended to be slow and contemplative can be played in unseemly haste, as in *Oops*, usually because musicians pumped up by adrenalin (or some-such) feel an urgency in front of the audience, and that their solos will have more fire if played at a greater pace. In *Self Portrait*, the beauty and energy of the studio track has been converted into a bland exercise devoid of emotion. On the positive side, this music is less electronic, which may help some listeners get into it. The chaos and culture of the war-torn city of *Beirut* comes across well in the opening track, but it is much diminished from the original. Also, the essence of the recording is dependent upon not just the musicians, but also the audience, the unpredictable acoustics of the hall, and the technicalities of the kit set-up. This one lacks the warmth and presence of *Smokin' in the Pit* (1980), which was outstanding. I frequently find it hard to detect Darryl Jones's bass presence, and although Steve Smith is very good, he's no substitute for Peter Erskine's playing on *Magnetic* (1986). As for Mike Stern, his solos on *Oops* and *Safari* are cliché-ridden and ordinary, whilst on *Cajun*, he sounds uncomfortable and inexperienced. (It is worth remembering that he had a bad drug habit around this time when he was hanging out with Jaco Pastorius during Jaco's dark days.) Part of the charm of *Cajun* was the Louisiana banjo sound, here substituted with a much inferior EWI sound that doesn't pretend to be a banjo. Mainieri's contributions are very good, especially on *Cajun* and *Sumo*, which is a good track thanks to the Mikes M and B. *Safari* approaches the quality of the original and is the best track, whilst *In a Sentimental Mood* is similarly well migrated, but no significant improvement on the original. It is used as a lead-in to *Trains*, the final track, which brings the album to a satisfactory finale. However, if you do not already possess any albums by Steps Ahead, this is a poor album with which to discover the band.

From 1987, as Michael was embarking on his solo career, Mainieri continued to establish a firm foundation for Steps Ahead in the archives of modern jazz music. However, much of the momentum that had existed with a band of the quality of the one that included Brecker, Gomez, Gadd and Erskine was lost. Continuity suffered, and the albums that followed were not quite up to the same standard as those early ones. Michael's place in Steps Ahead was taken by Bendik Hofseth (b1962, Norway). Bendik, as he is known, played on the next two albums, *NYC* (1989) and *Yin Yang* (1992). Steps Ahead recorded two further albums, *Vibe* (1995) and *Holding Together* (1999).

Randy Brecker: *Amanda* **– 1985 (***)**

Early in 1985, with Randy now free from contractual ties to Arista, he was a married man with a new baby daughter, Amanda. It is unsurprising that such a musically gifted individual like Randy should choose to marry another talented musician, especially one as beautiful as Eliane Elias, with the added bonus that the pianist was Brazilian and therefore instilled with the special sense of rhythm associated with that country.

After learning the piano from the age of seven, Elias (b1960, Sao Paolo, Brazil) moved to New York in 1981 where, the following year, she took the keyboard seat in Mike Mainieri's band, Steps Ahead, of which Michael Brecker was a part. Clearly, her close association with the Brecker Brothers led to surprise consequences. Thus, when Randy did finally achieve favourable circumstances to make a new album as leader, it is hardly surprising that he should choose to include his new family in the project. Though Amanda, due to her young age, could not yet play much other than a rattle, she still was able to contribute her name to much of the music. She would later grow up to be a talented musician in her own right.

Despite Randy's earlier difficulties with Arista, he was still not able to capture the kind of record deal that other musicians could command. His new record was released under the Passport Jazz imprint of a New Jersey company, Passport Records, set up by Jem Records in 1973 and closed in 1988. The chosen studio was Secret Sounds Studio in NYC. The limited distribution from this small company makes this CD hard to find today.

The album cover shows a beautiful couple wearing fine evening dress, and purveys a message of cool sophistication and a little mystery... There are few clues on the outside of the package that this could be a jazz record. So perhaps it isn't?

In February 1985, Randy and Eliane entered the Secret Sound Studios with friends from the BB days. Will Lee, Jeff Mironov and Chris Parker were there to record the album's opening track, *Splash*. With Mark Egan and Danny Gottlieb they recorded three tunes, *Para Nada*, *Guaruha*, and *Samba da Bamba*. A couple of months later, in May, they recorded *Pandamandium*, and *Amandamada*, with Will Lee, Barry Finnerty and Dave Weckl.

As I begin my analysis, I sense that I am already in sensitive territory. For *Splash* I need to make the heretical remark that this music fits the *Wikipedia* definition of smooth jazz, i.e. "down-tempo in the range 90-105 bpm (this one is 105), layering a lead (melody playing) instrument (electric trumpet) over a backdrop that typically consists of programmed rhythms and various pads and / or samples." [51] Well, there's a real drummer here, at least. The melody is catchy, the changes are interesting, the tempo is lively but not fast, and there is a richness of sound that provides colour and enthusiastic vibrancy. It is a happy piece of music, consistent with deliriously happy parents putting their child in the bath and watching it have lots of fun. Not macho – just nice. Smooth jazz haters beware!

The next track, *Para Nada (For Nothing)*, is a beautiful Brazilian ballad with lyrics sung in Portuguese. It provides Randy with an opportunity to play a pretty solo on trumpet.

In complete contrast, however, *Pandamandium* is a fully mature BB fusion tune with strong echoes of some of Chick Corea's Elektric Band post-1986. There are strong Brazilian rhythms, and Michael is on hand to blow a good solo, Will Lee is mixed superbly into the foreground, and it's a treat to listen to his top-line, inventive bass. Dave Weckl's presence (curiously, he would soon play in that Chick Corea ensemble) is powerful, with nothing routine about his contributions. No sentiment here, just strong, new jazz, and on that basis, this is the album's standout track.

Samba Da Bamba is exactly what it says on the maracas: an energetic Brazilian party song. It is led by Eliane's lyrics and accomplished acoustic piano. She is followed at 1.56 by a Randy trumpet solo, played with typical Amazonian zest. Some great scat singing leads into a straight-ahead jazz solo from Eliane. Then, at six minutes (no concession to radio airplay here, then!) there is a section of traditional Brazilian vocalising. The voices are accompanied by percussion provided by "Cyro and George of the New York Samba Band." It's hard to find out who they are, but it seems as if this is at least an early reference to the well-known Brazilian percussionist, Cyro Baptista.

Amandamada is definitely 'after-party' - a cool, melodic Brazilian schmooze on which Michael, in recreational mode, plays alto flute, and Sadao Watanabe plays a particularly sexy, alto saxophone solo. This is lush, poolside music direct from Copacabana that is always a pleasure to hear for its sketches of exotica.

Guaruja begins with an *a tempo* trumpet intro, before breaking into a gently-paced fusion piece led by trumpet and synthesiser. After a good piano solo from Eliane, Randy contributes some funkier, improvised electric trumpet work at the tail end of the piece, which goes out on a splendid high.

In summary, the album, *Amanda* (1985), is a commercial jazz-fusion album that ranges in style from popular Brazilian to jazz. The memory left is that this is the kind of music that would have been heard on public broadcast systems in the 1980s and 1990s. To some minds, that is a condemnation. For me, it is something to celebrate. Remember, Randy and Michael led the way into this new fusion style of music that made millions of people feel comfortable – indeed, happy - in their surroundings. Here, the trailblazing stuff is put to one side. This record is about enjoying the fruits of past labours.

Randy Brecker: *In The Idiom* **– 1987 (***)**

This is the album that Randy always wanted to make. It's a collection of his own compositions, inspired by the jazz musicians he always looked up to, and played by musicians he admires today. Joe Henderson is his chosen sax-man, Ron Carter is on bass and Al Foster on drums. Dave Kikoski plays piano.

It's an album without commercial pressures, under his total control and played live in the studio. In the notes [52], Randy tells writer Bill Milkowski that this is the time for a reinvention of the cool, laid back style of jazz from the '50s and '60s, a style that does not necessarily look towards the power playing he has recently become used to.

Randy's choice of Joe Henderson was to assist with the objective of creating cool jazz. Randy: "He's so relaxing when he plays. I knew Joe would have a calming influence on me in the studio." [52] Joe Henderson (1937-2001, Lima OH) was born into a large family that was no impediment to his embarking on a successful period of music study. After a long and distinguished career as a leading tenor saxophone player recording for the major jazz labels such as Blue Note and Milestone Records, Henderson played prolifically as a sideman and became a very in-demand musician. However, it was a late association with Verve that gave him his greatest successes, especially with albums such as *Lush Life* (1992) and *So Near, So Far (Musings for Miles* (1993). As a result, he won Grammys in those years for best jazz solo performances and topped a series of polls: 'Jazz Artist of the Year' for 1992 and 1993, 'Best Tenor' saxophone player three years running for 1992-94 and 'Jazz Album of the Year' for 1992 and 1993.

Henderson had had a brief association with the Miles Davis Quintet in 1967, in the times of Herbie Hancock, Ron Carter and Tony Williams, although the band never recorded together. No doubt, Randy's choice of Ron Carter for this gig was a meeting of old friends for Joe and Ron. Al Foster, too, had played for Miles, although in his post-Bitches Brew years. The odd-one-out – metaphorically, at least - was David Kikoski (b1961 New Brunswick, NJ), a young 25-year-old Berklee Music School graduate who had recently come to Randy's attention, and makes his recording debut here.

Milkowski reports that Randy seems "more concerned with the totality of the music than in any ego-gratifying grandstanding." Randy tells him, "That comes with maturity. I've always been a little too concerned with chops and speed. Some part of that has to do with playing alongside my brother for so long. That's *his* forte. I'm at my best when I play less notes, more melodies. I know that now." [52]

Recorded over two days 19 / 20 Oct 1986, this hour-long CD filled the yawning gap in Randy's output of serious jazz, and represents another milestone in his career. It still stands as an entertaining and fulfilling session of top quality jazz from musicians who were among the best at their chosen trade.

Michael Brecker: *Michael Brecker* **- 1987 (*****)**

Michael's belated solo career began in 1987, when, aged 38, his self-titled debut album was finally released. Even in 1980, he'd felt the record was overdue when he told *Crescendo* magazine, "I haven't recorded under my own name yet. I've been waiting for the right record deal. Yes, it's high time, it was high time five years ago." [53] Now it was 1987, and there was still no solo release.

It's not insulting to say that Michael was not a natural bandleader. Everyone who has met him describes him as Mr Nice Guy, a shy, delightful man with perfect manners and a friendly, engaging, humorous personality. These may be superb qualities to find in a human being, but they are not the ones that are necessary and sufficient to manage other humans, especially ones with large egos, who may have their own agendas, or others who have demanding artistic objectives. Besides, Michael had plenty of work that he found satisfying and was sufficiently rewarding, without taking on the extra responsibilities that came with the artistic management of a group of highly talented musicians. That's not to say, of course, that he didn't want to record a project of his own design. It was just that such an exercise did not require the formation of a band – only the choice of appropriate musicians (indeed, friends!) whom he could rely upon to impart their best efforts in the execution of his musical plans. He didn't necessarily need to compose all of the music, although he clearly had some new material up his sleeve. Making a solo record was all about securing the right business opportunity. Finally, in 1987, he found one, thanks to Ricky Schulz, Vice President of MCA Records.

It was a surprisingly intimidating opportunity at first. Much was made in the contemporary music press that he was nervous about recording for the same label as John Coltrane, Pharoah Sanders, and McCoy Tyner. "I never really felt prepared until I did it," he told *Jazz Times*. "I had always felt more comfortable working collaboratively with my brother Randy. Now the collaboration is a little different. Having my own band, I have to assume responsibility for a lot of things." [54]

The personnel on his first album as leader was star-studded. First of all, Michael chose his friend, Don Grolnick, not to play, but to produce. They had been close friends since those early days in the 1970s when they were both in Dreams. They had played together many times since, with Don playing in the Brecker Brothers, and Mike playing in Don's bands, and on his albums. Now, the two men sat down for three weeks beforehand to sketch out the ideas for the album.

With Don in the box instead of at the keyboard, Mike hired Kenny Kirkland, along with Pat Metheny, Charlie Haden and Jack DeJohnette. It was many people's "Dream Team." Kirkland (b1955, Brooklyn, NY) was a favourite pianist of many players. He had feet in both the mainstream and fusion camps, but could invent prolifically from other people's ideas, no matter how far out they might be. Charlie Haden (b1937, Shenandoah, Iowa) was a giant from the old school, rising rapidly to the top of his profession by playing *avant garde* freeform jazz with the likes of Carla Bley, Paul Bley, and Ornette Coleman. Drummer Jack DeJohnette (b1942, Chicago, Illinois) had also made his mark as a leading member of the new school of drummers who had broken free from the role of keeping rigid rhythm, like humanoid metronomes, and become creators in their own right - musical inventors, who produced unpredictable but sympathetic percussive accompaniments. Finally, there was Pat Metheny, a unique guitarist with his feet planted securely in mainstream jazz, alongside the likes of Gary Burton and Steve Swallow, but one who had also created his own unique brand of guitar jazz-fusion.

Michael is recorded as saying that he "wanted to make a record with some mystery, one that bears more than one listening." [55] His style of contemporary jazz relies heavily on the more academic style of modal jazz, a tool often used by purist jazzers to elevate themselves into exclusivity from the long grass of popularity and commercialism. Made, I'm sure for all the best motives, it's a strategic decision that firmly places him in the company of premier league jazz musicians and attracts that kind of hallowed respect from the fraternity of jazz purists. Forget any idea you might have formed from listening to an album by the Brecker Brothers or Steps Ahead. Here, the name of the game that Michael now plays is contemporary jazz. Typically, this design is a mostly blank canvas on which the artist can experiment with a wide range of styles and techniques. In a sense, this is his own personal brand of free jazz, and thanks to his high profile in the world of jazz, it was to prove as influential as anything else he did in his career. We could have guessed the angle of the new musical direction by simply looking at the musicians he chose to play alongside him. Metheny, Haden, DeJohnette and Kirkland were all partial to a freer brand of jazz than might be expected in what is generally referred to as the mainstream. In so doing, Michael was adopting the Miles Davis musical philosophy of being true to himself, and not capitulating to any particular genre, style or convention.

On the album's notes, *New York Times* reporter Steve Schneider correctly said that a jazz musician can be measured by the company he keeps. [56] This is clearly true in this case, for all his band-mates are members of the same exclusive club. It's the same kind of strategy chosen by Miles Davis during the period of his Second Great Quintet period of 1964-68. Then, the music on the albums became increasingly elevated above what the average jazz listener was used to hearing. However, the music performed at gigs was often significantly different with an injection of more conventional tunes selected to appeal more to the live audiences. Unlike Davis, who retained a constant band format during that period, Michael's group of musicians was not intended to be a band of his own, but a vehicle to assist him in establishing a body of recorded music that could withstand the test of time. Mike's 'band' would remain flexible, according to whoever was available at any particular moment. By the 1980s, all major jazz musicians had their own solo careers, so it was simply not practical to hold on to permanent band formations using the very best players. Pat Metheny, for example, was so busy with his own group that his place was frequently taken by Mike Stern. After the darkness of his days with Jaco, Mike had now dedicated himself properly to the furtherance of his career, and was starting to take his rightful place in the top rank of jazz-fusion guitarists.

Michael's style of contemporary jazz on this album might be regarded as broadening the mainstream. The result was that, today, this kind of playing is more in the centre of the stream. But the contents of this disc are not very different to the feel of the music on Michael's later 'solo' albums, right up to his last, *Pilgrimage* (2007). The style of this recording includes the use of the Akai EWI, first adopted in Steps Ahead. By the time this album was recorded, Michael had become irrevocably fond of playing it. Had it been invented ten years earlier, this device would have become the standard tool of the jazz-fusioneer. However, his use of the EWI in this context must be taken as merely the choice of just another instrument for the acoustic setting he has defined. The fact that it is an electronic device is irrelevant in this case.

Sea Glass is a descriptive title for an impressionistic piece. It's Michael's own composition, and a statement, in the first track of his first album as leader, that here is a very serious musician. The waltz-time melody has elements of natural beauty, but is mystical and atmospheric, with Mike's questing instrument finding unexplored caves and undersea features from which as-yet unseen creatures appear. For me, however, the most memorable aspect of this composition is Kirkland's depiction of the title. His beautiful, long sustained chords make a remarkably accurate representation of a flat, featureless seascape in which all sense of distance and dimension is lost. Of course, Michael completes the painting with his imaginative note work, but - in this piece at least - Kirkland is the star that crystallises the title perfectly.

At track 2, the unpronounceable *Syzygy* is appropriate for a piece that is bent on taking the listener on a sonic EWI excursion. The piece starts out with Mike on tenor sax entrained in a freewheeling duet with Jack. Michael once said that he had long ago reached a point where he didn't need to practice to improve his technique. [37] He did, however, feel the need to practise, so as to explore the harmonic relationships between notes. As I listen to this kind of discourse with just the drums to keep him on track, it is tempting to compare him with his hero John Coltrane who (it is said) spent most of his waking time, when he was not gigging, doing just this kind of thing. After an exposition of a theme from 2.30 to 4.00, Kirkland enters the fray to play in a similar freestyle fashion with Charlie and Jack. From 5.26, Michael is back, now with his EWI, and he plays it so as to match some of Kenny's chordal keyboard work. Some listeners find it hard to relate to this kind of sound, because it is a saxophone player using an instrument that just does not sound like a saxophone. We fusioneers, however, love it, the more so when we can appreciate just how difficult it is to make these new sounds. Next up is Pat Metheny who improvises over a cycling set of chords. Finally, there's a return to the theme before Michael picks up his tenor tube and takes the piece out to fade with more duet freeform playing over a repeated piano motif.

Choices is a number by Mike Stern that happens to fit Michael's needs for a sophisticated modal construct, and plenty of room for free improvisation. This is a difficult piece for most ears, and not typical of Stern's compositional style.

At times, it is spacey and atmospheric, serious and never in the least singable, yet thanks to careful orchestration that is not obvious at first. There is an evolution to the sound that removes it from repetitive verse / chorus formats and renders the whole composition explorative and original.

Nothing Personal is the first of two compositions provided by Don. A straightahead concept, the music is played with a wonderfully implied swing by Jack DeJohnette that contains an explosive rhythm, igniting from time to time when Charlie Haden presses the detonator. Yet it continues to deliver massive energy behind the lead instruments. Once the heads are cooked, Pat Metheny leads off with an improvised solo that moves speedily through the orchestration with nimble, unobtrusive fingerwork. Then Michael challenges Grolnick's themes with controlled aggression until 4.25 when the sharp bebop-inspired melody reappears.

The Cost of Living is the second composition by Don Grolnick, a more accessible piece, supremely well played as a doleful ballad, and much slower than it appeared in later form on Grolnick's own album, *Nighttown* (1992). This is by far the better of the two versions, a most perfect piece of interpretation that broadens the ideas expressed in the title way beyond simple worries about money. This rendition is of tragedy in epic proportions. Whether on Mike's saxophone or Charlie's gentle acoustic bass, the melodic theme is massaged into a variety of shapes in the quest for a solution to the question faced by many people – just how can I deal with what life has given me? The plaintive theme of six rising notes could not be simpler, but that is the core of its success. The remainder is found in Don's carefully researched accompanying chords, played so sensitively on Kenny's piano, and the sympathetic rhythm of Jack's drums. There is a striking awkwardness to the fractured motif that occurs at 1.14, 2.00 and 2.09. It's a broken life we are looking at. The motif somehow makes the lines more lovable, like a handicapped child that everyone feels sorry for and tries to be nice to, knowing that the child faces a life sentence for which money can never be adequate compensation. From 2.23 to 4.18, Charlie Haden's solo is both breathtaking and heartbreaking in equal measure. Then it's Michael's turn, and even Charlie's craft is eclipsed. Knowing him as we do, Michael's reputation for technical demolition work on any improvisation usually involves immense, dense sheets of sound, *à la mode de Coltrane*. Here, however, his improvisation is a masterpiece, without recourse to that approach. At 5.38, his saxophone simply cries out for help, on behalf of all those countless refugees from poverty, famine and civil war. It makes all of our concerns about rises in the price of gas seem so insignificant.

Original Rays is a three-way composition by Michael with Mike Stern and Don Grolnick, and is an advertisement of the possibilities offered by the EWI. It may be that this type of sound is anathema to many listeners who find it too far removed from the saxophone. It is, of course, just another synthesiser, and it hardly matters whether it looks like a sax or a piano, it is the music that matters. This music is at least conventionally harmonised, and so more user-friendly than the modal compositions that seem so inaccessible. The music is as close to a jazz-fusion piece as it is polite to admit in this context, and it illustrates that even contemporary jazzers, trying to build on the foundations of their art, cannot entirely deny their secret fusionist desires! Even though Michael uses normal tenor sax later on, the cat is out of the bag, and Pat's guitar work just serves to advertise it even more. On the vinyl, it was the twilight track, a position where you can get away with anything. On the CD, it's a dead giveaway.

I would especially have given the vinyl record five stars, as the six tracks work so well together. However, my CD has an extra 'bonus' track that some may feel destroys the ethos of the LP. The interloper is the standard piece *My One and Only Love*. It begins with an extended two-and-a-half minute unaccompanied improvisation before the band enters to take the piece through in a very conventional way.

Listeners coming to this album for the first time need to be aware that this music is at least one intellectual level higher than many other albums Michael plays on. It may be that the adopted harmonies and styles are too unusual to satisfy some tastes. One thing that you can be sure of is that, with this collection of recordings, master craftsmen at the very top of their profession strove to create something of lasting value. They sure did it.

A final curiosity is the GRP monogram that appears on the disc, despite it clearly being recorded under an MCA Impulse! label. In view of the venom with which the purists later attacked GRP products, it is ironic that one of the puritans' later heroes should be branded in this way.

Michael Brecker was voted "Jazz Album of the Year" in both *Down Beat* and *Jazziz* magazines. One observer noted, "What made *Michael Brecker* such a rewarding effort was both the creative breakthrough it represented and the almost limitless promise it held for the future. Freed from the often rigorous constraints that all studio session musicians must contend with, and given *carte blanche* to follow his muse, Brecker produced a project that bristled with the intensity and excitement of an artist revelling in the heady spirit of artistic liberation." [57]

Possibly as a result of the success of his debut album, Michael must have been high in Herbie Hancock's thoughts when he decided to form a new mainstream quartet in 1987. Mike had recorded for Herbie's *Magic Windows* (1981) album but the two men had had only casual acquaintances in the meantime. This time, Herbie had succeeded in reforming Miles's 1960s band, with Tony Williams on drums and Ron Carter on bass and Michael taking the place of Miles! The following summer, Al Foster and Buster Williams, replaced Tony and Ron, but no albums resulted from either band.

Michael Brecker: *Don't Try This at Home* – 1988 (****)

Michael also went ahead with his own band in 1987. His promotional tour would be extensive, including dates in the USA, Europe and Japan. It was always going to be a long shot to expect that the musicians who had appeared on his album could go on tour. However, he succeeded in recruiting a very strong team of musicians.

Joey Calderazzo (b1965, New Rochelle, NY) started to learn the piano when he was aged seven and growing up in a strongly musical household. He joined his brother's rock band when aged only 14, but once his older band mates had enrolled at Berklee, he started to study jazz seriously by listening to all the great jazz pianists. He first met Michael at a jazz clinic, and impressed him so much that Mike recruited him into his 1987 band as a newcomer. It turned out to be an inspired choice by Michael, for Joey would play consistently alongside Mike during the coming years.

Drummer Adam Nussbaum was a natural choice too. Nussbaum (b1955, NYC) grew up in Norwalk, Connecticut and started to play drums at age 12 after studying piano for 5 years, and playing bass and saxophone as a teenager. He moved to New York City in 1975 to attend College, and was soon an active member of the local jazz scene. In 1978 he joined Dave Liebman's quintet and went on his first European tour with John Scofield. During the early eighties he continued working with Sco in a celebrated trio with Steve Swallow. In 1983 he joined the Gil Evans Orchestra, and also played with Stan Getz. He later joined the Eliane Elias / Randy Brecker Quartet, and played with Gary Burton, and Toots Thielemans.

The respected jazz writer George Varga was already starting to suggest comparisons between Michael Brecker and John Coltrane when he wrote the notes for Michael's second album, *Don't Try This At Home* (1988). Was it just another example of the music press overindulging in hyperbolic analysis? Varga wrote, "Searching, probing, absorbing, experimenting, analysing – Brecker is in a constant state of artistic reflection and expansion. Never mind that he already possesses one of the most formidable arsenals of skills of any saxophonist in contemporary music: voluminous, full body tone that is unmistakably Brecker in any context; a consistent technique that enables him to perform swirling melodies, dense harmonies, jagged rhythmic punctuations and complex contrapuntal lines with grace and agility; a veteran painter's sense of texture, shading and balance; chops galore (to use the musical vernacular); and perhaps most importantly, exemplary taste and sensitivity, together with an unerring knack of capturing the essence of each composition he performs." [57] It was a description of Michael's remarkable powers that contained as many positive adjectives as there were notes in a sheet of sound. Such words were often used to describe John Coltrane, but were they justified here? Well, if you listen seriously to Michael's albums as leader, these are, indeed, the kinds of descriptions that come to mind.

Right from the off on this album there is humour and surprise. The title, *Itsbynne Reel*, shows a lot of thought. The play on words is typical of Michael: he never passes up an opportunity for a light-hearted jape. The music begins. Wow! This is nothing like Coltrane! Where's the saxophone? Not necessary. The EWI is part of the experiment to try out new things. It's a fusion: Irish reel that sounds like bluegrass, American folk music, the drone of the pipes from 0.20, some variations on piano at 0.30, the fiddle at 0.55, and then at 1.12, the first hint that this is heading somewhere else. At 1.40, things start to get a bit weird. A lot is going on when, at 2.12, a switch is flicked and a whole lot of new tones and textures appear from nowhere: strange hiccups in the rhythm; bizarre but nerve-tingling chords. By four minutes the whole tune is buzzing. Finally at 4.18, the tenor saxophone appears, like the delayed appearance of the lead actor in a Shakespearean drama. From now on, the soliloquy is delivered, unscripted, impromptu, majestic. The final minute is ordered chaos, and when it's over, all you can say is "OMG!" The music is all about Michael, and, to some extent Don Grolnick, the two conceptualisers of this remarkable piece. It's true that the other musicians are essential to the overall sound, but throughout, our attention is focussed on the breathtaking virtuosity of this main man, who perhaps, *really is* comparable to John Coltrane...

Chime This is a Grolnick composition, and he introduces his piece with a series of evolving chords that echo the title. The slow rhythm doesn't begin until 1.30, when Adam Nussbaum's steady cymbal beat, and Charlie Haden's pulse join Don's piano. At 2.38, the piece steps up in tempo, with Mike Stern's guitar playing the melody in unison with Michael's tenor. At 3.34, the piece finally breaks into a straightahead swing-time beat with Don extemporising. From 4.35, Mike starts to improvise Don's tune.

Scriabin was written by Vince Mendoza, and the sense of the title, named after Russian classical music composer Alexander Scriabin, comes through at the start. Scriabin was an especially inventive composer who devised a system of music that correlated musical keys with spectral colours. Both during his life, and afterwards, he was vilified and lauded in equal measure for his unique approach. This is a quartet played by the masters, Michael with Herbie Hancock, Charlie Haden and Jack DeJohnette. Varga describes it as "forlorn, yet ultimately beguiling," a perfect and succinct analysis of the mood created by this composition. [57]

The fourth track is *Suspone*, a cutely titled piece that conjures images of dance halls and Great Gatsby stylish living. This Mike Stern composition typifies his fetish for straightahead, bebop-style melodies, its inspiration drawn from something that Charlie Parker did all the time – taking a well-known standard, such as *I Got Rhythm*, and massaging it this way and that, until all that remains is the familiar chord structure. It is Michael's EWI that kicks things off with an abstracted big band sound that keeps stepping off the bandstand and going walkabout with the key of the melody. Just occasionally the stray musicians re-join their colleagues, but the gulf between the key centres of soloist and rhythm players is often quite wide. Mike Stern is comfortable improvising in his own environment, but MB doesn't care much for comfort. Today's boots will take him anywhere he chooses. Nussbaum is secure, Jeff Andrews' walking electric bass is both insistent and consistent, whilst Joey Calderazzo's acoustic piano solo is excellent and precedes the final run through the theme with EWI once more. Overall, this music swings, and is fun, but slightly off-the-wall.

Don't Try This At Home is another Brecker / Grolnick composition, whimsically titled with deadly serious intent. A unique piece of music, its linear, non-repetitive form begins with an introduction by the EWI, deftly doubled on tenor saxophone to a timeless, thrusting rhythm by Jack DeJohnette. At 1.45, the tone becomes ominous, thanks to Herbie's serious chords. From 1.53, Mike Stern takes the lead and by 2.25 is expressing a clear, but complex melody that Michael soon kidnaps. Then, with his band working tightly around him, he leads them deeper and deeper into a complex exploration of the sonorities they have set up. Thanks to the cream-of-the-crop '60s avant-gardists, the music becomes some four minutes of brilliant free improvisation, in the best traditions of Coltrane, although the band is clearly working as a unit. From 6.25, Herbie leads Charlie and Jack in an extended extemporised trio setting. At 8.35, Michael is back with his stomping, leaden steps looking for a path through the long grass of his densely vegetated garden. It's all over very quickly after that. I don't know about trying this at home – most of us wouldn't know where to start!

Everything Happens When You're Gone is Mike's own composition, played as a quartet with Charlie, Adam and Joey. There is a long, solo intro to 0.45 when Joey joins him, and this leads into a slow ballad. It becomes a template for later compositions, which twist and turn through unexpected sequences of chords. A long solo from Joey runs to 4.10, when Mike begins his extended improvisation through to the end of the piece, which never returns to the start.

It's something of a relief when I arrive at Grolnick's *Talking to Myself*. It's another opportunity for the producer / pianist to join Michael, Mike Stern and Jeff Andrews, now also with drummer Peter Erskine and synthesiser player, Jim Beard. Grolnick is a very accomplished composer, creating music that is carefully structured, but doesn't rely on traditional chorus and verse formats, and his changes never feel alien, as they sometimes do in Michael's compositions. Don's knack for finding attractive melodies and motifs is truly gifted, and his skills in arranging the instrumental resources to hand are exemplary. So this piece is a further example in which Michael is given yet another new context in which to operate.

Jim Beard's presence adds a new dynamic to the colour pattern, which now, underpinned by Jeff's electric bass, is more akin to fusion than to mainstream. Jim Beard (b1960, Philadelphia PA) came to prominence on Wayne Shorter's album *Phantom Navigator* (1987), and worked on Eliane's *So Far So Close* (1988). An expert in contemporary technology, Jim is not just at home on all types of keyboards, but he programs drum machines and bass lines too. He arranges and produces the sound schemes that form such an important part of recordings, and will go on to work with Peter Erskine, Mike Stern, Bill Evans and John McLaughlin.

On this track, a melancholy introduction is soon given more optimism by the bright tones of the band and a cheerful, energetic beat. From 2.30, Michael breaks out into a section of alternate improvised and ensemble lines. A minute later he is alongside a persuasive set of five, rich chords, and a repeat of a pleasant middle section. Finally, Don's cycling chords take the song to a fade, and leave me wishing for more. That's always a good way to end.

Jim Beard contributed the final track (not present on the LP), quaintly titled, *The Gentleman & Hizcaine*. Structured in a simple ABA format, the music is built on an A-section of four enigmatic, cycling chords that bring a curious melodic line to life. It could be a comic Charlie Chaplin walk, set to music. It could equally be a penguin on an ice floe, or more darkly, an observation of life through drug-distorted pupils. This peculiar 'bonus' is clearly a reserve player in a great team of seven.

So what of the Brecker / Coltrane comparison? If there is a difference between the two great tenor players, it is Michael's tendency to retain a measure of loyalty to the composition in hand, rather than simply heading off into outer space in the manner used by Coltrane in his later years. I am certain that Michael would have been embarrassed to be compared to Coltrane, but there is no doubt they have much in common, even if this giant benefitted by standing on the shoulders of his musical idol.

As for the album itself, well, all tunes were played live, except for some doubling of sax over EWI. The standout tracks are without doubt those that Michael had a hand in writing. The title track is utterly superb, even if free jazz may turn off some listeners. As physicists would agree, there are degrees of freedom and this music doesn't go as far into the void as Coltrane might have done. Mike could not have chosen better musicians with whom to do it. Jack, Charlie and Herbie are all masters of total improvisation, and Michael shows here how good he is too. The originality of *Itsbynne Reel* is remarkable, and his use of the EWI, once accepted as having a justifiable presence on the jazz bandstand, adds a new dimension, as well as a degree of freedom. (And, by the way, child prodigy Mark O'Connor (b1961, Seattle, WA) is a multi-award-winning fiddle player, amongst other things. His playing is exceptional here, too.) The variation of the menu makes the album continually interesting, and each new avenue of approach is developed to previously unexplored depth.

It was a great compliment from the music business when Michael's performance on *Don't Try This At Home* won the Grammy for "Best Jazz Instrumental Performance Soloist (On A Jazz Recording)" (1988). There are other tracks that could equally well have won.

Michael went on tour in the summer of 1988 with Herbie Hancock's Head Hunters II funk band.

Randy Brecker: *Live At Sweet Basil* **– 1989 (****)**

Late in the year of 1988, Randy played a straightahead gig at New York's famous jazz club, *Sweet Basil*. Tracks were recorded over three nights from 18-20 November and released on the Sonet label the following year. The band consisted of Bob Berg (saxophone), David Kikoski (piano), Dieter Ilg (bass) and Joey Baron (drums).

Bob Berg (1951-2002, Brooklyn, NY) began learning piano at six and saxophone at thirteen. He graduated from the Juilliard School Of Music and then became a professional saxophonist specialising in hard bop jazz on the NYC circuit. Joining the business, pretty much at the top in Horace Silver's band, as Randy had done, he appeared on three albums: *Silver 'n Brass* (1975), *Silver 'n Wood* (1976) and *Silver 'n Voices* (1977). In 1985, he was a member of Miles's band, and played on *You're Under Arrest* (1985).

Dieter Ilg (b1961, Offenburg Germany) was a classically trained acoustic bass student and graduate of Freiburg University of Music from 1981-86. Then he gained a postgraduate degree from the Manhattan School of Music in 1987 and caught the eye of Randy Brecker when he filled in for Marc Johnson at a gig. Randy describes Dieter's playing as "flawless." [58] In recent years, Ilg has returned to Germany where he now teaches at his old University.

Joey Baron (b1955, Richmond VA) is largely self-taught. He was influenced by a wide range of musicians and styles and has worked extensively in his own bands and as a session man with top pop and jazz musicians such as Tony Bennett, Michael Jackson, Al Jarreau and John Scofield . His style has been associated with *avant garde* and experimental music, largely due to his close association over many years with experimentalist John Zorn that started with Zorn's album *The Big Gundown* (1985). This adventurous mode of playing interested David Sanborn for his change of style during the recording of *Another Hand* (1991). Baron was a member of Bill Frisell's band from 1985-95. Joey was introduced to Randy thanks to Bob Berg, and Randy wrote that he had since become musically dependent on Joey's unique sensitivity. [58]

Randy had spotted Dave Kikoski playing in Roy Haynes's Quartet and had hired him for *In The Idiom* (1987). His place in Randy's band was secure. Randy pointed out that none of this band had played together before. "From the first note, it just clicked. The group is truly a labor of love and every moment is a special occasion for us." [58]

The Sleaze Factor is a wonderful opener. As a really mean, blue, soulful design, it is the track closest to Randy's fusion sensitivities. The composite is based around Randy's favoured cocktail of oddly parallel harmonies shaken with chord changes that taste like strawberries dusted with pepper – combinations that should never work, but actually do. On the case of it, the track is straightforward, with long, lingering sensations, but these flavours are deeply sophisticated. Wickedly, Randy remarked that the inclusion of a 5/4 bar into the otherwise slinky funk samba "should sufficiently confuse anyone trying to dance [to it]." [58]

Horace Silver is well known for his pecuniary awareness, and Randy's fond memories of working in Horace's bands led him to dedicate his tune, *Thrifty Man*, to Silver. All the soloing is first class, but Randy, in particular, excels himself in the early part of this track.

It may not be fusion, but the main theme of *Ting Chang* is extraordinarily complicated, yet played flawlessly in parallel by Randy and Bob. Set as a fast Latin piece, it shifts into swingtime in sixteen bar cycles as Dieter's four-in-a-bar walking (should that be running?) bass takes charge. Berg is first to take on the challenge of the solo, and he drives through the sequences like a JCB in a green field. Naked aggression seems to be the only means of survival in this, one of Randy's toughest settings. Probably the most successful is Ilg who comes up with a brilliant percussive approach from 5.12 to 6.40. Indeed, this is a good showpiece for him, as his solo leaves many lesser bass players aghast.

The tension is set free for Randy's ballad, *Incidentally*, which he describes as "a lot of altered chords pitted against a simple counter melody." [58] Just in case all this would prove to be too easy, in a fit of musical masochism, Randy wrote the piece in a particularly hard key that musicians rarely use. No-one appears to notice, but then we only have audio!

The backbeat is brought out of the cupboard for the exceptional *Hurdy Gurdy* in this hot rocker. Again the melody is out of kilter with the chord sequence, which sounds like it ought to be logical, but is of the unique Brecker brand. The vibe is changed too, by Dave Kikoski's use of an organ sound to reflect Randy's younger years playing in organ trios in Philadelphia clubs and bars. Once the simple thirty-second introduction has been presented, this time it is Baron's turn to thrive as he sets up a fantastic pulse and proceeds to extrude it into constantly varying shapes during the solos. Randy clearly enjoys his freedom to push out with a fiery improvisation that is set against Bob Berg's fearless interpretation.

Randy had included *Moontide* in the running order of *In The Idiom* (1987), and being recorded so closely together, the treatments are quite similar. Thus, the two versions offer a good opportunity to compare the approaches of Joe Henderson and Bob Berg to what Randy describes as "inside-outside modality." In this version, at least, Baron's rhythmic interpretation shows a lot more imagination than Al Foster achieved and is perhaps the reason why this recording trumps the earlier one.

Henderson comes to mind again in the final track, *Mojoe*, which Randy dedicated to his saxophone hero. This is fast closing statement of energetic motion that features all the players in a hard-nosed post-bop setting. It's so deep in the mainstream that fans of fusion and crossover will probably find the undercurrents too bumpy.

Once again, with this album, Randy presents a wonderful selection of music that is different from much of the other material described in this book. The only downside is the slightly inferior sound quality of the recording, although Baron's drumming is well presented.

Paul Simon: *The Rhythm Of The Saints* – 1990 (*****)

In 1991, Michael toured for most of the year with Paul Simon. The tour took them to Africa where Michael drew particular inspiration, especially having long conversations with some of the African musicians in Paul's band. Both Michael and Randy appeared on Paul Simon's eighth studio album, *The Rhythm Of The Saints* (1990), although it is hard to discern their contributions. Michael's task was to provide fills on his EWI, which he did on most of the tracks. Of course, since the EWI is a synthesiser, it is difficult to detect what sound he is making. One exception is when both brothers appear together on *She Moves On*, Michael playing saxophones and Randy piccolo trumpet. For *Graceland* (1986), Simon had worked mostly with South African musicians, but for this large project with its focus on World rhythms, he selected a large number of Latin American musicians, especially Brazilian. Much of the recording was done in Rio de Janeiro, but the final work was done at the Hit Factory, NYC, where Mike and Randy did their overdubs. The end product is a very sophisticated album with smooth, atmospheric songs that purvey enigmatic messages. They are beautifully recorded and mixed into an excellent collection of varied and entertaining music. Although there is little obvious evidence of jazz in the songs, this is nevertheless a fusion of complex, perfectly executed traditional rhythms from southern continents blended with modern harmonies and melodies. The amount of work involved in turning a large number of percussion tracks into this slick, World music is obviously enormous. The album was one of Simon's most commercially successful records and was rightfully nominated for "Album of the Year" at the Grammys in 1992 – beaten to the prize by Natalie Cole's *Unforgettable* (1991).

Randy Brecker: *Toe To Toe* **– 1990 (****)**

This CD is precisely of its time, lodged in what I would describe as the fusion mainstream. Synthesisers? Yes. Drum machines? Yes. Sorry if that disappoints. Try to get over it. This is an album of exciting and mostly beautiful music performed by masters of their trade. The sound is frequently warm and rich, like the taste of apple pie and cream.

Besides Randy, the main creative force of the album is Jim Beard, who, we have already seen, worked with Eliane and Michael on their 1988 albums. Jim's footprints are all over this album, as instrumentalist, arranger, programmer and producer. A common feature of music from this vintage is to know when to use synthetic drums, and when to use real ones. For example, having hired Dennis Chambers to appear on the album, it's really hard to understand how you could *not* use him on every track! Randy and Jim Beard were able to make good choices on this album for the right reasons. Chambers is a drummer who appears not to mind working alongside them.

Dennis Chambers (b1959, Baltimore MD) made a big impact playing in the P-Funk collaborations of the late 1970s, and then appeared on John Scofield's *Blue Matter* (1986) and *Loud Jazz* (1987). Like Jim Beard, Dennis would go on to play regularly for mainstream fusion musicians such as Mike Stern, Bill Evans and John McLaughlin. So great is his talent that, although a master of funk drumming, he has always been able to play far beyond that style, and has become well known for power drumming. Bashiri Johnson was the percussionist chosen for the album. Bassist Victor Bailey (b1960, Philadelphia PA) is another contemporary of both Chambers and Beard. Bailey's career was established when he succeeded the great Jaco Pastorius in Weather Report in 1982, and played up until the band's finale. Then he had played in Steps Ahead with Mike Brecker and Mike Mainieri on *Magnetic* (1986), and with Billy Cobham on *Picture This* (1987).

Randy's chosen guitarist was Jon Herington (b1954, Paterson NJ) who had moved to New York around 1985 and become something of a late starter by waiting until his thirties to appear on albums by the top artists. Already well known to the other members of the band, he had played on Bailey's CD *Bottom's Up* (1989). Later, he would become Steely Dan's favoured lead guitarist for their return albums *Two Against Nature* (2000) and *Everything Must Go* (2003), as well as playing on albums by Bill Evans and Mike Stern. The great Bob Mintzer, saxophonist of Yellowjackets and leader of his own Big Band, appears at the extreme ends of the sound spectrum as he plays bass clarinet on *Trading Secrets* and piccolo on *What Is the Answer*. In supporting roles, we find Mark Ledford and Regina Belle who provide backing vocals. Mark had impressed listeners with his all-round musicianship on Pat Metheny's *Still Life (Talking)* (1987), and appeared with Dennis Chambers on Victor Bailey's *Bottom's Up* (1989). The brilliant young singer, Regina Belle (b1963, Englewood NJ) had been awarded a gold record for her #1 R&B hit album *Stay With Me* (1989) and was a great choice for this session.

So here was a wonderful nucleus of young players, already some of the best in contemporary jazz-fusion, which, as is apparent, required significant experience in the use of electronic devices.

With the Beard composition, *Mr. Skinny*, the heads of the music sound like the introduction to a grander piece, but this intro just keeps going. I guess that's why it's skinny: the music is mostly thin, but it's funky and varied in its colour palette.

The second track, *Trading Secrets*, is quite the opposite, akin to opening a treasure chest only to be amazed at the awesome jewels inside. It's a combination of great chords, rich textures and beautiful melody. But the wonderful juxtaposition of trumpet with Mintzer's bass clarinet playing in unison is a choice that is quite inspirational.

It Creeps Upon You was written by Randy and has echoes of the BB hit record *Sneakin' Up Behind You*, but let that not be taken as a downside, for this is also funky and fun. The backing vocals are especially effective in giving the track the feel of a musical commentary or playlet. Randy has developed this type of music into his own insignia for vocal tracks. Whatever you think about vocal jazz, there is still plenty of great trumpet playing, and the record is further enhanced by a cameo appearance of brother Michael towards the end.

It's back to sophistication for Randy's tune, *The Glider*, a sound that is luscious and conventionally harmonic. The music soars high up into the summer sunshine, the golden rays reflecting and refracting through the cockpit glass, until, at 1.30, our wind-powered aircraft enters the clouds of grey. A swathe of uncertainty envelops us briefly, until we soon emerge back into the glorious transparent atmosphere. Jon Herington adds a beautiful guitar solo before the synthesisers take over the autopilot. Great flight, Randy. I'll take this ride anytime.

The title track, *Toe To Toe*, is another synthesiser-led creation that sets Randy's intricate composition into a smooth, glossy patent leather shoe that fits snugly around his inquisitive feet.

The Jim Beard piece, *It's Up To You*, is significantly more energetic, thanks to an up-tempo beat and Herrington's lively accompaniment. He continues in a vein that brings up good memories of Frank Gambale's work with

Chick Corea in the Elektric Band, as Randy freewheels above him. There are many moments of kaleidoscopic change throughout this brilliant arrangement.

Randy's vocal on *What Is The Answer* is very reminiscent of Donald Fagen's singing style, one that he himself didn't like, but which became familiar to Dan fans, and was considered to be part of the band's success. This blue composition is modern jazz with a story to tell, thanks to a gorgeous flugelhorn sound that intimately probes the twisting chord changes. Bob Mintzer's piccolo adds some pretty, top-end colours.

The album is rounded off by the Herington composition, *Lost 4 Words*, a title that (briefly) worked for me. The music is characterised by a mysterious atmosphere in which Randy's penetrating trumpet sentences are interwoven with keyboard grammar and a searching bass syntax. Then Herington's heavy rock guitar sound cuts through the pages to dispel briefly the questions until he gets to the middle section when further uncertainty arises. By four minutes, the full band is turning the pages of the report, but somehow the density of the prose is too much to resolve the search four the missing words.

Some commentators will no doubt find this album to be date-stamped, a property that often implies that its value has diminished with time. If your tastes are influenced by fickle, ever-changing fashion, then you may not like this disc. However, a sub-surface inspection of this music reveals a rich seam of musical skills and creativity.

Michael Brecker: *Now You See It...(Now You Don't)* – 1992 (****)

The period of the early 1990s was very much in the mature period of jazz-fusion. Most serious jazzers had come off the fence – one way or the other – and decided whether they loved or hated it. Smooth jazz was well established as a musical genre, and serious jazzers mostly hated that. For those who liked either (or both, like me!) it was a wonderful time. It was a purple patch, a time of great excitement in jazz. There was so much new material across a broad range of styles, and so many new sounds to enjoy. Universities and Colleges were generating many very talented musicians who were well grounded in electronics as well as music. Recording and playing techniques had become much influenced by digital technology, and things were moving forward rapidly with every new advance in computer-driven kit.

Michael was riding the crest of this wave, experimenting with many new ideas that might have been thought impossible only ten years earlier. His winning formula on his own albums continued with *Now You See It... (Now You Don't)*. Many of the same musicians were present: Jim Beard, Jon Herrington, Adam Nussbaum, Joey Calderazzo and Jay Anderson were all young enough to know how to interact perfectly in the latest situations. There were some newcomers too, such as drummer Omar Hakim, bassist Victor Bailey, and veteran percussionist, Don Alias.

But Michael's team had firmed up around some wonderfully gifted people who understood the new tools better than most, and who also had the musical acumen to apply them in the most artistic ways. Programmers had now joined the serried ranks of contributors to albums. Jason Miles (b1952, Brooklyn NY) was one such. Miles, like Mike and Randy, was a 1970s music graduate from University in Indiana. He formed a close relationship with Miles's late '80s collaborator, Marcus Miller, and contributed to synthesiser programming with Miles Davis on *Tutu* (1986), *Music From Siesta* (1987) and *Amandla* (1989). He was quickly recognised as one of the best in the business, and recruited by Mike Brecker for his projects. Then there was Judd Miller, who had become *the man* for all things concerning the EVI / EWI. Miller was an early participant in the development of electronic instruments. He became one of the first exponents of the EVI as well as a clever programmer for the EWI. Miller: "I got into doing soundtrack work around 1985. There were composers interested in the expressiveness and sound possibilities that the EVI had to offer. [59] Michael had been playing the EWI since around 1983 and was by now a virtuoso on it, but Miller's specialist expertise in programming was vital to Michael's continuing search for new levels of performance on the EWI, which would reach astonishing proportions on the road.

Michael used the EWI on half of the eight tracks on his latest album, including the opening piece, *Escher Sketch (A Tale Of Two Rhythms)*.

Back in 1970, I recall sitting with friends when one said, "Hey guys, Ginger Baker [the drummer for Cream] can play four different rhythms at the same time – two with his hands and two with his feet!" We were all incredulous. Most of us couldn't do two different rhythms with our hands. I remember that we all agreed to attribute this impossible skill to Ginger's roots as a jazzer. Such a skill is always impressive, wherever it is found, but its probably true to say that other drummers who could do this are more likely to be found in the jazz world: Billy Cobham and Steve Gadd spring immediately to mind.

Rarely has a piece of music been so obviously designed to have two different rhythms played simultaneously. It seems a shame that it was done here using synthetic drums instead of a real drummer, but that's part of the nature of the jazz-fusion beast. In any case, this is a remarkable piece of music. It starts off innocuously as Adam Nussbaum plays a straightahead swing jazz beat at 155 bpm on cymbal to accompany Michael's sweet tenor sax intro, and Jim Beard adds some synth chords. At 0.19, the second rock rhythm begins on drums at 116 bpm, a ratio that is 4/3 and very difficult to consciously deal with. There are plenty of songs in which a bar of 3/4 metre is fitted inside a bar of 4/4 metre, and musicians switch from one rhythm to another mid-flow. It's good, but that is not happening here: both rhythms are 4/4! If you can handle the overdubbed rhythms by tuning your ears to the first rhythm, and then the second, you will be able to hear how Michael plays inside both, cleverly doing it separately *and* concurrently. It is an amazing display of virtuosity. As if that were not enough, he adds a layer of EWI, mostly over the rock components, which is exaggerated by the Victor Bailey's electric bass and Jim's synthesisers.

Minsk is written in the identifiable style of Don Grolnick, beginning as a piece of classic straightahead jazz, but constructed around a theme that is unpredictable and fractured, with unusual intervals and staccato bursts. It's about as odd as a back pocket in a vest, but that's what makes Don's tunes so attractive. The mood is dark, and captures well the western stereotype of a Soviet city. From 1.16 to 1.32 the sun comes out briefly on the bridge, whereupon it's a return to the dark, cold, winter climate. At 4.00, Joey Calderazzo plays a solid improvisation that, by 5.15, is tensioned by the additional accompaniment of his military colleagues. The repeated theme is already memorable by the time it returns from 5.41. Then, as the armoured Soviet tank moves forward, Michael casts off all signs of restraint, and stands in front of it in defiant protest. The playing is, of course, amazing, but so is the production of this track. It may be Michael's record, but this is a Don Grolnick masterpiece.

Ostensibly, the next track is played by a quartet comprised of Michael with Jim Beard, Jon Herrington and Don Alias. Composed by Jim, *Ode To The Doo Da Day* is a curiously titled, unusual jazz-fusion piece, written in a Latin mood to which Don Alias contributes much of the rhythm. The problem in pieces like this that rely heavily upon electronics is the assignment of certain sounds to the players who make them. There is little doubt that Michael uses an overdubbed EWI track to play in unison with his tenor saxophone, a method that creates a particularly jazz-fusion tone for the saxophone. He also uses the EWI alone to play some of his lines in the loose guise of an electric oboe, but there are further sounds that may have been played by Jim or Michael. It's likely that the synthetic bass is from Jim's fingers, rather than Mike's. Whatever, this is a true jazz-fusion piece with both charm and interest.

There is no mention of EWI in the notes for *Never Alone*, a piece of Michael's work. As the title suggest, it's a moody ballad played by Victor on bass guitar, Omar on drums, and Don Alias on percussion, whilst Jim creates the electronic tonal backdrop via his keyboards. Michael weaves the kind of magic only he can achieve with his luscious saxophone, inspired by his own challenging melodies and chord patterns.

His next selection is a totally different animal and begins with the EWI to the fore. With the title, *Beep*, this could be an example of late 20th century bebop, or – dare I suggest – a little bopeep! This is certainly no nursery rhyme; this is a wolf in sheep's clothing and he's chasing the heroine across the fields, anticipating lunch as he does so. In the best jazz-fusion style, this really is a combination of acoustic sounds (Joey Calderazzo on piano, Jay Anderson on acoustic bass, and Michael's tenor leads) with the electronic mêlée from EWI, Beard's synthesisers, and Bailey's bass guitar.

Dogs In The Wine Shop is another of Don Grolnick's conceptions, in which a crazy title is attached to a most thoughtful, complex composition. Somehow he chose a Latin rhythm to accompany his themes, which demanded contributions from no less than three percussionists – Don Alias, Milton Cardona, and Steve Berrios. Calderazzo's acoustic piano mirrors the kinds of sounds Don might have made had he played on his own track, but once again Jim has a significant presence as he builds the colourful pastiche behind the lead instruments. Of course, it is Michael who fronts up, mostly playing the heads with discipline and the solos with loose invention. There are flashes of EWI in the accompaniment too, and the overall package, managed by Grolnick, is another joy to hear.

Jim Beard's second contribution is *Quiet City*, and he leads the tune with a bop-inspired melody that is staccato and sharply pointed. There is a Latin tint to the rhythm here too, thanks to the percussion from Hakim and Alias, whilst Jim's synthesisers are the only hint of electronics, as Michael drives down the straight streets of Gotham City on a holiday.

Michael decided to record a version of Bobby Troup's *The Meaning Of The Blues*, a straightahead jazz quartet piece played by Mike with Joey, Jay and Adam. The song is a minor standard, largely thanks to Miles Davis's version from 1957. Miles loved ballads, and Michael shows here how sensitively he can play mainstream jazz, despite his growing reputation for blowing his socks off in advanced settings.

I should not pass up the opportunity to say a few words about the accompanying cover art. Michael was inspired by the painting called *Sky and Water* (1938) by M. C. Escher, which shows blue geese in a green sky transforming into green fish in a blue sea. Michael attached his own interpretation, *Now You See It...(Now you Don't)*, as the title of the album – another superb insight that uses a well-known phrase from the world of magic to describe an artistic optical illusion. In addition, his use of the title, *Escher Sketch*, for the opening track is a 'typically Michael' play on words that matches the art to a popular toy that makes drawings disappear. The artistic association of the music to all this is a stroke of genius. Besides being a great sounding piece of jazz-fusion, in its own right, it is also a perfect musical *representation* of the fusion of rock and jazz – the first largely portrayed by electric instruments, the second by the usual acoustic sounds. I find this layering and weaving of ideas that blend words, art and music, truly awesome.

The Brecker Brothers: *Return of the Brecker Brothers* - 1992 (*****)

After the successes of the late 1970s, it was inevitable that the reformation of a band called the Brecker Brothers would generate much excitement. It had been a long wait. Michael said that he and Randy had been planning to regroup since around 1985; they just hadn't been able to get it together until now. This wasn't the kind of situation that so often arises in rock and pop where reformations were just about boosting the stars' pension funds with performances of old material that was as stale as microwaved pizza. Jazzers don't do that kind of thing. The Breckers had new, even better things to say.

There were some old friends present. Dave Sanborn was available to play on one track, *King Of The Lobby*, whilst Dennis Chambers was hired for those occasions when a real, live drummer was preferred. Don Alias and Bashiri Johnson were on hand to provide percussion. Mike Stern (b1953, Boston MA), like Randy, had played in BS&T, although Stern's residency had been later than Randy's. He attended Berklee Music School where he had already decided to study jazz. His breakthrough began when he joined Billy Cobham's band and appeared on the album *Stratus* (1981). He was lucky enough to become part of Miles's comeback band and played on *The Man With The Horn* (1981), *We Want Miles* (1982) and *Star People* (1983). His great potential was recognised, and thanks to a good contract with Atlantic Records, Mike embarked on a long series of very good albums beginning with *Neesh* (1983). Throughout the early 1980s, Mike had been associated with Jaco Pastorius, and had been part of Jaco's touring bands. His formal association with Michael Brecker began when he played on Michael's *Don't Try This At Home* (1988).

Stern's friend from Berklee, Dean Brown (b1955), is another popular session musician, who has had rather less visibility as a leader on albums. Dean started playing with Billy Cobham, and formed a professional relationship that has continued intermittently since then. He had to wait until *Here* (2001) for the first of his four solo CDs to be released, but over many years Dean has played alongside most of the top jazz-fusion and contemporary jazz musicians. He quickly became a top choice for BB bands.

By 1992, Max Risenhoover had built a solid reputation as a bass player, but perhaps more importantly was an excellent technician with the many electronic devices and computer-driven tools that were arriving fast in the top studios. He had already worked with Bob James and Kirk Whalum, and was a member of the Steps Ahead team for *Yin Yang* (1992).

As for bass, Will Lee would share duties with two newcomers, James Genus and Armand Sabal-Lecco. James Genus (b1966, Hampton VA) is one of the new generation of bass players, who is comfortable with both electric bass guitar and upright acoustic bass, which makes him a perfect modern session musician, and ideal for his work in the *Saturday Night Live* band on US TV.

After moving to New York, he soon started playing with jazz stars such as Horace Silver, Roy Haynes, Nat Adderley and Bob Berg. But he was still very much an up-and-coming player when Michael Brecker approached him. Genus, told an interviewer, "I was on the road, and I got a call from him. You know, I couldn't believe I was talking to him on the phone. They were putting together the Brecker Brothers Reunion Tour, and he told me that I was one of the bassists being considered for the tour. What can I say - my jaw just dropped to the floor. And then we got together, and it worked out, and we had a relationship together from that point on." [60] That phone call resulted in a couple of years working closely with the Brecker Brothers during the second important phase of their history.

Armand Sabal-Lecco is another of the amazingly gifted African players of electric bass. Like Richard Bona, Sabal-Lecco originated from the Cameroon, and had been chosen by Paul Simon to appear on his album *The Rhythm Of The Saint*s (1990). Michael and Randy quickly seized on his abilities and recruited him for the new Brecker Brothers recording.

One of the important new relationships for the Brecker Brothers was with George Whitty. Born and brought up in Oregon, George wanted to be a fusion musician during his time at High School, but there was something of a vacuum for that kind of jazz in his home district. Fortunately, his parents sent him to Berklee Music College for a couple of years, a step that proved vital in his career development. After a brief sojourn in New York, he took work on cruise ships where he got his first big break. "Matt 'Guitar' Murphy picked me up off those, and I did a year with him, and by the time I got back to New York I was playing pretty well, and I was already doing such electronic production as could be done in 1988. Things just kind of went from there." [61]

It was not long before his skills came to the attention of the Breckers. "A friend of mine, Joel Rosenblatt, recommended me to Eliane Elias as a second keyboard player in her band, and I did my best to impress her. She then recommended me to Randy to do some demos for that first *Return of the Brecker Brothers* record. They liked the demos, and decided to use parts of those as a framework for that CD." [61]

Besides his mastery of the electronic keyboard, George was soon proving his abilities in all other aspects of studio work, including as a programmer, composer, and producer. He has been closely associated with Michael and Randy ever since.

Song for Barry is cutting-edge jazz-fusion. The track begins with an addictive groove set up by Alias and Sabal-Lecco. Michael plays some little motifs on EWI that float freely like autumn leaves in the breeze. The groove steps up a gear at 0.22, thanks to the full bass rhythm, and Michael continues to embellish the groove with his electronic ornaments. At 0.45, the main theme starts, at another higher plane. The music is already special, so just hearing the theme repeated is pleasurable. At 1.20, the introduction of drums signals another step up to the next phase of the piece. All the flags are now blowing out in the wind as Mike's syncopated synth notes ring out in fanfare. From 1.52, it's Mike's tenor sax that takes on the challenge. A change up from 2.06 into a new written section is quite unexpected, and Randy's trumpet leads a jagged backing line as Mike shares groups of four bars. From 2.28, it's back to the main theme for eight bars until, at 2.42, a brooding vibe acts as a lead into a section from 2.58 that will receive development in the coda. From 3.30, Randy takes over the improvisation role over the main theme, which by now is becoming a new friend. But it's short lived for that coda section commences at 4.00. There follows some sixty seconds of spine-chilling climax, through which Mike Stern's white-hot guitar cuts like a thermal lance.

As an album opener (and as the first pukka BB track for years), this is out of the top drawer. The drumming, in particular, is as advanced as it gets. This was the sound of the early 90s. Just when Sanborn had made the astonishingly good *Close-up* (1988) but was about to temporarily retire into the outback with the poor album *Another Hand* (1991), the Brecker Brothers were set for a massive return to jazz-fusion. The main theme is pure rocket fuel. The second part of the tune just builds and builds to a screaming crescendo as the electric guitar winds increasingly skyward and the final note is devastating. Great stuff!

The reunion is entirely complete with the addition of David Sanborn to the front line for *King of the Lobby*. It also marks the return of Randy's humour, as little snippets of spoken words appear, scattered throughout to spice the tune up a little. But this piece is essentially a jazz-funk extension to the stuff that was going on in the 80s, extrapolated to the 90s with all the pizzazz you might expect from guys who've been at the cutting edge for over two decades. They're showing no sign of winding down: there's so much going on in the background as Randy and Michael make their solos. After you've had a good listen to the stunning solos, play it again and just absorb the beautiful details of all these great musicians. The clarity of the recording is so good, the tight ensemble playing of the horns, the neat, crisp funky guitar, the gorgeous funk bass and, of course, the wonderful 90s drum sound. Max Risenhoover must be given much credit for this great sound.

Big Idea moves farther out of the pure jazz idiom into the more popular genres. There is a watermark of the work of Maz and Kilgore on this music. Mary (Maz) Kessler was a student of economics in London before giving it up to become a musician in New York in the mid 1980s. She teamed up with Robbie Kilgore in an acid jazz band that impressed Michael and Randy. Kilgore had contributed a lot to the Steps Ahead album *Magnetic* (1986). Their obvious talents in a certain music genre led to their invitation to produce this track, and to add an entirely new dimension to the sound of the Brecker Brothers. Again, there are just occasional spoken lines behind the jazz, and echoes of Randy's hit song, *Some Skunk Funk*, put the music into the 'sampled' category. Besides Mike, Randy, and some additional Rhodes piano from George, the music is electronic. Listen out for the very nice sax and trumpet cadenza at the end, played over some great electronics.

Above and Below is a throbbing jazz piece that is modal, has a complex chord structure, and an extremely difficult melody of the kind we now expect from the brothers. This isn't jazz-fusion - just the very latest style of contemporary jazz. The harmonies are quite far out, and the pace is stunning. Just take this piece as an example of how far ahead Randy is. It's a brilliant piece of playing, fluid, creative and entirely unrestrained by the chord structure in which it operates. We have grown to expect saxophone pyrotechnics, but Randy tends not to make a big deal about his trumpet virtuosity. Not here, however. His sound at first, from 1.25 is electric and original, before he launches himself into a thrilling improvised solo from 1.55. After a reprise of the theme, Mike solos from 3.30, tearing up the music in a way that will surely please his fans. He rides the changes like the champion surfer we all know him to be. Both Michael and Randy are on top form and this piece absolutely burns. It all ends with a fiery drum solo from Dennis Chambers at 5.33. Throughout, the leaders are supported by the superb George Whitty, James Genus, Bashiri Johnson and Mike Stern, who takes on a rather low profile.

That's All There Is To It starts out as a kind of jazz-reggae piece, with a simple melody and staccato accompaniment. However, it's focussed on a humorous vocal from Randy. The theme is centred on an idea that Randy seems to enjoy - that of robots in human society. The *double entendres* jump out endlessly from a silly dialogue between an ageing man (who we might later identify as Randroid) and his girl. The fun is that you can also take it as a robot trying hard to behave like a human. It all comes to a head at 1.38 with the classic line, "I'm only human!" Randy does this again later with his Randroid character on *Hangin' in the City* (2001). But amongst all the fun, there is a great piece of music and some wonderful playing. It may not be everyone's cup of tea, but for me it's a very special track, - one of the few pieces of music that make me laugh out loud, especially, at 4.35, when the punch line is abbreviated to just, "Human!"

Wakaria (What's Up?) is Mike's composition and sounds like an ethnic African party. It's an ideal scenario for Sabal-Lecco to impart his African musical heritage. There's a simple basic rhythm but with lots of percussion and hand clapping that adds to the party spirit, with everyone having a great time. Michael plays a great soprano solo bridge section midway through. This piece is a wonderfully fresh, joyful ride through a new, constantly changing landscape.

Producers Maz & Kilgore are back in the studio again for *On the Backside*, another complex piece swathed in unusual harmonies, even if the construction of the piece itself is quite straightforward. It's a similar successful formula to the one used on *Big Idea*. Their particular style is outstanding when added to Randy and Michael's joint composition. Once again, there are different sections during which the mood changes from the harsh street level banter to the sophisticated penthouse chit-chat. Randy plays with the mute and sounds rather like Miles Davis, and is interlaced with Michael's slick tenor playing. But there are other sections with harmonies from outer space, always backed by the mesmerising hissy electronic rhythms. Layer upon layer of imaginative overdubs makes this piece a constantly evolving screensaver of great music.

Sozinho is Portuguese for 'alone', which gives a pretty good idea what this song is like. It's a poignant ballad, led by Randy, whose flugelhorn tone is doleful, but clean and gentle. Michael's improvisation is searching, but well considered. Mike Stern shows his soft side by playing gentle, acoustic guitar; even Dennis Chambers is wearing a pink vest. The result is a beautiful, conventional, love song in the jazz idiom that might even bring a tear to your eye.

Spherical is funky and fun, even without words. Randy plays muted trumpet to a jagged theme. The rhythm is funk, but with an emphasised syncopation to which the clever theme is applied scrupulously. The interwoven splatches of rhythm percolate through the entire piece, but are developed right through the final phase of the piece from 3.53, when Michael takes on a solo. This is a very clever, crafted piece of music that is far more detailed than it appears at a superficial level. Will Lee makes a welcome appearance playing a good brand of funky bass, while Chambers and Alias are responsible for the strong percussion. Stern is credited with playing, but is mostly unheard.

Randy's tune, *Good Gracious*, is amazing in a number of ways. It begins by pretending to be a modern version of that well-known Burlesque piece, *The Stripper*. This melody is a portrait of the kind of reaction that a straight-laced person might have on being confronted with salacious material in a dark, underground nightclub. As a result, there's a subtle kind of humour permeating this piece, despite the fact that it takes on a much more serious rock flavour as Mike Stern's electric guitar winds itself into a sexual frenzy. But it's never quite that simple. The heavy chordal arrangements are spectacular, the harmonies weird, and the rhythm a puzzle with a degree of difficult approaching a Rubik cube. Later, as the theme returns, you might discern that the four-beat rock rhythm is actually four and a half! (Actually it's 11/8, or 3x3 +2.) Even the final chord is crazy, and it's great!

Roppongi means 'six trees' in Japanese, and is district of Tokyo famous for expensive homes and lavish nightlife. Michael's EWI is played alongside the horns in a theme that combines the curious paralleling of harmonies that the brothers pioneered in the 70s. The rhythm section of Genus, Chambers and Alias lays down a solid swing beat, as the two leads interweave their solos in the style of traditional 'eights' duels. An occasional burst of Latin-swing breaks up the format, but quickly returns to the rapid-fire lines that penetrate the trees like tracer bullets.

There is justification for believing that the Brecker Brothers saved all their best material for ten years in the knowledge that when they finally put together a reunion record, it would be the best yet. Well, they succeeded. This album is superbly varied, with many different feels, rhythms, tempos, harmonic constructions and much colour. There is a lot of jazz-fusion, as well as some straightahead playing, but the latter plays second fiddle to the former, especially as there is such a strong presence of new generation musicians brought up in the contemporary electronic style. As if that were not enough, there is a brand of humour here that is stronger than on any other comparable album I can think of. At over an hour in length, the album is chock full of entertainment, as well as being bang up to date for 1992, and it made a great impact at the time. But with this amazing record, one of the most admired bands of the 1970s was back in business and, far from looking over their shoulders, they were as far ahead as ever.

The Brecker Brothers: The Return of the Brecker Brothers Live in Spain 1992 [DVD] – 1994 (*****)

After a hiatus of ten years, the band went on tour to promote the new album. The concert at the *Palau de La Musica* in Barcelona, Spain was recorded and is available on a rare DVD published by GRP. The band was a concentrated form of the one that had made the album, with Randy, Michael, Mike Stern, James Genus, Dennis Chambers and George Whitty.

Making comments about the band for the purposes of viewers who perhaps did not know much about the musicians, Randy said, "Dennis Chambers is the strongest drummer I've ever played with, he swings in every context. Mike Stern is a fantastic player, a real hard worker and is great to hang out with. George Whitty is a great find, both as a programmer, producer, player, and he also adds cohesive elements to the band. James Genus is a great both acoustic and electric player, and is probably one of the coolest people I've met." [62]

The video [63] begins with *Above and Below*, in which Randy plays a great solo. George is also shown playing a keyboard solo with Stern vamping alongside him on his Telecaster. This is one of the great advantages of being able to watch the music played, because we get to see why Randy describes Stern as "hard working." His constant chord vamping is physically demanding, with many combinations of jazz chords that require constantly changing fingering all over the keyboard. This is not a player who glides through a set of simple E7s, A7s and B7s, but a master craftsman who is intimately familiar with every position on his instrument. After an improvised solo from Michael, Dennis Chambers plays a great solo towards the end.

Michael's *Spherical* is next. Its format is one in which a beautiful, cool groove is set up using a gentle rhythm and a two-chord motif. There are sections in which the musicians insert cool guitar, trumpet and sax bursts, as in a conversation amongst friends. Added to this is the common formula of starting at a really low energy level, but max cool; then the tension is wound up to breaking point. It is a very popular and much used formula, and it works well here too. Stern endorses the scorched earth solo technique, first in trio with James and Dennis, and then with George added. Randy reboots the tune with a muted solo over the groove, and then winds up to full stretch without the mute. By minute ten, Michael is embarking upon the same strategy. The overall result is magnificent.

Some Skunk Funk is once again played at high velocity (157 bpm of crotchets / quarter notes) and the solo from Michael blisters the paintwork in my room. A change of vibe occurs at 3.05 when Michael finishes and Randy starts on electric trumpet. First, he introduces a slower, heavier feel; then a new rhythmic motif is taken up by the sidemen, and Randy blows really hard to the end. At 5.10, some ensemble motifs bring back the theme and the piece ends with high energy. It's the fastest funk you'll find anywhere.

Common Ground is a Stern composition that shows just how good a writer he is, as well as a player. Taken from his album, *Odds or Evens* (1991), this is a slow ballad, with Randy taking the first call and Mike the second. Randy plays a substantial, emotive solo comprised of sweet melodic lines, and takes the piece up several notches, but Michael's playing is a cut above with clean, slow lines, that flow smoothly and melodically. Then at 4.55 he moves into an R&B vibe as Dennis winds up tension. By 5.30, Mike is blowing his heart out, but brings it all back down at 6.20 for the reprise of the main theme. Mike Stern just stands majestically and plays the chords to his own tune. The ending to this very atmospheric, well-arranged piece is clean and perfectly suited to all that went before.

Song For Barry is by now well established as a competitor to the old crowd pleaser, *Some Skunk Funk*. With Mike taking the opportunity to kick it off with a long EWI solo (the one here seems unedifyingly short and may have been edited), it forms a major part of the programme to finish with. There is a great link from the end of Randy's solo into the theme, before Mike Stern solos, first on a single chord vamp, but then comes together with George, James and Dennis for an excellent set of evolving chords. This builds gradually into a superb climactic ending and the final motifs from all the players create a sonic explosion of epic proportions.

The tune played over the final credits is *Inside Out*, Randy's composition, first used on *Heavy Metal Bebop*, and a popular piece from the band's live repertoire.

The video programme was, on the whole, very well photographed, with some good opportunities to watch the players. The exceptions were for Michael's EWI solo, which was poorly shot, and for George, whose share of the footage was disappointing. On the other hand, the music and performance was of the highest order.

The Brecker Brothers playing at the North Sea Jazz Festival, Jul 10 1993. Photo: Louis Gerrits.

The Brecker Brothers: *Out of the Loop* - 1994 (*****)

When the Brothers' new album hit the streets, it was as if they had needed a trial run with the *Return* album to get fully into top gear. *Out of the Loop* was even better. But how could it be?

Most of the musicians from *Return Of The Brecker Brothers* were back. George Whitty had become an essential member of the team and was given an even bigger role in arranging and producing. James Genus and Dean Brown were back too. Robbie Kilgore and Maz Kessler had returned to impart some of their unique brand of street music to two tracks. There were some newcomers too. Steve Jordan returned in place of Dennis Chambers on drums. He was joined by Steve Thornton, who had played percussion for Miles Davis's *You're*

Under Arrest (1985), and had recently worked with Marcus Miller on *The Sun Don't Lie* (1993).

The opening track is *Slang*, another superb jazz-fusion piece. The rock rhythm kicks off. Two themes are superimposed, a simple slow theme based on three notes repeated, then a second that is faster and complex. From 2.02, the first solo on trumpet has Randy in his best straight-ahead jazz style sounding like Miles. This is jazz-fusion at its best, and as an opener for this album it is perfect. Just listen to Michael's solo from 3.45, which is one of his very best funky R&B creations. Beginning with just the rhythm for support, it soon picks up the bass and starts to catch fire at around 4.30. And it just goes on and on, developing and expanding, whilst always in touch with the underlying theme. Although the track does fade, it also does close tightly.

Evocations is a complete contrast. Although in 6/8 metre, the basic drum rhythm is beautifully slotted into the crack between the second and third beat. At 1.05 Michael's theme is exquisite, taking the piece to an entirely new level. It's a short but ecstatic theme that ends with a delightfully firm rapid double beat. There is a wonderfully executed high G that is part of the theme. It is off the top of the normal fingering on a saxophone, which illustrates the perfection of the playing on display. Then at 1.44 comes Randy's solo, again, a great example of beautiful trumpet playing. At 2.34 the piece becomes slightly detached during a short transitional section of super atmospherics, and then it's into a repeat of the theme at 3.10. From four minutes, Michael takes a solo that leads the piece out. This is the same kind of format that Sanborn was using for most of his pieces, whereby a basic ABAB song structure was developed incrementally so that a climax at the end of the piece was achieved through soloing.

With the help of old friends Maz Kessler and Robbie Kilgore, who both play on and produce the track, humour is back on the menu again with track 3, *Scrunch*. Over tinkling piano inserts, Michael and Randy take a really excellent theme that has a plethora of little interwoven phrases, some in unison, some played solo. The concept of this piece is utterly brilliant. It culminates with a fantastic climax at 2.25 (repeated again at 3.48). Then after a short bridge, Michael takes the solo. The rhythm is amusing, with the drums sounding like they're being played on dustbins, and swashed with all sorts of little percussive sounds, both acoustic and electric. Randy's trumpet also comes in with some little motifs that are really illuminating - precisely delivered comic asides like Groucho Marx one-liners.

A composition by Randy and Eliane Elias comes next. Eliane was invited back to play piano and to produce her track, *Secret Heart*, which is utterly different, and takes on a completely new level of sophistication. Michael comes in with a wonderfully smooth soprano solo that leads over an evolving chordal backdrop, and bubbles steadily upwards. Then, at 1.52, Randy comes in with one of his coolest entries on record. It's spine-tingling stuff. The kaleidoscopic accompaniment suffuses a stunningly executed solo, so perfectly played. Then there is another keyboard bridge - there are so many of these that you can become overwhelmed by the quality of the lead playing. From 3.56, Eliane takes over on acoustic piano, briefly sounding like Lyle Mays at 4.20, before entering the final fade-out phase. This piece is exquisite.

Next is *African Skies*, which later appeared on the album *Tales from the Hudson* (1996). This was a tune inspired by the wonderful skies Michael observed in Botswana during his 1991 tour with Paul Simon. Armand Sabal-Lecco had been invited back to play bass, and to add some authentic African sounds. Again, based in 6/8 there are overlying triplets. That's the subtle bit. The obvious bit is the wonderful, evocative, main melody, played in different ways; mostly Michael plays the tune, while Randy plays an unusual harmony. The second part of the theme is used as a backing for Mike's solo, and from 2.47 the main theme repeats, and leads into a second sax solo, complete with some elephantine interjections of the kind Michael does so well. Around 4.10, he is in the highest gear possible, playing runs and arpeggios like few others can imagine. It's stuff like this that provides the evidence for him being a member of a very small elite of the world's best saxophone players. It's very much a piece for Michael, with Randy taking a seat in the back of the Land Cruiser. From 5.50, a super cameo is developed that paints a wonderfully representative picture of an African landscape. An arrangement by Mike and George, this is truly wonderful stuff.

When it Was totally changes the vibe again, thanks to Maz & Kilgore's street production. The mood is casual, with a kind of urban party feel. Dean Brown and Robbie set up a great vamp on guitars. The melody is simple, if odd. The combination of guitar and Randy's muted trumpet adds to the casualness of it all. Around 2.10, the piece changes direction. At 3.12, the entry to Mike's short solo is brilliant, as he squeezes high notes from his tube. Then it's back to the main theme in a different key, and the play-out to their preferred faded end. (Michael admitted that he always had trouble with endings.) [64]

There is yet another change of mood for *Harpoon*, now to one in which a slightly darker, dangerous subject matter is addressed. This music can kill. Electronic effects from George's keys, coupled with Mike's EWI, form a large part of the improvised intro to 0.58. The rhythm, set up by Steve Thornton and Steve Jordan, with James's bass, is complex, as many Brecker pieces are. A theme comprised of a sequence of chord-based notes appears at 0.38 and 0.58, before solo instruments come in over the top at 1.13. The second minute is filled with incomprehensible rocket science. At 2.55 an electric entry from Randy heralds the start of a harmonically loose, precisely played and probing improvisation. Michael solos from 4.15 and it's mostly done with just rhythm for backing. Gradually, the keyboard begins to add content, and Michael becomes increasingly disturbed such that his lines are punctuated with profanity. If you could swear with a saxophone this is what it would sound like. No-one said harpoons had to be beautiful! At 6.30, an ensemble section commences that forms the basis of the final section. The lines, all written, become more and more urgent to bring the piece to a painful ending at 7.40. One word: awesome.

All things are possible with *The Nightwalker*, a descriptive piece that doesn't take much imagination. Michael takes the first solo at 2.40, cautiously at first, staying on the sidewalk, mostly in the monochromatic streetlights. As his perambulation proceeds, the characters he meets become stranger. He meets Randy at 4.34, another cloaked explorer of the night. At 6.02 both men are walking side-by side through the shadows in this rather strange world that most of us may find exciting, but that most of us probably fear. The piece ends with a piano cameo from George that acts like a warming cup of hot chocolate on a friend's front porch, compared to the cold personalities out on the streets.

And then She Wept is a ballad to bring this excellent album to a close. It's another of Randy's compositions filled with melody and fine performance. Both brothers can play the most achingly beautiful music, and this is no exception.

A feature of 1990s jazz that is perfectly demonstrated by this album is the entirely homogeneous mixture of styles. At a superficial level, you can just listen to this wonderful album and enjoy the wide variety of instrumental sounds - Randy has canned his vocals for this one. At a deeper level, however, when you analyse the content, you find that everything is here. Of course, this should not surprise us, for the Brecker Brothers were in at the start of jazz-fusion. Now, some 25 years later, the music has moved to new levels. There is absolutely no doubt that this should be regarded as one the very great albums of 1990s jazz. (I don't do six stars!)

George Whitty told an interesting story about *Harpoon*. "We got Steve Jordan to play drums on that one, and he called the night before, and said I don't want to play on that one - it's just not my bag really. He ended up doing a really cool thing on it, but there's lots of weird accents in it, and so on, and I don't think he felt ready to do it. He ended up doing this really great thing on a coke bottle." [61]

The Don Grolnick Group on tour in Southampton, UK (1995). Left to right: Don Grolnick (piano), Peter Washington (bass), Randy Brecker (trumpet).

Don Grolnick Group: *The London Concert* – rec. 1995; rel 2000 (***)

In January 1995, Don Grolnick took a band on tour for the last time. The trip included a number of gigs around the UK, and was sponsored by the Arts Council. I was lucky enough to be present at the band's gig at the University in Southampton. The concert played a few days later in London was recorded by the BBC and is available on a CD released in 2000. Forget fusion. This is a collection of superbly crafted straightahead jazz. The items were selected from Don's two albums, *Weaver Of Dreams* (1989) and *Nighttown* (1992). *Heart of Darkness* was used as the opener for the second album, and is played here, much as it appeared there. Humour is in the title of *Or Come Fog*, which, as Don explains on the recording, is based upon the structure of the jazz standard, *Come Rain Or Come Shine*. *Five Bars* and *Spot That Man* are mainstays of Don's first album as leader. The fifth track to be included is Don's arrangement of the Cole Porter number, *What Is This Thing Called Love*, or as my old friend used to call it crudely (with a different vocal inflexion), "What's *this* thing called, love?" Sounds like something Randroid might have said.

The Don Grolnick Group on tour in Southampton, UK. Left to right: Peter Erskine (drums, behind), Michael Brecker (tenor saxophone), Marty Ehrlich (flute), Don Alias (percussion, behind), Robin Eubanks (trombone, front).

Brecker Brothers: *Live in Tokyo U-Port Hall*, 1995 [DVD] – rec. 1995; rel. 2010 (***)

In 1995, the Brecker Brothers Band was still touring. As Michael said in an interview included on the DVD, they had never intended to take a ten or eleven year break. They tried out projects on their own, and became too busy. He admitted that they had been talking about it since 1985, and had actually briefly reformed the band at 7th Avenue South. But it wasn't until 1992 that they were able to make it happen. They originally intended for it to be only one album and a short tour, but the reformation of the band had proved to be extremely popular, and the guys found they were having so much fun that they decided to extend the band's lifetime. In this band, the brothers were extremely well supported by George Whitty, who remained on keyboards, whilst Dean Brown was guitarist, James Genus played bass, and Rodney Holmes drums.

On 13 March 1995, the Brecker Brothers band played at the U-Port Hall in Tokyo, and the gig is available on a DVD from the Jazz Door label. The filming is generally good, except that George Whitty's presence is almost ignored. There are some occasional sound issues, but the DVD is a reasonably good record of the band in this format. The five musical tracks are interspersed with short clips of a recorded interview with Randy and Michael just ahead of the gig. The set kicks off with novel versions of *Slang* and *Spherical*, tunes that have great variety and contrasting inputs from the band members. James is playing slap-funk bass throughout most of the material. Randy's tune, *Harpoon*, is darker and brings out his best playing. *Some Skunk Funk* is an encore, played fast in a crowd-pleasing mode that doesn't allow any room for finesse. But the encore is demanded after an explosive 30-minute rendition of *Song For Barry*, the undoubted highlight. Any reader who is still unsure of the scope of the EWI should watch this recording and prepare to be stunned. In the section of interview at track 6, Michael flags up that he is going to play the EWI. MB: "I play it because it's capable of doing so much in an expressive way that it has become almost as important to me as the saxophone." [66]

Randy Brecker: *Into the Sun* – 1995 (***)

It would seem that the return of the Brecker Brothers as a band was either undesirable or impractical because *Out of the Loop* was to be the duo's last album under that name. Perhaps the demands now placed upon them to perform as individuals were too great, or perhaps there were too many solo projects that tempted them away from what was now perceived, in the upper echelons of jazz, as an unfashionable style of playing.

Randy's next album was a curate's eggish collection of tracks, that were declared on the sleeve notes to be an "impression" of Brazilian music, inspired by his relationship with Eliane Elias. Much was made of the gains made by hiring appropriate musicians, but apart from Randy's friend and pianist Gil Goldstein, the bass player was Bakithi Kumalo, a South African; Jonathan Joseph was a drummer from the Hispanic community of Miami, and guitarist Adam Rogers was, well, American. Genuine Brazilian input was added in the usual way through percussion – in this case with Edson da Silva, aka Café. Indeed, it is only an impression of Brazil that is to be gained from this music. Track five is *After Love*, which is certainly melodically and harmonically similar to *Coisa Mais Linda*.

Randy chose Gil Goldstein to be his co-producer on this album. Goldstein (b1950, Baltimore MD) was a graduate of Berklee Music College, who, besides being a leading composer, arranger and producer, had distinguished himself as a pianist. From the age of five, he had also been a dedicated player of the accordion. In the 1980s, he appeared on several Billy Cobham albums, but perhaps made a more significant impression playing with Mark Egan, Dan Gottlieb and Bill Evans in their band Elements, a relationship that would continue into the years ahead. Apart from Gil, Randy chose musicians whom he did not know and who did not know each other. The purpose was, "to give this project the spontaneity one would find in a jazz context..." [67]

The young, jazz guitarist was Adam Rogers from New York, a versatile musician who had co-led the band Lost Tribe in the early 1990s. Chosen now to work with Randy and Gil, his future career would include joining Bill Evans's band, appearing on *Live in Europe* (1995), *Starfish and the Moon* (1997) and *Touch* (1999). Later, he would join Chris Potter's Underground to appear on *Travelling Mercies* (2002), *Underground* (2006), *Follow the Red Line* (2007) and others. He would also be called upon for further work with Randy, and win accolades with Michael's Quindectet album *Wide Angles* (2003).

Drummer, Jonathan Joseph (b1966, Miami FL) started drumming in church when aged six. His first big break came when he was chosen to play for Dizzy Gillespie's 70th birthday celebration. In 1988, he toured with Othello Molineaux to promote the Molineaux's CD, *It's About Time* (1988). After three years playing with vocalist Betty Wright, he joined Joe Zawinul's Syndicate in 1994, and then Pat Metheny's touring band briefly in late 1995. Around these years, he was playing with David Sanborn, Bill Evans, Mike Stern and Al Jarreau.

An unusual choice for bass was Bakithi Kumalo, a young South African born in Soweto. He had been selected to play on Paul Simon's album, *Graceland* (1986) and had worked regularly with Simon thereafter.

The only authentic Brazilian voice on the album was Café. Born in a small village in the state of Sao Paolo, Café was already an established musician in Brazil when he moved to the USA in 1985. Soon, he was appearing on Eliane's albums, *So Far, So Close* (1988), and *Cross Currents* (1989). He also worked with Mark Egan and Elements, appearing on several albums in the late 1980s.

The idea that this is an album of Brazilian music is inaccurate. Randy makes it clear in the notes that, "It was the intent of this project to present my impression of the music of Brazil mixed with my experiences in life and music as a North American who has travelled the world over and been influenced by many sights and sounds." [67]

The album commences with a nicely atmospheric piece called *Village Dawn* that has a main theme dominated by the gentle wordless singing of Maucha Adnet, another beautiful Brazilian singer from Rio de Janeiro translated into the USA. The American part of her career was successful, mostly through many years of close association with the great Brazilian musician, Antonio Carlos Jobim – he of *Girl From Ipanema* fame. Here, her confident vocalising is the perfect match to Randy's catchy melody. The result is a complete package of Brazilian colours and textures, whilst retaining its jazz credentials through the unusual chord sequences and Randy's rich solos.

Just Between Us is a slower, romantic piece written in Randy's preferred melodic style, where he takes loosely related sets of warm chord sequences and carefully stitches them together to create smooth, flowing line over which his meandering melodies waft like the scents of summer flowers in the breeze. If you like romantic music, this is fine stuff.

The Sleaze Factor is more of a flashback to the days of the funk band, and David Sanborn's presence as a guest on this track is a joy. The close, dissonant intervals between the trumpet and sax lines for the tune is just like Randy used on songs like *Some Skunk Funk*, yet this song didn't appear on a BB album. Instead, it was the favoured opening track for Randy's album, *Live At Sweet Basil* (1988) where it was given a different treatment. Here its role as a dark samba works perfectly, especially with the rough-edged lines of the alto saxophone.

The title track, *Into the Sun*, has lots of different fusion elements present in its construction. Latin inflexions are supplemented with rock, blues, funk and straight jazz. As the rhythmic foundation changes, so also do the chordal foci, and, as we approach the final three minutes, some listeners may find that the music becomes a feat of harmonic gymnastics as they try to keep up with the rapid changes that bend and twist their way through most of the available chords.

After Love is the kind of music that many people would associate with sitting at the poolside of a Rio hotel in the early evening following some afternoon delight. The main theme is romantic and perfumed, yet still retains an air of mystery that we always attach to our ladies. The middle sections are played with a slight increase in pelvic interest, especially when Rogers's electric guitar takes the lead, but overall, the music stays well focussed on the lady. A clinch and a gentle dance to the music is an obvious option here.

For conventional minds, the imagery conjured up by Randy's tune, *Gray Area*, is well matched to the title. The main idea is of a simple repeated motif, moulded like clay to higher and lower pitch and set to harmonic swatches that may or may not conform to standard methods. Then apply some heavy rock guitar textures and the result is a seedy part of town where the main activities are best avoided.

Tijuca is a district of Rio, named after a swampy region to the north of the city. So, for those of us unlucky enough not to have visited Rio, we rely upon the music of this impressionistic piece to offer us some idea about the place that clearly made an impression on Randy. Most listeners should interpret this as a fascinating place with many aspects to its character.

Buds is a reappearance of a piece that Randy played years before at Montreux, and it was published on the Arista All-Stars album, *Blue Montreux* (1978). This version retains its straight-ahead Brazilian sound, is played at a lively pace, and features a lovely, smooth solo from Randy and a more than competent acoustic guitar solo by Adam Rogers.

The penultimate tune, *Four Worlds*, is a feature for Gil's accordion. Jonathan Joseph's drumming is especially noticeable here, where it is very inventive and rhythmic.

The tenth and final track is a tribute to Randy and Michael's recently departed father, Bobby Brecker. In 1945, with Randy only three weeks old, his father recorded himself singing his own composition *The Hottest Man in Town*, written for his newborn son. Here, Randy reproduces his father's recording and he adds his own supplementary material to convert it into a significant track. The music is out of line with the rest of the album content, but we understand the need for it to be there.

For his work on this album, Randy won a Grammy for "Best Contemporary Jazz Performance" in 1997. It is a very fine achievement to gain that kind of recognition for working in a genre that is not the one you grew up with.

Michael Brecker: *Tales From the Hudson* – 1996 (****)

One of the best things to do when you visit New York is to take a boat trip around the island of Manhattan. All of us have our own take on this fantastic city, most mental images formed from what we have seen on TV. New York musos have their own tales to tell, the result of countless nights of playing music in a way that was largely formed in this city. Sure, New Orleans was the birthplace, but the Big Apple was where jazz went from nappies to long trousers, or perhaps I should say, diapers to pants. For his next album, *Tales From The Hudson* (1996) Michael was going home after a period away on the jazz-fusion cruise liner, avoiding the icebergs as he did so. In the wake of electrical storms and deep-water hazards, it was a comforting trip back to the safety of his hero, John Coltrane's record label, Impulse! No self-respecting jazzer could record a naked jazz-fusion album on that label, so this is a release of solid, mainstream quintet music, populated with his New Yorker friends Pat Metheny, Jack DeJohnette, Dave Holland and Joey Calderazzo. Additional guest, McCoy Tyner subs for Calderazzo on tracks 3 and 5, which also have Don Alias on percussion.) Having now become close friends with George Whitty, and confident in his production skills, Michael chose him to co-produce this album too.

The first track is *Slings and Arrows*, a mainstream piece with a fast swing tempo and conventional harmony. It's modal, in the Miles Davis late-fifties style that involves improvising freely over slowly evolving chords, but the chosen chords are in familiar modes. The theme is complex, the melody tight and it's a good start to the album.

Midnight Voyage is a Calderazzo number that is slower, mainstream, and has a slick, bluesy eight-bar theme. The AABA format is sometimes as pliant as a face in a fairground mirror. If ever an example was required of the use of syncopation in jazz, this could be it, for the delightful way in which the music departs from the standard 4/4 metre is a true delight on this track. It's beautiful playing in the cracks, and also great cool jazz for late night enjoyment. Michael's improvisation from 1.20 is a stunner, and Pat's contribution is perfectly modelled on the written harmonies.

Jazz-fusion is not entirely absent on the CD, for the third piece is Pat Metheny's *Song for Bilbao*, played similarly to the way he does on his own album, *Travels* (1983). Metheny and Brecker play the melody in unison, a unique sound, as Pat employs his well-known guitar synth sound, a departure from his normal 'Wes Montgomery' sound on this album. The construction of the melody is complex, and provides a challenging environment for the soloists - a challenge that both men rise to with consummate skill and artistry. McCoy Tyner's acoustic piano improvisation is a further bonus.

Track four is a Brecker-composed jazz ballad called *Beau Rivage*. There are unusual harmonies and constructions here that have become almost a trademark sound for Michael, and you will hear pieces on other albums that have similar characteristics. Pat's sensitive solo is beautifully recorded and exquisitely presented, in symbiosis with Dave, Jack and Joey. After this, Michael returns to develop his ideas more deeply, and then ends his work with an orchestrated finale.

African Skies is a brilliant Brecker composition, used to great effect on the Brecker Brothers' five-star album *Out of the Loop* (1994). It has a memorable, quirky melody, and Tyner's playing is quite exceptional, ably assisted by the rhythm section. This piece is a highlight, with Michael demonstrating beyond doubt that he is a master saxophonist in all respects. By the end of the fifth minute, his playing has become utterly devastating, a bubbling froth of notes, squawks, and contorted phrases that pour from his imagination.

The second half of the album begins with a longer piece called *Naked Soul*, which has a short intro improvised by Michael and Dave Holland. The early part of the theme deceives with a waltz feel, although the normal eights are comprised of a combination of 3+5 beats. After the twists and turns of the first minute, the piece settles down to a regular four-beat rhythm and the piece is cool, melodic and doleful. Brecker's style is intense and philosophical. It takes us to both highs and lows, but it's not joyous or beautiful in the sense that many would recognise. If you can make a connection with this through repeated listening, you're likely to fall in love with it forever. A bass solo by Dave Holland, assisted by Jack's sensitive drumming, helps a lot.

The eighth track is *Willie T*, a cool, swing piece based on a typical Grolnick tune that is entirely sympathetic to Mike Brecker's own style. In the simple modal style of Miles Davis's *So What*, it has a standard sequence of solos.

The final track is *Cabin Fever*, a hard-hitting blast of modal jazz with little in the way of theme – a freewheeling freak-out to blow away the cobwebs, just in case any jazz critics should think he was going soft!

Michael was not a prolific composer, preferring quality to quantity, and was therefore never afraid to include pieces by other musicians, especially Don Grolnick, whose music was challenging and therefore ideally suited to Michael's creative instincts. Unfortunately, this was to be the year of Don's untimely death from cancer on 1 June aged 46. The loss was a severe blow to Randy and Michael. Since their earliest years in New York, Don had been as close to them as it's possible for a jazz musician to be, and he had played a big part in a lot of their music.

So talented was he that he was in great demand, both as a performer and producer, but working on other people's projects rarely satisfies someone with such creative ability. In 1988 there came a change of emphasis. His wife wrote later, "As he began to approach 40, Don talked about realizing that 'you don't have forever to do what you want.'" It was a painfully prescient comment. His wife continues, "Don decided to take a complete break from jingles, pop tours, record dates, and producing, and make some space for the music that was building in his mind. For several months, he shut himself in a room with his Steinway, listening, playing and writing." [68] On February 14, 1989, Don went into the now-defunct Skyline Studio in Manhattan with an all-star ensemble, and recorded *Weaver of Dreams* (1990)...He said later, "It was the most fun I've ever had in my life." For the remaining years of his life, Don was able to work with his own music, played by his own band, when he was able to enhance substantially his reputation for being a brilliant jazz composer and pianist. He made four excellent albums containing mostly his own compositions, *Hearts and Numbers* (1985), *Weaver of Dreams* (1990), *Night Town* (1992) and *Medianoche* (1995). A posthumous live recording was also released, *The London Concert* (2000). Michael and Randy were two of his closest friends, and either or both of them played on all of Don's recordings.

Michael Brecker: *Two Blocks From the Edge* – 1998 (****)

In 1998, Michael released a straightahead quartet album in a format and style similar to his previous Impulse! release. Alongside him were Joey Calderazzo (piano), James Genus (bass) and Jeff 'Tain' Watts (drums). Don Alias, as usual, was on hand to add additional percussion.

It was the first outing on a Brecker album for Watts (b1960, Pittsburgh PA). Jeff was classically trained in percussion at the Duquesne University in his hometown of Pittsburgh, but then gained a place at Berklee to study jazz, where his friendship with Branford Marsalis developed into a close working relationship with both Marsalis brothers over the years from 1983 to 2009. In the early 1990s he also worked for three years in Los Angeles on the *Tonight Show* with Jay Leno, before returning to New York in 1995 to join Kenny Garrett's band. His experience playing drums for many of the top jazzers made him a perfect choice to join with Michael for this record.

The album's title, *Two Blocks From the Edge*, comes from Michael's best friend Don Grolnick, who once humorously told Mike that he liked "living close to the edge, as long as it was two blocks away… This album is dedicated to Don, whose presence I miss every day," wrote Michael. [69] Elsewhere, in an interview, he said, "He [Don] was my closest friend, and produced all of my records. We played in 12 or 13 different bands together. He had a way of smoothing my rough edges, and I could kind of ruffle-up his smooth edges. So we were a good team." [37]

It seems logical to deduce that, following his previous outing, Michael is continuing here to deepen his explorations into his more academic approach to jazz. The opening track is *Madame Toulouse*, a serious invention that inevitably involves some melodic gymnastics. The music begins with a strong focus on F major, played on bass to the backing of a lively percussive rhythm. As he improvises over this introduction, Michael's playing hops in and out of the chosen key, deviating quite wildly at times from the notes demanded by traditional rules of harmony, but always returning to his R&B sound. At 0.48, he begins a 'verse' that is written as if it changes key every two beats or so, but still returns to F major. For the second time through, his fantastic written melody is doubled by Joey, but diverges from James until they all come together for the final lines from 1.30. At 1.42, the sleek lines of the sixteen-bar chassis come into action, and Michael starts to push out into open country, employing steadily evolving machinations that soon involve the steel body panels of sound that are so often compared to Coltrane. With this French Madame in the passenger's seat, it is Michael's turn to drive.

It's a very serious business, living close to the edge of anything. I have a friend living in the Great Lakes area of the USA, and just two blocks from her house, barriers drop across the road several times each day to allow giant bulk carrier ships to pass through a tight canal. A photograph from her front porch would normally show a suburban road, just like many others, but when a ship passes through, the shadow of the leviathan looms large all around. It is exactly this kind of feeling created in Michael's title composition. The sense of the unexpected when you arrive at the edge is inescapable. He and his team first perform a difficult modal construction, and then embark upon an improvisation that is harmonically free, but holds on to the steady speed of the ship. After 8.32, the shadow is gone and the sunshine returns.

Bye George is a much lighter, medium-paced composition by Joey Calderazzo, in a format of eight bar cycles in the pattern AABBCA. Mike solos over this form from 1.16 to 3.45, after which Joey gets to take on his own writing. It's a good solid piece in the spine of the album, but not in the same league as Michael's compositions. A return to the original occurs at 5.24, and this is played through to the orchestrated ending.

El Niño is another unexceptional piece by Calderazzo that is given a Latin rhythm, boosted with Don's percussion, to accompany the theme. Around 3.10, Mike puts some fire into the mix and explodes into a life beyond mere samba prancing. His tube spouts sparks, and this encourages his band to follow him into a short, lively section that lasts to the end of Mike's solo at 4.05. Then it's Joey's turn, and he chooses to maintain the Latin feel throughout, whilst doubling up the tempo for a period. From 5.50, it's back to the theme, as expected. Joey adds some extra twists in the final bars to create a different, but faded, ending.

The album continues at track five with a third contribution from Joey, this time a slow ballad called *Cat's Cradle* that demands (and gets) a sensitive interpretation from its performers. James Genus plays a welcome acoustic bass solo that offers his translation of Joey's musical intent. The melody is in the style we have come to expect from jazzers from this period – a sequence of poetic phrases set to a backdrop of meandering (rather than evolving) chords. The answer to whether you find this beautiful or not is to be found inside your own head. It does not fire my imagination.

The Impaler is a well-written, hard bop composition from Jeff that is modal, and demanding in all respects. It is more of a full band piece this time, although Joey's chromatic improvisations form a memorable part of this tune, whilst composer Jeff's input is in line with his role at the centre of this piece. After a substantial drum solo, the piece concludes satisfactorily with some exciting unison lines by Joey and Michael.

Michael's ballad, *How Long 'Til The Sun*, is possibly more natural and evolutionary, compared to Joey's own slow tune with its more random choice of chords, and I certainly find this the more satisfying of the two. Michael's wonderful development of his own ideas is the perfect response to anyone unwise enough to pronounce that they prefer songs with words. It's all about emotion, rather than technique.

But hey! If you got it, flaunt it. Michael's piece, *Delta City Blues*, begins with a solo improvisation that seems as if he is planning to deliver a master-class in saxophone articulation. Of particular focus is his highly developed skill of jumping from one note to the next using intervals greater than an octave. This requires not just highly developed fingering practice, but also the more difficult skill of rapid alterations to his facial muscles and breathing, so as to execute the necessary changes to the column of air inside his instrument. Those of us who play the saxophone will marvel at this amazing display of technique, and it is hard for us to imagine sequences of notes that are more difficult to play than these. Some of the notes go off the top of the usual playing scale, others are 'burp' and 'parp' noises that require further skills, but they are tossed into the mix anyway, like seasoning casually sprinkled on salad. Then there are the wildly bent notes that swerve through a whole tone, when most of us need to press a different set of keys. But he doesn't. How does he do that?

Those listeners who don't play the instrument must surely understand that they are hearing something very special here. The overall effect is that of a cartoon depiction of a certain style of American life that will bring a smile to most faces. From 1.10, the band joins this colourful, clownish character who continues to stagger along the sidewalk, bumping into fire hydrants and newsstands along the way. It is only at 2.38 that, at last, Michael takes off his silly clothes and reveals the sophisticated musician beneath. From here on, the pace is fast and the articulation slick. Convention demands a reprise of the first idea, and he complies with a pragmatic, short statement. After all, there is simply nothing left to say about Mr. Delta. Amazing!

The Tin Pan Alley standard, *Skylark* (Mercer-Carmichael), begins with a stunning two-and-a-half minute saxophone cadenza. Even when he is joined for the second half of the track by Joey's solo acoustic piano, Michael continues to present a mesmerising interpretation of the original in the same *a tempo* style. It is the ideal closure to a very good album in which Michael's star, for once, totally eclipses his lunar colleagues.

The gulf in quality between Michael's compositions and the others is large. A slow starter in the field of composition, Michael had been studying hard, and is demonstrating some startling ideas on this album. It is probably unreasonable to expect him to contribute every track, so the album's overall effect is less impressive than it might have been. Michael always works his magic on the setting he is playing in, and brings wonderful invention to the briefest of contexts. He was clearly pleased to include Calderazzo's compositions, and in any other context, they would hold up well, but set alongside such immense writing, they seem diminished. The difference here, compared to other albums that I have awarded more stars, is that you *can* stop listening to this album before it is over. Purely on the basis of Michael's performance, however, it must rank amongst his best.

Michael Brecker: *Time is Of the Essence* **– 1999 (****)**

Michael migrated to the Verve label for his next album, and a project that was very different from his previous five albums. Its name might suggest a collection of tracks based upon weird time signatures and strange, unnatural rhythms, but that is only partly the case. Certainly, as a very serious student and experimenter in jazz technique, Michael now chose to focus on rhythm, and planned a set of nine tracks, grouped in threes with three different drummers. Jeff 'Tain' Watts had performed beautifully on his previous record, and Mike invited him to join this project too.

Mike also chose the amazing Elvin Jones as the top representative of the 'old school' of drummers. Born into a musical family, Elvin Jones (1927-2004, Pontiac MI) was brother of trumpeter, Thad Jones, and pianist, Hank Jones. Elvin had shown interest in percussion since watching circus bands as a child. He moved to New York in 1955 where he worked with jazz greats, Charles Mingus, Bud Powell and Miles Davis. Michael's admiration of Elvin stemmed perhaps from the fact that Elvin had played in John Coltrane's most famous quartets from 1960-66, and had performed on the masterpiece, *A Love Supreme* (1965).

Michael's third choice was Bill Stewart, a representative of the new generation of drummers and noted for his forward-looking approach to drumming. Stewart (b1966, Des Moines IA) was born the year after the release of *A Love Supreme*. Once he had decided to take up drums, he played in a wide range of musical contexts in Iowa, mostly in pop and R&B music. Then, after graduating, he enrolled at the University of Northern Iowa in Cedar Falls where he played in jazz and marching bands, as well as in the University orchestra. He then transferred to College in Wayne, New Jersey, where he studied with Dave Samuels, Rufus Reid and Harold Mabern. It was here that he met saxophonist Joe Lovano with whom he would later work extensively alongside John Scofield. In 1988, Bill moved to Brooklyn, New York, and was soon doing gigs with the Larry Goldings trio.

Coincidentally or not, Michael chose Goldings to play on all of the tracks of this album. Goldings (b1968, Boston MA) studied classical piano until the age of twelve. As a teenager, Larry studied privately with Keith Jarrett, the perfect master for a student making the transition from classical music to jazz. Then in 1986 he moved to NYC to study jazz at the New School. In 1988, Goldings began to play organ more seriously, during a regular gig with Peter Bernstein (guitar) and Bill Stewart at *Augie's* jazz bar on the Upper West Side of Manhattan, where there was no piano. His first album was *Intimacy Of The Blues* (1991). This trio continues to play together to this day, but when it does not, the guitar trio remains Larry's format of choice.

Last, but by no means least, was Michael's old friend, Pat Metheny who, like Goldings, would play on all tracks. There was no bass player; it's always a special circumstance when an organ is present, for it is taken for granted that the organist will take on the demands of providing bass notes. George Whitty was now Michael's preferred producer, and James Farber his talented recording engineer.

There are many musically interesting facets to the first track, *Arc Of The Pendulum*, that are worth describing, if only to gather data for analysis of the level of Michael's musical achievement. Michael chose a 3/4 metre for his composition, but the melody of his tune is played over two bars (six beats) with five notes, and four spaces, each of three quavers. It's not a difficult overlay of two different times for most musicians to engage with, but it is tricky when it pops in an out of view as it does here, surrounded by so many other features. In an overall F major setting, after a sixteen bar intro from Pat, Larry and Elvin, Michael and Larry play the first melody (A) twice over sixteen bars. It is played in two phrases of five notes, the first, a group of descending notes, A, G, F, C, G, A, followed by the ascending group G, G#, G#, A, A#. Even during the opening sequence, Michael's performance of the melody is aggressive, and he does not play the notes straight, choosing instead to present them in a kind of sawing action. The next sixteen bars constitute the second part of the theme (B). There are two fluid, racy lines of eight bars each, not without tricky twists and turns. It's not a blues, but it's not far away from a blues feel. The chord changes follow pathways (or progressions) that are common in jazz, and lead from one place to another in a fairly logical fashion. As they do so, they may descend by tones and semitones, which drive Michael to play chromatically for part of the time and to use many of his much-practised arpeggios for other parts. Next comes a repetition of melody A, harsher yet again, but the same in essence. The repetition of melody B is different, and much more difficult to play, with some very contorted bop-inspired long phrases that would challenge most players.

So, after this Intro-ABAB construct, Mike flows smoothly into his improvised solo from 1.40. Once again, it is remarkable for its fluid construction and the extremely long breaths he requires to play down through the scales. He applies his normal style of departure from his own harmonic structures to play in the long grass. By the three-minute mark, I hope you are aware that this is very special saxophone playing that just gets better and better, through to 4.15. It is a very fine solo indeed.

Meanwhile, Pat Metheny has a solid presence throughout, adding to Larry's backwash with a fine rhythmic chord pattern, until, at 4.15, he takes on an improvisation that is beautifully crafted. Elvin Jones's drumming is far from 'old school', especially as he has always been in the vanguard of inventive drumming. Here, he is continuously polyrhythmic, adding deep layers of complexity to the piece with his arms and legs often working independently. At 5.34, Larry, who has been dabbing chords throughout, as well as playing a quite satisfying bass rhythm, now takes over to play a solo that is solid and imaginative. The final pass through the main theme is made from 6.50, with the clear performance of that very tricky second theme, fast, discontinuous, hard bop, played in unison with Larry. From 7.42, the first theme is cut into smaller pieces and squirted into a finale that combines a drum solo with further wild speculation from Michael, followed by a faded ending.

Unlike some of the material on the previous album, in which Michael was extending himself amidst the somewhat unchallenging environment of his sidemen, now these musicians would have got to the end of the piece feeling that they had really achieved something extraordinary.

Sound Off is from Goldings' pen, and he seems to have taken some inspiration from *Arc of the Pendulum*. Jeff is now on drums, and his work is cut out with this fast 4/4 hard swinging composition. The main theme bears the same kind of rhythmic puzzle as in the first track – a juxtaposition of two competing metres, but this time it is a simple staccato phrase played in the cracks in a slick, syncopated fashion. The improvisations are sequenced with Mike going first. It's another inspired invention that thrills and amazes with its harmonic linkages. Larry is extremely proficient over his own changes, and comes across as a true organ specialist, despite being the youngest on the team. There is no space for a cigarette paper in the cracks between his fluid notes, and there is never an occasion where a designated bass player is frustratingly absent. A final flourish occurs at 5.12 when Pat Metheny plays his own solo phrase over the repeated theme, after which the piece comes to an ending that is both agreed and agreeable.

It's with a slight Latin rhythm that *Half Past Late* kicks off, its gentle lilting tune delivered once again between Pat, Mike and Larry, but with some parallel harmonies that give it a foreign accent like just another taxi driver. The intricacies of rhythms are explored here, more through the unusual structuring of the phrases than by explicitly odd rhythms. Once the improvisations begin in the third minute, Michael once more embarks upon a solo during which he adopts every conceivable trick of breath to generate notes that surprise and excite. Yes, the Brecker sheets of sound are here, but made from rough cottons and wools of distant and rare production. His music is about the weft, warp, weave and thread, rather than about the printed pattern. Pat Metheny, by contrast, has less to experiment with in that area, but makes the very best of his clean improvisation by skilful stitching with melody; it makes a suit that's as well cut as any Savile Row tailor could supply. Bill Stewart is a different kind of Elvin Jones. He takes his role seriously, adding as much polyrhythm as the piece deserves, but still holding the piece together expertly.

Jones is back in the seat for *Timeline*, a bluesy round of two, back-to-back, eight-bar designs. The first eight bars are delivered fairly straight, the second eight are played with an entirely different rhythmic pattern that fits into the same timeline. Pat takes the lead in his own composition, during which time Elvin's presence is clearly felt, his constantly searching polyrhythms pushing Pat forward. Then, by 2.30, Elvin is driving the piece high into clear air, at which point Mike is ready to assume the lead, blowing straight, hard jazz-blues as Elvin becomes ever more insistent and creative. For such a straightforward music setting, this recording is remarkable for the way the instrumentalists build so much into it. Elvin Jones's drumming is the highlight, which starts out so innocuously, and then grows into a demanding assault that, by five minutes, is leading all the others into the outback. There, unable to discover the path home, they disappear into the hot mist of their own making. Excellent!

The Morning of This Night is another outing for Jeff Watts and the boys. The early part of the music is challenging because of its lack of tempo, and the music is more about the feelings created by Michael's score. By the time Metheny is settled into his own delightful, melodic improvisation, Jeff's brushes have faded to a whisper. Michael's ballads don't always approach the kind of popular appeal of Pat's, although they are cleverly constructed and perfectly executed. This is true of *The Morning of This Night*, an idea that seems to be looking into the immediate future. The unpredictability of that is matched by the complex chord sequence that could go anywhere at anytime. It's one of Michael's few weaknesses.

Renaissance Man was written by producer, George Whitty, and dedicated to saxophonist Eddie Harris who had died in 1996. Michael kicks off with an improvised introduction to which the band joins, fully synched, to play a bluesy soulful melody that is sharp and shiny. A bridging section full of legato, tight, evolving chords makes an excellent return to the theme such that, by the time the sax-led band is in top gear, the funky music could easily have been found on an album by the Breckers or Dave Sanborn. Pat Metheny joins into the comfortable groove, and then it's Larry's turn to enjoy the rhythm, set up perfectly by Bill Stewart. Apart from some sax barks during the extended ending, there are not many tricks of the trade on view here, just good solid funky jazz and soulful organ.

Track seven is the next appearance of Jeff Watts, and of Michael's new fictional character, *Dr. Slate*. There's another superposition of detached theme and regular rhythm used in the tune's main theme, but this is soon dispatched in favour of the blues shuffle rhythm. At times, Michael plays like a man who walks along a narrow beam and then almost loses his balance. His notes swerve and sway in the wind of the rhythm section, but of course, the master acrobat is just fooling about, and he always retains his balance. By now, it is obvious that Mike couldn't fall anywhere: he'd simply float to a new place.

As I Am is a mojo major - a very slow tune written by Pat Metheny. It is played with extreme sensitivity and interpretation, in an environment where there is no requirement for displays of technical wizardry – just the utmost musicianship and gut feeling. Whether he is playing at the highest extremity allowed by his tenor sax, or at the quite difficult bottom end, where it is easy to squeeze the reed into delivering a bum note, Michael's playing is of the kind we have come to expect from this master. Larry and Bill are partners in the delivery of this fine music, but the plaudits are due to Mike and Pat on this one.

Outrance is Elvin's sunset, and it was probably a good decision to allocate this piece as the final track. Elvin enjoys an introductory flourish for 25 seconds, at which point we find that the advertisement to the garden tour is a simple bunch of flowers. A short bridge brings the heads around to the AABA format. The intrance to the jazz garden is thrown open at 1.40, and reveals a straightahead fast 4/4 swing-time design that's modal over some simple chords. It gives Mike the chance to forage around unrestrained. At 4.30, towards what surely is the end of his solo, he parts the darker foliage and finds some new strange growths; at 5.15, he launches into a lengthy session of pruning with just Elvin for company. By the time we arrive at 7.30, we've been witness to a duel with chainsaws at dawn. Then Mike sits down and leaves Elvin to find the outrance.

It is my feeling that, great drummers as they are, both Jeff and Bill are put in the shadow of Elvin Jones on this record. Perhaps they are insufficiently challenged; perhaps they simply don't see the opportunities that Elvin finds. Whatever is the truth, it leads to the feeling that this album might have been an incredible five star triumph had Elvin played on all tracks. Nevertheless, it is still very good indeed.

Bob Berg, Randy Brecker, Dennis Chambers, Joey DeFrancesco: *The JazzTimes Superband* **– 2000 (****)**

Around 2000, Glenn Sabin, publisher of the music magazine, *JazzTimes*, decided to mark the 30th Anniversary of his journal by affording himself of the luxury of a jazz group of his choosing. It was called The *JazzTimes* Superband, and consisted of Bob Berg, Randy Brecker, Joey DeFrancesco and Dennis Chambers. Three of the four, at least, were already well acquainted. By 2000, Berg and Chambers had a significant back catalogue of albums together and with Mike Stern. Both men had also appeared on Gary Willis's *Bent* (1998). So these two were also very familiar with Randy's playing during the 1990s.

If there was any unfamiliarity in the band, it was with the Hammond organist.

Joey DeFrancesco (b1971, Springfield PA) has the accolade of being invited to join Miles Davis's band from the time he graduated from High School in 1989 when he was just 18. This gifted player of the Hammond B-3 had met Miles on a local TV show and had impressed the maestro immensely. He toured with the band, and appeared on the Miles albums *Amandla* (1989) and *Live Around the World* (1996). Clearly a young virtuoso, he impressed Columbia Records too, because he was given a recording contract, and then began a series of releases as a leader for that label with *All Of Me* (1989). By the mid-1990s, Joey had established himself as a regular member of John McLaughlin's band, The Free Spirits, and appeared on McLaughlin's releases, *Tokyo Live* (1994), *After the Rain* (1995) and *The Promise* (1996).

It's time to feel rather sorry for guitarist, Paul Bollenback, who didn't make the line-up of the *JazzTimes* Superband, yet contributed a lot to this album. Bollenback (b1959, Chicago IL) spent part of his childhood in India, where he absorbed many of the sounds and influences of that style of music. On returning to the USA, he took up electric guitar, at which point the sound of Miles's mid-70s electric band converted him to fusion. He went on to study and graduate in music from the University of Miami. Through the 1980s, he continued to study and to play in bands in the Baltimore area, and later in the decade recorded for saxophonist Gary Thomas's album, *Seventh Quadrant* (1987). By 1990, he had formed a strong working relationship with Joey DeFrancesco, which continues to this day. So it is not surprising that he appears on this CD, albeit as a guest, rather than as a member of the band.

The opening track is Randy's composition, *Dirty Dogs*, a straightforward 12-bar blues for which there is an arrangement in the book by Abersold. [70] Most 12-bar blues tunes are readily likeable, and this is no exception, with a catchy tune. All the lead instrumentalists take turns to solo, including Bollenback. One of the peculiarities of recordings that feature the Hammond organ is that there is rarely a bass player, the low notes being provided by the organist's feet. Along with the fact that the sound of the B-3 is so immediately recognizable, listeners either like it or they don't, so if you don't, and you are likely to miss the presence of a real electric bass, then this album is probably not for you.

Berg leads off at the start of his own tune, *Silverado* with a pace that is urgent, but not leg-breaking, as defined by Joey's low-level activities. It's headed by a beguiling melody, with another straightforward sequence of chords to improvise over, based on a 16-bar blues. All the elements are present for an entertaining piece, especially a lively drum solo at the end.

Randy comes back with another of his tunes, *Jones Street*, a swinging straightahead construction. Randy, Joey, Bob and Paul take turns to improvise. This track is followed by the classic Sonny Rollins tune, *Oleo*, played at an astonishing 350 beats per minute. Since the soloists are playing eighth notes (quavers), this equates to a consistent pace of nearly twelve notes per second. What is even more remarkable is that they play the angular bebop melody at the same pace! It's both breathless and brilliant.

Friday Night At The Cadillac Club is a super-slick, singable tune written by Bob Berg that swings along with a rhythm that parallels pumping pistons. The next piece is also by Berg, *SoHo Sole*, a tune that rummages around in the minor keys to convey an atmosphere of anticipation, shady dealings and a hint of danger. Track seven is an indication of Randy's current interest in a certain female saxophone player. *The Ada Strut* is another of his compositions, light and colourful, bluesy, yet full of movement. No doubt, if we were familiar with the lady, we would recognise more. *Blue Goo* is a piece by Joey that sits solidly in the jazz 12-bar blues tradition, instantly recognisable and raising levels of excitement if you're into this kind of fun music. Paul Bollenback is allowed his own addition to the set with *Seven A.M. Special*, in which he establishes his personal guitar sound. It has elements of Mike Stern and John Scofield, although he doesn't solo himself. The final track is a version of the jazz standard, written by Eddie Harris, entitled *Freedom Jazz Dance*. This rendition is significantly freed up, in homage to the well-known version on Miles Davis's album, *Miles Smiles* (1966).

In summary, this is a very good album in which all band members contribute fairly equally to a lively, well recorded, atmospheric collection of mainstream jazz. Apart from the obvious exhibitions of brilliant playing, guitarist Paul Bollenback's contribution stands out because his particular, modern, electric sound adds greatly to the placement of this record at the end of the twentieth century, instead of several decades earlier.

Randy Brecker: *Hangin' In The City* – 2001 (****)

The release of the album, *Hangin' In The City* (2001), marks another evolutionary step in Randy's career. The old hallmarks are still present, as are many of his old musical friends, but from the first bars of the music it is clear that the influence of rap has entered Randy's thinking. I have described the influence of Maz & Kilgore on the BB records of the early 1990s, but Randy's good friend, Bill Evans, also made early strides in the assimilation of street music styles like rap and hip hop into the jazz on his albums *Push* (1994), *Escape* (1996) and *Starfish And The Moon* (1997). Of course, it was Herbie Hancock who trail-blazed this type of fusion in his work with Bill Laswell on *Rockit* (1983). The very mention of rap and hip hop is anathema to many readers, but the kind of jazz-street we get here is already mature and sophisticated. From all the evidence in the *Overture* that opens the album, it is also a great deal of fun.

Randy's singing style had always been his own, etched with some of the natural humour he possesses. Now, it seemed, it was time to formalise his voice into a kind of comical street character who could rap his way through what the album notes (and the lyrics of track 1) describe as "songs of rhyme, reason, romance and raunch." It was time for Randroid to take a bow.

Though he couldn't remember exactly when it came about, Randy explained to me how Randroid was created. "A very good friend of mine, Gary Bartz, invented Randroid. He came up to me and looked me in the eye early in the night when we were playing a gig and said, Randroid, Are you in there yet? No, I'm not there yet, I'll come back and talk to you later after a couple of shots. Hey Randroid! Are you here? OK, let's go hang out." [laughs] [5]

George Whitty's skills were now even more widely in use as he set up the sounds for much of the synthesised rhythms and textures. No dedicated drummer present (except Alias for some extra percussion). You would not know it unless you are experienced listener. As if that were not enough, George also acted as arranger, recording engineer, mixer and producer, all tasks being executed with the kind of professional yet humorous approach that put musicians at ease and made the music sound fun.

The album was Randy's first tie-up to Joachim Becker's Escape Records label, a relationship that offered many advantages of artistic license, as well as a good commercial structure to promote and sell the discs in a CD marketplace that was diminishing by the day.

Wayne Out is a fast, funky, instrumental that has a catchy theme that acts as an exciting wrapper to a hugely imaginative content of jazz. Both Randy and Adam stretch out in this piece and the ending is perfectly timed to leave us wanting more. It's a stunning track.

The lyrics to *Hangin' In The City* are well crafted to present a humorous view of life in the Big Apple, as seen from the eye of a New york native who can't imagine living anywhere else. This funky performance from Will Lee is quite sublime, mixed well to the front.

I Talk To The Trees is the antidote to the committed city dweller that put his materialistic case forward in the previous track. Now Randy chooses to recite his lyrics, which come dangerously close to expressing fine sentiment. It's a good decision, for the music is well produced to express good intent without getting slushy. In any case, the vocals, once presented, move to the rear as the instrumental work takes over. Randy's solo is searching, and Michael takes a generous slice of the action for the second half of this delicious piece. Richard Bona's bass contribution is perfectly fitted to the music, his fretless style and harmonics easily recognisable as part of his trademark.

Down 4 The Count supplements the Randroid catalogue with another piece of his sidewalk busking. Then, in contrast, track six is *Pastoral (To Jaco)*, a wonderful, but sober reflection of the passing of a great musician whose short life was proof of the as-yet undiscovered physical law that genius is directly proportional to tragedy. The beautifully melancholy 4/4 theme and improvisations are set against some faster 3/4 sections that invite Randy and Michael to remember some of the amazing notes they found whilst playing in Jaco's presence. Both of them succeed in capturing the excitement many of us remember from listening to Jaco's albums. Chris Minh Doky's bass playing is joyful and brilliant.

We come to the raunch with *Then I Came To My Senses*. This tune is a modern blues with some well-fitted guitar by Hiram Bullock that matches Randy's suggestive lyrics. It's impossible not to smile as you listen to this, but then, I am a bloke! However, strip out the obvious content and we are still left with a superbly arranged big band sound supporting one of the best kinds of guitar blues. Randy seems to have invented a new sub genre, 'class raunch'.

Seattle is the class without the raunch. Maybe a reminiscence of Randy's happy days in Seattle as a young musician, this is another sophisticated instrumental in the form of a guitar / trumpet / keyboard quintet. Randy and Adam play two generously proportioned solos.

Never Tell Her U Love Her is immediately commercial thanks to George's amazing backing. It could be said that the sentiments expressed in the lyrics, comic though they are, have a negative impact on the sophistication of the music. I can't imagine that the tone of the lyrics will make this track a smash hit with the ladies. It's one of those Guys Only tracks, and I, for one, love it.

I Been Through This Before is a gorgeous ballad that demonstrates the sincere, romantic side of Randy's music. It's a beautiful melody played over logical, interesting chord changes, and then lovely flugelhorn improvisation in which the notes pour out like dessert wine.

One Thing Led To Another is more successful at fitting raunchy lyrics to music, and even the trumpet – muted at first – sounds as if it's joining in the fun. The final part of the music features a great solo from Joe Caro (b1956, NYC), another friend of the BBs, and a session musician with many credits on top albums. It's a treat that keeps us tuned in right to the very end of this great album.

"This collection is inspired by 'the cats' their music and their wit," wrote Randy. [71] I do some brainstorming as I try to distil Randy's style. I jot down many comments about Randy's lyrics: humorous observations; New York City; serious musicality; contemporary (2001); tongue in cheek. I think of tree huggers who move out of the city to escape - but he doesn't need to. Everything he needs is in the city. Wanting to like trees and cows is like saying that you prefer them to your friends, to all the fun aspects of everyday life in the city – and especially to women. But the pastoral is taken very seriously, as in Tracks 4 and 6. So the city tracks are written with irony after all. Maybe the keyword is entertainment. Readers will have to make up their own minds on this one.

George Whitty's contributions are immense, and besides the fact that it's Randy's album, George deserves massive credit for making this collection sound as good as it does. In particular, it is common for bass to receive poor attention on CDs, but here the contributions of these gifted musicians, each different in their own way, but carefully created to match the feel of the music, get royal treatment from George's skilled hands.

Michael Brecker: Nearness of You – The Ballad Book – 2001 (***)

In December 2000, Michael turned up at New York's *Right Track* studios to record an album of 'ballads' with a group of musicians who were now all close friends: Pat Metheny, Herbie Hancock, Charlie Haden and Jack de Johnette. A ballad is usually sentimental and romantic, and expressed as a narrative poem is frequently sung. Right from the start, the album seems to be positioning itself more towards the commercial side of jazz where, hopefully, it might attract rather more attention.

The first track is *Chan's Song*, a cool, beautiful and logical piece by Herbie Hancock that won Michael a Grammy for the "Best Jazz Instrumental Solo" of the year. It gets the album off to a perfect start and acts as a warm-up for the main event. This is an appearance by Michael's friend James Taylor. Michael played on no less than seven of James' albums from 1972 to 1997, so now it was time for some payback. James's song, *Don't Let Me Be Lonely Tonight* is richly arranged, and allows Michael to show right away just how lusciously lyrical he can be when he is not chasing the next unusual chord change. Even James's singing has taken on a kind of new, laid-back, special-for-jazz tone, and if I were a woman I'd fancy him madly I'm sure, even at his age.

Nascente is a well chosen but little-known piece that is not really a ballad, but is certainly a beautiful piece of music. It's about now that we realise just how much Pat Metheny has contributed to this album, for besides being the album producer (along with Steve Rodby), and besides playing on all of the tracks, he has also written two songs, and arranged most of them. This is one. Pat plays his Roland guitar synthesiser overdubbed onto an acoustic guitar backing, before Herbie solos and finally Michael comes in. The music is interesting and constantly effervescent.

The lights are dimmed and the candles lit for an intimate dinner party with your loved one in *Midnight Mood*, a delicious ballad by Joe Zawinul. Recorded on Joe's first album, *Money in the Pocket* (1966), when he was still very much a cabaret accompanist, and before he was converted to electric playing, this is a very sexy piece with minimal playing and maximum feeling that oozes expression.

Then James Taylor returns for a spine-tingling version of *The Nearness of You*. It's a stunning highlight of the album, as James embarks on the first verse with just Pat Metheny's gentle Latin rumba accompaniment on acoustic guitar. Then when the band enters for the chorus, it becomes an exquisite whole as bass, drums, guitar and piano all play to perfection. A catchy little motif is used as a link into Michael's lead solo, played in a higher key that steps the whole piece up a notch, before falling back once more for a final verse from James and Herbie, played to the foxiest of foxtrots. The coda is improvised with a fade of slinky notes from Pat, Herbie and Michael and I feel like applauding out loud.

The idea of this being a Ballad Book leads to an arbitrary subdivision of the tracks into the meaningless *Chapter One* (tracks 1-5), *Chapter Two* (tracks 6-10) and *Epilogue* (track 11). Unfortunately, *Chapter One* is far better than the rest, as the album entirely loses its way after track five. The danger of a book of ballads is that all the tracks sound the same, and I can state categorically that this album is not guilty of that. It's hard to put a finger on just why the rest is so disappointing, but it always comes down to the selection of pieces. Michael's *Incandescence* returns to his format of chasing the chords, although his theme is not as disjointed as in some of his compositions. Pat Metheny's *Sometimes I See* provides a gentle lift, as the conventionally harmonic slow waltz, made up of logical changes, breaks into interesting counter-rhythms. It is the familiar Gil Evans arrangement of *My Ship*, taken from Miles Davis's album *Miles Ahead* (1957) that may or may not excite listeners most amongst *Chapter Two*. Gil Goldstein has a strong presence on this album as musical arranger and copyist, and he will work a lot for Michael in future years. His adaptation of Evans's arrangement for this band is very good, so it must be my familiarity with it that causes my lack of excitement on this occasion.

Irving Berlin's *Always* is an arrangement by Larry Goldings in which Jack DeJohnette monotonously plays triplets. Sadly, the arrangement is not enough to save the piece, which is just too much of a musical cliché to be appropriate in this context.

Pat Metheny might have saved the album with his own *Seven Days*, but the choice is too morose and the changes too unsettling at this stage in an hour of tender music; the music has an inappropriate presence here. Then, finally, Michael leads all the way through his own composition *I Can See Your Dreams*. With mostly just Herbie for accompaniment, this piece too fails to deliver with its schizophrenic design of short moody sections. Thus, the album ends in significant anti-climax, which is a great pity considering the obvious love and care that went into the making of it.

There's a little taste of Michael's humour on the cover of this CD, with a tiny human speck in the midst of a vast wilderness. I'm sure he laughed when he thought of that one!

Herbie Hancock / Michael Brecker / Roy Hargrove: *Directions in Music –* 2002 (*****)

Despite his irresistible urge to continue to develop new music based in electronics, as he did with *Future 2 Future* (2001), it is clear now that, as Herbie moved past his sixtieth year and into the 21st century, Miles Davis would never be far from his thoughts. Yet again, he chose to continue with his love of acoustic jazz in a further celebration, this time of both Miles Davis and John Coltrane. Both men were born in 1926, so in 2001 Herbie decided to create a project to celebrate the 75th anniversary of their birth. For this ambitious project

Herbie invited Michael Brecker to represent Coltrane's tenor saxophone and Roy Hargrove to represent Miles. Hargrove (b1969, Waco TX) had been carving a somewhat narrow groove with his own quartet on the New York jazz scene since 1989, and had already won a Grammy for *Habana* (1997) with a band called Crisol. Even so, it was a huge accolade for Roy to be invited to join such stellar company here, where his exceptional talent gained a new level of recognition in the acoustic jazz mainstream. Over the coming years, he would continue to play in Herbie's bands, as well as continue working with his own small group. Bass and drums were provided by the brilliant partnership of John Patitucci and Brian Blade, two men who had become first choice for Wayne Shorter's own quartet. Although the packaging of the project focuses on the three leading players, we should not underestimate the contributions made by this remarkable pairing.

As Herbie points out in the sleeve notes to this album, "We're not just playing the original chords of these pieces, but really moving beyond that, using our powers of concentration and our hearts and our trust in the ability of the others to respond to whatever happens and work outside the box. This philosophy is very much in keeping with what I believe to be the true spirit of Miles Davis and John Coltrane." [72] Herbie had, of course, always subscribed to this tenet – another he had learned from Miles. Herbie has frequently pointed out that Miles used to say that he employed musicians to experiment on the bandstand, not in rehearsal rooms, and this ethos is carried forward by this live recording in Toronto entitled *Directions in Music* (2002).

The album opens with Herbie's piece *The Sorcerer*, which he first played with Miles on the classic 1967 album of the same name. In other arenas, such a choice would be regarded as standard fare, but with these musicians there's no such interpretation. This version moves on as inevitably as any of the repeated recordings of Herbie's back catalogue.

So What / Impressions are two jazz compositions credited respectively to Miles and Trane that have enormous presence in the jazz repertoire. The chord sequence of both of these two famous pieces is identical: 16 bars of Dm7, 8 bars of Ebm7 and 8 bars of Dm7. This, of course, makes them easy to blend into one, as happens on this track. Both Miles and Trane would have been familiar with a cover version by Ahmad Jamal in 1955 of *Pavanne* by Morton Gould and this is indeed the origin of both songs. [73]

Transition (1965) was an album by Coltrane that bridged his traditional quartet work and some of the more experimental music of his last years. The title track is used as the basis for this band to develop. The theme is fast and penetrating and quickly lost as each soloist gives his take on the ideas. According to Wikipedia, the original Coltrane composition "exhibits an operatic dramatisation of the human search for meaning." [74] It now becomes clearer just how challenging it must have been for these three musicians (Brecker, especially) to take on the playing of this music and even dare to hope that they might approach it. Somehow, this kind of work could never be comparable with the playing of just another version of *Someday My Prince Will Come,* for example.

My Ship is in the same slow, beautiful vein as the original on *Miles Ahead* (1957), except that here it is given the slightest swing that pushes it into new territory. Hargrove's flügelhorn is at its luxurious best for this sweet music.

It is not enough, however, merely to reinterpret the music of the two icons. Instead, these musicians brought their own music to the project. Thus, Hargrove wrote the piece entitled *The Poet* with Miles in mind, saying that the piece was inspired by the Miles Davis quintet of the 1960s "when they were getting into a sound that went beyond traditional structure." [75] Michael wrote *D Trane*, which he said was "loosely based on a West African clave rhythmic structure and was influenced by Coltrane's compositions that drew upon African music." [76] As you listen to this rendition, it is quite possible to understand how this music could actually better represent the intellectual ideals of Coltrane's *Transition*. This piece is rightly positioned as the final track on the album, for it is a massive performance on the part of all those involved, and a *tour de force* for Brecker that draws a huge response from the audience.

The track entitled *Misstery* is a joint composition by Hancock, Brecker and Hargrove that adds a welcome freshness to a running order that contains plenty of well-known items. Yet, even as we ponder the up-coming *Naima*, a very well known piece from Trane's repertoire, we can have no idea what treat is in store. For any musician to stand alone on stage and perform Coltrane's *Naima* is daring in the extreme and beyond most sane players of the saxophone. For Michael Brecker to do so is a demonstration of his stratospheric pinnacle of achievement on his instrument. Even allowing for the fact that he must have wood-shedded this piece on countless occasions, it is a demonstration of tenor saxophone performance at an unparalleled level and, under any circumstances, we should feel privileged to listen. I could hardly imagine a better tribute to Trane.

There have been many tributes to Coltrane and Miles, not forgetting Herbie's own involvement with *A Tribute to Miles* (1994), and there will be many more in the future, but this must rank as one of the finest of all time. The whole concept of this album is a considerable challenge for everyone involved. As I have suggested above, it surely challenged its musicians. The members of the band, however, have the great advantage of knowing everything there is to know about the project – of knowing the origins of the music and playing it and developing it night after night on the bandstand. They even know it so well that they feel able to compose their own music in advance. Thus, as with Brecker's

D Trane or Hargrove's *The Poet*, we should never underestimate the challenge of presenting to the other musicians a self-penned work that might dare to approach the work of the two dead masters. During the performances, the musicians also experience and feel the intimate personal interactions, even if they are transitory and vary nightly with each re-working of a piece. For them to work together in such a way as to make it seem as if they are playing some perfectly scripted score even as they dodge and weave through the music in ways that are new even to them, is jazz craft at the highest level.

The album challenges us too, though not nearly as much. The great contradiction of music that is built upon improvisation, however, is in its permanence on a recording. We surely appreciate it more when we gain an understanding of the task at hand, yet the value of an improvised work must be lost in the repetition? I am at a loss to understand how the audience exposed to this for the first time could have gained anything more than the immediacy of living in their own personal moments. Some, unfamiliar with the music being performed, and of the artists in question, must surely gain little other than the instant aural experience, which they cannot be guaranteed to like. We, on the other hand, have the advantage of additional information such as I give you here, as well as the opportunity to listen again and to enjoy the moments we may have missed the first time around or to better understand those we did not miss first time around. Clearly, the benefit of retrospect pays dividends for the immense artistic achievement on this album, which is then better recognised. As a result, the album was rewarded by the decision of the jazz peer group when it not only won a Grammy for the "Best Jazz Instrumental Album", but got Herbie a personal Grammy for the "Best Jazz Instrumental Solo" on *My Ship*.

Charlie Haden with Michael Brecker: *American Dreams* **– 2002 (*****)**

The notes to this album tell us that the record was made over four days from 14-17 May 2002. Of course, that is far from the truth, for a huge amount of effort went into this album, the great proportion of it unseen beforehand. In a sense, that makes this an album that is far removed from the spontaneity of jazz and many listeners may not like this menu. Then, if I use the word 'orchestra' some readers will skip reading this and move on to the next section. A cursory description of this album might be enough to cause many readers to feel nauseous. How could Charlie Haden, he of the Carla Bley association, and *Escalator Over The Hill* fame, even contemplate such a syrupy, orchestral concoction? Even if I spell it out in detail, many readers will know this music is not for them. Well, if that's your bag, then so be it. The rest of you, please read on…

Charlie makes it quite clear in his notes that in this project he wanted to make music that represented the most beautiful desires of the American Dream, and that's quite clear from the title and packaging. This beauty is in the eyes of conventional beholders, the kind of people who represent the past, present and future of the USA. No crazy outlandish harmonies, rhythms or structures here, just page after page of the most beautifully crafted crotchets Charlie can uncover. Obviously, they are not all his, for this is very much a team project under his direction – and what a team!

With orchestral arrangements and conducting by Jeremy Lubbock, Alan Broadbent and Vince Mendoza on much of the album, the strings were always in safe hands. Lubbock described his own input as "a labor of love." [77]. Expert programming from Judd Miller (who happens to be Charlie's neighbour) is another strong pillar of support.

As for the musicians, Charlie chose three men at the very top of their trade. Brad Mehldau (b1970, Jacksonville FL) won the award of "Best All-Round Musician" from Boston's Berklee Music College from where he moved in 1988 to New York and began his own successful trio, as well as performing in numerous quartets with players such as Joshua Redman and Pat Metheny. Drummer Brian Blade (b1970, Shreveport LA) attended Loyola University in New Orleans, and then continued his musical apprenticeship in the home of jazz. By 2000, Brian had established himself as first choice drummer for the Wayne Shorter Quartet. When you are an acoustic bass player, like Charlie, you usually accept that you are going to have to turn over much of the lead instrument work to a conventional lead instrument player, and Charlie's choice of Michael Brecker for his main partner on this album was both natural and perfect.

Charlie's desire to capture his objective is achieved through an inspirational selection of songs. This record simply drips with love. From standards *Bittersweet*, *Young And Foolish*, *Love Like Ours* and *It Might Be You*, to modern jazz standards like Pat Metheny's composition, *Travels*, every second is exquisite perfection. Bebop is represented by a gentle, thoughtful version of Ornette Coleman's *Bird Song*. Brad contributes *Ron's Place*, whilst Charlie chooses two songs from Keith Jarrett's pen, *No Lonely Nights*, and *Prism*. He chooses two of his own numbers, *American Dreams* and *Nightfall*. The title track is Charlie's opportunity to stand out as the lead voice, and, without recourse to saxophone on this gorgeous track, he presents a sublime rendition of his song, bathed in some of the most deliciously devised chords from the orchestra under Broadbent's direction. Vince Mendoza's composition, *Sotto Voce*, is a wonderful ballad for jazz quartet supplemented by some rich synthesiser backing conceived by Judd Miller. The album could never be complete without a rendition of *America The Beautiful*, and this one is ... beautiful.

So, on this CD, don't expect Michael's saxophone fireworks or uncomfortable harmonies – just soak up an hour of outpouring of emotion such as only true artists can achieve. This album is pure joy from the first note to the last.

Michael Brecker Quindectet: *Wide Angles* – 2003 (*****)

'Quindectet' is a quaint old term for fifteen musicians, but don't expect a big band sound from this excellent album. This is more like a jazz orchestra in which wind, bass and rhythm is blended with strings. For much of the time, the album is just Brecker plus band, with a sprinkling of cameo solos from selected musicians. Although their names may be unfamiliar, don't think that these are just minor-leaguers. Aside from the superb playing, composing and arranging of Brecker, here is a very great effort from Gil Goldstein who, besides producing the album, wrote the magnificent arrangements for fifteen hungry musicians. The result is a great performance by a major star set in a wide variety of musical contexts. It's as if Michael is duetting with some kind of new instrument.

The album came about after Mike received an award to take part in a large ensemble tour of the UK during 2002. Back home in New York, Michael and Gil Goldstein worked together to design this set of songs for fifteen musicians. There is a great difference between composing a jazz tune, and having it in a form suitable for fifteen instruments. A lot of arranging and scoring is required, and Michael did not have the necessary depth of experience for this. So, although he composed nine of the ten tracks (he shared one of those with George Whitty; the tenth was by Don Grolnick), he leaned upon Goldstein to take on the heavy lifting. Goldstein was already well known to Mike, even though they had not recorded much together. Gil had carved out a high reputation as a performer, composer and an arranger, working many of Mike's friends on albums such as Billy Cobham's *Stratus* (1981), Mark Egan's *A Touch Of Light* (1988), Pat Metheny's *Secret Story* (1992), Randy's *Into The Sun* (1995), and Mike Stern's *Give And Take* (1997), to name just a few. Gil was just the man for the job.

As for the other musicians, there were some new names. John Patitucci (b1959, Brooklyn NY) is one of those bass players is as comfortable playing jazz-fusion on electric bass as he was playing straightahead on acoustic upright. He came to prominence as a virtuoso exponent of six-string electric bass in Chick Corea's Electric Band in the late 1980s and '90s, and starting with J*ohn Patitucci* (1988) and *On The Corner* (1989), found success with a string of his own albums of electric jazz-fusion. However, he kept up a strong profile on acoustic bass during this time, thanks largely to a long relationship playing acoustic bass in Wayne Shorter's quartets. In 2002 he was part of the wonderful Herbie Hancock project, *Directions in Music*, where he also played alongside Roy Hargrove, Brian Blade and Michael.

Though he had not played on Michael's records before, guitarist Adam Rogers had already played a great deal for brother Randy's bands, as well as

Randy's close associate, Bill Evans. Adam has been successful in creating his own sound, but has proved to be versatile, and sensitive to different situations, as well as extremely creative in his solos. Drummer Antonio Sanchez (b1971, Mexico City) excelled at Berklee Music School in the late 1990s, and was promptly hired by Pat Metheny for his album *Speaking of Now* (2002). Since then he has been Pat's first choice drummer for most of his projects.

Peter Gordon is perhaps the biggest unsung hero on the album, a classically trained musician who has been active since 1971 and has played for the Boston Symphony Orchestra and the Metropolitan Opera Orchestra. But his versatility on French horn soon made him the first choice session musician across the whole spectrum of music genres from pop to jazz. Peter has known the Breckers since their early days in New York, working together with artists such as Carole Hall, David Sanborn, Bob James, Luther Vandross, Chaka Khan, Peter Erskine and, especially, Jaco Pastorius' Word Of Mouth projects.

Trumpeter Alex Sipiagin (b1967, Yaroslavl, Russia) is a great-nephew of the famous Russian opera singer, Leonid Sobinov. At 12 years of age, he began playing in a children's orchestra. In 1990, Alex won first place in a Russian young jazz players' competition in Rostov City and visited the United States for the first time, performing with a Russian student jazz band, at the Corpus Christi Jazz Festival in Texas. He impressed many listeners with his playing, and when in 1991 he decided to pursue jazz and moved to New York City, he was able to stay in the USA. He was soon playing regularly at *Sweet Basil* with the Gil Evans Band directed by Miles Evans. Then in 1993 he became a member of Gil Goldstein's Zebra Coast Orchestra. Randy Brecker introduced Sipiagin to the Mingus Big Band in 1995, of which he is still a regular member, as well as the Mingus Dynasty and the Mingus Orchestra.

Steve Wilson started his saxophone training in the Hampton Virginia area where he lived as a boy. At University in Richmond VA, he played with many well-known jazz musicians, and became a touring musician in bands backing the likes of The Four Tops and Sophisticated Ladies. He moved to New York in 1987 and was soon part of the Lionel Hampton touring band. He has been a busy session man for musicians like Ralph Peterson, Jr., Marvin "Smitty" Smith, Joanne Brackeen, Leon Parker, and Buster Williams, and gained big band experience with the American Jazz Orchestra and the Mingus Big Band. In 1996 he joined the Dave Holland Quintet, and from 1998-2001 he was a member of Chick Corea's Grammy winning sextet, Origin. For his work on this album, he was asked to play the flute and alto flute.

Charles Pillow is a fluent performer and teacher of woodwind instruments, primarily saxophone, but equally at home on oboe, which he was asked to play on this CD. Over his long career, he has performed on over 100 recordings of jazz and pop artists, including those of Maria Schneider, David Sanborn, Joe

Henderson, John Scofield, Bob Mintzer, Bob Belden, Jay Z, David Liebman, Mariah Carey, Chaka Khan and Luther Vandross. English musician, Iain Dixon, had been a part of Michael's 2002 tour of the UK, and did so well that he was invited to take part in the recordings for this CD. Equally at home on clarinet or saxophone, his instruments here are clarinet and bass clarinet. Percussionist Daniel Sadownick was a native of the Bronx and obtained a Masters degree in music from New York University. When Michael hired him, he had already appeared on Steely Dan's *Two Against Nature* (2000) and Dennis Chambers' *Outbreak* (2002). Michael's string section consisted of Mark Feldman and Joyce Hammann (violins), Lois Martin (viola), Erik Friedlander (cello) and John Patitucci (bass).

It is perhaps Patitucci's bass that holds the music of *Broadband* together, for its presence is always clearly defined and, residing at the roots of pitch, it forms a secure foundation for this freewheeling piece. From the start, the theme is clearly presented in a shadowy mood with an edge of the unexpected, even though John holds on strongly to its 4/4 metre. However, as the piece proceeds, the wayward band seems to try increasingly hard, under Michael's leadership, to break free of Patitucci's rhythm. Indeed, it succeeds, even as the bass does its best to hold everyone tightly together. By halfway through, the piece is spectacularly off-piste, with Mike indulging himself, as usual. The music is as freely orchestrated as it can be without becoming total chaos, and for listeners who like the sound of rich chords and unusual harmonies, this track is a treat.

Don Grolnick's ghost hovers in the studio for the next track; he could easily have penned this one. The imagery suggested by the title *Cool Day in Hell* is a good fit to the music. After all, we imagine Hell to be a fiery place and it's supposed to be uncomfortable, to say the least. Michael has always been good at inventing melodies and themes that make the listener feel rather uneasy because of their unusual construction. The theme for this track certainly fits that description. As for it being cool, well paradoxically it's that too. The accompaniment has a strong symphonic element, leaving Michael to play the role of soloist throughout, which he does in the usual way, with a lengthy solo sandwiched inside his versions of the theme.

The accompaniment to the slow piece, *Angle of Repose*, is dominated by the string section, which imparts a majestic feel. The music is strong, proud, and bejewelled, so how could it also not be beautiful? I would nominate this for one of Michael's finest melodies, and it is so inspiring that John Patitucci's solo bass is a masterpiece in its own right. No saxophone fireworks here. This track is all about a wonderful tune and exquisite interpretation, especially at the gorgeously crafted end, which ought to bring a tear to most eyes.

Steve Wilson's flute leads off the music to *Timbuktu*. It soon becomes apparent that the infectious African rhythm is similar to *African Skies* from *Out*

Of The Loop (1994), and it also has similar rhythmic inflections in its simple melody. In the fifth minute, Michael starts to improvise aggressively, and the band vibe changes accordingly, but by the end of the sixth minute the music is back on track with the theme. This is not allowed to rest unaltered, for during the seventh and eighth minutes the theme is constantly manipulated through to the end.

There is a kind of craziness about *Night Jessamine* that has echoes of *Slang* from the same earlier album, with a strong percussive foundation and a rubberised bass line holding up the main theme. The middle section is very much more complicated with some cascading chords and drizzling sax notes. Michael's improvisation is in an unrelated key, which makes the piece sound even crazier.

Scylla is a joint composition by Michael and George Whitty. Scylla and Charybdis were sea monsters in Greek Mythology that inhabited the two sides of the Straits of Messina; to be caught between them was to be "between the Devil and the Deep Blue Sea." This tune is scary. Alex Sipiagin begins by taking a rare instrumental solo to a backing by Adam Rogers. The music has all the elements we are beginning to associate with one kind of Brecker composition: parallel and chromatic harmonies that disintegrate in front of us, and then move into free improvisation, such that by nine minutes, the music has become a truly frightening beast. It's a good thing Michael gets it back into its cage before the end.

Brexterity is not for the faint-hearted listener. If you have any sympathy with the saxophonist, you'll be feeling downright sorry for him after six minutes or so. Presumably inspired by the Charlie Parker number from the 1940s, *Dexterity*, Michael just keeps blowing throughout the entire length of this nearly seven-minute piece. An opening cadenza is improvised with Sanchez' drums to 0.36; then bass, guitar, and strings join in to 1.08 when the fifteen-second bebop theme begins, and is repeated with full band at 1.23, 1.49 and 2.04. (For less experienced listeners, when you hear the woodpecker sound, you are listening to the end of the first phrase.) From 2.15, Michael embarks on an improvisation over his structure, accompanied by drums, bass and guitar. In the world of superlatives inhabited by Michael (and Randy), it almost seems disingenuous to continue repeating words like 'amazing', 'remarkable', 'brilliant', etc. Listeners who are not used to hearing jazz, will simply not be able to comprehend just how amazing, remarkable, brilliant, this performance is. This is extremely complicated music, *for all of the players*. Although there are some repeated sections, as I have indicated, they are almost always played differently each time, so the music is constantly evolving throughout. In some places, musicians will have been invited to improvise; in others, they are playing music that does not move forward according to conventional rules of harmony. They will be constantly up against dissonance, which throws doubt into the musician's mind about whether or not he is playing the correct notes. Meanwhile, Michael is not overdubbing his track, as would often happen in such studio situations. This is being played live, and he is dealing with all of this constantly fluxing, dynamic harmony, never losing his place in the framework, but being creative to the highest possible level, playing fast, acrobatic sequences of notes that conform to the evolving harmonies he has already set down in the composition. Besides the extreme mental strain of making his brain function on so many levels without a break, the physical strain of never having a bar's rest to catch his breath makes him very physically fit. No matter how much woodshedding, this performance would tax almost every saxophone player to the limit. It is an excellent example of Michael's position at the top of the tree in his generation of saxophone players.

Don Grolnick's composition on this CD is a story of *Evening Faces*. We find them to be a depressing bunch, as this music begins in a sombre mood, without rhythm, for is there is none in this collection of sad, tired people, on their way home in the rush hour. At 1.25, the doors close on the subway train and the vehicle picks up speed to enter the tunnel. But even the train seems tired as driver Mike tries to coax a little speed out of it. Even co-driver Adam Rogers can barely maintain speed as, with their heads in newspapers, or eyes closed to absorb iPod music, the passengers nod and bump their way home.

In *Modus Operandy*, there are significant resonances with some of the rhythms and harmonies of hip hop used in saxophonist Bill Evans's unusual fusion album *Escape* (1996), for which reason alone, it is very worthwhile listening carefully to this track. There is nothing like this anywhere else in Michael's recorded repertoire. John Patitucci's unconventional electric bass playing is exceptional, as is the whole band arrangement, and especially the game of tag between the band and Robin Eubanks' trombone that is a particular highlight. Michael's creation is truly inspired.

The final track is *Never Alone*, which begins strongly with strings and tonal colour that could easily have been used for the sad scene in Bogey and Bergman's *Casablanca*. However, it quickly moves beyond that setting and into a jazz aria. And if the New York Metropolitan Opera had supplied their leading lady to sing this, the result could not match the eloquence with which Michael delivers one of his beautiful, melancholy ballads.

There is little else to say about this album except that it consists of seventy minutes of excellent, unique music.

Randy Brecker: *34th N Lex* – 2003 (****)

From the opening bars of Randy's album *34th N Lex* (2003) it is clear that we are witnessing the return of the 'A' Team, a full-on Brecker Brothers recording in disguise, complete with David Sanborn. If you were unaware of this before you bought the record, it brings a big smile to your face. Apart from the horns, Randy has retained the winning formula he adopted for *Hangin' In The City*, two years earlier, with George Whitty continuing to produce, mix, arrange and perform. Once again, there is no dedicated drummer or percussionist, although Clarence Penn plays drums on a couple of tracks. Will Lee is presumably unavailable, and Chris Minh Doky is the band's bassist for most of the tracks, except where Gary Haase sits in. Gary also assists with drum programming; Adam Rogers continues in the guitar seat. An extra bonus is the guest appearance of Fred Wesley on a number of tracks.

The boys' old friend Ronnie Cuber kicks off on the title track with a great, funky riff on baritone saxophone, and the unmistakable sounds of Michael Brecker and David Sanborn are close on his heels. The music has all the harmony hallmarks of the early albums. One of the great features of this music is the mixing, thanks to George, who succeeds in ensuring that all of the sounds are clear and balanced and, in particular, that he loves to hear the bass in all its glory. This kind of clarity is one of the real beauties of digital sound.

Streeange is a rich, modern fusion of street music and funk that is built on one of Randy's finest grooves. Adam Rogers and Gary Haase provide the real foundation of this tune, with the steady percussion somewhat secondary, whilst a background commentary by Makeeba Mooncycle is an excellent alternative to formal lyrics. Randy and Michael play a superb loose theme atop this pastiche, which sees the horns diverging and coming together in a way that the two brothers show their complete musical intimacy. Repeated listening is necessary to fully appreciate this opening. At one minute, new life is breathed into the piece as Michael improvises for a minute, and then the theme returns in a new form to serve as an intro to Randy's improvised section.

Shanghigh is a conventional, straightahead, acoustic composition that features the popular line-up of trumpet, tenor sax and trombone, played by Randy, Michael, and Fred Wesley, with Chris Minh Doky on acoustic bass, and Clarence Penn on drums. Despite the horn presence, George Whitty shows off his chops with some fine acoustic piano playing, supported by Adam's traditional electric guitar sound.

All 4 Love is a commercial production, written by Gary Haase, J Phoenix and Randy Brecker, with Randy in the lead, interspersed with vocals by J Phoenix. Haase provides most of the music, from keyboards, to bass, drums and percussion.

A full house of horns is used on *Let It Go*, with Randy, Michael, David, Fred and Ronnie. The drums and keyboard backing is due to George again, with yet more tricks from Gary Haase's computers. To many ears, this will sound like a big band track, with much of the space taken up by the ensemble repeating the catchy theme.

The beautiful ballad, *Foregone Conclusion*, is ethereal and uplifting, with Michael and Randy setting out the theme in woven strands of harmony. By around 2.30, the music has taken on an edge, before Randy reassures us that all is well from 3.10. The honeyed tones of his flugelhorn are joyful, yet retain that element of mystery as he masterfully negotiates his own chordal pathways. Randy leaves it to Michael to find a path out of the woods, and his short solo at the end of the piece is as magical as we have come to expect. The backing quartet of Whitty, Minh Doky, Rogers and Penn is beautifully placed – unobtrusive yet essential.

Hula Dula is a curious combination of a Latin rhythmic base with a driving four-horn theme that has the edge of a Swedish crime thriller. The harmony is raw and the low tones of Ronnie's baritone sax provide an ionic texture. It's not electric jazz, but Randy's solo makes sparks, and Adam Rogers adopts an electric guitar sound that leaks high voltage.

On 5 December 2002, Bob Berg was driving through a snowstorm on Long Island with his wife, when a truck hit his car. He was killed in the impact; his wife survived. It was a tragic loss to the jazz community, and to Randy, who dedicated *The Fisherman* (which had already been recorded) to his friend. The music is laid-back, but certainly not sad, and Randy plays optimistic, intricate lines to his usual high standard. Sanborn fans will love the track for a long-awaited full-blown solo set in the context that fans of his brand of jazz like best.

There's a certain *déjà-vu* to the start of *Give It Up*, which is great for all fans from BB days. Once again, it's a Randy / Mike / Fred trihorn blowout, and Fred gets first solo spot, which he fills with solid, joyful lines. Randy uses his mute in a Miles-like lead solo. Gary Haase is filling in much of the background once more as this funky tune wends its way to a faded finale.

Tokyo Freddie is a piece of fast acoustic jazz in the hard bop mould, played by a septet with George, Chris, Adam and Clarence in support of the horn frontline of Randy, Mike and Fred. Sadly, for Adam Rogers, his name is omitted from the credits, yet he plays an excellent electric guitar solo.

The final track is *The Castle Rocks* in which George alone provides the entire funky backdrop over which Randy, Mike and guest tenor saxophonist, Ada Rovatti, take turns to drive through this melody that's as hard and jagged as Cornish granite.

Overall, this album is a great success, capturing the times of the early 21st century, with its varied menu of sharp compositions, whilst always retaining the shadows of those fantastic days of Brecker Brothers fusion. Its success was properly recognised with the award of the top jazz Grammy for "Best Contemporary Jazz Album."

Bill Evans / Randy Brecker: *Soulbop Band Live* – 2004 (****)

In late November 2002 (*not* 2003, as indicated on the album notes), Randy was considering a 2003 tour, and he had discussed with Bob Berg the idea of his friend joining the band. Randy told jazz writer, Bill Milkowski, "Originally, I had this record *34th & Lex* slated to come out and I had just called Bob Berg and Ronnie Cuber to try to set up a tour to support the record. And a week later is when Berg was killed. At first I considered just scuttling the tour because Bob is kind of hard to replace... plus, he's such a close friend of mine. But one night by chance I was talking to Bill Evans, who I hadn't really thought of as a replacement... we were just kind of commiserating and he was telling me that he had just done a two-month tour of Europe with his regular band but was thinking of changing things up for another European tour the following summer. He had some gigs already booked, so we just kind of joined forces. I was going to call it New York Funk but Bill came up with the name Soul Bop, which really clicked with the promoters. It was short and to the point and gave a pretty good description of what this band was all about." [78]

Bill Evans loved the band. "The thing about this sort of band is when you have guys like Hiram Bullock and Dave Kikoski, you've got both ends of the spectrum there - the groove man and the serious jazz cat. And then you've got Victor Bailey and Steve, who can do both things, and you mix in Randy's sort of more intellectualized jazz stuff with my funk things... what you've got is a band that can do anything and go anywhere, depending on what kind of mood the band is in that night. We could rock out and tear it up in front of 8,000 people in Rome or just burn and simmer in a more straight ahead, introspective way in a nightclub in France. And that's the cool thing about the Soulbop Band. We can fit any occasion on any level." [79]

The Soulbop band performed first during the summer of 2003, and the concerts were so successful that a further series of gigs was planned for 2004. It was recordings from concerts on this extensive European tour during July and August, as well as from a set of gigs at the Iridium Club New York on 16-21 September, that appeared on the album *Soulbop Band Live* (2004).

Inevitably, Bill Evans (b1958, Clarendon Hills IL) has often been confused with his piano-playing namesake, especially since both men played with Miles. He has always been a first rank saxophone player whose fundamental orientation was jazz-fusion. Although they had known each other since Bill's earliest days playing with Miles Davis, this was the first time that Bill and Randy had formally joined forces for more than just a session or two. Bill had been a novice New York saxophonist when he befriended Miles during his dark days of seclusion. With others, he had helped the Master to regain his interest in performing, which started with his new musical phase of more accessible jazz-fusion captured on *The Man With The Horn* (1980). Evans continued with Miles for several more years, before taking his own direction and recording with the band Elements, featuring Mark Egan and Dan Gottlieb, and a new line-up of John McLaughlin's Mahavishnu. His own career as leader began with two remarkable albums, *Living In The Crest Of A Wave* (1984), and the amazing fusion CD, *Alternative Man* (1985), which marked him out as a true innovator. Since then, all of his many albums have been of very high quality, and in an evolving series of unusual styles.

The new Soulbop band was clearly of the highest quality. Every musician was not only an outstanding session player, but also a leader in his own right. Hiram Bullock had played alongside Randy since the early days of the Brecker Brothers, and over many years had been first choice for David Sanborn's bands. Victor Bailey was an old friend of both leaders, starting his career with Weather Report, and then joining Bill's bands from 1990 onwards. Drummer Steve Smith knew Victor Bailey well, but was a relative newcomer to Randy and Bill: this was his first recording for both men. Since 1986, Smith (b1954, Whitman MA), like Bailey, had been a long-standing member of Steps Ahead, but had also begun to establish himself as drummer-of-choice at the serious rock end of the jazz-fusion spectrum. He had played alongside such technical heavyweights as bassist Victor Wooten and guitarists Scott Henderson and Frank Gambale. Then he had joined one of a new kind of "supertrio" bands, along with Stuart Hamm and Frank Gambale. The three men would become well known for a series of very strong recordings under the group name GHS.

The opener, Bill's tune *Rattletrap*, first appeared on his album *Escape* (1996), played at the sedate speed of 125 bpm, compared to the scorching 150 bpm used here. The piece comes straight out of the box marked 'Skunk Funk Clones'. It boils with the kind of energy found at live sessions. The track is a stunning start to the album, and should bring a smile to most faces.

Early in 2002, Randy had joined Bill on a couple of tracks – *Road to Bilbao*, and *Midnight Creeper* on Bill's album *Big Fun* (2002). The title track of that album was included in the set list for this tour, where the soulful vamp was given a suit of supremely funky threads and some long, hot solos from Randy, Bill and Hiram.

In complete contrast to blowing over a single chord, Randy's fiercely difficult composition, *Above And Below*, is given a superb makeover, and Randy is clearly in top form as he opens the proceedings on this 150 bpm screamer taken from *Return of the Brecker Brothers* (1992). Bill makes a more-than-adequate job of subbing for Michael Brecker, and when the vibe shifts into straightahead fours for Dave Kikoski's solo, it becomes especially well oiled. After a drum solo from Steve Smith, the piece ends as scarily as it began.

Let's Pretend is a lovely ballad from Bill's pen that he has used on a number of recordings. Bill uses his soprano sax for the romantic tone he likes, and Dave Kikoski sounds like Herbie Hancock on acoustic grand piano as he stretches out on Bill's gorgeous melody. Randy provides delicious muted trumpet over the theme.

The Brecker Brothers anthem, *Some Skunk Funk*, is played next, at the comparatively sedate pace of 134 bpm, which allows the audience to pick up on the angular melody. This version is different as it is used as a showpiece for Victor Bailey, whose bass solo embraces all kinds of styles and skills, and includes a short homage to his Weather Report roots.

Lest we not forget the rest of the band, Hiram Bullock is allowed space to showcase his own deep skill with two compositions, the first of which is *Greed*, already recorded for his own album, *Try Livin It* (2003). Hiram had already proved himself to be a strong composer in his own right, with a steady stream of largely self-penned albums throughout the 1980s and 90s. *Greed* is a strong tune, led off with a powerful blues intro, and vocals expressing pointed lyrics. Before long, a cool funky R&B riff moves the piece on to allow the band members freedom to build their own grooves. Randy is well fired up for it, and develops a piercing tension that Bill is inspired to build on. After another verse, Hiram takes the final solo and enjoys creating his own sound of heavy guitar funk.

This two-volume set of CDs continues with *Soul Bop*, an Evans composition for which the title is only partly applicable. The tune is built upon Bill's developing style of blending lots of different genres such as straightahead, hip hop, fusion, soul, R&B and others. Randy is very much at home as he solos first to a fast vamp. All but drums drop out as Bill takes the wheel on soprano sax, a tool with which he is expert. The tension builds with the addition of more instruments, so that by the time his turn is over he is incandescent with ideas. Once again, Dave Kikoski seems more at home burning up the keys of his acoustic piano to a straightahead rhythm. The piece ends with some great ensemble playing, having perhaps, cast off everything but its bop apparel.

Tease Me is the second composition by Hiram Bullock. It's a funkfest, sung by Hiram, and well illustrated with colourful horn interjections. After hot solos by Dave, and a duel by Randy and Bill, Bullock once again sets out on a screaming electric guitar solo before ending with more lyrics and a tight workout from the ensemble. As a listener not too partial to vocal numbers, I feel that Hiram gets a good balance between instrument and voice in his arrangements.

The CD continues with Bill's tune, *Cool Eddie*. After a good intro by Bullock, Bill returns to his tenor sax for this one and expertly screws the tension from slack to buzzing inside a couple of minutes. Randy adopts a rather different tack as he explores the harmonic possibilities of this monochordal vamp, but his solo still attracts a strong reaction from the audience. Dave Kikoski shifts from organ to acoustic piano for his own improvisation that is full of complex rhythms, tinkling blue chords, and even a classical-style cadenza.

The next track is a previously unknown tune by Randy called *Mixed Grill*. Once again, it features a primary melody that is harmonically divorced from the underpinning chords, as well as a bridging section of tumbling notes played by the ensemble. The modal nature shoehorns the music into a slightly uneasy vibe for much of the improvisations, but the final bridges provide plenty of scope for imaginations to break loose.

Alongside in the running order comes Randy's *Hangin' In The City*. Randroid's rambling, strongly accented descriptions of life in NYC make a welcome humorous change in the mood of the programme, as well as a good lead into the final track, *Dixie Hop*, a selection that was included in Bill's album *Touch* (1999). Their jointly improvised duet at the start is a great intro to the superbly played bop theme that kicks the piece off. The bulk of the music at the core of this track is improvisation of intense drive and creativity. This is "soulbop" at its best.

There is a great deal to enjoy on this excellent album, with its varied and interesting menu, but we should remember that it is very much intended to be a record of live entertainment rather than a studio album with the kind of innovative cuts we may have become used to.

Randy Brecker with Michael Brecker: *Some Skunk Funk* **– 2005 (****)**

On 11 November 2003, a Brecker Brothers lookalike band played a live gig with the WDR Big Band Köln, under the direction of Vince Mendoza. It was Randy and Michael, with Will Lee, Jim Beard, Peter Erskine and the Argentinian percussionist, Marcio Doctor. The gig was part of the *Leverkusener Jazztage* Festival and is a significant event that now forms part of the recorded history of the Brecker Brothers. This is the only time that "the band" recorded with a large group, a key part of which is always the arrangements that will be used. It's a brave move to take a winning formula and change it. Rock bands don't dare to try. Jazzers, however, do it with joy and great care. It is a decision that is not without risk, for the music could be so strictly charted that it sounds restrictive and dull. With so many musicians involved, and without the experience gained by a band that has played together a lot, the discipline required to keep the music tight in a one-off gig such as this is considerable. So, much of the success of the gig is in the hands of the conductor / arranger – in this case, Vince Mendoza. But Randy had, as I said, chosen carefully.

Vince Mendoza (b1961, Connecticut) learned guitar and trumpet in his youth, and continued to play the latter in the Jazz Band of the Ohio State University where he graduated in music in 1983. He learned the art of arranging whilst running his own Big Band at University, and then moved to the

University of Southern California to further his studies in composition. His records as leader began with the release of *Start Here* (1990) and *Instructions Inside* (1991), and over the years since then he contributed to six Grammy award-winning albums, including Joni Mitchell's *Both Sides Now* (2000) and *Travelogue* (2002). He would win one for this record too.

The WDR Big Band of Cologne, whilst being around in its present form for over twenty years, has far older roots. Associated with German radio since the early post-war years, when it was a popular form of entertainment to broadcast big band dance music, the band was originally the Cologne Radio Dance Orchestra. Over the years from the late 1950s to the 1980s, it evolved into the WDR Big Band, thanks to the efforts of Kurt Edelhagen and Werner Muller. In the 2000s the band has become one of the most sought-after European groups to perform with, as this record testifies.

The album opens with a version of the BB theme tune, *Some Skunk Funk*, which has been played at seriously scary pace ("as fast as humanly possible!") over the years. Here, however, it is played at a somewhat calmer tempo necessitated by the large group, but is nonetheless full of fire and energy, thanks to the combined efforts of the rhythm section, and the tightness that is only seduced from the most experienced musicians. Michael takes a solo break from 1.26 in his inimitable fluid style, oozing raw energy. Randy's break begins with a change of mood to a quieter vibe from 3.25, and then, with his burning rhythm comrades, he proceeds to lead the remaining musicians to greater and greater performance levels. After a final run through the theme, the piece explodes with shrapnel.

The BB back-catalogue continues with *Sponge*, and some edgy harmonies from the band as the descending theme is played. Once again it is Mike's turn for first solo, and, as he improvises, the band takes the piece through its familiar paces behind him. The result is in the realms of organised chaos, which is exciting and different. Then, at 3.18, Randy changes the mood again, as he did previously, to improvise in one of his parallel harmony strategies. The piece ends with another of Vince's good climaxes.

The third track is a terrific arrangement of *Shanghigh*, one of Randy's tunes recorded on 34th *N Lex* (2002), and played here with solos from WDR musicians, Paul Shigihara (guitar), Heiner Wiberny (alto saxophone), Ludwig Nuss (trombone) and Jim Beard (piano). A loose, but fascinating, version of *Wayne Out*, a Randy tune that first appeared on *Hangin' In The City* (2000), is next in the running order. Besides some fantastic ensemble playing, and a pulsating solo from Randy, Olivier Peters plays a solo on soprano saxophone. The final bars are extraordinarily penetrating, especially when played at the appropriate volume. The contrast with the next track, *And Then She Wept* taken from *Out Of The Loop* (1994), is stunning as Randy fronts a luscious, smooth backwash of colourful harmony. Jim Beard plays a good solo on acoustic piano, but it is Randy's tune and he leads the band through six minutes of glorious ballad.

Another BB tune, not recorded since the original, is *Straphangin'*, and it is Mike who once again, stamps his presence over the first half of this super revision of the piece, but the listener should always keep one ear on the big band behind which, under Mendoza's direction, contribute significantly to the tense of this fine performance. The second half is under Randy's piercing lance, with the WDR boys winding things up to a glorious final section in which Mike and Randy play chicken in alternate four bar shouts. With the full band blowing hard behind them, this piece is nothing less than a triumph.

Randy's *Let It Go*, also from 34th *N Lex* (2002), is track 7, and is eminently suited to the Big Band format. Randy's solo during the third minute is electrified, and Will's strong, funky bass is fully in evidence, accompanying Jim Beard's organ solo. Ludwig Nuss's trombone solo is dextrous and in nice contrast with Michael's tenor sax finale. The last two minutes are given over to an ensemble arragement of the theme in which the soloists, come and go like will o' the wisps on a windy day.

Freefall, is a fast, straightahead piece, in best mould of late 20th century Big Band music, and it serves to remind listeners of just how far removed is the style from the new formats that grew out of 1970s fusion and are represented here on the other nine tracks of this CD. For all his fusion and electric credentials, Randy has never left the school of mainstream jazzers, and every so often he likes to remind us of it.

The penultimate track is *Levitate*, which was one of the first songs to appear on a BB album in 1975. Here, its overdue reappearance is given after a makeover in which it remains a superbly contemplative ballad, luxuriantly rich in new colour, thanks to Mendoza's creativity.

The more recent *Song For Barry*, taken from *Return Of The Brecker Brothers* (1992), begins with a percussion solo by Marcio Doctor which makes a good introduction to this ten-minute band spectacular. Mike's tenor and Randy's muted horn celebrate this great song together, with Paul Shigihara's guitar making a nice texture in the background. From four and a half minutes, the tenor saxophone remembers its animated alter ego, and succeeds in injecting high energy. By six minutes, the band is in full flight for thirty seconds as it introduces Randy with a samba rhythm that he loves to work with. At eight minutes, the pace has changed once more to accommodate Shigihara's rock guitar sound, through which Erskine & Co. lead the stampede towards a highly satisfying mega-climax. As all great CDs do, this one leaves all but the most fussy listener shouting out loud and pleading for more, as is proven by the concert hall audience. This CD sparkles and thrills from start to finish, and was justifiably awarded a Grammy in 2006 for "Best Large Jazz Ensemble Album." As Tony Williams once said, "Play It Loud."

Michael Brecker: *Pilgrimage* – 2007 (****)

On 29 August 2004, Michael Brecker was in Tokyo at the *Mount Fuji Jazz Festival* to take part in a Steps Ahead Reunion concert. He lined up alongside Mike Mainieri, Steve Gadd, Mike Stern, Daryll Jones and Adam Holzman. Whilst playing, it is said that he suffered from a severe pain in his back, and after seeking medical advice, he was diagnosed in 2005 with MDS (myelodysplastic syndrome), a blood disorder for which cures are mostly unknown. It was a severe shock, and, over the next couple of years, he and his family were subjected to a long fight against the disease.

Michael was planning a new album, and had collected nine songs to record, but his health was deteriorating rapidly and the project seemed impossible. He was close to death in November 2005, when his daughter Jessica became a donor for her dad in a new medical procedure. Sadly, any benefit he derived from it was only temporary. It began to look as if he would never play again. Then, in June 2006, Herbie Hancock persuaded Michael to make a surprise appearance with him at a concert in Carnegie Hall. They played Herbie's tune, *One Finger Snap*, and Michael received a standing ovation. It was his last public performance, but was a trigger for Michael to proceed with recording his last album. The sessions finally took place in August. [80]

The album was planned as a straightahead 'live' acoustic jazz project, but there would be no cover numbers, or retrospectives. The only association with the past would be his relationships with his fellow musicians, and the years of experience he had gained playing the saxophone. This was a collection of Michael's most advanced thinking to date, with interpretations by five of the finest creative minds in the jazz world. But it was the final appearance for this Dream Team. Every musician was the best in his own niche, but perhaps most importantly, all the players already knew each other very well. Herbie Hancock: uncontested first choice for Miles Davis during his finest years, and incomparable in all respects; Jack DeJohnette, super-inventive avant-gardist and polyrhythmic drummer; John Patitucci: one of the most creative jazz minds on acoustic bass; Pat Metheny: best jazz guitarist ever and one of the most original jazz musicians; Brad Mehldau: best jazz pianist of his generation. And let's not forget, once again, the brilliance of Gil Goldstein, who was Michael's right-hand man for the project and whose arrangements were from the top drawer.

There are numerous interpretations of the title of the opening track, *The Mean Time*. Certainly Michael has always been fascinated by rhythm, as we saw in his earlier albums. Listeners unfamiliar to jazz of this kind need to forget all they know about the typical plunk-plunk-plunk-plunk bass or the tum-tumty-tum-tumty drums playing four-in-a-bar swing-time rhythms of jazz from earlier decades. Ever since the 1960s, with the presence of Tony Williams in Miles's quintet and his polyrhythmic drumming techniques, exponents of the most advanced jazz have completely abandoned these old styles of rhythm. Throughout this track, but especially during the improvisation sections, it is instructive to listen to the work of bass and drums, and to see how instinctively they react to what is being played by the soloist.

Michael has always wanted to experiment in his work, but almost never to the total absence of musical form. From the start, we are presented with another of his unusual melodies, and Herbie interjects chimes, as if from a striking clock. Mike's melodies are often repeated, as here, and then sections of improvisation follow during which he may, depending upon the immediacy of the situation he detects from his band, deviate to a greater or lesser degree into uncharted tonal spaces. More likely is that he will go where he feels is best and hope his men follow. With these guys, they always do. After his own spot, Pat and Herbie follow him. At 5.50, there is a most remarkable orchestrated section that requires total concentration from all. It leads into a final recitation of the main melody and the coda. This kind of stuff is of exceptionally high quality and pretty much what we have come to expect from him.

With the second track, *Five Months From Midnight*, the number five seems to be a reference to a five beat rhythm that is clear later in the piece. However, the start is one of those constructions with a secret metric, unfathomable without the written music, and especially without the regular beat of drums or bass. Michael's melody floats in space, with its accompanying escorts, and we must simply relax and soak it up. His playing shows no sign of the weakness we might expect and the development of his themes is performed as perfectly as usual. Brad's presence is apparent by his strongly melodic accompaniment, much different from the more broken style of Herbie.

The third track, *Anagram*, resides in a rather more abstract musical space, mainly because of its modal design. From the start, a rhythmic phrase appears on bass, which seems like a good anchorage. The two main modes, separated by a musical fourth, are alternated, and provide the common chordal base – so far so good, but this is soon overwhelmed by Mike's unquantifiable 8-second melody line that defies all gravity. (The eight seconds from 0.14 to 0.22 or from 8.42 to 8.50 are good examples.) John and Jack set up a fast regular beat for the improvisations, with the two chord centres used to keep things together. A better idea of it can be gained from listening to the final section from 8.50, which focuses on a drum solo. But there is so much more in this extremely complex music. I guess you'll just have to solve your own puzzles with this one. Let's see now… agraman, amargan, argaman, gamarna, managra…

If you can catch it, *Tumbleweed* is more approachable. The rolling rhythm is set up from the start, and the theme enters after twenty seconds. There is a repeat, with Metheny added, as well as an unidentified voice. The third minute is filled with the sound of Pat's guitar synthesiser that builds a great tension into the fourth. By the fifth minute Michael is well into an improvised solo that simply gets better and better. Brad Mehldau's improvisation is heavy with chords and freethinking. The now familiar theme returns at 7.30, by which time the track has been marked out as one of the album's highlights.

When Can I Kiss You Again? is a ballad for grown-ups. On that basis, we might expect it not to meet everyone's expectations. It doesn't have any of the romance or sentimentality that many listeners might look for, but the melody meant a lot to Michael. In the circumstances, we'd all like this one to be special.

Cardinal Rule is another fine example of the complicated structures Michael uses. My analysis is clinical, but necessary in appreciating just how this music works. Needless to say, all links are so fluid that the uninformed listener should simply sit back and enjoy a single, exciting, original, music composition played by some of the best jazz musicians in the world. Identifiable sections are: 0 - 0.10 piano intro; theme A: 0.10 to 0.18 (8s); theme B: 0.18 to 0.30 (12s); theme A: 0.30 to 0.38 (8s); theme B: 0.38 to 0.50 (12s); theme C: 1.00 to 1.10 (10s); theme C repeated to 1.10 (10s); theme D: 1.10 to 1.22 (12s); repeated 1.22 to 1.34 (12s). A bass improvisation starts from 1.35; Michael takes it up from 2.30 for 26s, and then Mehldau at 2.56 for another 26s. Following this, Michael and Brad perform a very good improvised duet, especially when they stitch sheets together in the very exciting fifth minute. The pattern begins again at 5.25 with the sections outlined above. The repetition of theme D sounds like it's intended to be the end at 6.25, but there is an improvised coda from that point with Michael and drums exploring all points of the compass.

There is a slight Latin feel to the rhythm of *Half Moon Lane*, its gentle conventional pace staking out a position on the milder end of the spectrum of contents. The early playing is marked by a dichotomy of harmony between Pat and Mike, who occasionally come together, only to split again, like a tall and a short ballet dancer in a *pas de deux*. The main improvised section begins from 2.12, at which point the mood is most definitely of moonlight and romance. Then, like all good explorers, Michael moves the piece forward into a denser environment. Metheny takes it back a notch or two, through to 5.16, whereupon the original theme returns.

Loose Threads is the kind of thing Don Grolnick would have liked. Its perfectly synchronised collage of sonic ejaculations feels equivalent to a Jackson Pollock painting. Don was a devotee of the unexpected and the humorous. After all, when music is predictable, it must surely be less exciting? Musicians may choose to cut themselves off from the world, but Michael was never one of those. Neither was Don. Both thrived on connections with the audience, as well as with each other. They wanted to entertain and excite their listeners. They understood the need for syntax as an aid to understanding. So, unlike Pollock, you can find pattern and thought, and artistry, and message, and yes – occasionally humour, in this music, but you have to look for it. Most of us find the effort worthwhile. Just one more thing – Michael's improvisation on this track is exceptional. It caused Herbie to remark, "Wait a minute Michael, are you sure you're still sick?" [80]

Pilgrimage is a fitting final track. It is a conventional composition on which Herbie performs on electric keyboard, and Michael says good-bye with his EWI, a symbol of his contribution to the tech-age and a wholly new instrument that became an important part of his musical persona. But Michael will be remembered almost entirely for his devotion to the sound and development of saxophone playing. Fittingly, therefore, there are elements of John Coltrane's style in the opening 2 minutes and 45 seconds. The timeless, improvised saxophone incantation marks the end of one of the most wonderful careers in the history of jazz.

With hindsight, listeners will search for every indication of poignancy about this album, and there is, indeed, an undeniable sense of sadness that seeps out with its playing. Sure, everyone knew that Michael was a very sick man, but tried not to show it. Michael found everything hard, both physically and mentally, but the album is as good as any of the others in its class and better than some. We must credit the class of his sidemen, but the album is very much Michael's, through and through.

Given the timing and circumstances of the making of this record, there is an inevitable link with things beyond music. However, I am sure that Michael would not have wanted his album to carry the burden of association with anything other than being one of his best albums – and it is. So, looking for poignancy on this disc is an unrewarding search. During the recordings, Michael deliberately made light of the way he was feeling. He wanted to keep the focus on music, not on medical issues. So there was no concession to sickness – and it shows. Michael's wife, Susan, was amazed that Michael managed to get through it. "I believe it was his spirit, his wanting to complete the record, that kept him alive a lot longer than really was humanly possible given his physical condition," she said. [80]

Michael passed away on 13 January 2007. Five weeks later, on 20 February, a celebration of Michael's life was held in Manhattan Town Hall. Herbie Hancock and Paul Simon performed the song, *Still Crazy After All These Years*. Speaking during the service, Pat Metheny said, "His efforts to get this final message out to all of us on *Pilgrimage* will go down as one of the great codas in modern music history." [80]

Randy Brecker: *Randy in Brasil* – 2008 (*****)

In 2006, Randy began to plan yet another new kind of album in which he supplanted himself into a wholly Brazilian context thereby to follow his creative muse. It turned out to be a brilliant success. Thanks to his many Brazilian connections, he was able to assemble a band of the finest musicians, including Ruriá Duprat (keyboards), Teco Cardoso (saxophone), Ricardo Silveira (guitar) and Sizão Machado (bass).

The album was recorded in São Paolo in November 2006, under the direction of the multi-talented Brazilian musician, Ruriá Duprat. He was a nephew of Rogerio Duprat, who contributed to the highly influential album, *Tropicalia* (1968) from which arose a famous artistic movement known as Tropicalia or Tropicalismo, a fusion of Brazilian and foreign influences. When aged 21, Ruriá wrote to Quincy Jones using an address he took from the back cover of Michael Jackson's *Thriller* album. He sent samples of his work, and told Quincy that he would like to study at Berklee but couldn't afford it. Q kindly sponsored him through five years of study at Berklee. Finally, he was able to take the stage at the Grammy awards ceremony in 2009 to receive the award for "Best Contemporary Jazz Album." It was the first time a Brazilian producer had received such an award. He was chosen to be musical director of the Rio de Janeiro Orchestra for Diana Krall's *Live in Rio* (2008) concert tour.

Teco Cardoso (b1960, São Paolo) is widely regarded as the leading Brazilian saxophone player, a fact that is immediately apparent from the opening track, *Pedro Brasil*. Written by Djavan Viana, this piece is at once reminiscent of many performed by bands such as Spyro Gyra. After the catchy opening rhythmic phrase played on piano and guitar, Cardoso's soprano saxophone is the perfect match to Randy's sweet tones and the pair of instruments deliver the melody with grace. The sound is light, fresh and smooth, a true South American cocktail with that highly infectious rhythm that goes straight to a listener's feet. From 2.15, Randy's improvised solo is exquisite for its context, flawlessly invented on the fly yet with textbook compliance to conventional harmonies.

Gilberto Gil Moreira, simply known as Gilberto Gil (b1942) wrote the second tune on the album, *Ilê Ayê*. The music is much more animated, with Da Lua's energetic percussion that is surely typical of the partying street drummers. Meanwhile, the tune is dominated by a memorable melodic phrase that is repeated in different ways. Once again, Randy plays a couple of improvised choruses over the entire composition as Duprat's synthesiser backing converts the music from ethnic Brazilian into modern smooth jazz. His creative additions add much to the music, and Cardoso's saxophone playing is joyful.

Guaruja is the first of Randy's two compositions. Named after a beautiful coastal municipality to the south of São Paolo, the musical suggestion is of paradise and palm trees. Randy's melody is suitably delicious and supplemented by Ricardo Silveira who plays an atmospheric electric guitar solo, as well as some gentle acoustic guitar accompaniment. The chorus is sexy and perfectly fitted inside the structure of Randy's composition, whilst producer Duprat uses his experience with movie scores to add some atmospheric sounds of the seashore.

Me Leve (Take Me) is the second of Djavan's four pieces on the album. Another very melodic track with Randy playing a delightful tune in unison with Cardoso's soprano sax and Silveria contributing electric and acoustic guitar. Machado's bass playing is especially noticeable, and worth listening to see how different the style is from the usual jazz-funk bass lines. Besides another flawless improvisation from Randy, from 2.44, Duprat plays a great synthesiser solo.

Djavan's *Malásia* (Malaysia) is performed under the strong influence of Cardoso now playing flute, a lovely change of musical texture and colour. Some wonderful harmonies are now brought gloriously to the foreground, and matched against an embedded combination of 6-beat and 4-beat metres. From 1.25 (and again from 4.10), the aleady sombre, mystical sound is focussed into a chorus that is devastingly poignant. The track is a triumph of composition, arrangement and execution. However, I have to say that the accompanying notes are frustratingly inadequate, for there is a fine improvisation on fretless bass that is unrecognised therein, but we must assume is Machado. This is by no means the only error.

There are no prizes for guessing the derivation of the title of Randy's second contribution, *Sambop*, a lively tune with the flamboyant rhythm of the samba matched to an instantly likeable boppish tune voiced wordlessly by Rubinho Ribeiro who adds to Randy's headline melody. But the composition is not limited to that formula, for further interest is added by means of intervening sections that float rhythmlessly between the rocking solos. Each re-entry into the samba is achieved perfectly, especially at 3.13 when the transition to Duprat's acoustic piano solo is quite stunning.

Oriente (East) is the second of Gil's pieces, which, in this short arrangement, puts the Brazilian theme to one side and explores Gil's dark creation in the form of a jazz-fusion piece with lots of sound effects drawn from Duprat's special skills in producing film scores. The track is followed by *Maçã* (Apple), the fourth and last of Djavan's compositions, with Cardoso playing flute once more. After a straight performance of the simple tune, Randy ripens the fruit into stunning sweet, juicy, trumpet lines that are exciting and beautiful. The mixing on this, as on all tracks, is notably fine, with not just the star trumpter, but all musicians heard to perform in perfect balance.

Olhos Puxados (Slanted Eyes) was written by guitarist Joao Bosco (b1946). A gentle happy samba with Randy playing a sweet melody and embossed by smooth soprano saxophone from Cardoso. Perhaps a little predictable in harmonic structure, the piece is no less attractive if this kind of relaxed vibe is your thing. Once again, it is the sheer brilliance of Randy's improvised melodic lines that stands out, as he never seems to fail in creating the most inventive music that relates to both the listener and to the composer's intentions. The same mood continues with *Rebento* (Shoot), the third of Gil's tunes to make the track list. The prominence of the delightful acoustic guitar backing is strongly reminiscent of all those Getz / Byrd / Gilberto collaborations of the 1960s, except for the substitution of the gorgeous Getz sound by Randy's beautiful horn.

A change is introduced for *Fazendo Hora* (Doing Time), a composition by Gilson Peranzetta who is also present playing acoustic piano. Peranzetta is a classically trained musician who has worked extensively both inside and outside the borders of his native Brazil. He has worked with singers Shirley Horn, Sarah Vaughan and Diane Schuur, and is highly rated by Quincy Jones and George Benson. For this music, Duprat chose a different acoustic bass player called Rogerio, whilst retaining the services of Silveira playing nylon-stringed acoustic guitar. The title is most appropriate for this languid, lovely piece of Latin jazz, headlined by Randy's luscious flugelhorn sound.

There's no translation for *Aiaiai*, an onamatapoeic word that speaks for itself, though it is listed as *Ai Ai Ai de Mim* on the CD, another frustrating error in the package. The track was written by Ivan Lins (b1945) who since 1970 has become one of Brazil's leading songwriters. Lins became more famous outside of Brazil when he worked with Dave Grusin and Lee Ritenour on the successful GRP album *Harlequin* (1984). The music is sited less in the expected Brazilian ethnic mould, and is more of a fusion with American genres. Randy is animated and takes the album out on an energetic climax.

It could easily be the case that a high profile solo artist could take on a project such as this and totally dominate the performances. That is entirely not the case here. Randy knows well how frustrating it can be for great musicians to be frustrated by a lack of contribution to these kinds of projects. But here Randy blends superbly into each composition to create the different vibes required. As the lead artist he naturally comes into the foreground from time to time to play his allocated lead melody line or improvised solo, but space is always present for the other talented musicians to express themselves. Fans of Latin music will thoroughly enjoy this beautifully presented album. One of its great points - and there are many - is the fine balance in selection of material. The album maintains the extraordinarily high level of performance, arrangements, performance and mixing that is often so elusive. Low on machismo, and high on beautiful sounds, this album is likely to achieve a high position on the playlists of many listeners.

Randy Brecker: Nostalgic Journey: Tykocin Jazz Suite – 2009 (****)

In a search for his family roots, Randy found himself in northeast Poland and the small town of Tykocin. As a result of what turned out to be an emotional visit, Polish composer, pianist and jazz musician, Wlodek Pawlik composed an hour-long suite of music that he entitled *Nostalgic Journey*. The nine tracks contained on this CD are a synthesis of jazz with classical European music - what was named 'Third Stream' by Gunther Schuller in 1957.

Any search for information about Tykocin, immediately reveals a horror story that tells of the 1941 Nazi pogrom in which virtually all of the village's Jewish population was taken to the outskirts of the town and executed. It would be remarkable – even shameful - if a musical composition purporting to be about Tykocin did not refer to this terrible moment in its history. It is unsurprising, therefore, that there are Jewish references, and moments of great sadness contained herein. However, the music is generally uplifting, with sections of exquisite beauty. As Pawlik wrote on the notes, "This music is a great affirmation of life." [81] Much of the music contains Randy playing alongside Wlodek Pawlik on piano, Pawel Panita on double bass and Cezary Konrad on drums. There are also sections in which the quartet is joined by the Podlaise Opera and Philharmonic Orchestra. Readers who enjoy mainstream jazz with a soupcon of concert orchestra, will thoroughly enjoy this very different member of Randy's catalogue.

The orchestral opening, entitled *Introduction* is a good summary for anyone who has never visited this region. Randy then performs the joyful title track alongside the trio, with some fine blending with the orchestra. *Let's All Go To Heaven* is a celebration of an event for which I hope to postpone my visit to the booking office. I must admit, Pawlik's interpretation sounds like fun. *No Words* is a somewhat disappointing composition, unchallenging and derivative, it doesn't improve with further listening. The final two tracks, however, make up for that with some interesting and well-performed mainstream jazz. *Magic Seven* has allusions to Judaism, although the number seven is important in many civilisations. It is a substantial piece that is satisfying and dynamic. Whereas the composer could have chosen to end on the depressing note that rather sums up the region's dark clouds of history, instead, he goes out on a high, with the lively and energetic track, *Blue Rain*.

Randy further developed his relationship with Pawlik when he agreed to take part in celebrations for the 1850th anniversary of Kalisz, the oldest city in Poland. In June 2010, a concert called *Night in Calisia* was such a success that a decision was made to record the material played. As a result, the album entitled *Randy Brecker Plays Wlodek Pawlik's Night in Calisia* was released in 2013. The six tracks of this straightahead album were recorded with Pawlik's Trio, together with the Kalisz Philharmonic Orchestra conducted by Adam Klocek.

Randy Brecker: Jamey Abersold's Play Along Jazz, Volume 126 – 2009 (****)

For those of us fortunate enough to be able to read music, thirteen of Randy's wonderful compositions are brought alive in a different way by the written charts presented in Volume 126 of *Jamey Abersold's Jazz* series. Randy himself oversaw the creation of the written music and the play-along CDs. He also played the trumpet lines to the charts; where necessary, Ada Rovatti played the tenor saxophone lines. The tunes are all presented as straight ahead jazz compositions, with only occasional references to fusion. Even Randy's classic *Some Skunk Funk* is arranged in swing time rhythm, although the flavour of the original is well preserved. This is not a book for beginners. The music herein is perfectly designed for good students who already have well-developed instrumental skills, and the results, once learned, can easily be used for stage and club performances. Four charts are provided for each tune, in concert pitch (treble clef and bass clef), as well as in Bb and Eb pitch for transposing instruments. Chord sequences are also provided.

Randy Brecker With DR Big Band: *The Jazz Ballad Song Book* – 2011 (****)

In January 2010, Randy went to Copenhagen to record an album of ballads with the DR (Danish Radio) Big Band. Randy was following in the footsteps of a series of great guest musicians who had worked with the band, including Miles Davis, Stan Getz and Joe Henderson. The band had been formed in 1964 by DR's head of entertainment, Niels-Jørgen Kaiser, with the aim of supporting and promoting a thriving jazz community in Denmark. Since that time, the band's focus has always been artistic integrity over commercial interests. Following the 2008 appointment of MD Chris Minh Doky, the band has performed with Chris Potter and Mike Stern, as well as Randy.

On this very successful album a mix of traditional standards such as *'Round Midnight*, *Someday My Prince Will Come*, *All Or Nothing At All*, and Ella Fitzgerald's classic *Cry Me A River* are juxtaposed with less well known songs like Hoagy Carmichael's *Skylark*, and popular tunes like the James Bond theme to *Goldfinger*. The Andy Williams hit song, *This Is All I Ask* is also included, along with two of Randy's own tunes, *I Talk To The Trees*, and *Foregone Conclusion*. Needless to say, the recording is a must-listen CD for fans of the Big Band sound, and Randy's playing is quite exemplary.

Randy Brecker: The Brecker Brothers Band Reunion – 2013 (****)

At first sight, the album ID seems odd: How can this be a new album by the Brecker Brothers - without Michael? However, Randy has chosen his words carefully. This is a Randy Brecker record, and it documents the reuniting of some of the original members of the band. Once again, Randy's close friend and associate, George Whitty plays the major role of producer, as well as playing keyboards and creating some of the magical soundscapes. This is a superb package that consists of a CD crammed with 73 minutes of new music and a bonus DVD, 1 hour 38 minutes in duration, recorded live during the band's week-long 2011 gig at the *Blue Note*, New York. As such, it is one of the best value packages currently available.

Of the core members of the original band, Will Lee and David Sanborn make a welcome return. Old friend Mike Stern is back too, along with Dave Weckl, Adam Rogers, Chris Minh Doky, and Rodney Holmes.

Randy's wife, Ada Rovatti, takes on the unenviable task of playing tenor saxophone. When I suggested to George Whitty that it was the toughest act to follow, he replied, "Yeah, it's impossible, and in my opinion, she does the right thing, which is, you don't try to play Mike. To me, it's almost like, instead of taking someone who is a Mike fanatic, Ada is coming a little more out of, like a Wayne Shorter idea, especially on soprano. And, you know, play your own self on it, and that's exactly what she does. I could think of one or two guys who could step in there and try and play it the way Mike played it, but all that makes is comparisons, and any point where they're not as brilliant as Mike – it's a let down. Whereas, if you get in there, and play yourself, people are open to it. I know that Ada feels like it's a very hot, hot seat, you know, you're stepping right in the footprints of the icons." [61]

A wonderful new addition to the band is Oli Rockberger. Born in London, Rockberger took up residence in the USA after completing a scholarship at Berklee Music College from 1999-2004. Composer, keyboard player and vocalist, he has impressed many listeners with his solo albums, as well as appearing with such artists as Levon Helm, Jackie DeShannon, Gloria Gaynor, Jesse Harris, John Mayer, Les McCann and Charlie Hunter. George Whitty speaks very highly of his abilities. "When we did the gigs at the Blue Note he came up and sang a tune or two, and played… Oli Rockberger is a real genius. He's a songwriter right at the very top, in my book. There's a record of his called *Hush Now*. It's pretty much just him playing piano, and I think he made it in his apartment at Berklee, and I bought that a couple of years ago. When I found out that he was going to be involved with this CD, I said well, let me see who this is, and it's become one of my very favourite CDs in the interim. Couldn't be simpler, piano and voice, but just the strength of the song writing is crazy." [61]

Of the other new faces, fusion guitarist Mitch Stein is a very experienced session musician who first met the Brecker Brothers during gigs with the Don Alias All-Star Band in 2000. At the time of his appearance on this CD, Stein had become best known for his strong relationship with Rodney Holmes and Kip Reed in the band, Hermanators, formed in 1999 and their album *Twisted* (1999).

Multi-instrumentalist James Campagnola is a New Yorker and popular session player who knows all of these musicians well. On this CD, he plays baritone saxophone on two tracks.

The opening track is called *First Tune Of The Set*, a cut in the classic BB mould. After an up-tempo intro from keyboard that rocks between D# / G# and D / G, the main theme is played, Skunk-Funk-style, by Randy and Ada in series of variations that clash harmonically with the keyboard. Dean Brown fills the gaps in between with white-hot riffs that cover the first 1.10 of the track. Then a short middle section changes tack, before the original theme returns again. From 1.45, a new section begins with Weckl's drums and continues with George's keyboards. Repeated downward phrases catch the ear as they lead towards Randy's solo at 2.35, played to a high-energy samba rhythm. The whole vibe of the piece takes on a smoother cast for a minute, whereupon Stern takes over to play one of his characteristically fluid improvisations. Soon, Randy and Mike are sharing eights to great effect. From 5.25, it's George's turn, and the mood hardens into a dark, throbbing façade, with Will Lee's angry bass behind. The final repeat of the heads begins at 6.50, and the piece goes out on a neat high at 7.22. It's a great tune to open the set with - a position in which I assume it will be locked, *in perpetuity*.

Stellina is a lighter, more melodic, happy piece, built around some of Randy's most tuneful ideas, and dedicated to his young daughter. It is Latin-flavoured, with evolving chord sequences made more solid by Ada's tenor sax lines. Will Lee's crisp bass lines are nicely present in the foreground as Randy's mature flugelhorn tones wash cleanly over us like waves of warm water. From 3.40, Ada takes on an improvisation that is refreshingly different, but just as liquid. A minute later, George's electric piano develops the mood still further, and a minute after that, the piece runs through the original theme to conclude a most relaxing piece of modern jazz.

The third track is *The Dipshit*, a very different kind of child with 1970s parents. A cool, mid-tempo piece with a great bluesy gait, it lays off with Dave Sanborn joining Randy and Ada in the front line, and rendering one of his classic solos derived from times past. By four minutes, Adam Rogers has taken up the torch and shows a great deal of influence from John Scofield and Bill Frissell as he plays through his great solo. The whole pastiche is improved with the backing of George's Hammond B3 organ sound. It's a tune that will make all alumni from the old school feel extremely comfortable.

In the fourth slot is the first of two tracks featuring newcomer Oli Rockberger. *Merry Go Town* is a joint composition from Oli and Ada, in which Oli demonstrates the kind of brilliance that George referred to above. The melody is instantly catchy, with sticky phrases and wonderful chord sequences that are so good they should have been used years ago, but weren't. As such, this is a wholly uncharacteristic item in the BB repertoire, yet it could be voted best-on-album by many listeners. Essential to the mix are Ada's incredible creations on soprano saxophone, played with exquisite tone and mouth-watering technique. For once, the other musicians don't stand out, but that makes for the ultimate in musicianship, with each musician contributing exactly the right amount to George's beautiful sound-plan. This track is my idea of musical perfection.

The Slag is a seriously funky tune with elements from other genres thanks to the imagination of the players. Rodney Holmes's crisp drum accompaniment, Will Lee's strong funk bass lines, Mitch Stein's heavy metal rock guitar sounds, and George's honky-tonk piano - all support the sax and trumpet themes that once more hark back to earlier Brecker Brothers recordings. A superb descending, chromatic bridge-section has echoes of Weather Report's *Birdland* at 2.12 (and also at 5.22). Then, from 2.30, Randy begins a solo using his well-used electrified wah-wah sound, with George again using his Hammond sound. Mike Stern continues the wah-wah theme over a vamp as cold as an Arctic summer. Finally, from 5.55, the Birdland-style theme is developed into an excellent ending at 6.32.

Randy's humour is on display once again in *Really In For It*, as his alter ego, Randroid, makes an appearance. The piece is modelled on others that Randy wrote for *Hangin' In The City* (2001), although he actually wrote the original idea in the early 1970s. This one is wickedly funny. Much of the vibe is based upon the style developed by Maz & Kilgore in their streetwise constructions for *Return of the Brecker Brothers* and *Out Of The Loop*. Here, the style has been refined still further to give Randroid scope for serious mischief. Randy's muted trumpet is to the fore, whilst baritone sax licks and sharp bass riffs add to the rich sounds of a four-horn front line. A bonus is the presence of David Sanborn, whose acid tone etches a solo supported by the funkiest of backings by the rhythm section. This great groove takes the piece out with impeccable style.

The album would have been incomplete without proper reference to Michael Brecker, and it with his composition, *Elegy For Mike* that Randy says thanks to his brother. It's enough for me to describe it as a beautiful, personal statement, in which Ada once more demonstrates great lyricism.

Randy teams up with Oli in the composition *On The Rise*. The straightahead vocal from Oli is set against Randroid's more serious rap guise, but this tune is more about Oli's unique imagination than it is about oddball vocalising. From the start, Will Lee picks up an unusual bass line that underpins the richly diverse accompaniment. Adam Rogers's special style is added to great effect, horn ensembles splash colour everywhere, and, at the root of everything is George Whitty's masterful design.

The next track is *Adina*, named after Randy's wife. It begins with a slick, sophisticated blend of horns in the style of the best 1990s smooth jazz, but with Randy's unique harmonic stamp. As the music progresses through his solo, he leads the band farther and farther off-piste. There is something very special about the blend of tones from trumpet and soprano saxophone, and when these two instruments are played well together, as they are here, the tonality is like honey and ice cream. The overall effect of this piece is of a carefully crafted, delicious piece of home cooking.

In contrast, *R N Bee* is a strange insect, that occasionally makes rapid steps in unexpected directions, and whose sting is unpredictable both in timing and effect. After the ensemble description, Randy's interpretation is more scientific, and relates to a species and genus that is exciting rather than deadly. Ada's take adds further evidence that the beast is not as dangerous as he looks, but should be handled with care. Rodney Holmes masterfully takes over for the final couple of minutes, and the piece ends with a fade as Mr Bee disappears from view. Overall, this excellent composition has no direct competitors, and is a uniquely fine piece in the RB catalogue.

This already very good album concludes with a brilliantly funny classic blues tune called *Musician's Ol' Lady Dues Blues*, sung by Randroid to an accompaniment from Randy's shiniest blues trumpet and Adam Rogers' impeccably polished guitars. It completes an album of great variety and entertainment value that makes a perfect addition to the collection of modern jazz-fusion albums.

I suspect that many readers will be tempted to go straight to the bonus DVD for their first exposure to this album. If you do, you will find an excellent documentary of music, edited from the band's gigs at the *Blue Note*, New York. The band is the same on all tracks, and is composed of Randy and Ada, with Will Lee, George Whitty, Dave Weckl and Mike Stern. Oli Rockberger joins for a freer performance of *Merry Go Town*. On the whole, the music follows the formats of the equivalent tracks on the CD, except that the improvisations are, as usual, longer. The performances are even more 'electric' than on the CD with Ada, in particular, using lots of effects on her tenor sax. The filming and editing are both excellent, and Randy's light-hearted introductions between the tracks add greatly to the experience.

Of the tracks not included on the CD, there is a superb rendition of Michael's tune *Straphangin'*, in which Mike Stern's solo really smokes, Ada and Randy play wonderful electric solos, and the funk from Dave Weckl and Will Lee is of legendary proportions. The gig ends with Randy's blues, *Inside Out*, in which everyone plays a short solo. An encore, seemingly whipped up by a happy Mike Stern, concludes the show with the inevitable, *Some Skunk Funk*, played "as fast as humanly possible."

Summaries and Analysis

Randy and Michael Brecker are two musicians who have made unique contributions to music since the late 1960s, Randy playing trumpet and flugelhorn, Michael on tenor and soprano saxophones, flute and Electronic Wind Instrument. Over a period spanning some forty years, they frequently worked closely together, but also maintained successful careers with their own projects. Immensely talented and influential as individuals, there was (arguably) a synergistic effect when they worked together, and it was this strong closeness of their relationship that further enhanced their successes as progressive developers of jazz and jazz-fusion sub-genres. It is difficult to disentangle the intertwined threads of their long, complex careers. However, we can consider the following general headings:

1. Projects in which they worked together in a series of bands known as The Brecker Brothers;
2. Projects of their own design, with or without the other brother in the bands; these are often called, 'albums as leader';
3. Contributions to projects by other musicians, whether individually or together, in which either man could be considered as a member of the band; these are often called, 'albums as sideman';
4. Contributions to projects by other musicians, whether individually or together, in which either man was performing on individual tracks and not as a formal member of a band, i.e. as a 'session musician'.

These four categories will now be discussed.

1. The Brecker Brothers Band

There were many attempts to form successful jazz-fusion bands in the years from the late 1960s. I have described how Michael and Randy contributed greatly to the experiments from the very start of the process, and although the Brecker Brothers Band was not formed until January 1975, it was then *fully* formed with clear objectives from the start. Under Randy's leadership, the band recorded six albums of innovative music based upon experience already gained from working at the cutting edge. The band conformed to the advice and requirements of its management, during the series of six albums for Arista Records released in the period from 1975 to 1981 and the result was a coherent R&B jazz-fusion band that was as successful and influential as any similar band could be. For a time it was accepted that the song form was a part of the formula for success, but as time passed, the instinct to make instrumental jazz began to dominate. Michael told an interviewer: "Our music is instrumental music so there is no social message *per se*, there are no words. We deal mostly with colours, shapes and images. You know, the bottom line is swing and that is very important to us. It's very rhythmic music and we like to get that funk in there." [82]

Cook wrote about the Brecker Brothers, "The records were catchy enough to make the R&B charts, while satisfying musos with displays of prowess." [83] Cook had identified that the band's formula had been a fine balance between concessions to the industry, retention of the jazz ethos and appropriate levels of technical achievement, and a strong measure of entertainment value in the content.

By 1981, Randy and Michael both felt that it was time to take stock, and develop their careers in other directions. They never considered that the band's existence was permanently over, and were always open to the possibility of reforming at some point. Nevertheless, as they both became busy with other projects, the window of possibilities for returning to their original group began to grow narrow. Eventually, in 1992, the Brecker Brothers were able to regroup and restart the engine that had served them so well in the past. By this time, the market and the commercial factors thought necessary for success had changed enormously; single releases, for example, were in major decline, and jazz-fusion had become less popular as a stand-alone jazz form, yet more integrated into mainstream popular strands. Nevertheless, two albums were released in 1992 and 1994 that were, arguably, and with the benefit of a great deal more experience, in a higher league compared to those from the first tranche.

In 1995, Randy said, "What we do is interpret what is happening currently in music, and we try to offer our own interpretation, along with our own interpretation of music that we have listened to in our travels throughout the world, so a lot of that comes into play, particularly music of certain parts of Africa and Brazil, and along with interpreting American pop music within our own framework." [82]

As one of the driving factors of jazz-fusion, electronics had always been part of the band's ethos, and now took on an even stronger role, thanks to the development of computers and other devices, not just for playing, but for recording and mixing too. Musicians were greatly empowered by their knowledge of methods that utilised electronic devices, and Michael, in particular, became the leading exponent of the Electronic Wind Instrument.

A curious background to the story of the Brecker Brothers should also be noted. Randy is unequivocal that the name of the band resulted from a commercially motivated demand from his original producer, Steve Backer. It had always been Randy's intention to create records under his own name and leadership. Thus, his album, *Score* (1969), was a solo album, made with Michael at his side. Similarly, the discography lists many other occasions when Randy made records of his own with Michael in his band and/or contributing his own compositions. So Randy was the *de facto* bandleader in The Brecker Brothers, with all that that entails: writing and arranging most of the music, overseeing (to say the least) much of the production, not to mention many of the management functions. Thus, readers need to consider a far wider range of recordings when looking for music in the style of The Brecker Brothers.

2. Albums As Leaders

As we have seen, throughout his career, Randy wanted to make albums of his own design. Randy got a lucky break, thanks to his relationship with Duke Pearson, and recorded his first solo album, *Score* in 1969. Although the positions of Mike and Randy in Dreams were the result of an invitation to join someone else's project, Randy exerted a good measure of influence over the band's style, and he could equally have formed a band of his own at this point. For a time, it fitted well with his vision of what a jazz-fusion band could be, but over a period of two years and a couple of albums, the band wasn't good enough to survive long without strong, clear leadership. So, with invitations to join several other bands on the table, it wasn't until 1987 that his second album, *In The Idiom* was released. It was a similar story for Michael, except that he was four years behind his brother – a significant gap at this point in their lives. Their careers took similar (but not identical) paths for the years from 1971 to 1975, and from 1981 to 1987 diverged rather more. *Michael Brecker* (1987) was his first album as leader, an event that seemed long overdue even then. Randy's output on his mid-career albums was influenced by his marriage to Brazilian pianist, Eliane Elias, and Latin-based music has featured throughout his albums. Both Randy and Michael loved to play jazz-fusion music, but maintained their roots in straightahead jazz, so the output of both men contains recordings made in both genres. The discographies of their careers as leaders of their own projects show clearly a number of features.

Firstly, they made albums that included the other brother when possible. Presumably, availability was an issue, but there were other times when each brother made the most of an opportunity to play alongside players he admired and respected. For example, Michael worked a lot with Pat Metheny; Randy enjoyed playing with Bob Berg.

Secondly, their choice of musician was a good balance between acquiring the services of the most highly respected musicians from the older generation, and encouraging and developing careers by hiring the most promising up-and-coming musicians.

Thirdly, Randy's projects varied across a wide range of styles such as:

In The Idiom (straightahead, mainstream jazz);

Randy In Brasil (Latin jazz);

Nostalgic Journey: Tykocin Jazz Suite (orchestral, third stream jazz);

Soulbop Band Live (soul-funk-fusion);

Amanda (crossover, jazz-fusion)

The Jazz Ballad Song Book (jazz ballads);
Some Skunk Funk (big band jazz);
34th N Lex (acid or hip hop jazz, jazz-fusion)

Michael's project strategies were more focussed on recording albums of progressive, straightahead jazz, with some electronic content.

Fourthly, any given project had varied content, was usually intended to be innovative or progressive in some way, and performed at the highest levels of skill and musicianship. Projects were therefore usually challenging for the musicians to record, but humour was an essential element of time spent in the studio, as well as in the final performances.

3. Albums As Sidemen

Randy and Michael have served a great number of years as members of a number of jazz groups, full details of which are given in the discography. The length of service varies widely. It could be playing on just one album, playing gigs lasting days or weeks, extended national or international tours, or periods spanning more than one year in which numerous projects may have been completed.

There is a huge gulf between rock/pop music and jazz when it comes to bands. Rock/pop musicians are far more inclined to be associated with specific acts than jazz musicians. The characteristics of jazz on the New York scene were that jazz groups were often assembled for a particular project. (This of course, was facilitated by the great number of suitable musicians who were available in the New York area.) If the band was lucky, it might go on a tour, promoted by the record company. However, one of the complaints the Brecker Brothers had with Arista, was that they were not given enough resources to pay for the tour properly. Musicians might arrive back home at the end of a tour with debts. At the end of that particular cycle, musicians would think about their time with the band and decide whether to continue, or to accept an offer to join another band, in which case, the whole cycle would begin again.

In Randy's case, besides the Brecker Brothers, the most significant membership of bands was with Duke Pearson, Blood Sweat & Tears, Hal Galper, Horace Silver, Dreams, Larry Coryell's Eleventh House, Billy Cobham, Jaco Pastorius, Parliament / Funkadelic / P-Funk, Frank Zappa, Don Grolnick, Mingus Dynasty / Big Band, Bob Mintzer Big Band, GRP Big Band.

Michael's list of band memberships consists of many of the same bands as Randy: Hal Galper, Horace Silver, Dreams, Billy Cobham, Jaco Pastorius, Parliament / Funkadelic / P-Funk, Frank Zappa and Don Grolnick. It also includes Steps / Steps Ahead,

Sometimes memberships would overlap, and diaries would need to be carefully managed to weave busy schedules together.

4. Work As Session Musicians

Even the most cursory inspection of the discography at the end of this book is enough to tell you just how much Michael and Randy spent time working as session musicians, and it is not possible here to provide more than a superficial summary of the highlights of these two stellar careers. Proof of the great influence of both men within the wider world of music is demonstrated, at the very end of the discography, by the list of albums in which *both* Randy *and* Michael participated.

I am not aware of any other musicians who have participated in more albums, though common sense suggests there might be some. Precise numbers are difficult to obtain, because of uncertainty about the exact measure of participation and whether albums contained previously released material or not. However, the numbers indicate that Michael's time at work as a session musician led him to contribute to about 714 albums, with Randy on 862! From 1976 to 1979 the brothers were, on average, playing on more than one album every week.

Obviously, there are many instances in which they perhaps play on just one track of an album. This is usually a legitimate commercial ploy to enable the record company to put the name of a star musician on the front cover of the album, and therefore to attract more sales. I, for one, have frequently bought albums expecting my favourite musician to play a large part in it, only to find that he plays a single solo on a single track. For many years in pop music, a guest soloist might be used only for ten or twenty seconds. That's the minimum presence, and it applies to some cases in the discography. If the lead artist has a hit record, it's a boost for the session musician's career, but the album might bomb. In both cases, the session musician pockets the same one-off fee, usually a basic rate amount defined by the Musicians Union.

The session man might appear on some, but not all, of the album tracks in an expanded role as a 'guest musician'. This is often the case when the lead artist wants different combinations of musicians to enhance the colour palette of the album. Common practice with jazz musicians was to allow their guest to perform on one or two tracks, depending on whether the work could be fitted into a single day in the studio. Obviously, he might also perform on every track of the album. Even so, as a session musician, our man is not part of a formal band and is on a daily rate for studio time. It is, of course, quite possible that the session player never even gets to meet the lead artist! The job for which he has been hired is simply to turn up at the studio on the appointed day and play, as instructed, into a microphone that records him alone. Having finished, to the producer's satisfaction, he goes home.

Ronnie Cuber is today one of the great baritone saxophone players. A native New Yorker, he served his apprenticeship as a session musician. "Yeah, I became the first call baritone player in New York, starting the middle 70s, until it started to peter out, and there was a bunch of musicians that were the cream. When Randy and Mike were peaking with the Brecker Brothers they were getting to be the people to call - to go to for horns - so when an artist like Diana Ross or Bette Midler - Arif Martin [might be doing the] arrangements, he would put the call out for a horn overdub session at Atlantic records, and if Randy was writing the charts, then I would get the call. If there was a baritone saxophone, I was the one. So I got on a lot of sessions and there was a lot of work." [6]

Much of the available work was, of course, not necessarily for albums, but for TV commercials – jingles, as they are popularly known. Ronnie Cuber remembers it well. "I would be in the studios like four or five times a week. Like ten o'clock in the morning I would have a Burger King commercial, and in walked Michael, Randy, and a couple of other horn players, and we'd do that session. Then we'd have another one at, say, noon, up the street, and then another studio for another product for another company, and sometimes we would have three jingles sessions in one day." [6]

The same players would meet up at the different sessions and there became a cadre of professional musicians in the New York area amongst whom the work was shared out. It is startling to look through the range of recordings in the discography, some of them major hit records by world-class artists, and to see the same group of names filling the session musicians' chairs. (Unfortunately, this is a level of detail for which there was no room in this book.) It was as if there was a semi-formal 'session band' that turned up as a separate unit to play on everything that was going on. However, once you think about the processes going on behind the scenes, it is perhaps rather less surprising. Bookings were handled by a central agency called Radio Registry. Musicians' popularity was naturally a big factor in determining the amount of work they got, for it was often the case that someone who needed a tenor saxophone player would request (or even demand) Michael.

Of course, the session musician sees no correlation between his income and record sales. No matter how many millions of records are sold, after he walks, the musician makes nothing more from his work. This is how the business works. Whilst session musicians are doing their studio work, they are not making their own records. Whilst they are locked in studios for often ten to thirteen hours a day, they are not writing their own compositions that might earn them royalties.

Availability was a key issue, of course, and if Michael were unavailable, perhaps Bob Berg would be chosen instead. On any instrument, there might be five or ten premier league players from whom to choose. Few would disagree that Randy and Michael headed both lists. David Sanborn was first choice for alto sax. Steve Gadd was, for many years, the number one choice of drummer, whilst Will Lee was very high on the list for electric bass, Eddie Gomez for string bass, and Don Grolnick or Richard Tee for piano. On the fewer occasions when a tuba was required, it was usually Howard Johnson who got the job. Percussionists were usually Don Alias, Ralph MacDonald or Airto Moreira. For obvious reasons, there was a larger number of possible guitar players, with Cornell Dupree, Steve Khan, Mike Stern and John Abercrombie high in popularity. All of these men were at one time or another, part of the Brecker Brothers gang. Thus, with some permutation involved to deal with the unavailability issues, it was the same groups of guys who can be seen on albums recorded in New York studios. If or when players developed their own careers as solo artists in their own right, they might play a lesser part in session work to focus on their own projects. For example, George Benson was a very busy session musician at first, but once he had a smash hit with *Breezin'* (1976) the opportunities for him to appear as a session man were much reduced. To a lesser extent, a similar change happened to David Sanborn, although he was always keen to make guest appearances whenever his schedule allowed. The Brecker Brothers' appetite for work seemed almost unaffected over the years, and they have always been keen to take on as many guest appearances as they could possibly fit in, although the mid-1980s were rather less busy with typically about 10-15 guest appearances each year. Many of the other top session musicians continued in that way, making their own self-led albums when the opportunities arose. And, when they did, they formed their own 'dream team' of session men to stand alongside them.

One of the biggest occasions of the 1980s was to be hired for the recordings of Frank Sinatra's *L.A. Is My Lady* (1984). It turned out to be Sinatra's last studio album. The list of musicians credited is extensive. Of course, the Brecker Brothers (and Ronnie Cuber) were present. Ronnie was pleased because a video was made of the recordings and the final edit featured some close-ups of him. "There's one tune, *If I Should Lose You* with full band, Mike Brecker, Frank Wess, Frank Foster, George Young on lead alto, I'm playing baritone, bass clarinet. On that particular tune, after the vocal, with the horn ensemble, the camera shot right to me, and so I'm split screen with Sinatra. That was the only song that that happened on." [6]

However, the Breckers won the jackpot prize when Frank actually changed the lyrics of the last song to include naming the Brecker Brothers in his list of acknowledgements. I joked to Randy that this was the ultimate accolade. He agreed with me. "Well, you're right. We were proud of that of course. All our friends thought it was hysterical. We couldn't hear what he was singing, he was singing live in the studio, but we could only hear it in the playbacks. He sang, 'We have the Brecker Brothers...' All our friends - John Faddis, and

Soloff - [they] thought it was hysterical. But those sessions were very exciting because Frank was there, singing live. And of course, the greatest arrangers, the greatest musicians in New York, and Quincy [Jones] being there, so it was unforgettable." [5]

In his excellent autobiography, Bill Bruford tells a story about when he and Tony Levin were hired for a session with Al di Meola to record *Calliope* on Al's album, *Scenario* (1983). They both arrived at the studio on time, and then waited for nearly five hours until Al arrived. After spending some time carefully explaining what he wanted, Al noticed that Tony had still not taken his instrument (a special bass called a Chapman Stick) out of its case. He suggested that Tony "might like to get his instrument out of the case because this bit is going to get really tricky, as he lets rip a blazing run of notes that he is going to want Tony to double." Still there was no response from Tony, who was sitting stony-faced. After some irritation from Al, who had concluded that Tony didn't seem to be listening, everything was ready and the tape was rolled. Tony took out his instrument, plugged it in, and without a single note of testing, tuning or practising, blew the piece out of the water with a single shot. Bruford wrote, "He remembers the four-minute piece exactly, and produces a note-perfect bass part: no slips, no fluff, no guff. Then he doubles it. It is a remarkable feat of musicianship and establishes a different sense of authority in the studio." [84]

The story doesn't end there, for the engineer had made a bad mistake and had lost some bars from Tony's track. He needed another five minutes of Tony's time to repeat some of it. Tony, however, had his instrument packed and was going out of the door. The engineer pleaded with him to return. Somewhat grudgingly, Tony did so. Then the engineer found he still needed two notes. "Just two more notes!" he begged. But it was too late. Tony had completed his part of the deal and was gone.

It's an example of one end of the broad spectrum of session work – the kind where it is just work. The session musician doesn't care much about the music – or the lead musician either, especially if he has been messed about.

Concluding Remarks

Whilst Randy always performs at the highest technical level, it is the beautiful sound of his horn that continues to impress listeners with its frequent echoes of Miles Davis on a good day. Cook wrote, "He probably still likes the looseness and chopsmanship of R&B fusion best, but the dignity and calibre of his classical playing has never deserted him, and even when he doesn't sound as if he's trying all that hard, the lovely sound breaks through." [85]

Bill Evans wrote, "I met Randy years ago in the early 1980s in NYC when I was playing with Miles Davis. He was already an established player, writer, and innovator. I always wanted to get the chance to play with him. In reality, there are only a few players that really impressed me with their ability to reach an audience and perform at the highest level. Randy happens to be one of those guys." [86]

The general levels of Brecker Brothers performances has frequently confounded listeners, good musicians amongst them. One feature has been their use of "power play." At some point, the boys seem to have adopted the principle of playing at speeds they would call "as fast as humanly possible." How fast is this? Well, as a yardstick, lets us consider a composition of 4/4 metre where crotchets (quarter notes) are played at 150 bpm. The streams of semi-quavers (sixteenth notes) that Randy and Michael play is equivalent to playing ten notes per second, or six hundred sixteenth notes in one minute! There are few humans who could achieve this in a musically sensible way, let alone as creatively as these boys do. To adopt this method, *and also to play bebop-style melody lines*, is at the very highest level of performance. Guitar players usually have the edge over other instrumentalists because of their ability to pluck strings with alternating up and down strokes of the plectrum. Thus John McLaughlin, Frank Gambale, Allan Holdsworth and Al DiMeola are some of the fastest jazzmen. In the playing of wind instruments, however, the Brecker Brothers head the list. To really see what I mean, just try counting out loud from one to ten in one second! Then listen again to *Not Ethiopia* and see how well Randy and Mike do it.

Composition has always been another strong feature of Brecker pieces. Whilst Randy was keen to establish himself as a serious composer right from the beginning of his career, Michael felt less comfortable at first. However, in some regard, his desire to compete with his brother urged him towards developing his own skills, which he later achieved to a remarkable degree.

I asked Randy how he went about the process of writing. Randy replied, " I never studied composition, so when you're a studied writer you can use certain grids, certain methods, that will lead you down one path or another, so my method really was just to sit at the piano for hours and come up with little ideas, and it was like putting a puzzle together. I would get one idea here, and one idea there, and I was at the time very organised with recording everything, putting everything on cassettes, marking the cassettes, And I knew where everything was, so when I came up with an eight bar vamp, I would remember, Yeah I've got another piece that might fit good with this. Let's put the two pieces together. And then you make three pieces. It was really like putting a puzzle together. Now, with the advent of computers, the puzzle is a lot easier to fit together, and occasionally a tune would just come out, but I rarely had a plan in mind. I might have had a rhythm in mind at the start, it could have been anything, a bass line, a line on trumpet, *Skunk Funk* started [sings the line]. That was a line I found on the trumpet, so it was a little of everything all pieced together in a puzzle." [5]

I asked how he would describe the harmonies he so often uses? (The first thing that came to my mind was the word 'parallel'.) Randy: "There's some parallel voicings too. I tried to use rock rhythms. I had studied for a time -played with - Art Blakey, and I loved the three horn writing in jazz, I did a lot of transcriptions of, particularly the group of Wayne Shorter, Freddie Hubbard, and later Lee Morgan, and Curtis Fuller, so I utilised a lot of those voicings, in the three horn writing. And I took some chances with the harmony. I did a lot of things where the rhythm section is in one key and we might be a step up, or the guitar player was a step up, so it makes it kind of look askew, and it was all done on purpose to subtly extend the boundaries of funk and rock. The harmony was usually pretty thick, even though there was a pretty strong beat behind it." [5]

Michael and Randy Brecker playing at the North Sea Jazz Festival, 9 July 1993. Michael is playing the EWI. Photo: Louis Gerrits.

Michael Brecker's contributions to the art of performance are incalculable, notwithstanding his early adoption of an entirely new musical instrument – the EWI. He was excited by the new developing techno-world in music. With Mainieri and others, he had tried to develop the electronic style of jazz in Steps Ahead. "It was like playing in Technicolor instead of black and white. The issue isn't electronics, but the people who are playing it," he said. Although some of that is preserved on record, his performances at live gigs, where there is always so much more opportunity to 'stretch out', were unequalled in scope and technical achievement with a complicated advanced musical instrument like the EWI.

In a technical article for *Virtual Instruments* magazine in 2011, George Whitty described part of Michael Brecker's live show. "Mike had been on the road for 20 years with two 4-foot racks packed with synths, samplers, mixers, MIDI routers, loopers, and reverbs, topped off with an Oberheim Matrix 12 synth, from which he would perform a one-man EWI masterpiece every night in the middle of the set. It typically featured a couple hundred different sounds, layered ethnic bits, various lead sounds, drums, basses, percussion, a few beautiful polyphonic pieces (out of the monophonic EWI), and huge distorted guitars. Mike ended it with a big, layered jam, created one line at a time on Lexicon's Jam-Man, in which he would layer up a groove and a bunch of Brecker-only harmonic ideas and then blow over the whole thing. The EWI solo was always a show-stopper." [87]

By the late 1970s, popular music was integrating many strands of jazz into its format, led by Michael and Randy and many other jazz musicians who formed the backbone of session players. The massive growth of the music industry was driven by radio airplay and sales of albums in first vinyl and later CD formats. Thanks to FM radio, the big increase in airplay outlets, together with the massive increase in output of movies with associated soundtracks, absorbed all these influences from rock, pop, jazz, blues, funk, soul and even classical to create a pan-genre best described as simply 'fusion'. Thus, by 1985 when Randy's album *Amanda* was released, music such as the first track, *Splash*, had become the blueprint for what was view by many as a stereotype. There are many who would look down on this as something to be deprecated. Pop-fusion music often attracted much adverse criticism, such as when Piero Scaruffi said it was "...mellow, bland, romantic music" made by "mediocre musicians" and "derivative bands," in a tone that suggests this was all somehow against the law. In my own opinion, this is something to be applauded, for there is no contradiction in saying that music that is popular (i.e. non-elitist) is therefore, by definition, bad or without value. [88]

Michael Brecker's career is divided into a number of parts, each spanning a different sector of the musical firmament, each of them brilliant for different reasons: The Brecker Brothers, Steps and Steps Ahead, a formidable solo career, favoured sideman to the world's great musicians of all flavours, and a reputation for being the greatest session saxman. Perhaps the pinnacle of his achievement was achieved when he became the first musician to win Grammys for both the "Best Jazz Instrumental Performance" and "Best Jazz Instrumental Solo" two years in a row. In all, he won fifteen Grammys – more than any other saxophone player. All of these facets to Michael Brecker's life and work need to be examined.

There is a good case for the argument that Michael Brecker was the best saxophone player apart from John Coltrane. Ratliff rates Brecker and Grover Washington Jr. as "the two most influential saxophonists since Coltrane." [89]

Brecker, he says, "played on jazz and pop records that the average person knew." He might have added that, in so doing, he maintained a position at the top of the tree inside the jazz mainstream that Washington did not. Whilst I like Washington's music very much, I could never equate the two as saxophonists of equal power over the instrument and, of course, it is hard to imagine anyone ever eclipsing such an "artistic messiah figure" as Coltrane.

The classic example of a tall, dark, handsome man, Michael was immensely talented, yet surprisingly modest, polite man who shared a strong sense of humour with his brother. He was modest when it came to an understanding of just how talented he was. After all, he grew up in a family with such a deep vein of musical talent that he really believed everyone else was musical too! "I'm not a tremendously original player. I listen to things, I learn them until they get into my psyche and then I distort the hell out of them." [90]

In a sense, it was easier for him than perhaps it should have been. Some would argue that, in contrast to other, mainly black, jazz musicians, he grew up in a privileged family, sheltered from poverty and deprivation by his father's wealth. When he first went to New York, he was fortunate enough to follow in his brother's footsteps and to benefit from his brother's contacts. He was also fortunate enough to arrive there during the 'purple patch' for horn players – when the rock revolution had reached such a stage that it was ready to soak up every such musician it could find, and when technology had developed to the extent that it was pregnant with fantastic new electronic devices for musicians to explore. Even playing alongside his brother was advantageous to him, for not only did their duo double their desirability as sidemen for hire, but they were blessed with superb understanding that added immeasurably to the music. "We have some kind of weird intuitive communication. I never have to ask how he's going to phrase something." [90]

None of these arguments detract from the unrivalled skills that he was born with, that fabulous connectivity and co-ordination between brain, lungs, nerves and fingers that enabled him to make such unbelievable music. In a serious study of Coltrane, Ratliff acknowledges that even he was lucky. "His greatness wasn't all his own making. There were circumstances." [91].

Naturally, Michael had to work hard to get where he did. About practising, Michael said that he had never been "real good on discipline." He would "practice in spurts," playing a lot of arpeggios and playing as much as he could during the times when he was sufficiently motivated to do so. He tried to practice things that were going to be practical, rather than waste his time on stuff he would not use. He listened to records constantly, learned parts of solos, practising them in all the keys. However, he would not necessarily be able to play them verbatim afterwards, but the essence of the solos would later emerge somewhere from his subconscious – "usually two months later."

These arguments apply equally well to Randy. The sharing of DNA is obvious, but the distinction between nature and nurture is neither important nor illuminating in this case. It is logical to argue that the immense level of technical achievement they both soared to was partly a result of intense competition between the two men to outshine the other. Practice was a key element and both men practised remorselessly.

Michael practised a lot during his time with Horace Silver. He learned a lot playing with this jazz master. He also regularly took private music lessons during his career, including saxophone tuition from Joe Henderson. He studied composition during his time with Steps Ahead. Even when he was a saxophone 'star' he continued to seek lessons from other musicians, but he said that he found it hard to be taken seriously. [89]

Michael's tone is very like Sanborn's, even when you know that Sanborn plays exclusively alto saxophone, not tenor. Working closely together in the early years clearly made them listen carefully to each other and to feed off each other's playing. Both men have tones that are hard - not soft, richer in treble overtones, and electronically textured on most records. The contrast is with players like Getz whose tone is at the other extremity - very warm, soft and rounded. You can snuggle up to Getz's sound, whereas you'd cut yourself on Michael Brecker's incisive tone.

In contrast to popular music, since the 1960s, jazz musicians have continuously and thoroughly explored the value of complex rhythms, and the pages of this book make many references to that, perhaps more so with Michael. Michael felt that a deep understanding of time and rhythm was an essential part of his playing. He was, in fact, a very competent drummer, a skill that naturally helped in that regard.

The balance struck between involvement in all-out electronic jazz-fusion music and the purer qualities of mainstream jazz is a notable feature of both men. Michael, especially, said he enjoyed playing with Hal Galper because the acoustic music of the band helped to balance all the electronic experimentation that was going on in the Brecker Brothers music. But playing with credibility across a broad range of genres requires versatility, which comes from a combination of skill, vision and experience, three characteristics that Randy and Michael had in spades. Both of them wanted to have fun as well as to entertain. You could sum up their philosophy as "music without walls." James Genus: "I was fortunate to also be able to play on his [Mike's] solo records as well, and got to play both acoustic and electric on those recordings as we covered quite a few genres. After listening to him, and talking to him, and playing with him, I got to see that our approach to music in general was very similar. You know, the great ones always cross over musically, like Herbie and Miles, as well as Mike—it's just all about playing music—that's it! [33]

By all accounts, Michael was shier, and more self-effacing than his brother. There are many instances in the preceding pages where examples of his humble nature are evident. He did not seek fame or fortune *per se*, he never wanted to be idolised or treated differently in any way. He was totally dedicated to his music (and his family) and to being the best he could be. In 1980, Michael did not think he had done anything special. "As for the Mike Brecker school, I'm aware of that. Part of it comes from the fact that I'm basically just like an assimilator of things, and I just assimilated things a little earlier than some people did, in terms of influences. There are a lot of people that maybe play like me, but haven't really listened to me, they're assimilating the same influences now, and coming up with something similar. I think a way of playing was initiated by Dave Sanborn and myself, emotional? Alright, maybe that's the way to put it. But there's nothing amazingly ingenious about it though. It was all there to begin with. In other words, I'm saying I haven't really come up with anything that astounding! Yes it's a departure from the cool school, absolutely, I agree with that. It's a departure from previous approaches to playing the instrument also in certain ways. I always find it easier to play in a rock 'n' roll or R&B framework."

Michael would always seek to turn the spotlight away from himself onto others. For example, he said that playing with Pat Metheny on the Joni Mitchell tour was "one of the best experiences I ever had. That's where we found we had a real affinity…I love his playing and his conception and maturity in his playing. He's really a phenomenal musician." Of David Sanborn, Michael said, "He's one of my favourite living musicians. I'm a complete fan of his. The man can say more in one note than a lot of people can say in ten…He's a real voice. He has a unique sound…he's my favourite player to play with."

"Because in jazz there are so damn many great saxophone players, the lineage is so thick and strong that there is very little you can contribute that's new. All of a sudden, here's the new area of music, with very few people, other than King Curtis in it. So the field was wide open to find some other stuff to play I've tried to develop a voice of my own. [33]

"John Coltrane? It touched me real strongly for years. I listened to him for years, and I went through the whole thing, to the point where as much as I love it, I have trouble listening to it now, because it just takes me left. I had to consciously break away, yes. But the main thing I got from that was just a whole emotional approach. And spiritual things too. I have felt that a lot of jazz has lacked emotional content." [33]

Speaking of Michael's loss in 2009, James Genus told an interviewer, "He was an amazing person. I remember hearing a Pat Metheny record in '80 or '81 and going, who is that saxophone player—it just floored me. And beyond that, one of my favorite all-time records was one by Don Grolnick called *Hearts and*

Numbers. And that particular record is my favorite Michael Brecker recording of all time. He sounded amazing on that, and it had a major impact on me. I started listening to him all the time. He was an idol to me—his playing moved me so much, and I never thought I'd be able to play with him. That 'music for music's sake' philosophy was definitely my connection with him. Beyond that, Michael had a great sense of humor, and it seems there was no subject that we couldn't talk about in depth. He was always thirsting for different types of music, and he turned me on to a lot of different styles I hadn't been familiar with. Knowing him was one of the greatest experiences of my life. I'll never forget him… never." [60]

Randy continues to work as hard as ever, as he enjoys the freedom of working in whatever project area meets the constraints of family life and musical satisfaction. His recent project to reunite members of earlier BB bands, perfectly supported in Mike's absence by Ada Rovatti, was a great success, showing that he still has all his old verve. And Randy is a session musician to this day. (Had he lived, Michael would have been too.) I get a strong sense that Randy and Michael would not have behaved as Tony Levin did in Bill Bruford's story, related above. Suppose you wanted to hire Randy to appear on your record. Make contact, offer him a gig, find a date (that's probably the hardest part!), agree a fee, he's yours and will do what you ask. Chances are, he'll even offer free advice if he likes what you're doing. Just ask Janek Gwizdala, who successfully hired Randy to perform Randroid on Janek's album *Theatre By The Sea* (2013).

Appendix: George Whitty Discusses Working With The Brecker Brothers

George Whitty joined The Brecker Brothers Band for their project, *Return Of The Brecker Brothers* (1992). He was still in the band for the record and tour, *Brecker Brothers Band Reunion* (2013). I began by asking him about the first record.

KT: "So on that first record you were more of a player than you were a programmer?"

GW: "We based what we did on some of the programming I had done, and supplemented that with live musicians. The process on that one was a little chaotic. I don't think anyone could really tell you who the producer was on that disc."

KT: "Maz and Kilgore had a fantastic street music sound didn't they?"

GW: "Yeah. Those guys are really kinda geniuses, you know. Rob is as close to a Renaissance Man as anybody I've ever met. He was one of the top session players in New York for years. A lot of Steve Winwood's record *Higher Love* is Rob's doing; Hall & Oates: he did a lot of stuff for them. And then he got into the acid jazz thing, they were way out in the front of that, and then he took a break from doing that and he went to work for Microsoft where he designed a lot of the little animations that you see in the Windows Operating System, like when you go to search you see that little dog? It's like cartooning or something, but it's a completely different discipline, and he's now, as I understand it, Head of Voice Recognition Research at Ford, and he's just this laid back dude from Texas. Very talented musician, though. If you look him up on You-Tube you can see videos of him where he's created this little hardware box that does all this algorithmic harmony stuff, and he says, Well I had this old chip from a Texas Instruments Calculator and I pinched these knobs off an Akai drum machine... A very amazing dude."

KT: "But then, when you got onto the second album, you did a lot more production is that right?"

GW: "Yeah, we figured out how to do the second one after we did the first one. The second one [*Out of the Loop*] was a much better process, and in my opinion it's a much better CD."

KT: "On the subject of producing, at what point do you make a choice between a live drummer and a computer?"

GW: "It's always whether you can afford the live guy. Early on in my production career, I had a habit of getting wedded to what I had done, and as it progressed, and even by that second Brecker Brothers CD, I had learned to sketch it in, and get a vibe that I could play for people, but then to hire the right people and let them take it a couple of dimensions deeper. So the decision on that, I mean I'm working on it right now, is really more an issue of budget because if you can get any of those drummers who played on the Brecker Brothers CDs to play on your thing - if you can afford it by any stretch - you owe it to yourself to do it."

KT: "You had Dennis Chambers on the first record, but he was kind of balanced with synthesised drums. I wondered whether you chose the synthesised drums because you wanted a particular sound."

GW: Well I forget to be honest how I made any decisions like that, but I know that Maz and Kilgore (and Max [Risenhoover]) really wanted that sound that they had compiled. I think on Maz and Kilgore's cuts they might have had a guy come in and overdub stuff, but I remember Rob telling me at one point, that they had pinched a ride cymbal off a George Shearing record. So they are really round object people, but there's a genius in the objects they find."

KT: "Randy has almost invented a parallel harmony - you know, the harmonies are really skewed aren't they?"

GW: "Yeah, but that's the genius of Randy and there's no-one else who's ever approached him - maybe some of John Scofield's stuff, but the [Randy's] harmony violates every rule in the book, and yet it has this unbelievably strong interior logic that's unique to him. And everything he writes is like that. It's incredibly sophisticated, but there's no cadences that came from anyone with a powdered wig on their head. It's all stuff that he came up with. I guess Frank Zappa, might be another example of somebody that could write like that. If you look at the harmony that's in *Skunk Funk* it's in F minor for half a bar and then it's in D major for the next half of the bar, and you don't see that [in any other music]." *See Ref [70]*

KT: "Do you think weird harmony is just Randy's thing, because it seems to me that Michael did the same kind of thing?"

GW: "Mike told me once that [in] everything he wrote, the whole object of it was to get a rise out of Randy. Randy was definitely his ideal - I wouldn't say idol, but there was definitely a serious admiration there for Randy as a writer."

KT: "I suggest that Michael comes across as a serious composer in his own right. I could argue that Michael was as good a composer as Randy, yet here we are saying that Randy had a big influence over Michael."

GW: "Yeah, and I think Randy - just from who he was while Mike was growing up (and also by what he was listening to while Mike was growing up) - helped cultivate in Mike this idea that if it's just too simple and vanilla it's just not cool. And all the people that they listened to soloing had the same mentality, certainly all the saxophonists that Mike was listening to, all had the notion that the more extreme the 'out' stuff was, the more satisfying it was… You know, it's like, if you watch a gymnast work on the parallel bars, you don't want to see her just sitting on there, you want to see her doing these crazy flips way off there that you can't believe she's going to land, and that's the thrill of it. And a lot of musicians have that in their playing, but they don't have it in their writing. Mike and both Randy had it. Randy, of course, still has it. A lot of so-called modern jazz writing, it's one complex chord strung after the next, but there's no logic to it, there's no cadences there. And it's hard to play on because it's just not musical."

KT: "Would you comment upon the modern styles of ballad writing, which seems to me often to be a sequence of meandering chords."

GW: "I wouldn't agree with that. They were often very hard tunes to play on, but the harmony in both those guys' writing, to me, was specifically evocative. Pat's [Metheny] tunes, always take me on a real specific journey to a real specific place, and it's the wrinkles in the harmony that are as responsible as anything else, and then you bring it into a studio with Michael Brecker, and you know he's going to blow a great solo on it. Pat is another guy that, even from his very first CD, *Bright Size Life*, just completely threw the rulebook out. There's incredible logic in there, but it's definitely not your 2-5-1. For me, Pat is the most evocative writer, Pat and Lyle. Those things can really affect my mood. And it's the unusual harmony that does it for me."

KT: "How do you see the development of form and structure in Brecker Brothers compositions?"

GW: "Well the forms are always the kinds of Achilles heel of these things, because if there's anything that has musicians standing around, and scratching their heads at the rehearsal, and asking where the menu book is, it's the question of what should the form be. And that's part of the reason, I think, why Mike and Randy liked working with me, and working on the sequencer, was because we could vet all that stuff ahead of time. There's that essential part of a jazz musician where you don't want it to be AABA, especially when it's your own writing. But there's also kind of a mystery to how best to get something that's organic and flows right, but also pricks the ear."

KT: "Where does modal music presently stand in the jazz world? Do musicians still use it?"

GW: "Well, yeah. It's just like anything else, in the hands of real masters, they know what to do with it. It doesn't just sit there. If you listen to Branford Marsalis and Joey Calderazzo, there's an infinite number of places to take it. What I hear often is that people who don't have the imagination or the chops to take it somewhere interesting (this is mostly kind of funky bands)... I was at a Festival this year, and kind of couldn't believe - its almost like they're dirges you know, there's somebody playing a funk beat on it, but there's nobody making a journey out of it, so in my role as *de facto* Musical Director in Randy's band, I like to make sure that there's plenty of changes to blow on. There's modal sections too, but I think most of the tunes have some kind of progression."

KT: Michael made a speciality out of playing the EWI. Is it a dead duck now? Does anybody still play it?

GW: There are still guys who play it, Steve Tavaglione, here in Los Angeles, is a master of it. There's a guy named Judd Miller, who did a lot of the programming for Mike, who was incredible at it. I think the appetite for synthesiser soloing from a saxophonist - Mike had developed it into an extraordinary thing, it was kind of a calling card.

KT: I think he was *the* premier exponent of it, was he not?

GW: Yeah, No question about it. He enjoyed playing it on tunes, but mostly it was a thing that he did, you know, that big solo piece that was the result of many hundreds of hours of programming, and thinking, and constantly improving that.

KT: Do you think, if Mike had still been here, he would still be playing it?

GW: No question.

KT: I think I heard Michael say once that he put the two instruments on a par, that he loved playing the EWI almost as much as the tenor.

GW: Yeah, I don't doubt it.

KT: "What do you see as the differences in musicianship between Randy and Michael?"

GW: "It's a tough question, and because of Mike's admiration of Randy and Randy's aesthetic, they are similar, especially on the writing side. I think Mike was maybe a little more willing than Randy to let the tune be consonant, but then to play out against that, whereas Randy wants to have the tune itself that's very deep in the writing department, and always a challenge for your ear, and then to have the playing go outside of that. Mike wrote a lot of tunes that are closer to conventional harmony than Randy's stuff, which always has something unusual in it."

George said that the band had learned to use live performances to hone their playing before recording, a lesson learned from the sheer difficulty of playing *Harpoon* on *Out Of The Loop* (1994).

GW: "That [*Harpoon*] was one that didn't really flow organically in the studio on any of our parts, because its just a hard piece of music and that was probably the tune that convinced me that before we made any more records, we would learn the material and do some gigs first. So Randy's record that's about to come out, that's what we did. We worked up the demos, we got the whole thing ready, but then we went and played at the *Blue Note* in New York for a week, and once everybody knew the tunes, it was easy to go into the studio the next day and blow through them, being comfortable. So that was a lesson learned."

KT: "As a producer, what kinds of things do you consider when you are about to start the production of a record for Randy and Michael? Is there a discussion with them as to what they wanted first, and then you fill in the cracks, or do you have your own plan that you work to?"

GW: "Well, typically, back then they've always made these funny, very crunchy, little low-fi demos of their tunes, and they are always funny because they have funny little names on them, like Mike had one he called *Greedo*. He had another one called *Afroturd*. He was always unimpressed with his own writing. They would give me these little demos, and I think that's why they started using me, because I could get the essence out of the demo, but then produce it out to make it sound like a piece of finished music. But in the intervening years (and this was already underway by the time we did the second disc) I learned to figure out who the band was going to be, and then come up with an arrangement, and a demo that was going to be fun for them. And that is something that was missing off that first disc. At least for the tunes that I produced, I came up with the arrangement that I wanted, and then tried to get the guys to execute it. Whereas I think it's much better to come up with a good vibe and use the demo to get the arrangement figured out, you know, I put a lot of keeper keyboard parts and textures and maybe some percussion in there that we keep, but then just try to set it up so that the band can have the maximum fun. And Randy's record that just came out a couple days ago [Brecker Brothers Band Reunion] is a really good example of that. The live sessions in the studio were really fun and efficient, and it sounds like it. *African Skies*, from the second record, [Out Of The Loop] that's a good example of a track – it's a very complex track. The rhythm section parts especially were designed to be open enough so that everybody could just have fun, and Rodney and Armand just played insanely on that, and Dean as well, and as hard as it was, we actually pulled that arrangement off live in the studio, four different times. Yeah, the more you can give room for the musicians to get into gear and have fun with it, that translates directly to the experience of listening to it."

KT: "When Randy comes to you and says, I've got a piece here that we're going to do, does he present you with written music?"

GW: "Well he gives me a little logic file - the sequencing software that we both use, so if I need to, I can look at that and see what the part is. I always replay the stuff that he sends me, but I can print it up on the computer as notation, so that's typically what I get from him. There isn't a chart at that point, and the demo is only about a minute and a half long. All the important information is there in the demo, and even though its kind of Casio sounds, you get the vibe of the tune really clearly."

KT: "And was that the same with Michael when he came to you with a piece?"

GW: "Yeah. Often it was a great start on things. He had the three different sections of the tune, but it needed to be shaped into a thing, and then for both of them it was useful to hear it rendered up with something more like a real drummer. On the solo discs that I produced for Mike I did pretty elaborate, kind of swinging demos, even of the straightahead jazz stuff, so that he could take it home and assess it, and mess with it."

KT: "I'm a musician too, but I find it mysterious how you come up with such complex music. I've been listening to the stuff on the records and they are very complex pieces of music and I don't get how you do that without writing it all out. I guess it's all laid down on the computer, but then it wasn't always like that. The tools have changed a lot haven't they?"

GW: "The tools have changed, but then I keep heading back to the old process. If you have somebody like Will Lee on your session, you gotta just let him run with it, you know? He's unbelievably inventive, and he plays something and that gives the drummer an idea, and now the thing is poked off into a different direction, you know, that's the fun of it. The Brecker Brothers had a real habit, (and I think it was the most important criteria for them) that they got that kind of person in the band, you know - people who just like to sit down and play it different that day. There's an arrangement of *Sponge* that we do with Randy's band, and we did it some with the Brecker Brothers in the '90s, and when we get to the solo section, we always play this one vamp, and we'd probably done a hundred gigs with it like that. And Will came to one of the gigs and said, Gee, you guys have enshrined that thing, but I only played that one time in my life. It was recorded live at *My Father's Place* on Long Island and, he said, that was an arrangement that was just that night's output. And the more I do this stuff, the more I value getting out there on the road and taking a chance that it's not going to come together. But the more you do it, the more it comes together, and pretty soon you're at a point where it never fails. But that's Mike and Randy. I think that both those guys have a lot of [Thelonius] Monk mentality in there that, if its predictable, or if its the usual thing, just immediately there's no thrill any more, you know, they're not interested in it. At different times when I was producing stuff with Randy, who would be sitting in my apartment in Manhattan, and he'd be listening to the track, and now that I had it sounding good, it just wasn't weird enough for him. So he would say something like, Let's take that clavinet part and start transposing it around. And I would transpose it to what should be completely the wrong key, and I'd look back at him and he'd have this big smile on his face."

References

[1] Steps Ahead: *Copenhagen Live*, DVD, Storyville Films, 2007.

[2] Michael Cuscuna, *Down Beat*, 15 May 1969 p15.

[3] Larry Coryell: *Improvising – My Life In Music*, Backbeat Books, Hal Leonard Corporation, NYC, (2007) p57.

[4] Randy Sandke interviewed by Doug Ramsey: *Michael Brecker Remembered*, January 17, 2007 http://www.artsjournal.com/rifftides/ retrieved 2013.

2007/01/michael_brecker_remembered.html, retrieved 2013.

[5] Interview with Randy Brecker, 17 May 2013.

[6] Interview with Ronnie Cuber, 1 May 2013.

[7] Larry Coryell: p25.

[8] Larry Coryell: p69.

[9] R S Ginell, Larry Coryell bio, AllMusic.com, retrieved (2013).

[10] Al Kooper: *Backstage Passes and Backstabbing Bastards*, Backbeat Books, NY 2008 Hal Leonard Corporation.

[11] Michael Cuscuna, *Down Beat*, 15 May 1969 p15.

[12] Bone2Pick Randy Brecker Interview Pt 1 with Michael Davis hip-bonemusic.com 28 Sep 2012

[13] MB interviewed by Robert Palmer, *Down Beat*, 9 October 1975, p12, 13, 41.

[14] Michael Brecker talking to Tom Barlow, *Jazzwise* (2002) No. 55 p22-7.

[15] Randy Brecker, talking to Nat Hentoff, notes to *Score* (1969).

[16] Ken Trethewey, Jazz-Fusion and Miles Davis – Dark Prince, Jazz-Fusion Books.

[17] Randy Brecker: notes to *Score* (1969), Koch Jazz.

[18] Paul Stump, *Go Ahead John, The Music of John McLaughlin*, SAF Publishing (2000), p35.

[19] Brecker Brothers interviewed by Steve Bloom, *Down Beat*, June 1979, p24-26.

[20] Billy Cobham: in Stuart Nicholson, *Jazz Rock: A History*, Schirmer Books, New York (1998), p48.

[21] Stuart Nicholson, p43.

[22] Sam Rivers interviews, halgalper.com

[23] Larry Coryell: p91.

[24] Interview with Jim Schaffer, *Down Beat*, January 1974 p16.

[25] Larry Coryell: p92.

[26] Larry Coryell: p93-94.

[27] Tom Barlow, notes to Billy Cobham's *Spectrum* (2001), Atlantic Masters Edition.

[28] Mark Griffith, http://www.pas.org/experience/halloffame/CobhamBilly.aspx retrieved 2013.

[29] CliveDavis.com retrieved 2013.
[30] Miles Davis with Quincy Troupe; *Miles: The Autobiography* (1990), Picador p287.
[31] *New York Times* 17/2/1997.
[32] http://stevekhan.com/discog2.htm retrieved 2013.
[33] Michael Brecker reported in *Crescendo* (September, 1980) p22-3.
[34] Album review, *Down Beat*, August 1975, p24.
[35] Randy Brecker reported in *Blues & Soul*, 164 (1975) p41.
[36] Reported in *Blues & Soul*, 164 (1975) p28.
[37] Michael Brecker talking to Jason West (1999): http://www.allaboutjazz.com retrieved 2013.
[38] Wikipedia; *Heavy Metal Rock Music* retrieved 2013.
[39] *Jazz Hot*, September 1980, p37-38.
[40] Michael Brecker reported in in: Bill Milkowski, *Jaco: The Extraordinary and Tragic Life of Jaco Pastorius, The World's Greatest Bass Player* (1995) Backbeat Books, p90.
[41] Peter Erskine: Notes to *The Birthday Concert* (1994), Warner Bros. Masters Edition.
[42] Milkowski, p116.
[43] Milkowski, not referenced.
[44] Robert Baird, *Notes to the Storyville Archives*, Storyville Films, accompanying DVD, *Steps Ahead: Copenhagen Live* (2007).
[45] Mike Mainieri, sleeve notes to *Steps – A Collection*, 2000, NYC Records.
[46] Richard Cook, *Jazz Encyclopedia* (2005), Penguin Reference, p182.
[47] [http://www.patchmanmusic.com/NyleSteinerHomepage.html]
[48] The Louis Gerrits Michael Brecker Collection, personal communication, August 2013.
[49] http://www.synthtopia.com/content/2013/02/03/steinerphone-ewi-synth-jam/ retrieved 2013.
[50] Joel C Peskin: *The EWI Story* http://members.aol.com/Ireedman1/ewi.htm retrieved 2013.
[51] Wikipedia: Smooth jazz; retrieved June 2013
[52] Bill Milkowski interviews Randy Brecker, notes to *In The Idiom*, (1987) Denon Records.
[53] Michael Brecker writing in *Crescendo* (September, 1980) p22-3.
[54] Michael Brecker reported by Ken Frankling, *Jazz Times*, Nov 1988, 16-17.
[55] Michael Brecker, notes, *Michael Brecker* (1987) GRP Impulse! Records.
[56] Steve Schneider, notes to *Michael Brecker* (1987). GRP Impulse! Records.
[57] George Varga, notes to *Don't Try This at Home*, (1988) GRP Impulse! Records.
[58] Randy Brecker, notes to *Live At Sweet Basil* (1989) GNP Crescendo Records.
[59] Judd Miller, http://www.patchmanmusic.com/JuddMiller.html retrieved 2013.
[60] James Genus talking to Jake Cot for *Bass Musician Magazine*, http://bassmusicianmagazine.com/2009/04/conversation-with-james-genus/ retrieved 2013.

[61] Interview with George Whitty, 20 Sep 2013.

[62] Randy Brecker: in The Brecker Brothers: *The Return of the Brecker Brothers Live in Spain 1992* [DVD] (1994)

[63] Downloaded in 2013 at www.totallyfuzzy.net/ourtube/ brecker-brothers/live-in-barcelona-1992-video_061123dca.html

[64] Michael Brecker speaking in a lecture on DVD; The Louis Gerrits Michael Brecker Collection, personal communication, August 2013.

[65] Bill Bruford, *The Autobiography*, Jawbone Press (2009) p218.

[66] Michael Brecker in Brecker Brothers: *Live in Tokyo U-Port Hall*, 1995 [DVD] track 6 (2010).

[67] Randy Brecker in notes to *Into the Sun* (1995).

[68] Jeanne O'Connor-Grolnick, April 1997) Notes to *Don Grolnick: The Complete Blue Note Recordings* (1997), Blue Note Records

[69] MB, notes to *Two Blocks From the Edge* (1998), Impulse! Records.

[70] Jamey Abersold, *Play the Music of Randy Brecker*, (2009) Jamey Abersold Jazz, vol. 126.

[71] Randy Brecker: notes to *Hangin' In The City* (2001) ESC Records.

[72] Herbie Hancock, notes to Hancock, Hargrove, Brecker, *Directions in Music*, (2002), Verve.

[73] Wikipedia: *Impressions (composition) by John Coltrane*. en.wikipedia.org/wiki/Impressions_(instrumental), retrieved 2010.

[74] Wikipedia: *Transition (composition) by John Coltrane*. en.wikipedia.org/wiki/Transition_(John_Coltrane_album), retrieved 2010

[75] Roy Hargrove, notes to Hancock, Hargrove, Brecker, *Directions in Music*, (2002)Verve .

[76] Michael Brecker, notes to Hancock, Hargrove, Brecker, *Directions in Music*, (2002) Verve.

[77] Jeremy Lubbock: notes to Charlie Haden with Michael Brecker: *American Dreams* (2002) Verve.

[78] Randy Brecker talking to Bill Milkowski: reported in *Bill Evans Randy Brecker Soulbop Band;* http://www.bhm-music.de/bhm/en/ artists.php?upc=090204899654&s_name=7

[79] Bill Evans talking to Bill Milkowski: reported in *Bill Evans Randy Brecker Soulbop Band;* http://www.bhm-music.de/bhm/en/ artists.php?upc=090204899654&s_name=7

[80] http://www2.ljworld.com/news/2007/may/27/ facing_death_musician_michael_brecker_provides_mov; accessed Sep 2013

[81] Wlodek Pawlik, notes to *Nostalgic Journey: Tykocin Jazz Suite* (2009) Summit Records.

[82] Brecker Brothers: *Live in Tokyo U-Port Hall, 1995* (2010).

[83] Cook, p76

[84] Bill Bruford, p 154-156

[85] Cook, p77

[86] Bill Evans, notes to *Soulbop Band Live* (2004), BHM Records.

[87] George Whitty, *Michael Brecker's Logic Pro EWI Environment*, Virtual Instruments, June (2011) pp60-64. Also at:

http://ewilogic.com/wp-content/uploads/2011/06/Michael-Breckers-Logic-Environment.pdf

[88] http://www.scaruffi.com/history/jazz17h.html, downloaded, September 2013

[89] Ben Ratliff: *Coltrane – The Story of a Sound* (2007). Faber and Faber, London, p209

[90] Michael Brecker: lecture at the North Texas University, DVD, Spring 1984. Louis Gerrits Collection.

[91] Ben Ratliff, p216

Acknowledgements

I wish to offer my sincere thanks Randy Brecker for his interest and support throughout this project. Thanks are due also to Susan Brecker for her positive response and support.

I am very grateful to George Whitty for his valuable insights into the workings of the bands.

Thanks are due also to Ronnie Cuber, who provided me with a lot of background material about life as a session musician in New York City, and to his agent, Roberta Arnold, for her enthusiastic assistance.

A large debt of gratitude is owed to Louis Gerrits, who not only helped with photographs, but also did so much of the work in compiling the discography and generously allowed me to use material from his comprehensive collection.

Grammy Awards

*In December 2013, just prior to publication, Randy was nominated, along with the Włodek Pawlik Trio & the Kalisz Philharmonic for a Grammy Award for their album *Night in Calisia* (2013) in the category, "Best Large Jazz Ensemble."

2008: Best Contemporary Jazz Album, *Randy In Brasil*, Randy Brecker (artist), Eduardo Santos (engineer), Ruriá Duprat (producer).

2007: Best Jazz Instrumental Solo, *Anagram*, Michael Brecker (soloist).

2007: Best Jazz Instrumental Album, Individual or Group, *Pilgrimage*, Michael Brecker (artist), Joe Ferla (engineer), Gil Goldstein, Michael Brecker, Pat Metheny & Steven Rodby (producers).

2006: Best Jazz Instrumental Solo, *Some Skunk Funk*, Michael Brecker (soloist).

2006: Best Large Jazz Ensemble Album, *Some Skunk Funk*, Jim Beard, Marcio Doctor, Michael Brecker, Peter Erskine, Randy Brecker, Vince Mendoza, WDR Big Band & Will Lee (artists). Klaus Genuit & Peter Brandt (engineers / mixers), Joachim Becker & Lucas Schmid (producers).

2003: Best Contemporary Jazz Album, *34th N Lex*, Randy Brecker (artist), George Whitty (engineer / mixer), George Whitty (producer).

2003: Best Large Jazz Ensemble Album, *Wide Angles*, Michael Brecker Quindectet (Michael Brecker: artist), Jay Newland (engineer / mixer), Gil Goldstein (producer).

2003: Best Instrumental Arrangement, *Timbuktu*, Gil Goldstein & Michael Brecker (arrangers).

2002: Best Jazz Instrumental Album, Individual or Group, *Directions In Music*, Herbie Hancock, Michael Brecker & Roy Hargrove (artists), Doug Doctor, Jay Newland & Rob Griffin (engineers / mixers), Jason Olaine (producer).

2001: Best Jazz Instrumental Solo, *Chan's Song*, Michael Brecker (soloist).

1997: Best Contemporary Jazz Performance, *Into The Sun*, Randy Brecker (artist).

1996: Best Jazz Instrumental Solo, *Cabin Fever*, Michael Brecker (soloist).

1996: Best Jazz Instrumental Performance, Individual Or Group, *Tales From The Hudson*, Michael Brecker (artist).

1995: Best Jazz Instrumental Solo, *Impressions*, Michael Brecker (soloist).

1995: Best Jazz Instrumental Performance, Individual Or Group, *Infinity*, McCoy Tyner Trio (Aaron Scott, Avery Sharpe, McCoy Tyner) & Michael Brecker (artists).

1994: Best Contemporary Jazz Performance, *Out Of The Loop*, Brecker Brothers (Michael Brecker, Randy Brecker, artists).

1994: Best Instrumental Composition, *African Skies*, Michael Brecker (composer).

1988: Best Jazz Instrumental Performance Soloist (On A Jazz Recording), *Don't Try This At Home*, Michael Brecker (soloist).

Discography

Randy and Michael Brecker have played on, arguably, more published albums than any other artists in the history of recorded music, with Randy outstripping even his brother's efforts. That poses a great challenge to those who would try to catalogue their work. Fortunately, Randy has provided a comprehensive list of his own work; Louis Gerrits compiled the original list for Michael. Both Randy and Louis have allowed me to build upon this starting point. The discographies provided here are substantially revised and updated from the originals by reference to large Internet music databases at Allmusic.com and Discogs.com, as well as much other research by me. There is some vagueness regarding these musicians' recorded work in Japan, especially Michael, who has been unusually prolific there. Unfortunately, for reasons of space, it has not been possible to include all of the information collected. I have tried to list every album that Michael and Randy appeared on, although I have not included "compilation" albums, i.e. collections of previously published material, except in the case of albums with Randy or Michael as leader of the band. I have also not included information about multiple editions. The record label and number, and the UIN/UPC cited relate to editions published either in, or close to the first year of publication. In the case of albums published before CDs were available, I have either given the vinyl ID or the data for an early CD release, or both. Lists are generally in order of the year of recording. Sometimes this can differ significantly from the year of first publication. Where appropriate, star ratings are my own.

Errors and omissions are entirely my own responsibility and it is my intention to correct and improve the data in subsequent editions.

CDs by The Brecker Brothers: Randy and Michael Brecker as leaders

The Brecker Brothers
**** 1975 The Brecker Brothers
CD; Arista: BVCJ 37570; UIN/UPC: 886971118520
Length: (45.43); Album type: studio
Produced by: Randy Brecker
Musicians: Randy Brecker (trumpet), Michael Brecker (saxophone), David Sanborn (saxophone), Don Grolnick (piano), Bob Mann (guitar), Will Lee (bass), Harvey Mason Sr (drums), Chris Parker (drums), Ralph MacDonald (percussion)
Tracks: 1 Some Skunk Funk (5.50), 2 Sponge (4.04), 3 A Creature of Many Faces (7.40), 4 Twilight (5.42), 5 Sneakin' Up Behind You (4.53), 6 Rocks (4.37), 7 Levitate (4.31), 8 Oh My Stars (3.13), 9 D. B. B. (4.46)
Notes: Originally Arista AL 4037 (1975).

The Brecker Brothers Band
*** 1976 Back To Back
CD; Epic Legacy: 88697111812; UIN/UPC: 886971118124
Length: (48.44); Album type: studio
Produced by: Randy Brecker
Musicians: Michael Brecker (saxophone), Randy Brecker (trumpet), David Sanborn (saxophone), Don Grolnick (piano), Steve Khan (guitar), Will Lee (bass), Chris Parker (drums), Steve Gadd (drums), Ralph McDonald (percussion), Sammy Figueroa (percussion), Rafael Cruz (percussion), Lew Del Gatto (saxophone), David Friedman (vibraphone), Dave Whitman (keyboard), Luther Vandross (voice), Robin Clark (voice), Diane Sumler (voice), Patti Austin (voice), Allee Willis (voice)
Tracks: 1 Keep it Steady (Brecker Bump) (6.26), 2 If You Wanna Boogie...Forget It (3.58), 3 Lovely Lady (6.18), 4 Night Flight (6.15), 5 Slick Stuff (4.47), 6 Dig a Little Deeper (4.00), 7 Grease Piece (5.47), 8 What Can a Miracle Do (4.15), 9 I Love Wastin' Time With You (6.31)
Notes: Originally Arista AL 4061 (1976).

The Brecker Brothers
*** 1977 Don't Stop The Music
CD; Arista Legacy: 886971119022; UIN/UPC: 886971119022
Length: (41.33); Album type: studio
Produced by: Jack Richardson
Musicians: Michael Brecker (saxophone), Randy Brecker (trumpet), Don Grolnick (piano), Doug Riley (keyboard), Steve Khan (guitar), Hiram Bullock (guitar), Will Lee (bass), Chris Parker (drums), Ralph MacDonald (percussion), Lou Marini (saxophone), Alan Rubin (trumpet), David Taylor (trombone), Barry Rogers (trombone), Lew Del Gatto (saxophone)
Tracks: 1 Finger Lickin' Good (3.59), 2 Funky Sea, Funky Dew (6.12), 3 As Long As I've Got Your Love (4.13), 4 Squids (7.44), 5 Don't Stop the Music (6.31), 6 Petals (4.21), 7 Tabula Rasa (8.20)
Notes: Originally Arista AL 4122 (1977).

The Brecker Brothers
**** 1978 Heavy Metal Bebop
CD; Arista / BMG Japan: BVCJ 37471; UIN/UPC: 886971118322
Length: (42.33); Album type: live
Produced by: Randy Brecker, Michael Brecker
Musicians: Michael Brecker (saxophone), Randy Brecker (trumpet), Barry Finnerty (guitar), Neil Jason (bass), Terry Bozzio (drums), Sammy Figueroa (percussion), Rafael Cruz (percussion), Paul Schaefer (keyboard), Allen Schwarzberg (drums), Jeff Schoen (keyboard), Roy Herring (voice)
Tracks: 1 East River (3.37), 2 Inside Out (9.32), 3 Some Skunk Funk (7.01), 4 Sponge (6.24), 5 Funky Sea, Funky Dew (8.03), 6 Squids (7.56)
Notes: Japanese edition. Recorded live in 1978 at My Father's Place, Roslyn, Long Island, except for East River, recorded at The Power Station, NYC.

The Brecker Brothers
**** 1980 Détente
CD; Arista Legacy: 88697111822; UIN/UPC: 886971118223
Length: (43.25); Album type: studio
Produced by: George Duke

Musicians: Michael Brecker (saxophone), Randy Brecker (trumpet), Mark Gray (keyboard), George Duke (keyboard), Hiram Bullock (guitar), Neil Jason (bass), Steve Jordan (drums), Airto Moreira (percussion), Paulinho da Costa (percussion), Steve Gadd (drums), Don Grolnick (piano), Marcus Miller (bass), David Spinozza (guitar), Jeff Mironov (guitar), Ralph McDonald (percussion)
Tracks: 1 You Ga (Ta Give It) (4.30), 2 Not Tonight (3.56), 3 Don't Get Funny With My Money (4.34), 4 Tee'd Off (3.43), 5 You Left Something Behind (3.59), 6 Squish (5.51), 7 Dream Theme (5.40), 8 Baffled (5.22), 9 I Don't Know Either (5.49)
Notes: Originally Arista AB 4272 (1980).

The Brecker Brothers
***** 1981 Straphangin'
CD; Arista: ; UIN/UPC: 886971118421
Length: (44.42); Album type: studio
Produced by: Michael Brecker, Randy Brecker
Musicians: Michael Brecker (saxophone), Randy Brecker (trumpet), Barry Finnerty (guitar), Mark Gray (keyboard), Marcus Miller (bass), Richie Morales (drums), Sammy Figueroa (percussion), Manolo Badrena (percussion)
Tracks: 1 Straphangin' (8.06), 2 Threesome (6.24), 3 Bathsheba (6.58), 4 Jacknife (6.16), 5 Why Can't I Be There (5.00), 6 Not Ethiopia (5.40), 7 Spreadeagle (5.57)
Notes: Originally Arista AL 9550 (1981).

The Brecker Brothers
***** 1992 Return Of The Brecker Brothers
CD; GRP: GRD-96842; UIN/UPC: 011105968423
Length: (63.05); Album type: studio
Produced by: Randy Brecker, Michael Brecker, Max Risenhoover, George Whitty
Musicians: Michael Brecker (saxophone), Randy Brecker (trumpet), Mike Stern (guitar), Armand Sabal-Lecco (bass), Max Risenhoover (programming), Don Alias (percussion), George Whitty (keyboard), David Sanborn (saxophone), Dean Brown (guitar), Robbie Kilgore (keyboard), James Genus (bass), Dennis Chambers (drums), Bashiri Johnson (percussion), Will Lee (bass), Mary (Maz) Kessler (keyboard), Jason Miles (programming)
Tracks: 1 Song For Barry (5.07), 2 King of the Lobby (5.20), 3 Big Idea (4.20), 4 Above And Below (7.05), 5 That's All There Is To It (5.26), 6 Wakaria (What's Up?) (5.26), 7 On the Backside (6.25), 8 Sozinho (Alone) (7.36), 9 Spherical (5.58), 10 Good Gracious (5.13), 11 Roppongi (4.56)
Notes: Sanborn plays on 2.

The Brecker Brothers
***** 1994 Out Of The Loop
CD; GRP: GRD-97842; UIN/UPC: 011105978422
Length: (54.48); Album type: studio
Produced by: George Whitty
Musicians: Randy Brecker (trumpet), Michael Brecker (saxophone), George Whitty (keyboard), Dean Brown (guitar), James Genus (bass), Steve Jordan (drums), Steve Thornton (percussion), Larry Saltzman (guitar), Shawn Pelton (drums), Chris Botti (programming), Andy Snitzer (programming), Robbie Kilgore (keyboard), Mary (Maz) Kessler (keyboard), Armand Sabal-Lecco (bass), Rodney Holmes (drums), Eliane Elias (voice), Mark Ledford (voice)

Tracks: 1 Slang (6.11), 2 Evocations (5.16), 3 Scrunch (4.28), 4 Secret Heart (5.03), 5 African Skies (7.46), 6 When It Was (4.29), 7 Harpoon (7.43), 8 The Nightwalker (8.44), 9 And Then She Wept (4.53)
Notes: Awarded the Grammy for Best Contemporary Jazz Performance 1994.

The Brecker Brothers
***** 2012 The Complete Arista Albums Collection
8 CD; Sony: 886979796225; UIN/UPC: 886979796225
Length: (359.10); Album type: box set
Produced by: Randy Brecker
Musicians: Randy Brecker (trumpet), Michael Brecker (saxophone), Airto Moreira (percussion), Don Alias (percussion), Sanford Allen (violin), Lamar Alsop (viola), Patti Austin (voice), Manolo Badrena (percussion), Warren Bernhardt (keyboard), Doug Billard (voice), Beverly Billard (voice), Terry Bozzio (drums), Ariana Bronne (violin), Baron Browne (bass), Alfred Brown (viola), Josh Brown (voice), Hiram Bullock (guitar), Irene Cara (voice), Sue Ann Carlwell (voice), Carl Carlwell (voice), Robin Clark (voice), Larry Coryell (guitar), Rafael Cruz (percussion), Paulinho da Costa (percussion), Lew Del Gatto (saxophone), Peter Dimitriades (violin), George Duke (keyboard), Christine Faith (voice), Sammy Figueroa (percussion), Barry Finnerty (guitar), David Friedman (vibraphone), Jerry Friedman (guitar), Steve Gadd (drums), Paul Gershman (violin), Eddie Gomez (bass), Mark Gray (keyboard), Don Grolnick (piano), Roy Herring (voice), Neil Jason (bass), Steve Jordan (drums), Steve Khan (guitar), Harold Kohon (violin), Will Lee (bass), Tony Levin (bass), Jesse Levy (cello), Richard Locker (cello), Harry Lookovsky (violin), Guy Lumia (violin), Ralph MacDonald (percussion), Mike Mainieri (vibraphone), Bob Mann (guitar), Lou Marini (saxophone), Harvey Mason Sr (drums), Richard Maximoff (viola), Ullanda McCullough (voice), Paulette McWilliams (voice), Marcus Miller (bass), Jeff Mironov (guitar), Kash Monet (percussion), Richie Morales (drums), Chris Parker (drums), Matthew Raimondi (violin), William (Bill) Reichenbach (trombone), Doug Riley (keyboard), Barry Rogers (trombone), D. J. Rogers (voice), Aaron Rosand (violin), Alan Rubin (trumpet), David Sanborn (saxophone), Paul Schaefer (keyboard), Jeff Schoen (keyboard), Allen Schwarzberg (drums), David Spinozza (guitar), Diane Sumler (voice), David Taylor (trombone), Fonzie Thornton (voice), Sandy Torano (guitar), Luther Vandross (voice), Lenny White (drums), Dave Whitman (keyboard), Allee Willis (voice), Erik Zobler (percussion)
Tracks: 1 Some Skunk Funk (5.53), 2 Sponge (4.07), 3 A Creature of Many Faces (7.44), 4 Twilight (5.46), 5 Sneakin' Up Behind You (4.56), 6 Rocks (4.40), 7 Levitate (4.34), 8 Oh My Stars (3.16), 9 D. B. B. (4.47), 10 Keep it Steady (Brecker Bump) (6.29), 11 If You Wanna Boogie...Forget It (4.01), 12 Lovely Lady (6.21), 13 Night Flight (6.18), 14 Slick Stuff (4.50), 15 Dig a Little Deeper (4.04), 16 Grease Piece (5.49), 17 What Can a Miracle Do (4.17), 18 I Love Wastin' Time With You (6.32), 19 Finger Lickin' Good (4.02), 20 Funky Sea, Funky Dew (6.13), 21 As Long As I've Got Your Love (4.16), 22 Squids (7.46), 23 Don't Stop the Music (6.34), 24 Petals (4.23), 25 Tabula Rasa (8.19), 26 East River (3.37), 27 Inside Out (9.29), 28 Some Skunk Funk (6.59), 30 Funky Sea, Funky Dew (8.02), 31 Squids (7.53), 29 Sponge (6.23), 32 You Ga (Ta Give It) (4.32), 33 Not Tonight (3.56), 34 Don't Get Funny With My Money (4.34), 35 Tee'd Off (3.43), 36 You Left Something Behind (4.06), 37 Squish (5.51), 38 Dream Theme (5.40), 39 Baffled (5.23), 40 I Don't Know Either (5.48), 41 Straphangin' (8.07), 42 Threesome (6.28), 43 Bathsheba (7.01), 44 Jacknife (6.19), 45 Why Can't I Be There (5.04), 46 Not Ethiopia (5.45), 47 Spreadeagle (5.58), 48 Blue Montreux (8.50), 49 Rocks (7.56), 50 I'm Sorry (8.41), 51 Magic Carpet (5.37), 52 Buds (5.02), 53 Floating (7.56), 54 The Virgin and the Gypsy (8.25), 55 A Funky Waltz (6.02), 56 Candles (6.07), 57 Uptown Ed (6.39), 58 Love Play (10.54), 59 Cloud Motion (9.31)

Notes: Tracks 1-9 on CD1 45.48); tracks 10-18 on CD2 (48.44); tracks 19-25 on CD3 (41.37); tracks 26-31 on CD4 (42.25); tracks 32-40 on CD5 (43.37); tracks 41-47 on CD6 (44.45); tracks 48-54 on CD7 (52.59); tracks 55-59 on CD6 (39.15).

DVDs by The Brecker Brothers

The Brecker Brothers
1992 The Return of The Brecker Brothers: Live in Spain 1992
DVD; Pioneer LDC / GRP: PILJ-1124; UIN/UPC:
Length: (57.14); Album type: live
Produced by: Musicians: Randy Brecker (trumpet)
Michael Brecker (saxophone), Mike Stern (guitar), Dennis Chambers (drums), James Genus (bass), George Whitty (keyboard)
Tracks: 1 Above And Below (9.46), 2 Spherical (12.18), 3 Some Skunk Funk (6.20), 4 Common Ground (8.56), 5 Song For Barry (14.38), 6 Inside Out (n/k)
Notes: Recorded live at the Palau de la Musica, Barcelona, Spain.

The Brecker Brothers
*** 2010 Live In Tokyo, U-Port Hall, 1995
DVD; Jazz Door: JD 11046; UIN/UPC: 4250079741465
Length: (83.26); Album type: live
Musicians: Randy Brecker (trumpet), Michael Brecker (saxophone), George Whitty (keyboard), Dean Brown (guitar), James Genus (bass), Rodney Holmes (drums)
Tracks: 1 Slang (9.08), 2 Interview (1.57), 3 Spherical (15.37), 4 Interview (2.23), 5 Harpoon (13.33), 6 Interview (1.07), 7 Song For Barry (29.35), 8 Interview (1.42), 9 Some Skunk Funk (5.57)

Compilations of Previously Released Material (prm) by The Brecker Brothers

The Brecker Brothers
1990 The Brecker Bros. Collection, Vol. 1
CD; Novus / BMG: ND 90442; UIN/UPC: 0035629044227
Length: (70.17); Album type: prm
Musicians: Michael Brecker (saxophone), Randy Brecker (trumpet)
Tracks: 1 Some Skunk Funk (5.50), 2 Sponge (4.00), 3 Squids (7.45), 4 Funky Sea, Funky Dew (6.11), 5 Inside Out (9.27), 6 Dream Theme (5.37), 7 I Don't Know Either (5.47), 8 Bathsheba (7.00), 9 Straphangin' (8.05), 10 Threesome (6.21), 11 East River (3.33)

The Brecker Brothers
1991 The Brecker Bros. Collection, Vol. 2
CD; Novus / BMG: ND 83076; UIN/UPC: 0035628307620
Length: (68.52); Album type: prm
Musicians: Michael Brecker (saxophone), Randy Brecker (trumpet)
Tracks: 1 Rocks (4.39), 2 A Creature of Many Faces (7.42), 3 Funky Sea, Funky Dew (8.00), 4 Some Skunk Funk (6.55), 5 Sponge (6.19), 6 Squids (7.54), 7 Tee'd Off (3.43), 8 Squish (5.50), 9 Baffled (5.20), 10 Not Ethiopia (5.41), 11 Jacknife (6.18)

The Brecker Brothers
1997 East River
CD; Camden: 74321 511992; UIN/UPC: 743215119920
Length: (71.53); Album type: prm
Musicians: Michael Brecker (saxophone), Randy Brecker (trumpet)
Tracks: 1 East River (3.35), 2 Some Skunk Funk (5.51), 3 Inside Out (9.29), 4 Funky Sea, Funky Dew (6.12), 5 Straphangin' (8.07), 6 Threesome (6.19), 7 Rocks (4.39), 8 Baffled (5.21), 9 Jacknife (6.18), 10 Tee'd Off (3.43), 11 Not Ethiopia (5.43), 12 Keep it Steady (Brecker Bump) (6.17)

The Brecker Brothers
1998 Priceless Jazz 25: Brecker Brothers
CD; GRP; UIN/UPC: 011105994828
Length: (68.00); Album type: prm
Musicians: Randy Brecker (trumpet), Michael Brecker (saxophone)
Tracks: 1 Big Idea (4.20), 2 King of the Lobby (5.20), 3 And Then She Wept (4.53), 4 Slang (6.11), 5 Above And Below (7.05), 6 African Skies (7.46), 7 Song For Barry (5.07), 8 Harpoon (7.43), 9 Good Gracious (5.13), 10 Spherical (5.58), 11 Sozinho (Alone) (7.36)

The Brecker Brothers
2006 Sneakin' Up Behind You: The Very Best of The Brecker Brothers
CD; Arista Legacy: 82876 84865-2; UIN/UPC: 828768486528
Length: (66.54); Album type: prm
Musicians: Michael Brecker (saxophone), Randy Brecker (trumpet), David Sanborn (saxophone), Don Grolnick (piano), Bob Mann (guitar), Will Lee (bass), Chris Parker (drums), Harvey Mason Sr (drums), Ralph MacDonald (percussion), Doug Riley (keyboard), Steve Khan (guitar), Hiram Bullock (guitar), Sammy Figueroa (percussion), Lenny White (drums), Barry Finnerty (guitar), Marcus Miller (bass), Mark Gray (keyboard), Richie Morales (drums), George Duke (keyboard), Steve Jordan (drums), Airto Moreira (percussion), Neil Jason (bass), Manolo Badrena (percussion), Rafael Cruz (percussion)
Tracks: 1 Sneakin' Up Behind You (4.52), 2 Some Skunk Funk (5.49), 3 Funky Sea, Funky Dew (6.11), 4 Tabula Rasa (8.18), 5 Threesome (6.24), 6 Squish (5.52), 7 Baffled (5.23), 8 Straphangin' (8.08), 9 Jacknife (6.18), 10 Inside Out (9.27)

Unofficial Releases of Brecker Brothers Material

The Brecker Brothers
1994 The Brecker Brothers - Live
CD; Jazz Door: JD 1248; UIN/UPC: 4011778600466
Length: (n/k); Album type: live
Musicians: Michael Brecker (saxophone), Randy Brecker (trumpet), George Whitty (keyboard), Mike Stern (guitar), Dennis Chambers (drums), James Genus (bass)
Tracks: 1 Some Skunk Funk (7.20), 2 Common Ground (14.02), 3 Sponge (7.00), 4 Song For Barry (20.36), 5 Spherical (12.21), 6 N.Y. Special (5.49)
Notes: Recorded in NYC.

CDs by Randy Brecker as leader

Randy Brecker
**** 1969 Score
CD; Koch Jazz: KOC CD 51416; UIN/UPC: 65240514162
Length: (38.09); Album type: studio
Produced by: Duke Pearson
Musicians: Randy Brecker (trumpet), Michael Brecker (saxophone), Jerry Dodgion (flute), Hal Galper (piano), Larry Coryell (guitar), Eddie Gomez (bass), Chuck Rainey (bass), Bernard (Pretty) Purdie (drums), Mickey Roker (drums)
Tracks: 1 Bangalore (4.32), 2 Score (7.17), 3 Name Game (5.13), 4 The Weasel Goes Out to Lunch (1.19), 5 Morning Song (4.08), 6 Pipe Dream (4.31), 7 The Vamp (5.13), 8 The Marble Sea (5.41)
Notes: Originally released on Blue Note. Rainey and Purdie replace Gomez and Roker on 2,7. Dodgion plays on 5,6,8. Coryell plays on 2,5,6,7,8. Galper plays on 1,2,3,7. This record has also been issued by Jazz Door as Score, CD JD1211, UIN 4011778600107, credited to The Brecker Bros.

Randy Brecker, Eliane Elias
*** 1985 Amanda
CD; Passport: PJCD 88013; UIN/UPC: n/a
Length: (40.49); Album type: studio
Produced by: Randy Brecker, Eliane Elias
Musicians: Randy Brecker (trumpet), Eliane Elias (voice), Michael Brecker (saxophone), Dave Weckl (drums), Danny Gottlieb (drums), Manolo Badrena (percussion), Mark Egan (bass), Cyro Baptista (percussion), Will Lee (bass), Jeff Mironov (guitar), Chris Parker (drums), Barry Finnerty (guitar), Sadao Watanabe (saxophone)
Tracks: 1 Splash (5.23), 2 Para Nada (For Nothing) (7.08), 3 Pandamandium (6.22), 4 Samba de Bamba (8.16), 5 Amandamada (4.47), 6 Guaruja (8.51)
Notes: Michael Brecker, Lee, Finnerty, Weckl and Badrena play on 3, 5, both recorded May 1985. All other tracks recorded Feb 1985. MB plays alto flute on 5; Watanabe plays alto sax on 5.

Randy Brecker
*** 1987 In The Idiom
CD; Denon: 33CY-1483; UIN/UPC: 4988001085232
Length: (58.21); Album type: studio
Produced by: Randy Brecker
Musicians: Randy Brecker (trumpet), Joe Henderson (saxophone), Ron Carter (bass), Al Foster (drums), David Kikoski (keyboard)
Tracks: 1 No Scratch (5.45), 2 Hit Or Miss (9.20), 3 Forever Young (5.59), 4 Sang (6.37), 5 You're In My Heart (6.49), 6 There's A Mingus A Monk Us (6.29), 7 Moontide (7.31), 8 Little Miss P (9.23)

Randy Brecker
**** 1989 Live At Sweet Basil
CD; GNP Crescendo: GNPD 2210; UIN/UPC: 052824221024
Length: (62.34); Album type: live
Produced by: Randy Brecker
Musicians: Randy Brecker (trumpet) Joey Baron (drums), Bob Berg (saxophone), Dieter Ilg (bass), David Kikoski (keyboard)

Tracks: 1 The Sleaze Factor (7.34), 2 Thrifty Man (9.35), 3 Ting Chang (8.08), 4 Incidentally (8.15), 5 Hurdy Gurdy (10.20), 6 Moontide (7.40), 7 Mo' Joe (11.02)
Notes: This edition 1991. Originally released by Sonet (1989) SNTF 1011; UIN/UPC: 045395101116

Randy Brecker
**** 1990 Toe To Toe
CD; MCA: MCAD 6334; UIN/UPC: 076732633427
Length: (43.37); Album type: studio
Produced by: Jim Beard, Randy Brecker
Musicians: Randy Brecker (trumpet), Jim Beard (keyboard), Dennis Chambers (drums), Jon Herington (guitar), Victor Bailey (bass), Darryl Jones (bass), Bashiri Johnson (percussion), Bob Mintzer (saxophone), Michael Brecker (saxophone), Mark Ledford (voice), Regina Belle (voice)
Tracks: 1 Mr. Skinny (5.39), 2 Trading Secrets (5.10), 3 It Creeps Up on You (4.53), 4 The Glider (6.04), 5 Toe to Toe (4.54), 6 It's Up to You (5.50), 7 What is the Answer (4.41), 8 Lost 4 Words (6.14)

Randy Brecker
*** 1995 Into The Sun
CD; Concord: CCD-4761-2; UIN/UPC: 013431476122
Length: (58.51); Album type: studio
Produced by: Gil Goldstein, Randy Brecker
Musicians: Randy Brecker (trumpet)
Gil Goldstein (keyboard), Adam Rogers (guitar), Bakithi Kumalo (bass), Jonathan Joseph (drums), Edson Aparecido (Café) da Silva (percussion), David Sanborn (saxophone), Dave Bargeron (trombone), David Taylor (trombone), Lawrence Feldman (saxophone), Keith Underwood (flute), Bob Mintzer (saxophone), Richard Sussman (keyboard), Maucha Adnet (voice)
Tracks: 1 Village Dawn (6.23), 2 Just Between Us (5.48), 3 The Sleaze Factor (4.47), 4 Into the Sun (6.54), 5 After Love (7.27), 6 Gray Area (6.42), 7 Tijuca (5.18), 8 Buds (3.55), 9 Four Worlds (7.18), 10 The Hottest Man in Town
Notes: Awarded the Grammy for Best Contemporary Jazz Performance 1997.

Bob Berg, Randy Brecker, Dennis Chambers, Joey DeFrancesco
**** 2000 The JazzTimes Superband
CD; Concord: CCD-4889-2; UIN/UPC: 013431488927
Length: (65.46); Album type: studio
Produced by: Nick Phillips
Musicians: Bob Berg (saxophone), Randy Brecker (trumpet), Dennis Chambers (drums), Joey DeFrancesco (keyboard), Paul Bollenback (guitar)
Tracks: 1 Dirty Dogs (6.17), 2 Silverado (8.25), 3 Jones Street (6.08), 4 Oleo (5.36), 5 Friday Night at the Cadillac Club (4.47), 6 SoHo Sole (7.14), 7 The Ada Strut (6.16), 8 Blue Goo (6.24), 9 Seven A.M. Special (6.08), 10 Freedom Jazz Dance (8.12)
Notes: Randy Brecker plays flugelhorn on 4, Oleo, and on 7, The Ada Strut.

Randy Brecker
**** 2001 Hangin' In The City
CD; ESC Records: ESC/EFA 03674-2; UIN/UPC: 718750367426
Length: (62.08); Album type: studio
Produced by: George Whitty
Musicians: Randy Brecker (trumpet), Michael Brecker (saxophone), Dean Brown (guitar), Adam Rogers (guitar), Chris Minh Doky (bass), Hiram Bullock (guitar), Will Lee (bass), Richard Bona (multi), Don Alias (percussion), George Whitty (keyboard), Richard Locker (cello), Joe Locke (vibraphone), Katreese Barnes (voice), Michael Harvey (voice), Joe Caro (guitar)
Tracks: 1 Overture (5.11), 2 Wayne Out (4.28), 3 Hangin' In The City (5.46), 4 I Talk to the Trees (7.19), 5 Down 4 The Count (4.41), 6 Pastoral (To Jaco) (7.11), 7 Then I Came 2 My Senses (5.27), 8 Seattle (5.24), 9 Never Tell Her U Love Her ('Less She's 3000 Miles Away) (4.58), 10 I Been Through This Before (5.56), 11 One Thing Led to Another (5.45)

Randy Brecker
**** 2002 34th N Lex
CD; ESC Records / Victor: VICJ 61085; UIN/UPC: n/a
Length: (56.53); Album type: studio
Produced by: George Whitty
Musicians: Randy Brecker (trumpet), Michael Brecker (saxophone), David Sanborn (saxophone), Ronnie Cuber (saxophone), George Whitty (keyboard), Adam Rogers (guitar), Chris Minh Doky (bass), Gary Haase (bass), Zach Danziger (drums), Adam Rogers (guitar), Chris Taylor (guitar), Clarence Penn (drums), Fred Wesley (trombone), Ada Rovatti (saxophone), Makeeba Mooncycle (voice), J Phoenix (voice)
Tracks: 1 34th N Lex (6.29), 2 Streeange (4.21), 3 Shanghigh (5.37), 4 All 4 Love (3.36), 5 Let It Go (3.57), 6 Forgone Conclusion (7.40), 7 Hula Dula (5.09), 8 The Fisherman (5.33), 9 Give It Up (5.00), 10 Tokyo Freddie (4.34), 11 The Castle Rocks (4.48)
Notes: Awarded the Grammy for Best Contemporary Jazz Album 2003. This is a Japanese edition.

Bill Evans, Randy Brecker
**** 2004 Soulbop Band Live
2 CD; BHM: BHM 1003-2; UIN/UPC: 090204899654
Length: (96.55); Album type: live
Produced by: Bill Evans, Randy Brecker
Musicians: Bill Evans (sax) (saxophone), Randy Brecker (trumpet), Hiram Bullock (guitar), David Kikoski (keyboard), Victor Bailey (bass), Steve Smith (drums)
Tracks: 1 Rattletrap (7.37), 2 Big Fun (8.55), 3 Above And Below (11.15), 4 Let's Pretend (7.43), 5 Some Skunk Funk (6.41), 6 Greed (9.11), 7 Soul Bop (9.51), 8 Tease Me (6.18), 9 Cool Eddie (9.30), 10 Mixed Grill (6.01), 11 Hangin' in the City (6.37), 12 Dixie Hop (7.16)
Notes: Tracks 1-6 on CD1; tracks 7-12 on CD2.

Randy Brecker, with Michael Brecker
**** 2005 Some Skunk Funk
CD; Telarc: SACD-63647; UIN/UPC: 089408364761
Length: (68.48); Album type: live
Produced by: Lucas Schmid, Joachim Becker

Musicians: Randy Brecker (trumpet), Michael Brecker (saxophone), Jim Beard (keyboard), Will Lee (bass), Peter Erskine (drums), Marcio Doctor (percussion), WDR Big Band (band), Vince Mendoza (conductor)
Tracks: 1 Some Skunk Funk (6.26), 2 Sponge (6.46), 3 Shanghigh (6.26), 4 Wayne Out (4.56), 5 And Then She Wept (6.07), 6 Straphangin' (8.18), 7 Let It Go (8.02), 8 Freefall (6.17), 9 Levitate (4.58), 10 Song For Barry (10.32)
Notes: Awarded the Grammy for Best Large Jazz Ensemble Album 2006. Michael Brecker awarded the Grammy for Best Jazz Instrumental Solo 2007 for Some Skunk Funk. Recorded during the Leverkusener Jazztage at the Forum, Leverkusen.

Randy Brecker
***** 2008 Randy In Brasil
CD; MAMA Records: MAA 1035; UIN/UPC: 734956103521
Length: (56.30); Album type: studio
Produced by: Ruria Duprat
Musicians: Randy Brecker (trumpet), Teco Cardoso (saxophone), Ruria Duprat (keyboard), Paulo Calazans (keyboard), Gilson Peranzetta (piano), Andre Mehmari (piano), Ricardo Silveira (guitar), Sizao Machado (bass), Rogerio (bass), Da Lua (percussion), Joao Parahyba (percussion), Robertinho Silva (percussion), Edu Ribeiro (drums), Caito Marcondes (percussion), Rubinho Ribeiro (voice)
Tracks: 1 Pedro Brasil (4.29), 2 Ile Aye (4.18), 3 Guaruja (6.03), 4 Me Leve (4.22), 5 Malasia (5.30), 6 Sambop (5.11), 7 Oriente (3.30), 8 Maca (3.49), 9 Othos Puxados (4.26), 10 Rebento (5.14), 11 Fazendo Hora (4.20), 12 Aiaiai (5.03)
Notes: Won Grammy for Best Contemporary Jazz Album 2008.

Randy Brecker
**** 2009 Nostalgic Journey: Tykocin Jazz Suite
CD; Summit: DCD 527; UIN/UPC: 099402527925
Length: (60.06); Album type: studio
Produced by: Darby Christensen, Kip Sullivan
Musicians: Randy Brecker (trumpet), Bialystok Podlasie Opera Philharmonic (orchestra), Wlodek Pawlik (piano), Cezary Konrad (drums), Pawel Panita (bass), Marcin Nalecz-Niesiolowksi (conductor)
Tracks: 1 Introduction: Movement 1 (2.30), 2 Introduction: Movement 2 (3.14), 3 Introduction: Movement 3 (2.51), 4 Nostalgic Journey (10.27), 5 Let's All Go To Heaven (10.44), 6 Piano Introduction To No Words (2.26), 7 No Words (9.39), 8 Magic Seven (12.55), 9 Blue Rain (5.18)
Notes: Recorded at the Podlasie Opera and Philharmonic Concert Hall in Bialystok, July 2008.

Randy Brecker with the DR Big Band
**** 2011 The Jazz Ballad Song Book
CD; Red Dot Music: RDM012; UIN/UPC: 5709498208831
Length: (70.38); Album type: studio
Produced by: Chris Minh Doky
Musicians: Randy Brecker (trumpet), DR Big Band (band)
Tracks: 1 All or Nothing at All (7.55), 2 Cry Me A River (5.20), 3 Someday My Prince Will Come (7.00), 4 Foregone Conclusion (6.29), 5 Goldfinger (5.23), 6 Skylark (7.78), 7 I Talk To The Trees (6.25), 8 This Is All I Ask (8.18), 9 The Immigrant / Godfather (8.14), 10 Round Midnight (7.51)

Notes: Nominated for Grammy for Best Large Jazz Ensemble Album (2011). Recorded at DR Byen Studios 2 and 3, Copenhagen, Denmark.

Randy Brecker
**** 2013 The Brecker Brothers Band Reunion
CD+DVD; Piloo Records: PR007; UIN/UPC: 616892156048
Length: (73.07); Album type: studio
Produced by: George Whitty
Musicians: Randy Brecker (trumpet), Ada Rovatti (saxophone), David Sanborn (saxophone), Will Lee (bass), Dave Weckl (drums), George Whitty (keyboard), Mike Stern (guitar), Dean Brown (guitar), Adam Rogers (guitar), Oli Rockberger (keyboard), Mitch Stein (guitar), Rodney Holmes (drums), Chris Minh Doky (bass), Jim Campagnola (saxophone)
Tracks: 1 First Tune Of The Set (7.33), 2 Stellina (7.40), 3 The Dipshit (6.07), 4 Merry Go Town (5.17), 5 The Slag (6.38), 6 Really In For It (7.47), 7 Elegy For Mike (7.41), 8 On The Rise (5.37), 9 Adina (6.19), 10 R. N. Bee (7.27), 11 Musician's Ol' Lady Dues Blues (5.01), 12 First Tune Of The Set (13.28), 13 The Slag (9.14), 14 Introduction (1.15), 15 Adina (12.01), 16 Introduction (0.38), 17 Really In For It (7.49), 18 Introduction (0.51), 19 Straphangin' (11.40), 20 Introduction (1.08), 21 Stellina (9.38), 22 Introduction (0.54), 23 Merry Go Town (8.15), 24 Introduction (5.46), 25 Inside Out (7.01), 26 Introduction (1.46), 27 Some Skunk Funk (6.08), 28 Introduction (0.26)
Notes: 1-11 on music CD; 12-20 on bonus DVD. Sanborn plays on 3, 6; Rogers plays on 2, 3, 6, 8, 11; Weckl plays on 1, 2, 3, 4, 7, 8, 9; Holmes plays on 5, 6, 10; Rockberger plays on 4, 8; Minh Doky plays on 7, 9; Lee plays on all except 7, 9, 10. Brown plays on 1, 3, 7, 9; Stern plays on 1, 5, 6; Stein plays on 5, 6, 10; Whitty, Rovatti play on all except 11.

Randy Brecker, Wlodek Pawlik
**** 2013 Randy Brecker Plays Wlodek Pawlik's Night in Calisia
CD; Summit: 612; UIN/UPC: 099402612928
Length: (63.37); Album type: studio
Musicians: Wlodek Pawlik (piano), Randy Brecker (trumpet), Pawel Panita (bass), Cezary Konrad (drums), Kalisz Philharmonic Orchestra (orchestra), Adam Klocek (conductor)
Tracks: 1 Night In Calisia (10.54), 2 Amber Road (9.44), 3 Orienthology (10.17), 4 Follow The Stars (11.17), 5 Quarrel of The Roman Merchants (10.59), 6 Forgotten Song (10.26)

DVDs by Randy Brecker

Randy Brecker, with Michael Brecker
**** 2005 Some Skunk Funk
DVD; BHM: DVD 01 / BHM 1020; UIN/UPC: 090204899937
Length: (115.00); Album type: live
Produced by: Lucas Schmid, Joachim Becker
Musicians: Randy Brecker (trumpet), Michael Brecker (saxophone), Will Lee (bass), Jim Beard (keyboard), Peter Erskine (drums), Vince Mendoza (conductor), Marcio Doctor (percussion), WDR Big Band (band)
Tracks: 1 Shanghigh (6.26), 2 Wayne Out (4.56), 3 And Then She Wept (6.07), 4 Freefall (6.17), 5 Straphangin' (8.18), 6 Sponge (6.46), 7 Let It Go (8.02), 8 Levitate (4.58), 9 Some Skunk Funk (6.26), 10 Song For Barry (10.32)
Notes: Filmed live at the Leverkeusener Jazztage Festival 2003.

Randy Brecker
2007 The Geneva Concert
DVD; SKU/ Inakustik /New Morning: SKU23100; UIN/UPC: 0707787646277
Length: (120.00); Album type: live
Produced by:
Musicians: Randy Brecker (trumpet), Neils Lan Doky (keyboard), Alvin Queen (drums), Pierre Boussaguet (bass)
Tracks: 1 On Green Dolphin Street, 2 Star Eyes, 3 The Target, 4 Softly As In A Morning Sunrise, 5 That's It, 6 Blue Moon
Notes: Recorded at the Geneva Jazz Festival 1994.

CDs by Michael Brecker as leader

Michael Brecker
***** 1987 Michael Brecker
CD; GRP/Impulse!: GRP 01132; UIN/UPC: 011105011327
Length: (54.26); Album type: studio
Produced by: Don Grolnick, Michael Brecker
Musicians: Michael Brecker (saxophone), Jack DeJohnette (drums), Charlie Haden (bass), Kenny Kirkland (piano), Pat Metheny (guitar), Don Grolnick (piano),
Tracks: 1 Sea Glass (5.49), 2 Syzygy (9.44), 3 Choices (8.06), 4 Nothing Personal (5.29), 5 The Cost Of Living (7.49), 6 Original Rays (9.04), 7 My One And Only Love (8.16),
Notes: Originally on MCA Impulse! as MCAD 5980. Recorded at Power Station, NYC, 1987.

Michael Brecker
**** 1988 Don't Try This At Home
CD; GRP Impulse!: 050-114-2; UIN/UPC: 011105011426
Length: (55.31); Album type: studio
Produced by: Don Grolnick
Musicians: Michael Brecker (saxophone), Mike Stern (guitar), Don Grolnick (piano), Charlie Haden (bass), Jeff Andrews (bass), Jack DeJohnette (drums), Mark O'Connor (multi), Adam Nussbaum (drums), Herbie Hancock (keyboard), Judd Miller (programming), Joey Calderazzo (piano), Peter Erskine (drums), Jim Beard (keyboard),
Tracks: 1 Itsbynne Reel (7.41), 2 Chime This (7.50), 3 Scriabin (7.45), 4 Suspone (4.59), 5 Don't Try This at Home (9.30), 6 Everything Happens When You're Gone (7.11), 7 Talking to Myself (5.10), 8 The Gentleman and Hizcaine (5.19),
Notes: Herbie Hancock plays on 3 and 5. Joey Calderazzo plays piano on 4, 6. Jeff Andrews plays electric bass on 1,4,7,8; Charlie Haden plays acoustic bass on 1, 3, 5. Adam Nussbaum plays drums on 2, 4, 6; Jack de Johnette plays drums on 1, 3,5,8; Peter Erskine plays drums on 7. Jim Beard plays on 7, 8. Originally on MCA Impulse! as MCAD 42229.

Michael Brecker
**** 1992 Now You See It (Now You Don't)
CD; GRP: GRP 96222; UIN/UPC: 011105962223
Length: (52.08); Album type: studio
Produced by: Don Grolnick
Musicians: Michael Brecker (saxophone), Joey Calderazzo (piano), Victor Bailey (bass), Don Alias (percussion), Jon Herington (guitar), Jim Beard (keyboard), Jason Miles (programming), Judd Miller (programming), Jimmy Bralower (programming), Adam Nussbaum (drums),

Omar Hakim (drums), Jay Anderson (bass), Milton Cardona (percussion), Steve Berrios (percussion),
Tracks: 1 Escher Sketch (A Tale of Two Rhythms) (5.23), 2 Minsk (9.03), 3 Ode to the Doo Da Day (5.51), 4 Never Alone (5.35), 5 Peep (7.25), 6 Dogs in the Wine Shop (6.33), 7 Quiet City (6.04), 8 The Meaning of the Blues (5.57),

Michael Brecker
**** 1996 Tales From The Hudson
CD; Impulse!: 11105-1191-2; UIN/UPC: 011105119122
Length: (60.23); Album type: studio
Produced by: George Whitty, Michael Brecker, Pat Metheny
Musicians: Michael Brecker (saxophone), Pat Metheny (guitar), Jack DeJohnette (drums), Dave Holland (bass), Joey Calderazzo (piano), McCoy Tyner (piano), Don Alias (percussion),
Tracks: 1 Slings and Arrows (6.19), 2 Midnight Voyage (7.17), 3 Song for Bilbao (5.44), 4 Beau Rivage (7.38), 5 African Skies (8.12), 6 Introduction to Naked Soul (1.14), 7 Naked Soul (8.43), 8 Willie T (8.13), 9 Cabin Fever (6.59),
Notes: Recorded at Power Station, NYC, January, 1996. Tyner replaces Calderazzo on 3, 5. Alias on 3, 5 only.

Michael Brecker
**** 1998 Two Blocks from The Edge
CD; Impulse!: 11105-1261-2; UIN/UPC: 011105126120
Length: (60.48); Album type: studio
Produced by: Michael Brecker, Joey Calderazzo
Musicians: Michael Brecker (saxophone), Joey Calderazzo (piano), James Genus (bass), Jeff (Tain) Watts (drums), Don Alias (percussion),
Tracks: 1 Madame Toulouse (5.19), 2 Two Blocks from the Edge (8.32), 3 Bye George (6.59), 4 El Nino (7.41), 5 Cat's Cradle (6.43), 6 The Impaler (7.13), 7 How Long 'Til the Sun (7.39), 8 Delta City Blues (5.37), 9 Skylark (5.04),

Michael Brecker
**** 1999 Time Is Of The Essence
CD; Verve: 314547844-2; UIN/UPC: 731454784429
Length: (69.57); Album type: studio
Produced by: George Whitty
Musicians: Michael Brecker (saxophone), Pat Metheny (guitar), Larry Goldings (organ), Elvin Jones (drums), Jeff (Tain) Watts (drums), Bill Stewart (drums),
Tracks: 1 Arc of the Pendulum (8.59), 2 Sound Off (6.04), 3 Half Past Late (7.54), 4 Timeline (6.05), 5 The Morning of This Night (7.42), 6 Renaissance Man (8.36), 7 Dr. Slate (7.40), 8 As I Am (6.49), 9 Outrance (10.08),
Notes: Recorded at Right Track Studios, NYC, 1999.

Michael Brecker
*** 2001 Nearness Of You: The Ballad Book
CD; Verve: 549 705-2; UIN/UPC: 731454970525
Length: (60.18); Album type: studio
Produced by: Pat Metheny, Steve Rodby
Musicians: Michael Brecker (saxophone), Pat Metheny (guitar), Herbie Hancock (keyboard), Charlie Haden (bass), Jack DeJohnette (drums), James Taylor (voice)

Tracks: 1 Chan's Song (5.15), 2 Don't Let Me Be Lonely Tonight (4.43), 3 Nascente (6.18), 4 Midnight Mood (6.22), 5 The Nearness of You (4.32), 6 Incandescence (5.21), 7 Sometimes I See (5.26), 8 My Ship (7.10), 9 Always (5.37), 10 Seven Days (5.32), 11 I Can See Your Dreams (3.50)
Notes: Recorded at Right Track Recording, NYC, December 18-20, 2000.

Michael Brecker Quindectet
***** 2003 Wide Angles
CD; Verve: 0044007614228; UIN/UPC: 044007614228
Length: (70.23); Album type: studio
Produced by: Michael Brecker, Gil Goldstein
Musicians: Michael Brecker (saxophone), Alex Sipiagin (trumpet), Robin Eubanks (trombone), Peter Gordon (french horn), Steve Wilson (saxophone), Iain Dixon (clarinet), Charles Pillow (oboe), Mark Feldman (violin), Joyce Hammann (violin), Lois Martin (viola), Erik Friedlander (cello), Adam Rogers (guitar), John Patitucci (bass), Antonio Sanchez (drums), Daniel Sadownick (percussion)
Tracks: 1 Broadband (6.48), 2 Cool Day in Hell (7.51), 3 Angle of Repose (6.42), 4 Timbuktu (7.58), 5 Night Jessamine (5.23), 6 Scylla (10.40), 7 Brexterity (6.41), 8 Evening Faces (7.14), 9 Modus Operandy (5.27), 10 Never Alone (5.42)
Notes: Recorded live at Bennett Studios, Englewood NJ.

Michael Brecker
**** 2007 Pilgrimage
CD; Wa Records: 0602517263512; UIN/UPC: 602517263512
Length: (77.42); Album type: studio
Produced by: Michael Brecker, Gil Goldstein, Steve Rodby, Pat Metheny
Musicians: Michael Brecker (saxophone), Pat Metheny (guitar), Herbie Hancock (keyboard), Brad Mehldau (piano), John Patitucci (bass), Jack DeJohnette (drums)
Tracks: 1 The Mean Time (6.55), 2 Five Months from Midnight (7.40), 3 Anagram (10.09), 4 Tumbleweed (9.36), 5 When Can I Kiss You Again? (9.42), 6 Cardinal Rule (7.31), 7 Half Moon Lane (7.17), 8 Loose Threads (8.34), 9 Pilgrimage (10.02)
Notes: Awarded the Grammy for Best Jazz Instrumental Solo 2007 for Anagram. Awarded the Grammy for Best Jazz Instrumental Album, Individual or Group 2007 for Pilgrimage. Herbie Hancock plays on 1, 5, 8, 9. Brad Mehldau plays on 2, 3, 4, 6, 7.

DVDs by Michael Brecker

Michael Brecker Quindectet
2011 Angle of Repose / Live in Japan
DVD; Jazz Door: JD11058; UIN/UPC: 4250079741588
Length: ; Album type: live
Musicians: Michael Brecker (saxophone), Gil Goldstein (keyboard), Alex Sipiagin (trumpet), Peter Gordon (french horn), Robin Eubanks (trombone), Bob Sheppard (saxophone), Dan Willis (oboe), Roger Rosenberg (clarinet), Joyce Hammann (violin), Meg Okura (viola), Lois Martin (viola), David Eggers (cello), Adam Rogers (guitar), Boris Kozlov (bass), Antonio Sanchez (drums), Daniel Sadownick (percussion)
Tracks: 1 Syzygy, 2 Broadband, 3 Scylla, 4 Timbuktu, 5 Itsbynne Reel, 6 Angel Of Repose
Notes: Recorded at the Blue Note, Tokyo on 12 Feb 2004.

Unofficial Releases of Michael Brecker Material

The Michael Brecker Band
1993 Live
CD; Jazz Door: JD 1230; UIN/UPC:
Length: ; Album type: live
Musicians: Michael Brecker (saxophone), Mike Stern (guitar), Joey Calderazzo (piano), Jeff Andrews (bass), Adam Nussbaum (drums)
Tracks: 1 Gossip (6.23), 2 Nothing Personal (14.55), 3 Original Rays (22.23)

Michael Brecker Group
1999 The Cost Of Living
CD; Jazz Door: JD 1260; UIN/UPC:
Length: ; Album type: live
Musicians: Michael Brecker (saxophone), Adam Nussbaum (drums), Jay Anderson (bass), Joey Calderazzo (piano)
Tracks: 1 Itsbynne Reel, 2 Chime This, 3 Choices, 4 The Cost Of Living, 5 Nothing Personal

CDs and DVDs with Randy and/or Michael Brecker as sidemen (in approximate order of recording).

Horace Silver
1969 You Gotta Take A Little Love
CD; Blue Note: BST 84309; UIN/UPC: 0946 3 74222 2 4
Length: (39.06); Album type: studio
Produced by: Francis Wolff
Musicians: Horace Silver (piano), Randy Brecker (trumpet), Bennie Maupin (saxophone), Billy Cobham (drums), John Williams (bass) (bass)
Tracks: 1 You Gotta Take A Little Love (5.24), 2 The Risin' Sun (4.37), 3 It's Time (6.42), 4 Lovely's Daughter (4.14), 5 Down And Out (4.30), 6 The Belly Dancer (7.25), 7 Brain Wave (6.14)
Notes: Recorded at Rudy Van Gelder Studio, Englewood Cliffs, NJ

Horace Silver
1970 That Healin' Feelin'
Vinyl; Blue Note: BST 84352
Length: (n/k); Album type: studio
Musicians: Horace Silver (piano), Randy Brecker (trumpet), George Coleman (saxophone), Bob Cranshaw (bass), Jimmy Lewis (bass), Mickey Roker (drums), Idris Muhammad (drums), Houston Person (saxophone), Andy Bey (voice), Gail Nelson (voice), Jackie Verdell (voice)
Tracks: 1 That Healin' Feelin', 2 The Happy Medium, 3 The Show Has Begun, 4 Love Vibrations, 5 Peace, 6 Permit Me To Introduce You To Yourself, 7 Wipe Away The Evil, 8 Nobody Knows, 9 There's Much To Be Done

Dreams
*** 1970 Dreams
CD; Sony Music Special Products: A28334; UIN/UPC: 079892833423
Length: (40.12); Album type: studio

Produced by: Fred Weinberg
Musicians: Randy Brecker (trumpet), Michael Brecker (saxophone), Billy Cobham (drums), Barry Rogers (trombone), Jeff Kent (keyboard), John Abercrombie (guitar), Edward Vernon (voice), Doug Lubahn (bass)
Tracks: 1 Devil Lady (3.32), 2 15 Miles to Provo (3.00), 3 The Maryanne (2.23), 4 Holli Be Home (5.41), 5 Try Me (5.07), 6 Dream Suite: Asset Stop / Jane / Crunchy Grenola (14.45), 7 New York (5.32)

Dreams
*** 1971 Imagine My Surprise
CD; Sony Music Special Products: A28333; UIN/UPC: 079892833324
Length: (40.37); Album type: studio
Produced by: Steve Cropper
Musicians: Randy Brecker (trumpet), Michael Brecker (saxophone), Will Lee (bass), Billy Cobham (drums), Barry Rogers (trombone), Don Grolnick (piano), Bob Mann (guitar), Edward Vernon (voice), Steve Cropper (guitar)
Tracks: 1 Calico (3.17), 2 Why Can't I Find A Home (3.40), 3 Child of Wisdom (5.20), 4 Just Be Ourselves (4.32), 5 I Can't Hear You (3.48), 6 Here She Comes Now (4.01), 7 Don't Cry My Lady (3.41), 8 Medicated Goo (3.53), 9 Imagine My Surprise (8.01)

Hal Galper
*** 1971 Wild Bird
Vinyl; Mainstream: MRL-354
Length: (39.06); Album type: studio
Musicians: Hal Galper (piano), Michael Brecker (saxophone), Randy Brecker (trumpet), Victor Gaskin (bass), Bill Goodwin (drums), Billy Hart (drums), Bob Mann (guitar)
Tracks: 1 Trilogy 1: Convocation (7.05), 2 Trilogy 2: Wild Bird (8.03), 3 Trilogy 3: Change Up (5.04), 4 This Moment (11.40), 5 Whatever (7.14)

Mike Mainieri and Friends
*** 1972 White Elephant Vol 1
CD; NYC Records: 6008-2; UIN/UPC: 4011687600823
Length: (48.44); Album type: studio
Produced by: Mike Mainieri
Musicians: Michael Brecker (saxophone), Randy Brecker (trumpet), Mike Mainieri (vibraphone), Jon Faddis (trumpet), Lew Soloff (trumpet), Ronnie Cuber (saxophone), Frank Vicari (saxophone), Barry Rogers (trombone), Jon Pierson (trombone), Steve Gadd (drums), Tony Levin (bass), Warren Bernhardt (keyboard), Joe Beck (guitar), David Spinozza (guitar), Hugh McCracken (guitar), Sam Brown (guitar), Nick Holmes (guitar), Sue Manchester (voice), Bob Mann (guitar), Donald MacDonald (drums), Paul Metzke (guitar), Nat Pavone (trumpet), George Young (saxophone)
Tracks: 1 Peace Of Mind (4.52), 2 The Jones (7.11), 3 Battle Royal (5.13), 4 Look In His Eyes (7.10), 5 White Elephant (12.03), 6 Easy On (2.43), 7 Animal Fat (5.21), 8 Monkey (5.13)
Notes: Originally released on Just Sunshine JSS-3000 as a double LP.

Mike Mainieri and Friends
*** 1972 White Elephant Vol 2
CD; NYC Records: 6011-2; UIN/UPC: 4011687601127
Length: (50.24); Album type: studio

Produced by: Mike Mainieri
Musicians: Mike Mainieri (vibraphone), Michael Brecker (saxophone), Joe Beck (guitar), Warren Bernhardt (keyboard), Randy Brecker (trumpet), Sam Brown (guitar), Nick Holmes (guitar), Tony Levin (bass), Sue Manchester (voice), Bob Mann (guitar), Hugh McCracken (guitar), Donald MacDonald (drums), Paul Metzke (guitar), Nat Pavone (trumpet), Jon Pierson (trombone), Barry Rogers (trombone), Lew Soloff (trumpet), David Spinozza (guitar), Frank Vicari (saxophone), George Young (saxophone), Ann E. Sutton (voice), Ronnie Cuber (saxophone)
Tracks: 1 More To Love (4.40), 2 Broadway Joe (4.36), 3 Dreamsong (5.33), 4 Gunfighter (6.19), 5 Right Back (5.03), 6 Sunshine Clean (3.23), 7 Save The Water (3.39), 8 Auld Lang Syne (7.16), 9 Field Song (6.25), 10 Battle Royal (3.18)
Notes: Originally released on Just Sunshine JSS-3000 as a double LP.

Horace Silver
*** 1972 In Pursuit Of The 27th Man
CD; Blue Note RVG Edition: 7243-5-35758-2; UIN/UPC: 7243-5-35758-2
Length: (40.43); Album type: studio
Produced by: George Butler
Musicians: Horace Silver (piano), Randy Brecker (trumpet), Michael Brecker (saxophone), David Friedman (vibraphone), Bob Cranshaw (bass), Mickey Roker (drums)
Tracks: 1 Liberated Brother (5.23), 2 Kathy (4.17), 3 Gregory Is Here (6.21), 4 Summer In Central Park (4.41), 5 Nothin' Can Stop Me Now (9.44), 6 In Pursuit Of The 27th Man (9.44), 7 Strange Vibes (5.02)

Hal Galper
**** 1972 The Guerilla Band
Vinyl; Mainstream: MRL 337
Length: (36.42); Album type: studio
Musicians: Don Alias (percussion), Hal Galper (piano), Randy Brecker (trumpet), Michael Brecker (saxophone), Victor Gaskin (bass), Steve Haas (drums), Bob Mann (guitar)
Tracks: 1 Call (6.05), 2 Figure Eight (7.37), 3 Black Night (3.16), 4 Welcome To My Dream (4.50), 5 Rise And Fall (9.05), 6 Point Of View (5.49)
Notes: Recorded also as a release on P-Vine PCD-23922 (1970)

Eleventh House
*** 1974 Introducing The Eleventh House With Larry Coryell
CD; Vanguard : VMD 79342-2; UIN/UPC: 090204400126
Length: (44.47); Album type: studio
Produced by: Daniel Weiss
Musicians: Larry Coryell (guitar), Randy Brecker (trumpet), Alphonze Mouzon (drums), Mike Mandel (keyboard), Danny Trifan (bass),
Tracks: 1 Birdfingers (3.07), 2 The Funky Waltz (5.10), 3 Low-Lee-Tah (4.17), 4 Adam Smasher (4.30), 5 Joy Ride (6.08), 6 Yin (6.03), 7 Theme for a Dream (3.26), 8 Gratitude 'A So Low' (3.21), 9 ISM-Ejercicio (3.59), 10 Right on Y'all (4.21),
Notes: Originally vinyl disc VSD 79342.

Billy Cobham
**** 1974 Crosswinds
CD; Atlantic: 8122-73528-2; UIN/UPC: 081227352820
Length: (35.11); Album type: studio
Musicians: Billy Cobham (drums), John Abercrombie (guitar), Michael Brecker (saxophone), Randy Brecker (trumpet), Garnett Brown (trombone), George Duke (keyboard), Lee Pastora (percussion), John Williams (bass) (bass)
Tracks: 1 Spanish Moss (4.08), 2 Savannah the Serene (5.09), 3 Storm (2.46), 4 Flash Flood (5.05), 5 The Pleasant Pheasant (5.11), 6 Heather (8.25), 7 Crosswind (3.39)
Notes: Originally released as Atlantic SD 7300 (1974).

Billy Cobham
**** 1974 Total Eclipse
CD; Atlantic: 8122-76585-2; UIN/UPC: 081227658526
Length: (44.05); Album type: studio
Musicians: Billy Cobham (drums), John Abercrombie (guitar), Randy Brecker (trumpet), Michael Brecker (saxophone), Glenn Ferris (trombone), David Earl Johnson (percussion), Sue Evans (percussion), Cornell Dupree (guitar), Milcho Leviev (keyboard)
Tracks: 1 Solarization (3.00), 2 Second Phase (1.43), 3 Crescent Sun (2.40), 4 Voyage (2.56), 5 Solarization - Recapitulation (0.50), 6 Lunarputians (2.32), 7 Total Eclipse (5.59), 8 Bandits (2.30), 9 Moon Germs (4.55), 10 The Moon Ain't Made of Green Cheese (0.58), 11 Sea of Tranquillity (10.44), 12 Last Frontier (5.22)

Billy Cobham
*** 1975 Shabazz (Recorded Live In Europe)
CD; Atlantic / Rhino: 8122733372; UIN/UPC: 081227333720
Length: (39.38); Album type: live
Musicians: Billy Cobham (drums), Michael Brecker (saxophone), Randy Brecker (trumpet), Alex Blake (bass), Glenn Ferris (trombone), Milcho Leviev (keyboard), John Scofield (guitar), John Abercrombie (guitar)
Tracks: 1 Shabazz (13.48), 2 Taurian Matador (5.28), 3 Red Baron (6.37), 4 Tenth Pinn (14.00)

Parliament
1975 Mothership Connection
CD; Casablanca: 842 502-2
Length: (41.26); Album type: studio
Musicians: Randy Brecker (trumpet), Michael Brecker (saxophone), George Clinton (voice), William (Bootsy) Collins (bass), Gary (Mudbone) Cooper (drums), Joe Farrell (saxophone), Maceo Parker (saxophone), Fred Wesley (trombone), Bernie Worrell (keyboard), Reginald (Rasputin) Boutte (voice), Sidney Barnes (voice), Bryan Chimenti (voice), Raymond Davis (voice), Debbie Edwards (voice), Glen Goins (guitar), Michael Hampton (guitar), Clarence (Fuzzy) Haskins (voice), Archie Ivy (voice), Taka Khan (voice), Cordell Mosson (bass), Garry Shider (voice), Grady Thomas (voice), Pamela Vincent (voice), Deborah Wright (voice)
Tracks: 1 P-Funk (Wants To Get Funked Up) (7.39), 2 Mothership Connection (Star Child) (6.11), 3 Unfunky UFO (4.24), 4 Supergroovalisticprosifunkstication (5.04), 5 Handcuffs (4.03), 6 Give Up The Funk (Tear The Roof Off The Sucker) (5.46), 7 Night Of The Thumpasorus Peoples (5.11), 8 Star Child (Mothership Connection) (3.08)
Notes: Originally Casablanca 7022.

Billy Cobham
*** 1975 A Funky Thide Of Sings
CD; Atlantic: 7567-80766-2; UIN/UPC: 075678076626
Length: (44.43); Album type: studio
Produced by: Billy Cobham, Mark Meyerson
Musicians: Billy Cobham (drums), John Scofield (guitar), Alex Blake (bass), Randy Brecker (trumpet), Glenn Ferris (trombone), Walt Fowler (trumpet), Michael Brecker (saxophone), Tom (Bones) Malone (trombone)
Tracks: 1 Panhandler (3.50), 2 Sorcery (2.26), 3 A Funky Thide of Sings (3.23), 4 Thinking of You (4.12), 5 Some Skunk Funk (5.07), 6 Light at the End of the Tunnel (3.37), 7 A Funky Kind of Thing (9.24), 8 Moody Modes (12.16)
Notes: One of Ahmet Ertegun's 50 selections for reissue to commemorate the 50th Anniversay of Atlantic Records.

Jaco Pastorius
***** 1976 Jaco Pastorius
CD; Epic : CDEPC 81453; UIN/UPC:
Length: (41.55); Album type: studio
Produced by: Bobby Colomby
Musicians: Jaco Pastorius (bass), Don Alias (percussion), Randy Brecker (trumpet), Michael Brecker (saxophone), Ron Tooley (trumpet), David Sanborn (saxophone), Howard Johnson (sax) (saxophone), Herbie Hancock (keyboard), Narada Michael Walden (drums), Alex Darqui (keyboard), Lenny White (drums), Bobby Economou (drums), Michael Gibbs (orchestrator), Wayne Shorter (saxophone), Othello Molineaux (steel pans), Leroy Williams (steel pans), Peter Gordon (french horn),
Tracks: 1 Donna Lee (2.27), 2 Come On, Come Over (3.52), 3 Continuum (4.32), 4 Kuru / Speak Like A Child (7.41), 5 Portrait of Tracy (2.23), 6 Opus Pocus (5.28), 7 OkonKole Y Trompa (4.24), 8 (Used To Be A (Cha-Cha) (8.55), 9 Forgotten Love (2.13),

The Eleventh House featuring Larry Coryell
*** 1976 Aspects
Vinyl; Arista: AL 4077
Length: (n/k); Album type: studio
Produced by: Randy Brecker
Musicians: Larry Coryell (guitar), Michael Brecker (saxophone), Randy Brecker (trumpet), Steve Khan (guitar), Gerry (The Gov) Brown (drums), David Sanborn (saxophone), James Mtume (percussion), Mike Mandel (keyboard), John Lee (bass), Danny Toan (guitar), Terumasa Hino (trumpet)
Tracks: 1 Kowloon Jang, 2 Titus, 3 Pyramids, 4 Rodrigo Reflections, 5 Yin-Yang, 6 Woman Of Truth And Future, 7 Ain't It Is, 8 Aspects

Parliament
1976 The Clones Of Dr. Frunkenstein
CD; Casablanca: 842 620-2
Length: (40.11); Album type:
Musicians: Randy Brecker (trumpet), Michael Brecker (saxophone), Maceo Parker (saxophone), Fred Wesley (trombone), George Clinton (voice), Gary (Mudbone) Cooper (drums), Jerome Brailey (drums), William (Bootsy) Collins (bass), Glenn Collins (guitar), Gary (Mudbone) Cooper (drums), Raymond Davis (voice), Debbie Edwards (voice), Rick Gardner (saxophone), Glen Goins (guitar), Michael Hampton (guitar), Clarence (Fuzzy)

Haskins (voice), Eddie Hazel (guitar), Taka Khan (voice), Cordell Mosson (bass), Garry Shider (voice), Calvin Simon (voice), Grady Thomas (voice), Bernie Worrell (keyboard)
Tracks: 1 Prelude (1.40), 2 Gamin On Ya! (3.01), 3 Dr. Funkenstein (5.46), 4 Children Of Productions (3.57), 5 Getten' To Know You (5.18), 6 Do That Stuff (4.47), 7 Everything Is On The One (3.47), 8 I've Been Watching You (Move Your Sexy Body) (6.00), 9 Funkin' For Fun (5.55)
Notes: Originally Casablanca NBLP 7034 (1976).

Hal Galper
*** 1977 Reach Out!
Vinyl; Inner City: IC-2067
Length: (50.52); Album type: studio
Musicians: Hal Galper (piano), Randy Brecker (trumpet), Michael Brecker (saxophone), Billy Hart (drums), Wayne Dockery (bass)
Tracks: 1 Reach Out (9.12), 2 I'll Never Stop Loving You (7.15), 3 Spidit (5.57), 4 My Man's Gone Now (3.51), 5 Waiting For Chet (8.09), 6 I Can't Get Started (3.14), 7 Children Of The night (13.14)

Hal Galper
*** 1978 The Hal Galper Quintet Live: Redux '78
CD; Concord Jazz: CCD-4483
Length: (n/k); Album type: live
Produced by: Musicians: Hal Galper (piano)
Randy Brecker (trumpet), Michael Brecker (saxophone), Wayne Dockery (bass), J.C. Moses (drums)
Tracks: 1 Introduction / Triple Play, 2 My Man's Gone Now, 3 Another Jones, 4 I'll Never Stop Loving You, 5 Tune of the Unknown Samba, 6 Shadow Waltz, 7 This Is The Thing

Mike Nock
1978 In Out And Around
Vinyl; Timeless: SJP119
Length: (45.45); Album type:
Musicians: Mike Nock (keyboard), Michael Brecker (saxophone), Al Foster (drums), George Mraz (bass)
Tracks: 1 Break Time (7.05), 2 Dark Light (5.50), 3 Shadows Of Forgotten Love (9.30), 4 The Gift (7.05), 5 Hadrians Wall (7.35), 6 In Out And Around (8.40)
Notes: Recorded at Sound Ideas Studio, NYC.

Frank Zappa
1978 Zappa In New York
Vinyl, Warner Brothers: 2D 2290
Length: (74.52), Album type: live
Musicians: Frank Zappa (guitar), Michael Brecker (saxophone), Lou Marini (saxophone), Ronnie Cuber (saxophone), Terry Bozzio (drums), Eddie Jobson (keyboard), Dave Samuels (vibraphone), Russell Malone (guitar), Randy Brecker (trumpet), Ray White (guitar), Patrick O'Hearn (bass), Ruth Underwood (percussion), Don Pardo (voice), John Bergamo (percussion), Ed Mann (percussion), Lou Ann Neill (harp)
Tracks: 1 Titties and Beer (5.39), 2 I Promise Not To Come In Your Mouth (aka Läther) (2.50), 3 Punky's Whips (10.51), 4 Sofa (3.15), 5 Manx Needs Women (1.40), 6 The Black Page Drum Solo / Black Page #1 (4.06), 7 Big Leg Emma (2.17), 8 Black Page #2 (10.31), 9

Honey, Don't You Want A Man Like Me? (4.15), 10 The Illinois Enema Bandit (12.31), 11 The Purple Lagoon (16.57)
Notes: The Brecker Brothers were in the band for this album of live cuts recorded December 1976 at the Palladium, NYC. Some of this material also appears on Läther. Due to censorship issues, there has been a complex series of reissues and releases.

Charles Mingus
1979 Me Myself An Eye
CD; Atlantic: 7567930682; UIN/UPC: 075679306821
Length: (57.19); Album type: studio
Produced by: Ilhan Mimaroglu, Raymond Silva
Musicians: Charles Mingus (bass), Park (Pepper) Adams III (saxophone), Randy Brecker (trumpet), Michael Brecker (saxophone), Joe Chambers (drums), George Coleman (saxophone), Larry Coryell (guitar), Ronnie Cuber (saxophone), Michael Davis (trumpet), Ted Dunbar (guitar), Sammy Figueroa (percussion), Ricky Ford (saxophone), Steve Gadd (drums), Eddie Gomez (bass), Jimmy Knepper (trombone), Lee Konitz (saxophone), Ray Mantilla (percussion), George Mraz (bass), Akira Ohmori (saxophone), Keith O'Quinn (trombone), Craig Purpura (saxophone), Kenneth Hitchcock (saxophone), Yoshiaki Malta (saxophone), Daniel Block (saxophone), John Tank (saxophone), Jack Walrath (trumpet), Locksley Wellington (Slide) Hampton (trombone), Jack Wilkins (guitar), Bob Neloms (piano), Danny Richmond (drums), Paul Jeffrey (conductor)
Tracks: 1 Three Worlds Of Drums (30.21), 2 Devil Woman (9.24), 3 Wednesday Night Prayer Meeting (9.50), 4 Carolyn 'Keki' Mingus (7.44)
Notes: Trumpet

Warren Bernhardt, Michael Brecker, Randy Brecker, Mike Mainieri
**** 1979 Blue Montreux
Vinyl; Arista: AB4224; UIN/UPC: 078635657326
Length: (52.29); Album type: live
Produced by: Mike Mainieri
Musicians: Michael Brecker (saxophone), Randy Brecker (trumpet), Warren Bernhardt (keyboard), Steve Jordan (drums), Steve Khan (guitar), Larry Coryell (guitar), Tony Levin (bass), Mike Mainieri (vibraphone)
Tracks: 1 Blue Montreux (8.44), 2 Rocks (7.52), 3 I'm Sorry (8.36), 4 Magic Carpet (5.32), 5 Buds (4.58), 6 Floating (7.51), 7 The Virgin and the Gypsy (8.22)

Warren Bernhardt, Michael Brecker, Randy Brecker, Mike Mainieri
**** 1979 Blue Montreux II
Vinyl; Arista: AB4225; UIN/UPC: 4988017648285
Length: (39.15); Album type: live
Produced by: Mike Mainieri
Musicians: Michael Brecker (saxophone), Randy Brecker (trumpet), Warren Bernhardt (keyboard), Mike Mainieri (vibraphone), Larry Coryell (guitar), Eddie Gomez (bass)
Tracks: 1 A Funky Waltz (6.03), 2 Candles (6.07), 3 Uptown Ed (6.39), 4 Love Play (10.54), 5 Cloud Motion (9.31)

Steps
*** 1980 Step By Step
CD; NYC Records: NYC 6028
Length: (37.27); Album type:
Produced by: Mike Mainieri Musicians: Michael Brecker (saxophone)
Mike Mainieri (vibraphone), Steve Gadd (drums), Eddie Gomez (bass), Don Grolnick (piano)
Tracks: 1 Uncle Bob (11.00), 2 Kyoto (6.58), 3 Belle (7.48), 4 Bullet Train (5.31), 5 Six Persimmons (6.10)

Steps
***** 1980 Smokin' In The Pit
CD; NYC Records: NYC 6027-2
Length: (149.22); Album type:
Produced by: Mike Mainieri
Musicians: Michael Brecker (saxophone), Mike Mainieri (vibraphone), Eddie Gomez (bass), Steve Gadd (drums), Don Grolnick (piano), Kazumi Watanabe (guitar)
Tracks: 1 Tee Bag (13.44), 2 Uncle Bob (11.00), 3 Fawlty Tenors (10.46), 4 Lover Man (8.34), 5 Fawlty Tenors (Alternate Take) (12.30), 6 Song to Seth (13.02), 7 Momento (2.56), 8 Young and Fine (16.32), 9 Not Ethiopia (10.59), 10 Soul Eyes (12.15), 11 Recordame (10.10), 12 Not Ethiopia (Alternate Take) (12.00), 13 Sara's Touch (13.59)

Joni Mitchell
***** 1980 Shadows And Light
2 CD; Elektra/Asylum: BB 704
Length: (72.16); Album type: live
Produced by: Joni Mitchell
Musicians: Joni Mitchell (voice), Michael Brecker (saxophone), Pat Metheny (guitar), Jaco Pastorius (bass), Lyle Mays (keyboard)
Tracks: 1 Introduction (1.51), 2 In France They Kiss on Main Street (4.14), 3 Edith and the Kingpin (4.09), 4 Coyote (4.56), 5 Good-bye Pork Pie Hat (6.04), 6 The Dry Cleaner from Des Moines (4.33), 7 Amelia (6.39), 8 Pat's Solo (3.10), 9 Hejira (7.45), 10 Dreamland (4.38), 11 Band Introduction (0.52), 12 Furry Sings the Blues (5.14), 13 Why Do Fools Fall in Love (2.53), 14 Shadows and Light (5.24), 15 God Must Be a Boogie Man (5.03), 16 Woodstock (5.08)
Notes: Recorded at the County Bowl, Santa Barbara, CA, September, 1979. Available as a DVD. Three other tracks, Black Crow, Don's solo and Free Man in Paris, were omitted from the CD edition.

Parliament
1980 Trombipulation
CD; Casablanca: 842 623-2
Length: (43.47); Album type:
Musicians: Michael Brecker (saxophone), Randy Brecker (trumpet), Jerome Ali (guitar), Jimmy Ali (bass), Danny Cahn (trumpet), Gordon Carlton (guitar), David Lee Chong (keyboard), Jessica Cleaves (voice), George Clinton (voice), Kenny Colton (drums), Benny Cowan (trumpet), Lige Curry (voice), Raymond Davis (voice), Tony Davis (voice), Darryl Dixon (trumpet), Ronald Dunbar (voice), Janice Evans (voice), Ron Ford (voice), Mallia Franklin (voice), Lawrence Fratangelo (percussion), Lonnie Greene (drums), Richard (Kush) Griffith (trumpet), Larry Hatcher (trumpet), Shirley Hayden (voice), Sheila Horne (voice), Larry Heckstall (voice), Nina Hoover (voice), Cheryl James (voice), Robert (P-Nut) Johnson

(voice), Tyrone Lampkin (drums), Tracey Lewis (voice), Little Sonny (harmonica), David Majal II (trumpet), Jeanette McGruder (voice), Stevie Pannall (voice), Maceo Parker (saxophone), Michael (Clip) Payne (voice), Anthony Posk (violin), Barry Rogers (trombone), Jerome Rogers (voice), Manon Saulsby (keyboard), Kevin Shider (voice), Garry Shider (voice), Linda Shider (voice), Dawn Silva (voice), Carl (Butch) Small (percussion), Don Sterling (bass), David Taylor (trombone), Greg Thomas (trumpet), Dave Tofani (saxophone), Patti Walker (voice), Jeanette (Baby) Washington (voice), Fred Wesley (trombone), Andre Williams (voice), Ernestro Wilson (keyboard), Bernie Worrell (keyboard), Phillippe Wynne (voice)
Tracks: 1 Crush It (3.51), 2 Trombipulation (4.34), 3 Long Way Around (5.40), 4 Agony Of Defeet (6.23), 5 New Doo Review (5.55), 6 Let's Play House (3.39), 7 Body Language (5.57), 8 Peek-A-Groove (7.48)

Jaco Pastorius
**** 1981 Word Of Mouth
CD; Warner Bros: 3535 2; UIN/UPC: 075992353526
Length: (44.06); Album type:
Musicians: Jaco Pastorius (bass), Jack DeJohnette (drums), Peter Erskine (drums), Herbie Hancock (keyboard), Othello Molineaux (steel pans), Robert Thomas Jr (drums), Dave Bargeron (trombone), Chuck Findley (trumpet), Jim Pugh (trombone), William (Bill) Reichenbach (trombone), Michael Brecker (saxophone), Hubert Laws (flute), Tom Scott (saxophone), Wayne Shorter (saxophone), Toots Thielemans (harmonica), Peter Gordon (french horn), Brad Warnaar (french horn), David Taylor (trombone)
Tracks: 1 Crisis (5.20), 2 3 Views of a Secret (6.09), 3 Liberty City (11.59), 4 Chromatic Fantasy (3.01), 5 Blackbird (2.47), 6 Word of Mouth (3.53), 7 John and Mary (10.53)

Jaco Pastorius
**** 1994 The Birthday Concert
CD; Warner Bros Masters: 81227 3671 2; UIN/UPC: 081227367121
Length: (69.22); Album type: live
Musicians: Jaco Pastorius (bass), Michael Brecker (saxophone), Bob Mintzer (saxophone), Don Alias (percussion), Peter Erskine (drums), Dave Bargeron (trombone), Othello Molineaux (steel pans)
Tracks: 1 Soul Intro / The Chicken (8.00), 2 Continuum (2.34), 3 Invitation (17.43), 4 Three Views Of A Secret (5.56), 5 Liberty City (8.11), 6 Punk Jazz (4.35), 7 Happy Birthday (1.48), 8 Reza (10.36), 9 Domingo (5.39), 10 Band Intros (2.37), 11 Amerika (1.43)
Notes: Also reproduced on the Jazz Door release, The Florida Concert. Recorded at Mr. Pips, Deerfield Beach, Fort Lauderdale.

Jaco Pastorius
**** 1982 The Florida Concert
CD; Jazz Door: JD12135; UIN/UPC: 4250079712014
Length: (67.21); Album type: live
Musicians: Jaco Pastorius (bass), Michael Brecker (saxophone), Bob Mintzer (saxophone), Dan Bonsanti (saxophone), Gary Lindsay (saxophone), Randy Emerick (saxophone), Ken Faulk (trumpet), Brian O'Flaherty (trumpet), Brett Murphey (trumpet), Jerry Peel (french horn), Peter Gordon (french horn), Russ Freeland (trombone), Mike Katz (trombone), Dave Bargeron (trombone), Peter Graves (trombone), Othello Molineaux (steel pans), Peter Erskine (drums), Don Alias (percussion), Oscar Salas (percussion)

Tracks: 1 Soul Intro / Chicken (8.01), 2 Continuum (2.34), 3 Invitation (17.43), 4 Three Views Of A Secret (5.47), 5 Liberty City (8.12), 6 Punk Jazz (4.35), 7 Reza (10.34), 8 Domingo (5.36), 9 Band Intros (2.36), 10 Amerika (1.43)
Notes: on the Warner Bros. release, The Birthday Concert. Recorded at Mr. Pips, Deerfield Beach, Fort Lauderdale.

Steps
** 1982 Paradox
CD; NYC Records: NYC 6028
Length: (70.49); Album type: studio
Produced by: Mike Mainieri
Musicians: Michael Brecker (saxophone), Mike Mainieri (vibraphone), Peter Erskine (drums), Don Grolnick (piano), Eddie Gomez (bass)
Tracks: 1 NL 4 (8.45), 2 The Aleph (9.56), 3 Patch of Blue (7.49), 4 Four Chords (10.52), 5 Take a Walk (11.56), 6 Nichka (2.25), 7 The Aleph (Alternate Take) (19.06)
Notes: Japanese edition: Jroom COCB 53306 (1982)

Claus Ogerman with Michael Brecker
*** 1982 Cityscape
CD; Warners: 8122-73718-2; UIN/UPC: 081227371821
Length: (53.45); Album type: studio
Produced by: Tommy LiPuma
Musicians: Claus Ogerman (conductor), Michael Brecker (saxophone), Warren Bernhardt (keyboard), Steve Gadd (drums), Eddie Gomez (bass), Marcus Miller (bass), John Tropea (guitar), Howard (Buzz) Feiten (guitar), Paulinho da Costa (percussion)
Tracks: 1 Cityscape (8.47), 2 Habanera (8.08), 3 Nightwings (7.45), 4 In the Presence and Absence of Each Other Pt 1 (8.57), 5 In the Presence and Absence of Each Other Pt 2 (6.49), 6 In the Presence and Absence of Each Other Pt 3 (6.41), 7 In the Presence and Absence of Each Other Pt 3 (Alt take) (6.38)

Bob Mintzer
*** 1985 Source
CD; Explore Records: 789140-0033; UIN/UPC: 878914000337
Length: (38.02); Album type: studio
Produced by: Teruo Nakamura
Musicians: Bob Mintzer (saxophone), Don Grolnick (piano), Mark Gray (keyboard), Jaco Pastorius (bass), Will Lee (bass), Tom Barney (bass), Hugh McCracken (guitar), Bill Washer (guitar), Lew Soloff (trumpet), Alan Rubin (trumpet), Alan Raph (trombone), Tom (Bones) Malone (trombone), Carla Poole (flute), Brian Brake (drums), Peter Erskine (drums), Frank Malabe (percussion), Manolo Badrena (percussion), Chuggy Carter (percussion), Carter Cathcarte (voice), Lillias White (voice), Randy Brecker (trumpet)
Tracks: 1 Late Night With You (4.17), 2 Don't Lock the Door (5.53), 3 The Source (4.23), 4 I Don't Know (5.11), 5 Mr Fone Bone (7.07), 6 Centering (4.10), 7 Spiral (6.50)

Jaco Pastorius
2006 Live In Montreal [DVD]
DVD; Decca:; UIN/UPC: 602517078963
Length: (n/k); Album type: live
Musicians: Jaco Pastorius (bass), Peter Erskine (drums), Don Alias (percussion), Othello Molineaux (steel pans), Randy Brecker (trumpet), Bob Mintzer (saxophone)

Tracks: 1 Chicken, 2 Donna Lee, 3 Bass Solo (6.08), 4 Mr. Fonebone, 5 Fannie Mae
Notes: This DVD is exactly the same performance as the Live and Outrageous DVD. Recorded at the Montreal International Jazz Festival 1982.

Jaco Pastorius
2007 Live And Outrageous [DVD]
DVD; Shanachie:
Length: (60.00); Album type: live
Musicians: Jaco Pastorius (bass), Don Alias (percussion), Randy Brecker (trumpet), Othello Molineaux (steel pans), Bob Mintzer (saxophone), Peter Erskine (drums)
Tracks: 1 Portrait of Tracy, 2 Mr. Fonebone, 3 Bass Solo (6.08), 4 Donna Lee, 5 Chicken
Notes: This DVD is exactly the same performance as the Live in Montreal 1982 DVD. Recorded at the Montreal International Jazz Festival 1982.

Jaco Pastorius
2008 Live In Japan And Canada 1982 [DVD]
DVD; Jazz VIP: 133
Length: (137.05); Album type: live
Musicians: Jaco Pastorius (bass), Randy Brecker (trumpet)
Tracks: 1 Invitation (9.35), 2 Soul Intro / The Chicken (8.13), 3 Donna Lee (12.14), 4 Continuum (1.56), 5 Sophisticated Lady (9.25), 6 Liberty City (11.00), 7 Three Views Of A Secret (6.14), 8 Percussion solo (4.27), 9 Okonkole Y Trompa (6.40), 10 Reza (7.19), 11 Giant Steps (1.59), 12 Reza (1.30), 13 The Chicken (6.31), 14 Donna Lee (14.29), 15 Bass Solo (6.08), 16 Mr. Fonebone (18.01), 17 Fannie Mae (11.24)
Notes: Tracks 1-12 recorded at Budokan, Tokyo 1 September 1982. Contains music from the albums Twins I and II. Tracks 13-17 recorded at Montreal Jazz Festival 2/3 July 1982.

Jaco Pastorius & Word of Mouth Big Band
2007 Live At The Aurex Jazz Festival
DVD; Jazz Door: (n/k)
Length: (80.00); Album type: live
Musicians: Jaco Pastorius (bass), Randy Brecker (trumpet), Bob Mintzer (saxophone), Peter Erskine (drums), Othello Molineaux (steel pans), Don Alias (percussion), Toots Thielemans (harmonica), Elmer Brown (trumpet), Forrest Buchtel (trumpet), Jon Faddis (trumpet), Ron Tooley (trumpet), Peter Graves (trombone), Wayne Andre (trombone), William (Bill) Reichenbach (trombone), Dave Bargeron (trombone), Alex Foster (saxophone), Mario Cruz (saxophone), Randy Emerick (saxophone), Paul McCandliss (saxophone), Peter Gordon (french horn), Brad Warnaar (french horn)
Tracks: 1 Invitation, 2 Soul Intro / The Chicken, 3 Donna Lee, 4 Continuum, 5 Sophisticated Lady, 6 Liberty City, 7 Three Views Of A Secret, 8 Percussion Solo, 9 Okonkole Y Trompa, 10 Reza, 11 Giant Steps, 12 Reza (Reprise)
Notes: Recorded live at the Aurex Jazz Festival at the Budokan in Tokyo Japan on September 1st, 1982.

Jaco Pastorius
**** 1983 Invitation
CD; Warner Bros: 7599 23876 2; UIN/UPC: 0759923876-2
Length: (43.08); Album type: live
Produced by: Jaco Pastorius
Musicians: Jaco Pastorius (bass), Don Alias (percussion), Randy Brecker (trumpet), Peter Erskine (drums), Bob Mintzer (saxophone), Othello Molineaux (steel pans), Toots

Thielemans (harmonica), Elmer Brown (trumpet), Forrest Buchtel (trumpet), Jon Faddis (trumpet), Ron Tooley (trumpet), Wayne Andre (trombone), Dave Bargeron (trombone), Peter Graves (trombone), William (Bill) Reichenbach (trombone), Mario Cruz (saxophone), Randy Emerick (saxophone), Alex Foster (saxophone), Paul McCandliss (saxophone), Peter Gordon (french horn), Brad Warnaar (french horn)
Tracks: 1 Invitation (6.57), 2 Amerika (1.09), 3 Soul Intro / The Chicken (6.49), 4 Continuum (4.28), 5 Liberty City (4.35), 6 Sophisticated Lady (5.17), 7 Reza / Giant Steps / Reza (10.23), 8 Fannie Mae / Eleven (2.38)
Notes: This is the US shortened single CD version of the double album Twins I & II. Despite the labelling of this album, the music was part of the tour of Japan by the Word of Mouth Big Band. Recorded at Budokan, Tokyo on 1982/9/1; Osaka Festival Hall on 1982/9/4; Yokohama Stadium on 1982/9/5.

Jaco Pastorius Big Band
**** 1999 Twins I & II: Live In Japan 1982
2 CD; Warner Music Japan: WPCR-10609/10; UIN/UPC: 93624757-2
Length: (89.49); Album type: live
Produced by: Jaco Pastorius, Michael Knuckles
Musicians: Jaco Pastorius (bass), Don Alias (percussion), Randy Brecker (trumpet), Peter Erskine (drums), Bob Mintzer (saxophone), Othello Molineaux (steel pans), Toots Thielemans (harmonica), Elmer Brown (trumpet), Forrest Buchtel (trumpet), Jon Faddis (trumpet), Ron Tooley (trumpet), Wayne Andre (trombone), Dave Bargeron (trombone), Peter Graves (trombone), William (Bill) Reichenbach (trombone), Mario Cruz (saxophone), Randy Emerick (saxophone), Alex Foster (saxophone), Paul McCandliss (saxophone), Peter Gordon (french horn), Brad Warnaar (french horn)
Tracks: 1 Invitation (8.31), 2 Soul Intro / The Chicken (6.50), 3 Continuum (4.30), 4 Liberty City (11.37), 5 Three Views Of A Secret (5.57), 6 Sophisticated Lady (7.07), 7 Amerika (1.13), 8 Okonkole Y Trompa (6.53), 9 Reza / Giants Steps / Reza (14.49), 10 Elegant People (12.44), 11 Twins (6.04), 12 Pac-Man Blues (Fannie Mae) (2.38), 13 Eleven (0.48)
Notes: Despite the labelling of this album, the music was part of the tour of Japan by the Word of Mouth Big Band. Recorded at Budokan, Tokyo on 1982/9/1; Osaka Festival Hall on 1982/9/4; Yokohama Stadium on 1982/9/5.

Steps Ahead
*** 1983 Steps Ahead; UIN/UPC: 07559601682
CD; Elektra Musician: 7559-60168-2
Length: (46.59); Album type: studio
Produced by: Steps Ahead
Musicians: Mike Mainieri (vibraphone), Michael Brecker (saxophone), Eddie Gomez (bass), Peter Erskine (drums), Eliane Elias (voice)
Tracks: 1 Pools (11.15), 2 Islands (6.23), 3 Loxodrome (5.25), 4 Both Sides of the Coin (6.10), 5 Skyward Bound (4.03), 6 Northern Cross (5.50), 7 Trio (An Improvisation) (7.32)

Bob Mintzer and the Horn Man Band
***** 1983 Papa Lips
CD; Explore Records: 789140-0020; UIN/UPC: 878914000207
Length: (42.17); Album type: studio
Produced by: Teruo Nakamura
Musicians: Bob Mintzer (saxophone), Don Grolnick (piano), Michael Brecker (saxophone), Randy Brecker (trumpet), Lawrence Feldman (saxophone), Roger Rosenberg (clarinet), Pete

Yellin (saxophone), Carla Poole (flute), Marvin Stamm (trumpet), Lew Soloff (trumpet), Laurie Frink (trumpet), Dave Bargeron (trombone), Bob Smith (trombone), Keith O'Quinn (trombone), David Taylor (trombone), George Moran (trombone), Will Lee (bass), Tom Barney (bass), Peter Erskine (drums), Frank Malabe (percussion)
Tracks: 1 Papa Lips (6.29), 2 Lazy Day (9.29), 3 I Hear a Rhapsody (4.11), 4 Latin Dance (7.58), 5 Truth (7.17), 6 Mr Fonebone (6.42)

Gil Evans & Orchestra
1983 Live in Lugano 1983 [DVD]
DVD; Arthaus Musik: 107113; UIN/UPC: 807280711394
Length: (58.00); Album type: live
Musicians: Gil Evans (composer), Michael Brecker (saxophone), Randy Brecker (trumpet), Billy Cobham (drums), Mike Mainieri (vibraphone)
Tracks: 1 Copenhagen Sights, 2 Friday the 13th, 3 Variations on Misery, 4 Waltz, 5 Orange Was The Color Of Her Dress, Then Blue Silk, 6 Stone Free, 7 Honey Man, 8 Gone
Notes: Recorded at the Palazzo dei Congressi, Lugano on 27 Jan 1983

Steps Ahead
****2007 Copenhagen Live [DVD]
DVD; Storyville Films: 80491-26036; UIN/UPC: 880491260363
Length: (56.00); Album type: live
Produced by: Kjeld Gronberg
Musicians: Mike Mainieri (vibraphone), Michael Brecker (saxophone), Eddie Gomez (bass), Peter Erskine (drums), Eliane Elias (voice)
Tracks: 1 Islands, 2 Pools, 3 Skyward Bound, 4 Northern Cross, 5 Loxodrome, 6 Sara's Touch, 7 Duo (In Two Parts), 8 Both Sides of the Coin
Notes: Also released as Steps Ahead In Europe, Idem (2003). Recorded 1/4/1983

Frank Sinatra with Quincy Jones and Orchestra
1984 L.A. Is My Lady
CD; Qwest/WarnerBrothers: 25145-1
Length: (36.35); Album type: studio
Musicians: Michael Brecker (saxophone), Randy Brecker (trumpet), Frank Sinatra (voice), Wayne Andre (trombone), George Benson (guitar), George Bohanon (trombone), Oscar Brashear (trumpet), Ray Brown (bass) (bass), Ndugu Chancler (drums), John Clark (french horn), Buddy Collette (saxophone), Bob Crenshaw (bass), Ronnie Cuber (saxophone), David Duke (french horn), Jon Faddis (trumpet), Frank Foster (saxophone), Steve Gadd (drums), Peter Gordon (french horn), Gary Grant (trumpet), Urbie Green (trombone), William Green (saxophone), Lionel Hampton (vibraphone), Jerry Hey (trumpet), Major Holley (bass), Kim Hutchcroft (saxophone), Bob James (keyboard), Qunicy Jones (conductor), Ralph MacDonald (percussion), Lew McCreary (trombone), Marcus Miller (bass), Tony Mottola (guitar), Sidney Muldrow (french horn), Joe Newman (trumpet), Joe Parnello (keyboard), Jerry Peel (french horn), Benny Powell (trombone), Tony Price (tuba), William (Bill) Reichenbach (trombone), Lee Ritenour (guitar), John Robinson (drums), Margaret Ross (harp), Alan Rubin (trumpet), Jim Self (tuba), Henry Sigismonti (french horn), Lew Soloff (trumpet), Neil Stubenhaus (bass), David Taylor (trombone), Ed Walsh (keyboard), Bill Watrous (trombone), Frank Wess (saxophone), Larry Williams (saxophone), George Young (saxophone)
Tracks: 1 L.A. Is My Lady (3.12), 2 The Best of Everything (2.45), 3 How Do You Keep The Music Playing? (3.49), 4 Teach Me Tonight (3.44), 5 It's All Right With Me (2.39), 6 Mack The Knife (4.50), 7 Until The Real Thing Comes Along (3.03), 8 Stormy Weather (3.38), 9 If

I Should Lose You (2.36), 10 A Hundred Years From Today (3.04), 11 After You've Gone (3.15)
Notes: Sinatra's last complete studio album.

Steps Ahead
*** 1984 Modern Times
CD; Elektra Musician: 7559 60351-2; UIN/UPC: 075596035125
Length: (47.30); Album type: studio
Produced by: Steps Ahead
Musicians: Mike Mainieri (vibraphone), Michael Brecker (saxophone), Warren Bernhardt (keyboard), Eddie Gomez (bass), Peter Erskine (drums)
Tracks: 1 Safari (6.58), 2 Oops (6.20), 3 Self Portrait (6.02), 4 Modern Times (6.17), 5 Radioactive (8.49), 6 Now You Know (6.25), 7 Old Town (6.19)

Don Grolnick
**** 1985 Hearts And Numbers
CD; Hip Pocket / VeraBra: HP 106
Length: (39.08); Album type: studio
Produced by: Don Grolnick
Musicians: Don Grolnick (piano), Randy Brecker (trumpet), Peter Erskine (drums), Will Lee (bass), Marcus Miller (bass), Hiram Bullock (guitar), Tom Kennedy (bass), Michael Brecker (saxophone), Jeff Mironov (guitar), Clifford Carter (keyboard)
Tracks: 1 Pointing At The Moon (6.18), 2 More Pointing (3.11), 3 Pools (5.18), 4 Regrets (5.14), 5 The Four Sleepers (5.27), 6 Human Bites (5.23), 7 Act Natural (5.05), 8 Hearts And Numbers (3.07)

Bob Mintzer Big Band
*** 1985 Incredible Journey
CD; DMP Records: CD-451; UIN/UPC: n/a
Length: (67.57); Album type: studio
Produced by: Bob Mintzer
Musicians: Bob Mintzer (saxophone), Marvin Stamm (trumpet), Randy Brecker (trumpet), Laurie Frink (trumpet), Bob Millikan (trumpet), Dave Bargeron (trombone), Bob Smith (trombone), Keith O'Quinn (trombone), David Taylor (trombone), Lawrence Feldman (saxophone), Pete Yellin (saxophone), Michael Brecker (saxophone), Bob Malach (saxophone), Roger Rosenberg (clarinet), Don Grolnick (piano), Lincoln Goines (bass), Peter Erskine (drums), Frank Malabe (percussion)
Tracks: 1 Incredible Journey (7.42), 2 The Ring (5.55), 3 Flying (9.22), 4 Computer (9.19), 5 Tribute (10.30), 6 Latin Dance (8.30), 7 Lazy Day (11.40), 8 Slo Funk (4.54)

Bob Mintzer Big Band
*** 1986 Camouflage
CD; DMP Records: CD-456
Length: (60.00); Album type: studio
Produced by: Bob Mintzer, Tom Jung
Musicians: Bob Mintzer (saxophone), Peter Erskine (drums), Lawrence Feldman (saxophone), Laurie Frink (trumpet), Don Grolnick (piano), Frank Malabe (percussion), Bob Malach (saxophone), Bob Millikan (trumpet), Keith O'Quinn (trombone), Roger Rosenberg (clarinet), Chris Seiter (trombone), Bob Smith (trombone), Marvin Stamm (trumpet), David Taylor (trombone), Pete Yellin (saxophone), Zev Katz (bass), Randy Brecker (trumpet)

Tracks: 1 Techno Pop (5.38), 2 Mr Fone Bone (6.18), 3 A Long Time Ago (8.22), 4 After Thought (1.43), 5 Camouflage (7.51), 6 One Man Band (5.44), 7 Truth (9.35), 8 Hip Hop (6.06), 9 In The Eighties (8.16)

Steps Ahead
**** 1986 Magnetic
CD; Elektra Musician: WPCR-25073
Length: (47.53); Album type: studio
Produced by: Steps Ahead
Musicians: Mike Mainieri (vibraphone), Michael Brecker (saxophone), Victor Bailey (bass), Hiram Bullock (guitar), Peter Erskine (drums), Kenny Kirkland (piano), Chuck Loeb (guitar), Warren Bernhardt (keyboard), Mitch Forman (keyboard), Robbie Kilgore (keyboard), Paul Jackson (bass), Dianne Reeves (voice), Peter Schwimmer (banjo)
Tracks: 1 Trains (7.31), 2 Beirut (8.17), 3 Cajun (6.18), 4 In A Sentimental Mood (3.35), 5 Magnetic Love (5.35), 6 Sumo (5.52), 7 All the Tea in China (5.06), 8 Something I Said (4.13), 9 Magnetic Love (reprise) (1.26)
Notes: This CD is a Japanese Edition.

Steps Ahead
** 1986 Live In Tokyo 1986
CD; NYC Records: VACF 1006; UIN/UPC: 4011778979807
Length: (64.15); Album type: live
Produced by: Mike Mainieri
Musicians: Mike Mainieri (vibraphone), Michael Brecker (saxophone), Mike Stern (guitar), Darryl Jones (bass), Steve Smith (drums)
Tracks: 1 Beirut (9.53), 2 Oops (8.47), 3 Self Portrait (7.30), 4 Sumo (9.01), 5 Cajun (8.14), 6 Safari (6.23), 7 In a Sentimental Mood (4.26), 8 Trains (9.32)

Bob Mintzer Big Band
*** 1988 Spectrum
CD; DMP Records: CD-461
Length: (n/k); Album type: studio
Produced by: Bob Mintzer
Musicians: Bob Mintzer (saxophone), Dave Bargeron (trombone), Randy Brecker (trumpet), Peter Erskine (drums), Lawrence Feldman (saxophone), Laurie Frink (trumpet), Lincoln Goines (bass), Don Grolnick (piano), Frank Malabe (percussion), Bob Malach (saxophone), Phil Markowitz (piano), Bob Millikan (trumpet), Keith O'Quinn (trombone), Jim Riley (percussion), John Rosenberg (trumpet), Bob Smith (trombone), Marvin Stamm (trumpet), David Taylor (trombone), Pete Yellin (saxophone)
Tracks: 1 Like A Child, 2 Spectrum, 3 My Romance, 4 Hanky Panky, 5 Mr Funk, 6 Mine Is Yours, 7 Frankie's Tune, 8 The Reunion, 9 Heart Of The Matter, 10 I Hear A Rhapsody, 11 Solo Saxophone, 12 Cowboys and Indians

Herbie Hancock Quartet
*** 1994 The Herbie Hancock Quartet Live
CD; Jazz Door: JD 1270
Length: (74.38); Album type: live
Musicians: Herbie Hancock (keyboard), Charles (Buster) Williams (bass), Al Foster (drums), Michael Brecker (saxophone), Greg Osby (saxophone), Bobby McFerrin (voice)

Tracks: 1 Just One of Those Things (25.24), 2 Air Dancing (13.51), 3 The Sorcerer (17.18), 4 Jammin' (18.05)
Notes: Tracks 1,2,4 recorded live in New York 23/5/1992; track 3 recorded live in Belgrade 31/10/88. Michael Brecker plays on 1,2,4; Greg Osby plays on 3; Bobby McFerrin sings on 4.

Peter Erskine
**** 1988 Motion Poet
CD; Denon: CY-72582; UIN/UPC: 081757258227
Length: (53.31); Album type: studio
Produced by: Don Grolnick
Musicians: Peter Erskine (drums), Michael Brecker (saxophone), John Abercrombie (guitar), Dave Bargeron (trombone), Jim Beard (keyboard), Randy Brecker (trumpet), John Clark (french horn), Eliane Elias (voice), Lawrence Feldman (saxophone), Matt Finders (trombone), Peter Gordon (french horn), Don Grolnick (piano), Marc Johnson (bass), Will Lee (bass), Jeff Mironov (guitar), Joe Mosello (trumpet), Jerry Peel (french horn), Roger Rosenberg (clarinet), Lew Soloff (trumpet), Bob Mintzer (saxophone)
Tracks: 1 Erskoman (6.25), 2 Not A Word (6.43), 3 Hero With A Thousand Faces (6.23), 4 Dream Clock (7.22), 5 Exit Up Right (6.00), 6 A New Regalia (4.04), 7 Boulez (3.22), 8 The Mystery Man (7.43), 9 In Walked Maya (5.09)
Notes: Randy Brecker plays on 2, Not A Word, on 4, Dream Clock, and on 8, The Mystery Man. Michael Brecker plays on 3, Hero with A Thousand Faces. Bob Mintzer solos on 4, Dream Clock and on 8, The Mystery Man. Mintzer plays ensemble on 1 and 3 - 6. Recorded 25/4 to 1/5/1988 at Master Sound Astoria, Queens, NYC.

Herbie Hancock
2004 Herbie Hancock Special with Bobby McFerrin And Michael Brecker [DVD]
DVD; TDK / Loft: 5 450270 008131
Length: (54.12); Album type: live
Musicians: Herbie Hancock (keyboard), Bobby McFerrin (voice), Michael Brecker (saxophone)
Tracks: 1 Air Dancing (8.30), 2 Oleo (18.41), 3 Improvisation (2 hands) (8.42), 4 Improvisation (4 hands) (8.49), 5 Cantaloupe Island (2 hands) (5.01), 6 Cantaloupe Island (4 hands) (4.29)
Notes: Recorded live at the Munich Philharmonie, 15/7/1988.

Bob Mintzer
*** 1989 Urban Contours
CD; DMP Records: CD-467
Length: (n/k); Album type: studio
Produced by: Bob Mintzer
Musicians: Bob Mintzer (saxophone), Dave Bargeron (trombone), Randy Brecker (trumpet), Peter Erskine (drums), Lawrence Feldman (saxophone), Laurie Frink (trumpet), Lincoln Goines (bass), Don Grolnick (piano), Chuck Loeb (guitar), Frank Malabe (percussion), Bob Malach (saxophone), Ray Marchica (programming), Bob Millikan (trumpet), Jeff Mironov (guitar), Joe Mosello (trumpet), Keith O'Quinn (trombone), Jim Pugh (trombone), John Rosenberg (trumpet), Bob Smith (trombone), Marvin Stamm (trumpet), David Taylor (trombone), Pete Yellin (saxophone)
Tracks: 1 8th Avenue March, 2 Urban Contours, 3 I Heard It Through The Grapevine, 4 The Tunnel, 5 Papa Lips, 6 Empty Streets, 7 Happy Song, 8 Lincoln Center, 9 The Way I Feel, 10 MacDougal Street, 11 Little Help From My Friends, 12 Beyond the Limit

Don Grolnick
*** 1989 Weaver Of Dreams
CD; Blue Note: CDP 0777 7 94591 2 6
Length: (51.14); Album type: studio
Produced by: Don Grolnick
Musicians: Don Grolnick (piano), Randy Brecker (trumpet), Michael Brecker (saxophone), Peter Erskine (drums), Dave Holland (bass), Bob Mintzer (saxophone), Barry Rogers (trombone)
Tracks: 1 Nothing Personal (5.44), 2 What is This Thing Called Love (8.41), 3 A Weaver of Dreams (4.40), 4 His Majesty The Baby (6.47), 5 I Want to be Happy (5.45), 6 Persimmons (6.54), 7 Or Come Fog (5.23), 8 Five Bars (7.20)

Bob Mintzer Big Band
*** 1991 Art Of The Big Band
CD; DMP Records: CD-479; UIN/UPC: 089672047926
Length: (62.21); Album type: studio
Produced by: Bob Mintzer, Tom Jung
Musicians: Bob Mintzer (saxophone), Marvin Stamm (trumpet), Randy Brecker (trumpet), Laurie Frink (trumpet), Bob Millikan (trumpet), Dave Bargeron (trombone), Keith O'Quinn (trombone), Michael Eugene Davis (trombone), David Taylor (trombone), Matt Finders (trombone), Pete Yellin (saxophone), Lawrence Feldman (saxophone), Scott Robinson (saxophone), Roger Rosenberg (clarinet), Phil Markowitz (piano), Lincoln Goines (bass), Peter Erskine (drums), John Riley (drums), Frank Malabe (percussion), Chuck Loeb (guitar)
Tracks: 1 Without A Song (4.47), 2 Brazilian Affair (5.00), 3 Christopher Columbus (7.20), 4 Easy Living (6.26), 5 Art of the Big Band (7.54), 6 Moonlight Serenade (6.44), 7 Elvin's Mambo (6.38), 8 Weird Blues (4.40), 9 Paul's Call (7.53), 10 But Not For Me (4.19)

Don Grolnick
*** 1992 Nighttown
CD; Blue Note: CDP 0777 7 98689 2 6
Length: (57.19); Album type: studio
Musicians: Don Grolnick (piano), Randy Brecker (trumpet), Joe Lovano (saxophone), Marty Ehrlich (clarinet), Steve Turre (trombone), Dave Holland (bass), Bill Stewart (drums)
Tracks: 1 Heart of Darkness (6.31), 2 What is This Thing Called Love (6.13), 3 One Bird, One Stone (6.20), 4 Nighttown (8.15), 5 Genie (7.25), 6 Spot That Man (5.25), 7 The Cost Of Living (8.09), 8 Blues for Pop (9.01)
Notes: Recorded 1991/12 at Skyline Studios NYC by James Farber.

Bob Mintzer and Michael Brecker
*** 1994 Twin Tenors
CD; Novus / RCA: 01241-63173-2; UIN/UPC: 012416317320
Length: (59.02); Album type: studio
Produced by: Takao Ogawa, Yoshihiro Kumagai
Musicians: Bob Mintzer (saxophone), Michael Brecker (saxophone), Don Grolnick (piano), Michael Formanek (bass), Peter Erskine (drums)
Tracks: 1 The Saxophone (5.48), 2 Giant Steps (6.07), 3 Three Pieces (3.45), 4 Tenorman's Lament (6.32), 5 Two Ts (8.16), 6 Sonny (5.26), 7 Body and Soul: Everything Happens To Me (12.24), 8 Three Little Words (5.27), 9 Giant Steps (5.00)
Notes: Also published as The Saxophone featuring Two T's. Michael Brecker plays only on 2, Giant Steps, 5, Two Ts, and 7, Body and Soul: Everything Happens To Me.

Marc Copland Quintet
1995 Stompin' with Savoy
CD; Savoy:
Length:; Album type:
Produced by: Musicians: Marc Copland (piano)
Randy Brecker (trumpet), Bob Berg (saxophone), Dennis Chambers (drums), James Genus (bass)
Tracks: 1 Equinox, 2 I Got Rhythm, 3 I Loves You Porgy, 4 Footprints, 5 Easy To Love, 6 Lover Man, 7 Woody 'n' You, 8 Blue in Green, 9 One Finger Snap, 10 All Blues

Don Grolnick
*** 1995 Medianoche
CD; Warner Bros: 9 46287-2
Length: (56.29); Album type: studio
Musicians: Don Grolnick (piano), Michael Brecker (saxophone), Dave Valentin (flute), Mike Mainieri (vibraphone), Andy Gonzales (bass), Don Alias (percussion), Steve Berrios (percussion), Milton Cardona (percussion)
Tracks: 1 Catta (4.09), 2 Rainsville (5.26), 3 Water Babies (7.08), 4 Medianoche (5.21), 5 Cape Verdean Blues (4.54), 6 Heart of Darkness (6.00), 7 If Ever I Should Leave You (7.20), 8 Rojo Y Negro (4.54), 9 Oran (5.31), 10 Night Song (5.33)

Don Grolnick Group
*** 2000 The London Concert
CD; Fuzzy Music: PEPCD008; UIN/UPC: 650130000823
Length: (64.38); Album type: live
Musicians: Don Grolnick (piano), Michael Brecker (saxophone), Randy Brecker (trumpet), Marty Ehrlich (clarinet), Robin Eubanks (trombone), Peter Washington (bass) (bass), Don Alias (percussion), Peter Erskine (drums)
Tracks: 1 Intro (0.24), 2 Heart of Darkness (11.59), 3 Band Intro (2.04), 4 Or Come Fog (12.44), 5 Five Bars (10.56), 6 Spot That Man (11.05), 7 Don Alias Intro (1.18), 8 What is This Thing Called Love (11.18)
Notes: Recorded Jan 1995.

Bob Mintzer Big Band
**** 1996 Big Band Trane
CD; DMP Records: CD-515; UIN/UPC: 089672051527
Length: (61.51); Album type: studio
Produced by: Bob Mintzer
Musicians: Bob Mintzer (saxophone), Lawrence Feldman (saxophone), Bob Malach (saxophone), Roger Rosenberg (clarinet), Pete Yellin (saxophone), Randy Brecker (trumpet), Laurie Frink (trumpet), Tony Kadleck (trumpet), Bob Millikan (trumpet), Michael Mossman (trumpet), Marvin Stamm (trumpet), Michael Eugene Davis (trombone), Keith O'Quinn (trombone), Larry Farrell (trombone), David Taylor (trombone), Phil Markowitz (piano), Jay Anderson (bass), John Riley (drums)
Tracks: 1 My Favourite Things (4.56), 2 A Love Supreme - Acknowledgement (7.00), 3 Run For Your Life (5.18), 4 Prayer for Peace (6.16), 5 One People (5.31), 6 Impressions (5.42), 7 Spirits (7.22), 8 Ancestors (6.00), 9 Softly Spoken (7.13), 10 Trane's Blues (5.56)

Smappies
1996 Rhythmsticks
CD; Victor: VICP8165
Length: (n/k) ; Album type: studio
Musicians: Randy Brecker (trumpet), Michael Brecker (saxophone), Mike Mainieri (vibraphone), Will Lee (bass), Jay Beckenstein (saxophone), Dave Valentin (flute), Arturo Sandoval (trumpet), David Spinozza (guitar), Philippe Saisse (keyboard)
Tracks: 1 James Bond Theme, 2 Working People, 3 Won't Stop Raining, 4 Pain, 5 Pensando em Voce, 6 Muchacha Bonita, 7 Part Time Kiss, 8 I Wish You'll Be Happy, 9 Morning, 10 Happy Birthday
Notes: A Japanese edition. The Brecker Brothers play on tracks 1, and 2. Mainieri plays on 3. Lee plays on 3, 7, 9. Beckenstein solos on 4, 9. Valentin and Sandoval play on 6.

Herbie Hancock & The New Standard All Stars
2009 One Night In Japan [DVD]
DVD; Immortal:
Length: (74.00); Album type: live
Musicians: Herbie Hancock (keyboard), John Scofield (guitar), Michael Brecker (saxophone), Dave Holland (bass), Jack DeJohnette (drums), Don Alias (percussion)
Tracks: 1 New York Minute (13.31), 2 Norwegian Wood (9.05), 3 Mercy Street (12.52), 4 You've Got It Bad Girl (15.39), 5 Love is Stronger Than Pride (14.42)
Notes: Recorded at Lake Stella Theater, Kawaguchi, Japan, 3/8/1996.

Tony Williams
**** 1997 Wilderness
CD; ARK 21: 7243-8-54571-2-8; UIN/UPC: 724385457128
Length: (64.59); Album type: studio
Produced by: Tony Williams
Musicians: Tony Williams (drums), Michael Brecker (saxophone), Herbie Hancock (keyboard), Pat Metheny (guitar), Stanley Clarke (bass)
Tracks: 1 Wilderness Rising (7.35), 2 China Town (8.33), 3 Infant Wilderness (2.31), 4 Harlem Mist '55 (4.03), 5 China Road (2.46), 6 The Night You Were Born (8.05), 7 Wilderness Voyager (2.07), 8 Machu Picchu (6.42), 9 China Moon (3.24), 10 Wilderness Island (2.49), 11 Sea of Wilderness (3.06), 12 Gambia (6.13), 13 Cape Wilderness (7.15)

Elvin Jones Jazz Machine
2004 The Truth: Heard Live At The Blue Note
CD; Half Note:
Length: (60.24); Album type: live
Musicians: Elvin Jones (drums), Michael Brecker (saxophone), Robin Eubanks (trombone), Carlos McKinney (piano), Antoine Roney (saxophone), Gene Perla (multi), Darren Barrett (trumpet)
Tracks: 1 E.J.'s Blues (8.22), 2 Straight No Chaser (7.39), 3 Body And Soul (9.47), 4 Truth (7.17), 5 A Lullaby Of Itsugo Village (7.42), 6 Wise One (12.27), 7 Three Card Molly (7.10)
Notes: Recorded at the Blue Note, NYC, 11,12/11/1999.

Bob Berg, Randy Brecker, Dennis Chambers, Joey DeFrancesco
**** 2000 The JazzTimes Superband
CD; Concord: CCD-4889-2; UIN/UPC: 013431488927
Length: (65.46); Album type: studio

Produced by: Nick Phillips
Musicians: Bob Berg (saxophone), Randy Brecker (trumpet), Dennis Chambers (drums), Joey DeFrancesco (keyboard), Paul Bollenback (guitar)
Tracks: 1 Dirty Dogs (6.17), 2 Silverado (8.25), 3 Jones Street (6.08), 4 Oleo (5.36), 5 Friday Night at the Cadillac Club (4.47), 6 SoHo Sole (7.14), 7 The Ada Strut (6.16), 8 Blue Goo (6.24), 9 Seven A.M. Special (6.08), 10 Freedom Jazz Dance (8.12)
Notes: Randy Brecker plays flugelhorn on 4, Oleo, and on 7, The Ada Strut.

Herbie Hancock
***** 2002 Directions In Music
CD; Verve: 589 654 2
Length: (78.19); Album type: live
Produced by: Michael Brecker, Jason Olaine, Herbie Hancock
Musicians: Herbie Hancock (keyboard), Roy Hargrove (trumpet), Michael Brecker (saxophone), John Patitucci (bass), Brian Blade (drums)
Tracks: 1 The Sorcerer (8.53), 2 The Poet (6.35), 3 So What/ Impressions (12.51), 4 Misstery (8.16), 5 Naima (7.29), 6 Transition (10.26), 7 My Ship (8.40), 8 D Trane (15.09)
Notes: Recorded live at the Massey Hall, Toronto, Canada on 25 Oct 2001.

Charlie Haden with Michael Brecker
***** 2002 American Dreams
CD; Universal France / Verve: 064 096-2; UIN/UPC: 044006409627
Length: (74.18); Album type: studio
Musicians: Charlie Haden (bass), Michael Brecker (saxophone), Brad Mehldau (piano), Brian Blade (drums)
Tracks: 1 American Dreams (4.50), 2 Travels (6.44), 3 No Lonely Nights (5.16), 4 It Might Be You (4.52), 5 Prism (5.19), 6 America The Beautiful (5.21), 7 Nightfall (5.06), 8 Ron's Place (7.27), 9 Bittersweet (6.43), 10 Young And Foolish (5.36), 11 Bird Food (7.29), 12 Sotto Voce (5.10), 13 Love Like Ours (4.25)

Tom Scott
**** 2006 Bebop United
CD; MCG Jazz: MCGJ1021; UIN/UPC: 612262102127
Length: (59.22); Album type: live
Produced by: Tom Scott
Musicians: Tom Scott (saxophone), Ronnie Cuber (saxophone), Phil Woods (saxophone), Randy Brecker (trumpet), Gil Goldstein (keyboard), Jay Ashby (trombone), Duane Burno (bass)
Tracks: 1 Children of the Night (6.39), 2 Silhouettes (5.31), 3 Tones For Joan's Bones (6.56), 4 His Eyes, Her Eyes (8.14), 5 Sack O' Woe (8.13), 6 Back Burner (9.53), 7 Close View (6.39), 8 The Song Is You (8.22)
Notes: Woods plays on 2, 7. Recorded May 2002.

Saxophone Summit
*** 2004 Gathering Of Spirits
CD; Telarc: 83607; UIN/UPC: 089408360725
Length: (65.56); Album type: studio
Produced by: Richard Seidel
Musicians: Billy Hart (drums), Cecil McBee (bass), Phil Markowitz (piano), Dave Liebman (saxophone), Joe Lovano (saxophone), Michael Brecker (saxophone)

Tracks: 1 Alexander The Great (6.51), 2 The 12th Man (9.56), 3 India (14.14), 4 Peace On Earth (5.05), 5 Tricycle (17.30), 6 A Gathering Of Spirits (12.17)

Marc Copland, Randy Brecker
*** 2006 Both / And
CD; Nagel-Heyer: 2067
Length: (62.54); Album type: studio
Musicians: Marc Copland (piano), Randy Brecker (trumpet), Victor Lewis (drums), Ed Howard (bass)
Tracks: 1 Through the Window (8.29), 2 I Loves You Porgy (8.16), 3 Over the Hills (8.27), 4 The Sidewinder (6.29), 5 Both/And (8.20), 6 Round the Horn (5.07), 7 When the Wind Stops (8.51), 8 Bookends (8.55)

Oliver Strauch's Groovin High
2011 Live With Randy Brecker
CD; Jazz 'n' Arts:; UIN/UPC: 4260089370388
Length: (72.13); Album type: live
Musicians: Oliver Strauch (drums), Randy Brecker (trumpet), Johannes Muller (saxophone), August-Wilhelm Scheer (saxophone), Gautier Laurent (bass), Pierre-Alain Goualch (piano)
Tracks: 1 Joshua (7.43), 2 Eighty-One (10.29), 3 You Don't Know What Love Is (12.10), 4 September Boy (3.40), 5 Transition (4.42), 6 Holy Forest (7.32), 7 Funky Beta One (12.27), 8 Bye Bye Blackbird (11.26)

Randy Brecker, Wlodek Pawlik
****2013 Randy Brecker Plays Wlodek Pawlik's Night in Calisia
CD; Summit: 612; UIN/UPC: 099402612928
Length: (63.37); Album type: studio
Musicians: Wlodek Pawlik (piano), Randy Brecker (trumpet), Pawel Panita (bass), Cezary Konrad (drums), Kalisz Philharmonic Orchestra (orchestra), Adam Klocek (conductor)
Tracks: 1 Night In Calisia (10.54), 2 Amber Road (9.44), 3 Orienthology (10.17), 4 Follow The Stars (11.17), 5 Quarrel of The Roman Merchants (10.59), 6 Forgotten Song (10.26)
Notes: In December 2013, Randy was nominated, along with the Włodek Pawlik Trio & the Kalisz Philharmonic for a Grammy Award for their album *Night in Calisia* (2013) in the category, "Best Large Jazz Ensemble."

Randy Brecker Discography (excluding albums of previously released material)

1967 Duke Pearson: Introducing Duke Pearson's Big Band
1968 Blood, Sweat & Tears: Child Is Father To The Man
1968 Duke Pearson: Now Hear This
1968 The McCoys: The Infinite McCoys
1968 Jazz Composer's Orchestra: The Jazz Composer's Orchestra
1969 Randy Brecker: Score
1969 Gary McFarland: America The Beautiful
1969 Horace Silver: You Gotta Take A Little Love
1969 Joe Beck: Nature Boy
1969 Paul Sylvan: Good Paul Sylvan
1970 Horace Silver: That Healin' Feelin'
1970 Jack McDuff: Who Knows What Tomorrow's Gonna Bring?
1970 Oliver Nelson: Black, Brown And Beautiful
1970 Johnny Hodges, Leon Thomas, Oliver Nelson: Three Shades of Blue
1970 Dreams: Dreams
1971 Prairie Madness: Prairie Madness
1971 Lotti Golden: Lotti Golden
1971 Lena Horne: Nature's Baby
1971 David Pomeranz: Time To Fly
1971 Hal Galper: Wild Bird
1971 Dreams: Imagine My Surprise
1971 Harlem River Drive: Harlem River Drive
1971 Air: Air
1971 Carole Hall: If I Be Your Lady
1972 Mike Mainieri and Friends: White Elephant Vol 2
1972 James Brown: Get On The Good Foot
1972 James Taylor: One Man Dog
1972 Gary Burton: In The Public Interest
1972 Hal Galper: The Guerilla Band
1972 Full Moon: Full Moon
1972 Mike Mainieri and Friends: White Elephant Vol 1
1972 The Free Design: One by One
1972 Horace Silver: In Pursuit Of The 27th Man
1972 Todd Rundgren: Something/Anything?
1973 Todd Rundgren: A Wizard, A True Star
1973 John Simon: Journey
1973 Luiz Bonfa: Jacaranda
1973 Mark Murphy: Bridging A Gap
1973 Michael Wendroff: Michael Wendroff
1973 Lou Reed: Berlin
1973 The Fabulous Rhinestones: Free Wheelin'
1973 Crowbar: Crowbar
1973 Mark James: Mark James
1973 Nick Holmes: The Soulful Crooner
1973 Joao Donato: Donato Deodato (EP)
1973 The Cecil Holmes Soulful Sounds: Music For Soulful Lovers
1973 Mike Gibbs & Gary Burton: The Public Interest
1973 Stanley Turrentine: Don't Mess with Mister T
1973 Alphonse Mouzon: Funky Snakefoot
1973 Borderline: Sweet Dreams And Quiet Desires / The Second Album
1973 Don Sebesky: Giant Box
1974 Borderline: The Second Album
1974 Average White Band: AWB
1974 Aerosmith: Get Your Wings
1974 Arif Mardin: Journey
1974 Felix Cavaliere: Felix Cavaliere
1974 Hubert Laws: Chicago Theme
1974 Todd Rundgren: Todd
1974 B. J. Thomas: Longhorn And London Bridges
1974 Billy Cobham: Total Eclipse
1974 Luiz Bonfa: Manhattan Strut
1974 Johnny Winter: John Dawson Winter III
1974 Eleventh House: Introducing The Eleventh House With Larry Coryell
1974 Rachel Faro: Refugees
1974 Bob James: One
1974 Jerry Lacroix: Second Coming
1974 Johnny Winter: Saints & Sinners
1974 Billy Cobham: Crosswinds
1974 Grover Washington Jr.: Mister Magic
1974 James Taylor: Walking Man
1974 Gato Barbieri: Chapter Three: Viva Emiliano Zapata

1974 Idris Muhammad: Power Of Soul
1975 The Manhattan Transfer: The Manhattan Transfer
1975 Judy Collins: Judith
1975 Esther Phillips: Esther Phillips And Joe Beck
1975 George Benson: Pacific Fire
1975 George Benson: Good King Bad
1975 Mike Longo: 900 Shares Of The Blues
1975 Black Heat: Keep On Runnin'
1975 Luther Allison: Night Life
1975 Stark & McBrien: Big Star
1975 Don Sebesky: The Rape Of El Morro
1975 Bazuka: Bazuka
1975 Mark Dimond, Frankie Dante: Beethoven's V
1975 Billy Cobham: Shabazz (Recorded Live In Europe)
1975 Ruth Copeland: Take Me To Baltimore
1975 Parliament: Mothership Connection
1975 Russel Morris: Russel Morris
1975 Hank Crawford: Don't You Worry 'Bout A Thing
1975 Ron Carter: Anything Goes
1975 Barry Miles: Magic Theater
1975 Mark Murphy: Mark Murphy Sings
1975 Charles Earland: Odyssey
1975 Bob James: Two
1975 David Sanborn: Taking Off
1975 The Brecker Brothers: The Brecker Brothers
1975 Eric Gale: Forecast
1975 Grover Washington Jr: Feels So Good
1975 Esther Phillips: What A Diff'rence A Day Makes
1975 Steve Satten: Whatcha Gonna Do For Me?
1975 Bruce Springsteen: Born To Run
1975 Billy Cobham: A Funky Thide Of Sings
1975 Bob Moses: Bittersuite In The Ozone
1975 Al Kooper: Al's Big Deal / Unclaimed Freight
1976 The Brecker Brothers Band: Back To Back
1976 Barry Miles: Sky Train
1976 Gato Barbieri: Caliente!

1976 Average White Band: Soul Searching
1976 Jun Fukamachi: Spiral Steps
1976 Rosie: Better Late Than Never
1976 Dan Hartman: Images
1976 The Eleventh House featuring Larry Coryell: Aspects
1976 Jaco Pastorius: Jaco Pastorius
1976 Bootsy Collins: Stretchin' Out In Bootsy's Rubber Band
1976 Ben Sidran: Free In America
1976 Patti Austin: End Of A Rainbow
1976 Gerry Brown & John Lee: Still Can't Say Enough
1976 Blue Oyster Cult: Agents Of Fortune
1976 Ringo Starr: Ringo's Rotogravure
1976 Jack Wilkins: You Can't Live Without It
1976 Phil Woods: The New Phil Woods Album
1976 Hubert Laws: Romeo & Juliet
1976 Elton John: Blue Moves
1976 Parliament: The Clones Of Dr. Frunkenstein
1976 Roland Prince: Color Visions
1976 Martee Lebous: The Lady Wants To Be A Star
1976 O'Donel Levy: Windows
1976 Weldon Irvine: Sinbad
1976 Webster Lewis: On The Town
1976 George Benson: Cast Your Fate To The Wind
1976 Esther Phillips: For All We Know
1976 Laura Nyro: Smile
1976 Manhattan Transfer: Coming Out
1976 Grover Washington Jr: A Secret Place
1976 Roy Buchanan: A Street Called Straight
1976 Bob James: Three
1976 Diana Marcovitz: Joie De Vivre!
1976 Esther Phillips: Capricon Princess
1976 John Tropea: John Tropea
1976 Andy Harlow: Andy Harlow's Latin Fever
1976 Bette Midler: Songs For The New Depression
1976 Bill Amesbury: Can You Feel It
1977 Coal Kitchen: Thirsty Or Not...Choose Your Flavor

1977 Malcolm Tomlinson: Coming Outta Nowhere
1977 Andy Pratt: Shiver In The Night
1977 Bootsy's Rubber Band: Ahh...The Name Is Bootsy, Baby!
1977 Joe Thomas: Here I Come
1977 Tornader: Hit It Again
1977 Domenic Troiano: Burnin' At The Stake
1977 Phoebe Snow: Never Letting Go
1977 Joe Farrell: La Catedral Y El Toro
1977 John Tropea: Short Trip To Space
1977 Fred Wesley: A Blow For Me, A Toot To You
1977 J. Geils Band: Monkey Island
1977 Harold Vick: After The Dance
1977 Garland Jeffreys: Ghost Writer
1977 Pezband: Pezband
1977 Peter Bliss: Peter Bliss
1977 Eric Gale: Ginseng Woman
1977 The Manhattan Transfer: Pastiche
1977 Hal Galper: Reach Out!
1977 Idris Muhammad: Camby Bolongo
1977 Idris Muhammad: Turn This Mutha Out
1977 Joao Donato: Joao Donato
1977 Jimmy McGriff: Red Beans
1977 Kiki Dee: Kiki Dee
1977 Jun Fukamachi: Jun Fukamachi Live At The Triangle Theatre
1977 Maynard Ferguson: Conquistador
1977 Odyssey: Odyssey
1977 Fania All-Stars: Rhythm Machine
1977 Charles Earland: Revelation
1977 Jun Fukamachi: Evening Star
1977 Zbigniew Seifert: Zbigniew Seifert
1977 Jun Fukamachi: Jun Fukamachi
1977 Bob James: Heads
1977 Steve Khan: Tightrope
1977 Billy Cobham: Inner Conflicts
1977 Hank Crawford: Tico Rico
1977 Jun Fukamachi: Triangle Session
1977 Jun Fukamachi: The Sea Of Dirac
1977 Average White Band: Benny & Us
1977 Ringo Starr: Ringo The 4th
1977 William Eaton: Struggle Buggy
1977 Wild Cherry: Electrified Funk
1977 Meco: Star Wars And Other Galactic Funk
1977 Don Pullen: Tomorrow's Promises

1977 David Matthews: Dune
1977 Jimmy McGriff: Tailgunner
1977 The Brecker Brothers: Don't Stop The Music
1978 Flora Purim: Walking Away
1978 Hal Galper: The Hal Galper Quintet Live: Redux '78
1978 Kate Taylor: Kate Taylor
1978 Joe Thomas: Platos Retreat And Other Funky Delights
1978 Various Artists: The Wiz [Original Soundtrack]
1978 The Brecker Brothers: Heavy Metal Bebop
1978 Marilyn McCoo & Billy Davis Jr: Marilyn & Billy
1978 Richard Tee: Strokin'
1978 Wild Cherry: I Love My Music
1978 Ralph MacDonald: The Path
1978 Breakwater: Breakwater
1978 Rupert Holmes: Pursuit Of Happiness
1978 Jun Fukamachi: Jun Fukamachi & The New York All Stars Live
1978 Paul Mauriat Plus: Overseas Call
1978 John Tropea: To Touch You Again
1978 Deodato: Love Island
1978 Jon Faddis: Good And Plenty
1978 Tina Turner: Love Explosion
1978 Alessi Brothers: All For A Reason
1978 Melanie: Phonogenic Not Just Another Pretty Face
1978 Walter Bishop Jr.: Cubicle
1978 Garland Jeffreys: One-Eyed Jack
1978 David Spinozza: Spinozza
1978 Chaka Khan: Chaka
1978 Eric Gale: Multiplication
1978 Ben Sidran: Live At Montreaux
1978 David Sanborn: Heart To Heart
1978 Chris Hinze Combination: Bamboo Magic
1978 Hal Galper Quintet: Children Of The Night
1978 Bill Chinnock: Badlands
1978 Fania All-Stars: Spanish Fever
1978 Hal Galper: Speak with A Single Voice
1978 George Benson: Space
1978 Scarlet Rivera: Scarlet Fever
1978 Steve Khan: The Blue Man

1978 Jack Wilkins: Merge
1978 Carly Simon: Boys In The Trees
1978 Mark "Moogy" Klingman: Moogy II
1978 Flora Purim: Everyday Everynight
1978 Various Artists: Starmania: l'Opera Rock de Michel Berger et Luc Plamondon
1978 Robert Palmer: Double Fun
1978 Thijs van Leer: Nice To Have Met You
1978 Bob James: Touchdown
1978 The Average White Band: Warmer Communications
1978 Odyssey: Hollywood Party Tonight
1979 Ronnie Dyson: If The Shoe Fits
1979 Yusef Lateef: In A Temple Garden
1979 Masahiko Satoh: All-In All-Out
1979 Bob James: Lucky Seven
1979 Kleeer: I Love To Dance
1979 Narada Michael Walden: Awakening - The Dance Of Life
1979 Bad News Travels Fast: Look Out
1979 The Average White Band: Feel No Fret
1979 Bad News Travels Fast: Ordinary Man
1979 David Matthews: Digital Love
1979 Charles Mingus: Me Myself An Eye
1979 Steve Khan: Arrows
1979 Niteflyte: Niteflyte
1979 Teddy Pendergrass: Live! Coast To Coast
1979 Ralph MacDonald: Counterpoint
1979 Warren Bernhardt, Michael Brecker, Randy Brecker, Mike Mainieri: Blue Montreux II
1979 Casiopea: Casiopea
1979 Desmond Child And Rouge: Desmond Child And Rouge
1979 The Tony Williams Lifetime: The Joy Of Flying
1979 Alec R. Costandinos & The Syncophonic Orchestra: Winds Of Change: A Musical Fantasy
1979 Bette Midler: Thighs And Whispers
1979 Richard T. Bear: Red Hot & Blue
1979 Wilbert Longmire: Champagne
1979 Mongo Santamaria: Red Hot
1979 Candi Staton: Chance
1979 Kleeer: Winners
1979 Charles Earland: Coming To You Live
1979 Saint & Stephanie: Saint & Stephanie
1979 Spyro Gyra: Morning Dance
1979 John Mayall: Bottom Line
1979 Warren Bernhardt, Michael Brecker, Randy Brecker, Mike Mainieri: Blue Montreux
1979 Poussez!: Poussez!
1979 Michael Franks: Tiger In The Rain
1979 Original Soundtrack: The Warriors
1979 Herbie Mann: Yellow Fever
1979 Carly Simon: Spy
1979 Terumasa Hino: City Connection
1979 David "Fathead" Newman: Scratch My Back
1980 Joao Donato: Spirit Of Deodato
1980 Yoshiaki Masuo: Song Is You And Me
1980 The Spinners: Love Trippin'
1980 Richard Tee: Natural Ingredients
1980 George Clinton and the P-Funk All-Stars: Plush Funk
1980 Spyro Gyra: Catching The Sun
1980 Charles Mingus: Something Like A Bird
1980 Stone Alliance: Heads Up
1980 Chaka Khan: Naughty
1980 Patti Austin: Body Language
1980 Bob James: H
1980 Manu Dibango: Gone Clear
1980 J. D. Drews: J. D. Drews
1980 The David Chesky Band: Rush Hour
1980 Jun Fukamachi: On The Move
1980 Ray Gomez: Volume
1980 Cameo: Feel Me
1980 The Brecker Brothers: Détente
1980 David Liebman: Pendulum
1980 Parliament: Trombipulation
1980 Paul Simon: One Trick Pony
1980 Jimmy Maelen: Beats Workin'
1980 Hank Crawford: Cajun Sunrise
1980 Far Cry: The More Things Change
1980 Spyro Gyra: Carnaval
1980 Bunky Green: Places We've Never Been
1980 Various Artists: Fame [Original Soundtrack]
1981 Herbie Mann: Mellow
1981 Mike Mainieri: Wanderlust

1981 J. Geils Band: Freeze Frame
1981 Diana Ross: Why Do Fools Fall In Love
1981 The Brecker Brothers: Straphangin'
1981 Garland Jeffreys: Escape Artist
1981 Carly Simon: Torch
1981 Chic: Take It Off
1981 Chaka Khan: What Cha' Gonna Do For Me
1981 Masaru Imada: Carnival
1981 Manu Dibango: Ambassador
1981 George Benson: GB
1981 Phoebe Snow: Rock Away
1981 Rickie Lee Jones: Pirates
1981 Hubert Laws: Pavane
1982 Ron Carter: El Noche Sol
1982 Barry Finnerty: New York City
1982 Michael Franks: Objects Of Desire
1982 The Average White Band: Cupid's In Fashion
1982 Jim Carroll Band: Dry Dreams
1982 Change: Sharing Your Love
1982 Janis Siegel: Experiment In White
1982 Mark Gray: Boogie Hotel
1982 Narada Michael Walden: Confidence
1982 David Matthews: Grand Cross
1982 Bugatti & Musker: The Dukes
1982 Peter Erskine: Peter Erskine
1982 Bob James: Hands Down
1982 Luther Vandross: Forever, For Always, For Love
1982 Donald Fagen: The Nightfly
1983 George Benson: In Your Eyes
1983 Various Artists: Digital Big Band Bash!
1983 Bob Mintzer and the Horn Man Band: Papa Lips
1983 Jaco Pastorius: Invitation
1983 Lew Tabackin: Lew Tabackin Quartet
1983 Gil Evans & Orchestra: Live in Lugano 1983 [DVD]
1983 Michael Franks: Passionfruit
1983 Bob James: The Genie
1984 Barry Gibb: Now Voyager
1984 Steely Dan: Gaucho
1984 Jukkis Uotila: Introspection
1984 Mingus Dynasty: Live At The Village Vanguard
1984 Joe Cocker: Civilized Man
1984 Diana Ross: Swept Away
1984 Frank Sinatra with Quincy Jones and Orchestra: L.A. Is My Lady
1984 Mark Gray & Super Friends: The Silencer
1984 Lou Reed: New Sensations
1984 Martha and the Muffins: Mystery Walk
1985 Bob Mintzer Big Band: Incredible Journey
1985 Don Grolnick: Hearts And Numbers
1985 James Brown: The CD Of JB: Sex Machine & Other Soul Classics
1985 Hank Crawford: Roadhouse Symphony
1985 Randy Brecker, Eliane Elias: Amanda
1985 Dolby's Cube: May The Cube Be With You
1985 James Taylor: That's Why I'm Here
1985 Dire Straits: Brothers In Arms
1985 Patti Austin: Gettin' Away with Murder
1985 Michael W. Smith: Big Picture
1985 Carla Bley: Night-Glo
1985 Bob Mintzer: Source
1985 Jennifer Holliday: Say You Love Me
1985 Teruo Nakamura: Super Friends
1985 Taeko Ohnuki: Copine
1986 Hank Crawford: Mr. Chips
1986 Ronnie Cuber: Live At The Blue Note
1986 Michael W. Smith: The Big Picture
1986 Ornella Vanoni: Ornella E...
1986 Paul Simon: Graceland
1986 Eric Clapton: August
1986 Bob James: Obsession
1986 Bob Mintzer Big Band: Camouflage
1986 Chaka Khan: Destiny
1986 Original Soundtrack: A House Full Of Love: Music From The Cosby Show
1986 Grover Washington Jr: House Full Of Love: Music from The Cosby Show
1986 Cameo: Word Up!
1986 Rare Silk: New Weave
1986 Steve Winwood: Back In The High Life
1987 Randy Brecker: In The Idiom
1987 Jill Jones: Jill Jones

1987 Various Artists: Total Happiness (Music from The Bill Cosby Show, Vol. 2)
1987 Michael Franks: The Camera Never Lies
1987 Jukkis Uotila: Avenida
1987 Go West: Dancin' On The Couch
1987 Glenn Alexander: Glenn Alexander
1987 Various Artists: Lost In The Stars: The Music Of Kurt Weill
1987 Billy Cobham: Picture This
1987 Hiram Bullock: Give It What U Got
1988 Cameo: Machismo
1988 Luther Vandross: Any Love
1988 Bob Mintzer Big Band: Spectrum
1988 Various Artists: Denon Jazz Sampler, Vol. 3
1988 Eric Clapton: Crossroads
1988 Loren Schoenberg Jazz Orchestra: Solid Ground
1988 Eliane Elias: So Far So Close
1988 Soundtrack: Punchline
1988 Various Artists: Implosions
1988 Peter Erskine: Motion Poet
1988 Dire Straits: Money For Nothing
1988 The Mingus Dynasty: Mingus' Sounds Of Love
1988 Gillan & Glover: Accidentally On Purpose
1988 Jorge Dalto: Listen Up!
1988 B. B. King: King Of Blues: 1989
1988 Lyle Mays: Street Dreams
1988 Big Band Charlie Mingus: Live At The Theatre Boulogne-Billancourt, Paris Vol. 2
1988 Andy Sheppard: Andy Sheppard
1988 The SOS All-Stars: New York Rendezvous
1988 Hue And Cry: Remote
1989 Randy Brecker: Live At Sweet Basil
1989 Eliane Elias: Cross Currents
1989 Randy Brecker: Mr. Max!
1989 Toninho Horta: Moonstone.
1989 Eddie Gomez: Street Smart
1989 Don Grolnick: Weaver Of Dreams
1989 Rickie Lee Jones: Flying Cowboys
1989 Bob Mintzer: Urban Contours
1989 Phoebe Snow: Something Real
1989 Various Artists: Charles Mingus: Epitaph [DVD]
1989 D'Atra Hicks: D'atra Hicks
1989 Mike Catalano: A Rio Affair
1989 Bianca Ciccu: The Gusch
1989 Third World: Serious Business
1989 Vince Mendoza: Vince Mendoza
1989 Various Artists: Echoes Of Ellington, Vol. 2
1989 Richie Beirach: Some Other Time - A Tribute To Chet Baker
1990 Bob Berg: In The Shadows
1990 Michael Colina: Rituals
1990 Claus Ogerman: Claus Ogerman Featuring Michael Brecker
1990 Niels Lan Doky: Dreams
1990 George Benson: Big Boss Band
1990 Mitch Farber: Star Climber
1990 Hypersax: Stepdance
1990 Charles Mingus: Epitaph
1990 Caifanes: El Diablito
1990 Kenny Werner: Uncovered Heart
1990 CTI All-Stars: Rhythmstick
1990 Nick Brignola: What It Takes
1990 Randy Brecker: Toe To Toe
1990 Paul Simon: The Rhythm Of The Saints
1990 Bob James: Grand Piano Canyon
1991 John Scofield: Grace Under Pressure
1991 Alex Gunia: Alex Gunia's Groove Cut
1991 David Wilcox: Home Again
1991 Big Band Charlie Mingus: Live At The Theatre Boulogne-Billancourt, Paris Vol. 1
1991 Various Artists: Colors Of Jazz: For Sunday Morning
1991 Various Artists: Colors Of Jazz: For Tropical Nights
1991 James Taylor: New Moon Shine
1991 Dieter Ilg: Summerhill
1991 Various Artists: Colors Of Jazz: From Dusk Till Dawn
1991 Chroma: Music On The Edge
1991 Bob Mintzer Big Band: Art Of The Big Band
1991 Acoustic Alchemy: Back On The Case
1991 Trudy Desmond: Tailor Made
1991 Tom Scott: Keep This Love Alive
1991 Dave Kikoski: Persistent Dreams
1991 Various Artists: From Hollywood
1991 L. J. Reynolds: L. J. Reynolds

1992 David Sanborn: Upfront
1992 Bruce Williamson: Big City Magic
1992 Jenni Muldaur: Jenni Muldaur
1992 Toshinobu Kubota: Neptune
1992 John Simon: Out On The Street
1992 Jay Anderson: Next Exit
1992 The Brecker Brothers: The Return of The Brecker Brothers: Live in Spain 1992 [DVD]
1992 Ray Simpson: Ray Simpson
1992 Don Grolnick: Nighttown
1992 Michael Musillami: Glass Art
1992 Niels Lan Doky: Paris by Night
1992 J Geils Band: Houseparty: Anthology
1992 Sandy Bull: Vehicles
1992 Dave Weckl Band: Heads Up
1992 Eero Koivistoinen: Altered Things
1992 Carly Simon: This Is My Life
1992 Various Artists: After The Dance
1992 Chris Minh Doky: Letters
1992 Various Artists: Enja 20th Anniversary Sampler
1992 GRP All-Star Big Band: GRP All-Star Big Band
1992 The George Gruntz Concert Jazz Band: Blues 'n Dues Et Cetera
1992 Tom Scott: Born Again
1992 Peter Erskine: Sweet Soul
1992 The Brecker Brothers: Return Of The Brecker Brothers
1992 LaVern Baker: Woke Up This Mornin'
1992 Garland Jeffreys: Matador & More.
1992 Conrad Herwig Quintet: The Amulet
1992 Milky Way: Milky Way
1993 Cornell Dupree: Child's Play
1993 Jimmy Haslip: Arc
1993 O.C. Smith: After All Is Said And Done
1993 Jay Leonhart & Friends: Live At Fat Tuesday's: May 13-16, 1993
1993 Love X 3: Love X 3
1993 Mingus Big Band: Mingus Big Band 93: Nostalgia In Times Square
1993 Donald Fagen: Kamakyriad
1993 Idris Muhammad: My Turn
1993 Othello Molineaux: It's About Time
1993 Laura Nyro: Walk The Dog & Light The Light
1993 George Benson: Love Remembers
1993 Mike Stern: Standards And Other Songs
1993 Leslie Mandoki: People
1993 GRP All-Star Big Band: Live
1993 GRP All-Star Big Band: Dave Grusin Presents GRP All-Star Big Band Live!
1993 Byron Olson: Sketches Of Miles: Arrangements For Chamber Players And Jazz Soloists
1993 Beatnik Rebel: Science: Featuring Tony Verderosa
1993 Various Artists: World Of Contemporary Jazz Groups
1993 Will Lee: Oh!
1994 Marc Beacco: Scampi Fritti
1994 Various Artists: Carnegie Hall Salutes The Jazz Masters: Verve At 50
1994 Mose Allison: The Earth Wants You
1994 Julie Eigenberg: Love Is Starting Now
1994 Mike Longo: El Moodo Grande
1994 Kenneth Sivertsen: Remembering North
1994 Robin Eubanks: Mental Images
1994 Al Kooper: Rekooperation
1994 Dr. John: Television
1994 Robert Miller: Child's Play
1994 Dave Stryker: Nomad
1994 Ben Sidran: Life's A Lesson
1994 The McCoys: Psychedelic Years
1994 GRP All-Star Big Band: All Blues
1994 Various Artists: Denon Hi-Fi Check CD
1994 Various Artists: Cole Porter In Concert: Just One Of Those Live Things
1994 Ray Drummond: Continuum
1994 Aerosmith: Box Of Fire
1994 Sergio Salvatore: Tune Up
1994 Urbanator: Urbanator
1994 Hank Crawford: Heart And Soul: The Hank Crawford Anthology
1994 Jonathan Butler: Head To Head
1994 Caecilie Norby: Caecilie Norby
1994 BFD: BFD
1994 The Brecker Brothers: The Brecker Brothers - Live
1994 The Brecker Brothers: Out Of The Loop
1994 Various Artists: A Tribute To Curtis Mayfield

1995 Toko Furuuchi: Strength
1995 Steve Million: Million To One
1995 Al Kooper: Soul Of A Man: Al Kooper Live
1995 Manhattan Jazz Quintet: Moritat
1995 Matalex: Wild Indian Summer
1995 Frank Mantooth: Sophisticated Lady
1995 Michael Franks: Abandoned Garden
1995 Alan Pasqua: Dedications
1995 Tom Grant: Instinct
1995 Herbie Mann: Peace Pieces: The Music Of Bill Evans
1995 Marc Copland Quintet: Stompin' with Savoy
1995 Various Artists: Jazz To The World
1995 Randy Brecker: Into The Sun
1995 John Scofield: Groove Elation
1995 Elton John: Empty Skies
1995 Roberta Flack: Roberta
1995 McCoy Tyner Trio Featuring Michael Brecker: Infinity
1995 Mingus Big Band: Gunslinging Birds
1995 Laura Theodore: Tonight Is The Night
1995 Raw Stylus: Pushing Against The Flow
1995 Eric Felten: Gratitude
1995 Doky Brothers: Doky Brothers
1996 Leslie Mandoki: People In Room No.8
1996 Spyro Gyra: Heart Of The Night
1996 Liza Minnelli: Gently
1996 Lenny White: Renderers Of Spirit
1996 Smappies: Rhythmsticks
1996 Bob Mintzer Big Band: Big Band Trane
1996 Nils Landgren Funk Unit: Paint It Blue
1996 Common Ground: Common Ground
1996 John Scofield: Quiet
1996 Tony Verderosa: Beatnik Rebel Science
1996 Hue And Cry: JazzNotJazz
1996 Barbara Dennerlein: Junkanoo
1996 Tim Sessions: And Another Thing...
1996 Mingus Big Band: Live In Time
1996 Janet Burgan: Janet Burgan
1996 Chuck Bergeron: Loyalties
1996 Bernard Purdie: Bernard Purdie's Soul To Jazz
1996 The Chartbusters: Mating Call
1996 Various Artists: Jazz Central Station: Global Jazz Poll Winners Vol. 1
1996 Steve Turre: Steve Turre
1996 Nora Nora: Electric Lady
1996 David Sanborn: Songs From The Night Before
1996 Caecilie Norby: My Corner Of The Sky
1996 Various Artists: Big Band Renaissance
1996 Lew Tabackin: Tenority
1997 Various Artists: CTI Records: Acid Jazz Grooves
1997 Steve Million: Thanks A Million
1997 Various Artists: Vanguard Collector's Edition
1997 Linda Eder: It's Time
1997 Leslie Mandoki: The Jazz Cuts
1997 Lionel Hampton: The Lionel Hampton International Jazz Festival 1997 [DVD]
1997 Various Artists: The Art Of Jazz Saxophone: Impressions
1997 Horace Silver: A Prescription For The Blues
1997 Various Artists: Sleep Warm: The Jazz Slumber Project
1997 Don Braden: The Voice Of The Saxophone
1997 Herbie Mann: 65th Birthday Celebration: Live At The Blue Note In New York City
1997 Various Artists: Heirs To Jobim: A Musical Tribute
1997 Ann Hampton Callaway: After Ours
1997 Tim Ries: Imaginary Time
1997 Rolf Kuhn & Friends: Affairs
1997 Various Artists: Jazz Fusion Vol. 2
1997 Andy LaVerne: Four Miles
1997 Matalex: Jazz Grunge
1997 Herbie Mann: America / Brasil
1997 Mose Allison: Jazz Profile: Mose Allison
1997 Yoko Ono: A Story
1997 Mike Longo: Like A Thief In The Night
1997 Bob Berg: Another Standard
1997 Peter Linhart Group: Nailin'
1997 Mike Longo: New York '78

1997 Various Artists: RCA Victor 80th Anniversary
1997 Various Artists: CTI Records: The Birth Of Groove
1997 Carmen Lundy: Old Devil Moon
1997 Mingus Big Band: Que Viva Mingus!
1997 Joe Chindamo: Reflected Journey
1997 Karrin Allyson: Daydream
1998 Eijiro Nakagawa: Peace
1998 Fritz Renold & The Bostonian Friends: Starlight
1998 Peter Erskine: Behind Closed Doors, Vol. 1
1998 Chris Minh Doky: Minh
1998 Billy Cobham: Focused
1998 The Kerry Strayer Septet: Jeru Blue: Tribute To Gerry Mulligan
1998 Various Artists: Jazz Central Station: Global Jazz Poll Winners Vol. 2
1998 Various Artists: Pulp Fusion, Vol. 2: Return To The Tough Side
1998 Chuck Bergeron: Compositions Coast To Coast
1998 Various Artists: Priceless Jazz Sampler, Vol. 4
1998 Various Artists: Discover an American Original: The Jazz Sampler
1998 Tony Lakatos: Generation X
1998 Rolf Kuhn: Music For Two Brothers
1998 Thilo Wolf: Swinging Hour In New York
1998 Sanne Salomonsen: In A New York Minute
1998 Cornell Dupree: Double Clutch
1998 Matalex: Jazz Grunge Tour '96: Live
1998 Gerry Mulligan All-Star Tribute Band: Thank You, Gerry! Our Tribute To Gerry Mulligan
1998 Various Artists: Hipbop 'N' Funk
1998 Chuck Jackson: I'll Never Get Over You
1998 Mark Murphy: Jazz Standards
1999 Michel Berger: Voyou
1999 Mingus Big Band: Blues & Politics
1999 Eileen Ivers: Crossing The Bridge
1999 Steve Million: Truth Is…
1999 Various Artists: Groove Jammy, Vol. 2

1999 Jaco Pastorius Big Band: Twins I & II: Live In Japan 1982
1999 Rick Shadrach Lazar: The Call
1999 Michael Franks: Barefoot On The Beach
1999 Gary LeMel: Moonlighting
1999 Philip Bailey: Dreams
1999 Various Artists: Mile by Jazz Mile
1999 Mark Murphy: Mark Murphy Sings Nat King Cole And More
1999 Linda Eder: It's No Secret Anymore
1999 Nomad: Songman
1999 Fabrizio Sotti: This World Upside Down
1999 70s Jazz Pioneers: Live At The Town Hall, New York City
1999 Martin Taylor: Kiss & Tell
1999 Various Artists: The Other Side Of Standards
1999 Mark Murphy: Songbook
1999 David Lahm: Jazz Takes On Joni Mitchell
1999 Frank Catalano: Pins 'n' Needles
2000 Bob Berg, Randy Brecker, Dennis Chambers, Joey DeFrancesco: The JazzTimes Superband
2000 Various Artists: Celebrating The Music Of Weather Report
2000 Slim Man: All I Want For Christmas
2000 Don Grolnick Group: The London Concert
2000 John Nugent Quintet: Live At The Blue Note (N.Y.C.)
2000 Richard Cole: The Forgotten
2000 Various Artists: Jazz Sampler, Vol. 1
2000 Lew Del Gatto: Katewalk
2000 The Hector Martignon Trio: The Foreign Affair
2000 Chris Minh Doky: Listen Up!
2000 James Brown: James Brown's Funky People Pt. 3
2000 Bill Deal & Ammon Tharp: The Original Rhondels: The Sound Of Virginia Beach
2000 Rex Rideout: Club 1600
2000 Carman: Heart Of A Champion
2000 Various Artists: Wave Music Volume 3
2000 Michael Davis: Brass Nation

2000 David Lahm: More Jazz Takes On Joni Mitchell
2000 Various Artists: Blow! Jazz Trumpet And Saxophone Virtuosos
2000 Andy Summers: Peggy's Blue Skylight
2001 B.B. King: Here And There: The Uncollected B.B. King
2001 Teo Macero: Impressions Of Miles Davis
2001 Dalia Faitelson: Global Sound-Diamond
2001 T.K. Blue: Eyes Of The Elders
2001 Dean Brown: Here
2001 Laura Nyro: Angel In The Dark
2001 Jack Wilkins: Reunion
2001 Randy Brecker: Hangin' In The City
2001 Frank Catalano: Live At The Green Mill
2001 Poul Reimann: New York Sessions
2001 Randy Waldman: UnReel
2001 Doc Powell: Life Changes
2001 Hiram Bullock: Color Me
2001 Bill O'Connell Latin Jazz Project: Black Sand
2001 Curtis Stigers: Baby Plays Around
2002 Mingus Big Band: Tonight At Noon: Three Or Four Shades Of Love
2002 Various Artists: Play Jaco: A Tribute To Jaco Pastoruis
2002 Larry Coryell: Birdfingers
2002 Various Artists: Colors Of Latin Jazz: Shades Of Jobim
2002 Randy Brecker: 34th N Lex
2002 Various Artists: The Art Of Jazz: Saxophone [Slimline]
2002 Christos Rafalides: Manhattan Vibes
2002 Mike Pope: The Lay Of The Land
2002 Dennis Chambers: Outbreak
2002 Will & Rainbow: Over Crystal Green
2002 Bill Evans: Big Fun
2002 Dalia Faitelson: Point Of No Return
2002 Anton Fig: Figments
2002 Billy Cobham: Drum 'n' Voice, Vol. 1
2002 Eliane Elias: Kissed by Nature
2002 Various Artists: A Great Night In Harlem
2003 Jaco Pastorius: Punk Jazz: The Jaco Pastorius Anthology

2003 Chuck Loeb: eBop
2003 Aretha Franklin: So Damn Happy
2003 Ricky Sebastian: The Spirit Within
2003 Ada Rovatti: Under The Hat
2003 Various Artists: Bubbles, Brazil & Bossa Nova
2003 The Dynamic Superiors: The Sky's The Limit
2003 Linda Eder: Broadway My Way
2003 Aaron Neville: Nature Boy: The Standards Album
2003 Caribbean Jazz Project: Birds Of A Feather
2003 Streetwize: Work It!
2003 Michael Davis: Trumpets Eleven
2003 Ada Rovatti and the Elephunk Band: For Rent
2003 Various Artists: Concord Records 30th Anniversary
2003 Stanley Jordan: Dreams Of Peace
2003 David Sanborn: Timeagain
2004 Mike Gibbs: Nonsequence
2004 GRP All-Star Big Band: Rediscovery On GRP
2004 Soul Generation: Stop, Look And Listen
2004 Bill Evans, Randy Brecker: Soulbop Band Live
2004 James Silberstein: Song For Micaela
2004 Ian Gillan: Mercury High: The Story Of Ian Gillan
2004 Machan: Machan
2004 g.org: A New Kind Of Blue
2004 Patrick Arnold: From The Ashes
2004 David Garfield: Giving Back
2004 Bill O'Connell: Latin Jazz Fantasy
2004 Claus Ogerman: A Man And His Music
2004 Martha Redbone: Skintalk
2004 Ann Hampton Callaway: Slow
2004 Joris Teepe: Going Dutch
2004 Manhattan Jazz Orchestra: Moanin'
2004 Various Artists: Sax In The City
2005 Jason Miles: Miles To Miles: In The Spirit Of Miles Davis
2005 Mingus Big Band: I Am Three
2005 Rupert Holmes: Cast Of Characters: The Rupert Holmes Songbook
2005 B.D. Lenz: Tomorrow's Too Late

2005 Pat LaBarbera Quintet: Crossing The Line
2005 Various Artists: Hit The Rhodes, Jack
2005 Randy Brecker / Michael Brecker: Some Skunk Funk [DVD]
2005 Ronaldo Folegatti: Jamming!
2005 Linda Eder: By Myself: The Songs Of Judy Garland
2005 Beatlejazz: With A Little Help From Our Friends
2005 Randy Brecker, Michael Brecker: Some Skunk Funk
2005 Woody Witt Quintet: Square Peg, Round Hole
2005 Andrea Giuffredi: L' Anacoreta
2005 Man Doki: Soulmates
2005 Various Artists: Progressions: 100 Years Of Jazz Guitar
2005 Servulo Augusto: Coletivo
2005 Jaco Pastorius: Live In Japan [DVD]
2005 Roger Ball: Childsplay
2005 Mica Paris: If You Could Love Me
2005 Phishbacher: Infinity Ltd.
2005 Tha' Hot Club: In The V.I.P. Room
2005 David Gibson: The Path To Delphi
2005 Cyndi Lauper: The Body Acoustic
2005 Johnny Rodgers: Box Of Photographs
2006 Various Artists: Fusion with Attitude
2006 Tom Scott: Bebop United
2006 Garland Jeffreys: I'm Alive
2006 Maucha Adnet: The Jobim Songbook
2006 Various Artists: Funk Academy
2006 Gil Parris: Strength
2006 Marc Copland, Randy Brecker: Both / And
2006 Jaco Pastorius: Live In Montreal [DVD]
2006 Ultrablue: Ultrablue
2006 Gil Goldstein: Under Rousseau's Moon
2006 Manhattan Jazz Orchestra: Swing Swing Swing
2006 The Dizzy Gillespie All-Star Big Band: Dizzy's Business
2006 Various Artists: Chesky 20th Anniversary
2006 Pirineos Jazz Orchestra & Randy Brecker: Transatlantic Connection
2006 Chris Minh Doky: The Nomad Diaries
2006 Various Artists: Sunshine On Your Back Porch: A Celebration Of Gennett Records
2006 Eliane Elias: Around The City
2006 Ada Rovatti: Airbop
2006 Charlie Barnet: Live At Basin Street East
2007 Randy Brecker: The Geneva Concert [DVD]
2007 Richard Cole: Shade
2007 Jaco Pastorius & Word of Mouth Big Band: Live At The Aurex Jazz Festival
2007 Jaco Pastorius: Live And Outrageous [DVD]
2007 Miroslav Vitous: Universal Syncopations II
2007 Jeff Lorber: He Had A Hat
2007 Caecilie Norby: Slow Fruit
2007 Machan: Motion Of Love
2007 Danny Lerman: Meowbaby
2007 Igor Butman Big Band: Magic Land
2007 Paul Bollenback: Invocation
2007 Keiko Lee: In Essence
2007 Mike Catalano: A Manhattan Affair
2007 Blue Oyster Cult: Discover
2007 Rob Fried: Wind Song
2007 Igor Butman Big Band: The Eternal Triangle
2007 Bill Evans: The Other Side Of Something
2007 Various Artists: Swedish Jazz: Live from The Swedish Jazz Celebration 2007
2007 Vince Seneri: The Prince's Groove
2007 The Jimmy Amadie Trio: The Philadelphia Story
2007 Gary Haase: String Theory
2008 Delirium Blues Project: Serve Or Suffer
2008 Randy Brecker: Randy In Brasil
2008 Jaco Pastorius: Live In Japan And Canada 1982 [DVD]
2008 Chip White: Double Dedication
2008 Saxophone Summit: Seraphic Light
2008 Yoichi Murata Soul Brass & Big Band: Tribute To The Brecker Brothers
2008 Karen Blixt: Mad Hope

2009 Various Artists: Sweethearts: Oceanlight Records Multi-Artist Pop Hits CD, Vol. 1
2009 Leslie Mendelson: Swan Feathers
2009 Mauri Sanchis: Groovewords
2009 Mike Stern: Big Neighbourhood
2009 Chuck Owen & The Jazz Surge: The Comet's Tail
2009 Brian Bromberg: It Is What It Is
2009 The CTI Jazz All-Star Band: Montreux Jazz Festival 2009 [DVD]
2009 Randy Brecker: Nostalgic Journey: Tykocin Jazz Suite
2009 George Robert Jazztet: Remember The Sound: Homage To Michael Brecker
2009 The Norbotten Big Band: The Avatar Sessions
2009 Gil Parris: A Certain Beauty
2009 Various Artists: Jazz Lounge Vol. 13
2009 Lynne Arriale: Nuance: The Bennett Studio Sessions
2010 Bartosz Hadala Group: The Runner Up
2010 Fahir Atakoglu: Faces & Places
2010 Arif Mardin: All My Friends Are Here
2010 Ratko Zjaca: Continental Talk
2010 The Brecker Brothers: Live In Tokyo, U-Port Hall, 1995 [DVD]
2010 Chie Imaizumi: A Time Of New Beginnings
2010 Conrad Herwig: The Latin Side Of Herbie Hancock
2010 Pendulum: Live At The Village Vanguard 1978
2010 The Jeff Lorber Fusion: Now Is The Time
2010 Ben E. King: Heart & Soul
2010 Richard Cole: Inner Mission
2010 Brigitte Zarie: Make Room For Me
2010 Sinne Eeg: Remembering You
2011 Randy Brecker with the DR Big Band: The Jazz Ballad Song Book
2011 Eliane Elias: Light My Fire
2011 The J.B.s and Fred Wesley: The Lost Album Featuring Watermelo Man
2011 Sophie Millman: In The Moonlight
2011 Kenny Werner: Ballons: Live At The Blue Note
2011 Makoto Ozone: Live & Let Live - Love For Japan
2011 Oliver Strauch's Groovin High: Live With Randy Brecker
2012 Brian Bromberg: Compared To That
2012 Ratko Zjaka: Now & Then: A Portrait
2012 Richard Sussman Quintet: Continuum
2012 Felipe Salles: Departure
2012 Jaiman Crunk: Encounters
2012 Jimmy Mulidore: Jimmy Mulidore & His New York City Jazz Band
2012 The Fusion Syndicate: The Fusion Syndicate
2012 Gianni Bardaro: Soul Blueprint
2012 Steve Tyrell: I'll Take Romance
2012 Metropole Orkest: Better Get Hit In Your Soul: A Tribute To The Music Of Charles Mingus
2012 Bruno Marinucci Trio: Nal Tarahara
2012 Doug Belote: Magazine St.
2012 Mike Stern: All Over The Place
2012 Sean O'Bryan Smith: Reflection
2013 Nilson Matta: Black Orpheus
2013 Randy Brecker: The Brecker Brothers Band Reunion
2013 Eliane Elias: I Thought About You: A Tribute To Chet Baker
2013 Randy Brecker, Wlodek Pawlik: Randy Brecker Plays Wlodek Pawlik's Night in Calisia
2013 Janek Gwizdala: Theatre By The Sea
2013 AMC Trio with Randy Brecker: One Way Road To My Heart

Michael Brecker Discography (excluding albums of previously released material)

1966 Ramblerny: School 66 (Summer Big Band Camp)
1969 Paul Sylvan: Good Paul Sylvan
1969 Randy Brecker: Score
1970 Dreams: Dreams
1971 Hal Galper: Wild Bird
1971 Prairie Madness: Prairie Madness
1971 Air: Air
1971 Dreams: Imagine My Surprise
1972 Mike Mainieri and Friends: White Elephant Vol 2
1972 Darius Brubeck: Chaplin's Back
1972 Horace Silver: In Pursuit Of The 27th Man
1972 Gary Burton: In The Public Interest
1972 Hal Galper: The Guerilla Band
1972 Mike Mainieri and Friends: White Elephant Vol 1
1972 James Taylor: One Man Dog
1972 Todd Rundgren: Something/Anything?
1972 Paul Simon: Paul Simon
1972 The Section: The Section
1972 James Brown: Get On The Good Foot
1973 Mark Murphy: Bridging A Gap
1973 The Fabulous Rhinestones: Free Wheelin'
1973 James Brown: Think (Alternate Take)
1973 James Brown: Think/Something
1973 Pacific Gas & Electric: Starring Charie Allen
1973 John Lennon: Mind Games
1973 Borderline: Sweet Dreams And Quiet Desires / The Second Album
1973 Lou Reed: Berlin
1973 Crowbar: Crowbar
1973 Mike Gibbs & Gary Burton: The Public Interest
1973 Michael Wendroff: Michael Wendroff
1973 Mark James: Mark James
1973 Todd Rundgren: A Wizard, A True Star
1974 Gato Barbieri: Chapter Three: Viva Emiliano Zapata
1974 Borderline: The Second Album
1974 Hubert Laws: Chicago Theme
1974 Billy Cobham: Crosswinds
1974 B. J. Thomas: Longhorn And London Bridges
1974 Luiz Bonfa: Manhattan Strut
1974 Billy Cobham: Total Eclipse
1974 Rachel Faro: Refugees
1974 Aerosmith: Get Your Wings
1974 James Taylor: Walking Man
1974 Arif Mardin: Journey
1974 Esther Phillips: Performance
1974 Johnny Winter: John Dawson Winter III
1974 Average White Band: AWB
1974 Todd Rundgren: Todd
1974 Carly Simon: Hotcakes
1975 Mark Murphy: Mark Murphy Sings
1975 The Manhattan Transfer: The Manhattan Transfer
1975 Stark & McBrien: Big Star
1975 Don Sebesky: The Rape Of El Morro
1975 Bruce Springsteen: Born To Run
1975 Black Heat: Keep On Runnin'
1975 Billy Cobham: A Funky Thide Of Sings
1975 The Brecker Brothers: The Brecker Brothers
1975 David Sanborn: Taking Off
1975 Randall Bramblett: That Other Mile
1975 Russel Morris: Russel Morris
1975 Bazuka: Bazuka
1975 Billy Cobham: Shabazz (Recorded Live In Europe)
1975 George Benson: Good King Bad
1975 Felix Cavaliere: Destiny
1975 Luther Allison: Night Life
1975 George Benson: Pacific Fire
1975 Esther Phillips: Esther Phillips And Joe Beck
1975 Parliament: Mothership Connection
1975 Esther Phillips: What A Diff'rence A Day Makes
1975 Steve Satten: Whatcha Gonna Do For Me?
1975 Esther Phillips: What A Diff'rence A Day Makes
1975 Ron Carter: Anything Goes

1975 Ruth Copeland: Take Me To Baltimore
1975 Paul Simon: Still Crazy After All These Years
1976 Don Cherry: Hear & Now
1976 Bette Midler: Songs For The New Depression
1976 Parliament: The Clones Of Dr. Frunkenstein
1976 James Taylor: In The Pocket
1976 Grant Green: The Main Attraction
1976 Average White Band: Soul Searching
1976 Martee Lebous: The Lady Wants To Be A Star
1976 Jaco Pastorius: Jaco Pastorius
1976 Elliott Murphy: Night Lights
1976 Ish: Ish
1976 George Benson: Cast Your Fate To The Wind
1976 Laura Nyro: Smile
1976 John Tropea: Tropea
1976 Candi Staton: Young Hearts Run Free
1976 Jun Fukamachi: Spiral Steps
1976 Bootsy Collins: Stretchin' Out In Bootsy's Rubber Band
1976 Orleans: Waking & Dreaming
1976 Gerry Brown & John Lee: Still Can't Say Enough
1976 Manhattan Transfer: Coming Out
1976 Michael Franks: The Art Of Tea
1976 Blue Oyster Cult: Agents Of Fortune
1976 The Brecker Brothers Band: Back To Back
1976 Freddie Hubbard: Windjammer
1976 Ben Sidran: Free In America
1976 Jack Wilkins: You Can't Live Without It
1976 Esther Phillips: For All We Know
1976 Patti Austin: End Of A Rainbow
1976 Joe Thomas: Feelin's From Within
1976 Idris Muhammad: House Of The Rising Sun
1976 Ringo Starr: Ringo's Rotogravure
1976 Weldon Irvine: Sinbad
1976 Chris Hinze: Parcival
1976 Michael Franks: Sleeping Gypsy
1976 Diana Marcovitz: Joie De Vivre!
1976 Esther Phillips: Capricon Princess
1976 Elton John: Blue Moves
1976 Roy Buchanan: A Street Called Straight
1976 The Claus Ogerman Orchestra: Gate Of Dreams
1976 Rosie: Better Late Than Never
1976 The Eleventh House featuring Larry Coryell: Aspects
1976 Pavlov's Dog: At The Sound Of The Bell
1976 Lorraine Frisaura: Be Happy For Me
1976 John Tropea: John Tropea
1977 Tornader: Hit It Again
1977 Jun Fukamachi: Jun Fukamachi
1977 Jun Fukamachi: Triangle Session
1977 Jun Fukamachi: The Sea Of Dirac
1977 Chet Baker: You Can't Go Home Again
1977 Sunshine: Sunshine
1977 Andy Pratt: Shiver In The Night
1977 Charles Earland: Revelation
1977 John Tropea: Short Trip To Space
1977 Fred Wesley: A Blow For Me, A Toot To You
1977 Kumiko Hara: No Smoking
1977 Phoebe Snow: Never Letting Go
1977 Jun Fukamachi: Jun Fukamachi Live At The Triangle Theatre
1977 Zbigniew Seifert: Zbigniew Seifert
1977 Garland Jeffreys: Ghost Writer
1977 Eric Gale: Ginseng Woman
1977 J. Geils Band: Monkey Island
1977 Idris Muhammad: Turn This Mutha Out
1977 Wild Cherry: Electrified Funk
1977 Mel Lewis: Mel Lewis And Friends
1977 Steve Khan: Tightrope
1977 Bob James: Heads
1977 The Brecker Brothers: Don't Stop The Music
1977 Ringo Starr: Ringo The 4th
1977 William Eaton: Struggle Buggy
1977 Bootsy's Rubber Band: Ahh...The Name Is Bootsy, Baby!
1977 Hal Galper: Reach Out!
1977 Mike Mainieri: Love Play
1977 Coal Kitchen: Thirsty Or Not...Choose Your Flavor
1977 Joanne Brackeen: Tring-A-Ling: Joanne Brackeen Meets Michael Brecker
1977 Kiki Dee: Kiki Dee

1977 Domenic Troiano: Burnin' At The Stake
1977 Hank Crawford: Tico Rico
1977 Frankie Valli: Lady Put The Light Out
1977 Average White Band: Benny & Us
1977 Phoebe Snow: Against The Grain
1977 Billy Cobham: Inner Conflicts
1977 Harold Vick: After The Dance
1977 Joe Farrell: La Catedral Y El Toro
1977 Bruce Fisher: Red Hot
1977 Odyssey: Odyssey
1977 Malcolm Tomlinson: Coming Outta Nowhere
1977 Peter Bliss: Peter Bliss
1977 Jimmy McGriff: Red Beans
1977 Patti Austin: Havana Candy
1977 Carol Grimes: Carol Grimes
1977 Al Foster: Mixed Roots
1977 Joe Beck: Watch The Time
1978 Paul Mauriat Plus: Overseas Call
1978 Flora Purim: Everyday Everynight
1978 Garland Jeffreys: One-Eyed Jack
1978 Scarlet Rivera: Scarlet Fever
1978 Lori Lieberman: Letting Go
1978 Sylvia Syms: She Loves To Hear The Music
1978 The Brecker Brothers: Heavy Metal Bebop
1978 Wild Cherry: I Love My Music
1978 Melanie: Phonogenic Not Just Another Pretty Face
1978 Henry Gaffney: On Again, Off Again
1978 Rupert Holmes: Pursuit Of Happiness
1978 Robert Palmer: Double Fun
1978 Allen Harris: Oceans Between Us
1978 Hal Galper: The Hal Galper Quintet Live: Redux '78
1978 Angela Bofill: Angie
1978 Jack Wilkins: Merge
1978 Richard Tee: Strokin'
1978 Steve Khan: The Blue Man
1978 Baby Grand: Baby Grand
1978 Larry Coryell: Difference
1978 David Clayton-Thomas: David Clayton-Thomas
1978 John Tropea: To Touch You Again
1978 Chaka Khan: Chaka
1978 Tina Turner: Love Explosion

1978 Kate Taylor: Kate Taylor
1978 Various Artists: The Wiz [Original Soundtrack]
1978 Alessi Brothers: All For A Reason
1978 Carly Simon: Boys In The Trees
1978 Marilyn McCoo & Billy Davis Jr: Marilyn & Billy
1978 The Players Association: Born To Dance
1978 The Average White Band: Warmer Communications
1978 Various Artists: The Atlantic Family Live In Montreux
1978 Ralph MacDonald: The Path
1978 Quincy Jones: Sounds ... And Stuff Like That!!
1978 Mike Nock: In Out And Around
1978 Rainbow: Crystal Green
1978 Jun Fukamachi: Jun Fukamachi & The New York All Stars Live
1978 Harris Simon: New York Connection
1978 Neil Larsen: Jungle Fever
1978 David Sanborn: Heart To Heart
1978 Bill Chinnock: Badlands
1978 Ben Sidran: Live At Montreaux
1978 Hal Galper: Speak with A Single Voice
1978 Various Artists: Starmania: l'Opera Rock de Michel Berger et Luc Plamondon
1978 David Spinozza: Spinozza
1978 Chris Hinze Combination: Bamboo Magic
1978 Jon Faddis: Good And Plenty
1978 Hal Galper Quintet: Children Of The Night
1979 Bad News Travels Fast: Ordinary Man
1979 Michele Freeman: Michele Freeman
1979 Pages: Future Street
1979 Neil Larsen: High Gear
1979 Niteflyte: Niteflyte
1979 Kenny Loggins: Keep The Fire
1979 Bad News Travels Fast: Look Out
1979 Cheryl Lynn: In Love
1979 Ian Lloyd: Goose Bumps
1979 Maxine Nightingale: Lead Me On
1979 Bob James: Lucky Seven
1979 Jimmy Mack: On The Corner
1979 Charles Mingus: Me Myself An Eye
1979 Jan Akkerman: 3

1979 The Tony Williams Lifetime: The Joy Of Flying
1979 Alec R. Costandinos & The Syncophonic Orchestra: Winds Of Change: A Musical Fantasy
1979 Bette Midler: Thighs And Whispers
1979 Charles Earland: Coming To You Live
1979 Warren Bernhardt, Michael Brecker, Randy Brecker, Mike Mainieri: Blue Montreux
1979 Warren Bernhardt, Michael Brecker, Randy Brecker, Mike Mainieri: Blue Montreux II
1979 Carly Simon: Spy
1979 Michel Colombier: Michel Colombier
1979 Carillo: Street Of Dreams
1979 Herbie Mann: Yellow Fever
1979 Original Soundtrack: The Warriors
1979 Brooklyn Dreams: Sleepless Nights
1979 John Mayall: Bottom Line
1979 Kleeer: Winners
1979 The Brothers Johnson: Blam!!
1979 Diana Ross: The Boss
1979 Players Association: Turn The Music Up!
1979 Candi Staton: Chance
1979 Ben Sidran: The Cat And The Hat
1979 Wilbert Longmire: Champagne
1979 The Calello Orchestra: The Charlie Calello Serenade
1979 The Average White Band: Feel No Fret
1979 Fotomaker: Transfer Station
1979 Tom Browne: Browne Sugar
1979 Casiopea: Casiopea
1979 Desmond Child And Rouge: Desmond Child And Rouge
1979 Michael Johnson: Dialogue
1979 The Writers: All In Fun
1979 Mongo Santamaria: Red Hot
1979 Richard T. Bear: Red Hot & Blue
1979 Patti Austin: Live At The Bottom Line
1979 Ralph MacDonald: Counterpoint
1979 Jason Miles: Cozmopolitan
1979 Spyro Gyra: Morning Dance
1979 David Matthews: Digital Love

1979 Narada Michael Walden: Awakening - The Dance Of Life
1979 The Writers: All In Fun
1979 Saint & Stephanie: Saint & Stephanie
1979 Sadao Watanabe: Morning Island
1979 Yusef Lateef: In A Temple Garden
1979 Steve Khan: Arrows
1979 Art Garfunkel: Fate For Breakfast
1979 Roger Voudouris: Radio Dream
1980 Parliament: Trombipulation
1980 Pat Metheny: 80/81
1980 Kazumi Watanabe: To Chi Ka
1980 Gladys Knight & The Pips: About Love
1980 Tommy James: Three Times In Love
1980 Ray Gomez: Volume
1980 Circus: Wonderful Music
1980 The Brecker Brothers: Détente
1980 Pussez!: Leave That Boy Alone!
1980 The Spinners: Love Trippin'
1980 Steps: Step By Step
1980 Spyro Gyra: Carnaval
1980 Steps: Smokin' In The Pit
1980 J. D. Drews: J. D. Drews
1980 Harris Simon Group: Swish
1980 James Last Band: Seduction
1980 Chaka Khan: Naughty
1980 Jun Fukamachi: On The Move
1980 Patti Austin: Body Language
1980 Charles Mingus: Something Like A Bird
1980 Yoshiaki Masuo: Song Is You And Me
1980 Terumasa Hino: Day Dream
1980 Stone Alliance: Heads Up
1980 Googie And Tom Coppola: Shine The Light Of Love
1980 Don Schlitz: Dreamers Matinee
1980 George Clinton and the P-Funk All-Stars: Plush Funk
1980 Candi Staton: Candi Staton
1980 Joni Mitchell: Shadows And Light
1980 Paul Simon: One Trick Pony
1980 Manu Dibango: Gone Clear
1981 Herbie Hancock: Magic Windows
1981 Mike Mainieri: Wanderlust
1981 Chick Corea: Three Quartets
1981 Jaco Pastorius: Word Of Mouth
1981 Joachim Kuhn: Nightline New York
1981 Art Garfunkel: Scissors Cut

1981 Garland Jeffreys: Escape Artist
1981 The Brecker Brothers: Straphangin'
1981 Yoko Ono: Season Of Glass
1981 Funkadelic: The Electric Spanking Of War Babies
1981 Henry Gross: What's In A Name
1981 Carly Simon: Torch
1981 Chic: Take It Off
1981 ACOM: Cozmopolitan
1981 Masaru Imada: Carnival
1981 Lena Horne: The Lady And Her Music - Live On Broadway
1981 Dan Fogelberg: The Innocent Age
1981 Chaka Khan: What Cha' Gonna Do For Me
1981 Alphonse Mouzon: Morning Sun
1981 Diana Ross: Why Do Fools Fall In Love
1981 Various Artists: Montreux Jazz Festival -25th Anniversary
1981 George Benson: GB
1981 Manu Dibango: Ambassador
1981 Spyro Gyra: Freetime
1981 Herbie Mann: Mellow
1982 Fagner: Sorriso Novo
1982 Various Artists: Casino Lights - Live At Montreux
1982 David Matthews: Grand Cross
1982 Peter Erskine: Peter Erskine
1982 Ron Carter: El Noche Sol
1982 Mark Gray: Boogie Hotel
1982 Minako Yoshida: Light'n Up
1982 Donald Fagen: The Nightfly
1982 Claus Ogerman with Michael Brecker: Cityscape
1982 Jaco Pastorius: The Florida Concert
1982 Michael Franks: Objects Of Desire
1982 UZEB: Fast Emotion
1982 Barry Finnerty: New York City
1982 Luther Vandross: Forever, For Always, For Love
1982 Steps: Paradox
1983 Melissa Manchester: Emergency
1983 Steps Ahead: Steps Ahead
1983 Franco Ambrosetti: Wings
1983 Peter Brown: Back To The Front
1983 Bob Mintzer and the Horn Man Band: Papa Lips
1983 Georges Acogny: Guitars On The Move

1983 Kenny Wheeler: Double, Double You
1983 Larry Carlton: Friends
1983 Gil Evans & Orchestra: Live in Lugano 1983 [DVD]
1983 Terumasa Hino: New York Times
1983 Bob James: The Genie
1983 Gerry Mulligan: Little Big Horn
1983 George Benson: In Your Eyes
1983 Billy Joel: An Innocent Man
1983 Carly Simon: Hello Big Man
1983 Urszula Dudziak: Sorrow Is Not Forever ... But Love Is
1983 Mark Knopfler: Local Hero (Original Sound Track)
1984 Diana Ross: Swept Away
1984 Julian Lennon: Valotte
1984 Ashford & Simpson: Solid
1984 John Abercrombie: Night
1984 Lou Reed: New Sensations
1984 Martha and the Muffins: Mystery Walk
1984 Barry Gibb: Now Voyager
1984 David Sanborn: Straight To The Heart
1984 Frank Sinatra with Quincy Jones and Orchestra: L.A. Is My Lady
1984 Roger Daltrey: Parting Should Be Painless
1984 Jane Fonda: Prime Time Workout
1984 Original Soundtrack: Footloose
1984 Steps Ahead: Modern Times
1984 Barry Finnerty: Lights On Broadway
1984 Steely Dan: Gaucho
1984 Mark Gray & Super Friends: The Silencer
1985 Michael W. Smith: Big Picture
1985 Mitchel Forman: Train Of Thought
1985 Michael Franks: Skin Dive
1985 Teruo Nakamura: Super Friends
1985 Taeko Ohnuki: Copine
1985 Franco Ambrosetti: Tentets
1985 Eddie Gomez: Discovery
1985 James Taylor: That's Why I'm Here
1985 Don Grolnick: Hearts And Numbers
1985 Patti Austin: Gettin' Away with Murder
1985 Dolby's Cube: May The Cube Be With You

1985 Bob Mintzer Big Band: Incredible Journey
1985 Dire Straits: Brothers In Arms
1985 Kazumi Watanabe: Mobo Splash
1985 Randy Brecker, Eliane Elias: Amanda
1986 Randy Bernsen: Mo' Wasabi
1986 Rare Silk: New Weave
1986 Kazumi Watanabe: Mobo I
1986 Steps Ahead: Live In Tokyo 1986
1986 Eddie Gomez: Mezgo
1986 Original Soundtrack: A House Full Of Love: Music From The Cosby Show
1986 Bonnie Tyler: Secret Dreams And Forbidden Fire
1986 Ornella Vanoni: Ornella E...
1986 Earl Klugh: Life Stories
1986 Original Soundtrack: 9 1/2 Weeks
1986 Kenia: Initial Thrill
1986 Kimiko Itoh: A Touch Of Love
1986 Steps Ahead: Magnetic
1986 Grover Washington Jr: House Full Of Love: Music from The Cosby Show
1986 Michael W. Smith: The Big Picture
1986 Bob James: Obsession
1986 Hugh Marsh: The Bear Walks
1986 Billy Joel: The Bridge
1986 Kazumi Watanabe: Mobo II
1986 Kimiko Kasai: My One And Only Love
1986 Chaka Khan: Destiny
1986 Tramaine: The Search Is Over
1986 Hiram Bullock: From All Sides
1986 Eric Clapton: August
1986 Cameo: Word Up!
1987 Kimiko Itoh: For Lovers Only
1987 Michael Franks: The Camera Never Lies
1987 David Sanborn: A Change Of Heart
1987 Members Only: Members Only
1987 Charnett Moffett: Net Man
1987 Neil Larsen: Through Any Window
1987 Hiram Bullock: Give It What U Got
1987 Michael Brecker: Michael Brecker
1987 Hiram Bullock: Give It What U Got
1987 Various Artists: A Homeless Children's Medical Benefit Concert
1987 Dan Fogelberg: Exiles
1987 Various Artists: Brastilava Jazz Days
1987 The Gadd Gang: The Gadd Gang

1987 Carly Simon: Coming Around Again
1988 Patti Austin: The Real Me
1988 Roberto Gatto: Notes
1988 Art Garfunkel: Lefty
1988 Alexander Zonjic: Romance With You
1988 Jorge Dalto: Listen Up!
1988 Cameo: Machismo
1988 Michael Brecker: Don't Try This At Home
1988 Peter Erskine: Motion Poet
1988 Dire Straits: Money For Nothing
1988 John Abercrombie: Getting There
1988 Gary Burton: Times Like These
1988 Mike Lawrence: Nightwind
1988 Eliane Elias: So Far So Close
1988 Donny Osmond: Donny Osmond
1988 Eddie Gomez: Power Play
1988 James Taylor: Never Die Young
1988 Hue And Cry: Remote
1988 John Patitucci: John Patitucci
1988 The SOS All-Stars: New York Rendezvous
1988 Toshiki Kadomatsu: Before The Daylight
1988 Simone: Seducao
1988 Michael Colina: Shadow Of Urbano
1988 Mike Stern: Time In Place
1989 Various Artists: Select Live Saxophone Workshop
1989 Mike Stern: Jigsaw
1989 Victor Bailey: Bottom's Up
1989 Don Grolnick: Weaver Of Dreams
1989 Vince Mendoza: Vince Mendoza
1989 Tolvan Big Band: Colours
1989 John Patitucci: On The Corner
1989 Karizma: Forever In The Arms Of Love
1989 Third World: Serious Business
1989 Holly Knight: Holly Knight
1989 Carole King: City Streets
1989 Richie Beirach: Some Other Time - A Tribute To Chet Baker
1989 Torsten de Winkel: Mastertouch
1989 Regina Belle: Stay With Me
1989 Mark O'Connor: On The Mark
1990 Little Feat: Representing The Mambo
1990 Eugene Pao: Outlet
1990 Dave Weckl Band: Master Plan

1990 Carly Simon: Have You Seen Me Lately?
1990 Carly Simon: My Romance
1990 John Patitucci: Sketchbook
1990 Michael Colina: Rituals
1990 Niels Lan Doky: Friendship
1990 Chuck Loeb: Life Colors
1990 Jim Beard: Song Of The Sun
1990 Jonathan Butler: Deliverance
1990 Randy Brecker: Toe To Toe
1990 Orleans: Still The One
1990 Claus Ogerman: Claus Ogerman Featuring Michael Brecker
1990 Everything But The Girl: The Language Of Life
1990 Paul Simon: The Rhythm Of The Saints
1990 Bob James: Grand Piano Canyon
1991 Joey Calderazzo: In The Door
1991 Jennifer Holliday: I'm On Your Side
1991 L. J. Reynolds: L. J. Reynolds
1991 Paul Simon: Paul Simon's Concert In The Park
1991 Garland Jeffreys: Don't Call Me Buckwheat
1991 James Taylor: New Moon Shine
1992 Michael Brecker: Now You See It (Now You Don't)
1992 Toshinobu Kubota: Neptune
1992 John Simon: Out On The Street
1992 Jenni Muldaur: Jenni Muldaur
1992 The Brecker Brothers: Return Of The Brecker Brothers
1992 Garland Jeffreys: Matador & More.
1992 Various Artists: After The Dance
1992 The Brecker Brothers: The Return of The Brecker Brothers: Live in Spain 1992 [DVD]
1992 Sandy Bull: Vehicles
1993 Laura Nyro: Walk The Dog & Light The Light
1993 Jay Leonhart & Friends: Live At Fat Tuesday's: May 13-16, 1993
1993 John Patitucci: Another World
1993 Charles Blenzig: Say What You Mean
1993 Beatnik Rebel: Science: Featuring Tony Verderosa
1993 Kimiko Itoh: Standards My Way

1993 The Mendoza / Mardin Project: Jazzpana
1993 David Friesen: Two For The Show
1993 Leslie Mandoki: People
1993 Peter Delano: Peter Delano
1993 Flying Monkey Orchestra: Back In The Pool
1993 Carly Simon: Carly Simon's Romulus Hunt, A Family Opera
1993 The Michael Brecker Band: Live
1994 Jaco Pastorius: The Birthday Concert
1994 Al Jarreau: Tenderness
1994 Bob James: Restless
1994 Alan Pasqua: Milagro
1994 Mariko Takahashi: Couplet
1994 Edie Brickell: Picture Perfect Morning
1994 Kenneth Sivertsen: Remembering North
1994 Urbanator: Urbanator
1994 Marc Beacco: Scampi Fritti
1994 Jason Miles: World Tour
1994 The Brecker Brothers: Out Of The Loop
1994 Vincent Nguini: Symphony-Bantu
1994 Sergio Salvatore: Tune Up
1994 Mike Stern: Is What It Is
1994 The Brecker Brothers: The Brecker Brothers - Live
1994 Jonathan Butler: Head To Head
1994 Michael Cusson: Wild Unit 2
1994 BFD: BFD
1994 Aerosmith: Box Of Fire
1994 Julie Eigenberg: Love Is Starting Now
1994 Randy Sandke: Chase
1994 Herbie Hancock Quartet: The Herbie Hancock Quartet Live
1994 Jan Hammer: Drive
1994 Bob Mintzer and Michael Brecker: Twin Tenors
1995 Yasuaki Ide: Cool Blue
1995 Toko Furuuchi: Strength
1995 Georg Pommer: Coast To Coast
1995 Thursday Diva: Follow Me
1995 Kimiko Itoh: Sophisticated Lady
1995 Dave Brubeck: Young Lions & Old Tigers
1995 Miwa Yoshida: Beauty And Harmony

1995 Alan Pasqua: Dedications
1995 Chris Botti: First Wish
1995 Flying Monkey Orchestra: Mango Theory
1995 Don Grolnick: Medianoche
1995 Michael Franks: Abandoned Garden
1995 T-Square and Friends: Miss You In New York
1995 Toshinori Yonekura: Cool Jamz
1995 John Basile: Frankly Speaking
1995 Doky Brothers: Doky Brothers
1995 SIXUN: Lunatic Taxi
1995 Rick Rhodes: Indian Summer
1996 Julian Coryell: Without You
1996 Various Artists: For Our Children Too
1996 Michael Brecker: Tales From The Hudson
1996 Chris Walden Orchestra: Ticino
1996 Eugene Pao: By The Company You Keep
1996 Misato Watanabe: Spirits
1996 Herbie Hancock: The New Standard
1996 Lenny White: Present Tense
1996 Wolfgang Schalk Bandet: The Second Third Man featuring Michael Brecker
1996 Chris Hinze: Senang
1996 Jason Miles: Mr. X
1996 Hue And Cry: JazzNotJazz
1996 Ralph MacDonald: Just The Two Of Us
1996 Smappies: Rhythmsticks
1996 John McLaughlin: The Promise
1996 Kenji Hayashida: Marron
1996 Caecilie Norby: My Corner Of The Sky
1996 Nils Landgren Funk Unit: Paint It Blue
1996 Natalie Cole: Stardust
1996 Bernard Purdie: Bernard Purdie's Soul To Jazz
1996 Tom Coster: From The Street
1996 Arturo Sandoval: Swingin'
1996 Lenny White: Renderers Of Spirit
1996 Chuck Loeb: The Music Inside
1996 Leslie Mandoki: People In Room No.8
1996 Michal Urbaniak: Urbanator II
1997 John Patitucci: One More Angel

1997 Tony Williams: Wilderness
1997 The Michael White Project: Take That
1997 Mike Stern: Give And Take
1997 Joe Chindamo: Reflected Journey
1997 Kenny Rankin: Here In My Heart
1997 Till Bronner: Midnight
1997 Original Soundtrack: Midnight In The Garden Of Good And Evil
1997 Ryo Kawasaki: Mirror Of My Mind
1997 Doky Brothers: Doky Brothers, 2
1997 Yoshiko Kishino: Randezvous
1997 Sergio Salvatore: Point Of Presence
1997 Leslie Mandoki: The Jazz Cuts
1997 Alex Riel: Unriel
1997 Wallace Roney: Village
1997 Dave Grusin: West Side Story
1997 Yoko Ono: A Story
1997 Horace Silver: A Prescription For The Blues
1997 Andreas Vollenweider: Kryptos
1997 James Taylor: Hourglass
1998 Chris Minh Doky: Minh
1998 Kevin Mahogany: My Romance
1998 Mark Murphy: Jazz Standards
1998 Tony Reedus and Urban Relations: People Get Ready
1998 The Randy Waldman Trio: Wigged Out
1998 Arturo Sandoval: Hot House
1998 Sanne Salomonsen: In A New York Minute
1998 Mark Ledford: Miles 2 Go
1998 Super Nova: Brazilian Jazz - The music And lyrics Of Claudia Villela
1998 Marc Copland: Softly...
1998 John Patitucci: Now
1998 Michael Brecker: Two Blocks from The Edge
1998 Eijiro Nakagawa: Peace
1998 Rick Rhodes: Deep In The Night
1998 Eliane Elias: Eliane Elias Sings Jobim
1998 Jacky Terrason: What It Is
1999 Smappies: Smappies II
1999 Michel Berger: Voyou
1999 XL: Jukola
1999 Mark Murphy: Songbook
1999 Papo Vazquez: At The Point V. One
1999 Richard Bona: Scenes From My Life

1999 David Sanborn: Inside
1999 Kimiko Kasai: My Favorite Songs Vol. 1
1999 Gary LeMel: Moonlighting
1999 Michael Brecker: Time Is Of The Essence
1999 Michael Brecker Group: The Cost Of Living
1999 Vince Mendoza: Epiphany
1999 Michael Franks: Barefoot On The Beach
1999 Jan Lippert: Imprints
1999 Mark Murphy: Mark Murphy Sings Nat King Cole And More
1999 Gonzalo Rubalcaba: Inner Voyage
2000 Don Grolnick Group: The London Concert
2000 Various Artists: Celebrating The Music Of Weather Report
2001 Michael Brecker: Nearness Of You: The Ballad Book
2001 Dean Brown: Here
2001 Richard Bona: Reverence
2001 Harvie S & Eye Contact: New Beginning
2001 Randy Brecker: Hangin' In The City
2001 Randy Waldman: UnReel
2001 Mike Stern: Voices
2001 Jane Monheit: Come Dream With Me
2001 Laura Nyro: Angel In The Dark
2001 Jack Wilkins: Reunion
2002 Randy Brecker: 34th N Lex
2002 Billy Cobham: Drum 'n' Voice, Vol. 1
2002 Charlie Haden with Michael Brecker: American Dreams
2002 James Taylor: October Road
2002 Will & Rainbow: Over Crystal Green
2002 Dennis Chambers: Outbreak
2002 Herbie Hancock: Directions In Music
2002 Mike Pope: The Lay Of The Land
2003 Carmen Cuesta-Loeb: Dreams
2003 Marc Copland: Marc Copland And
2003 Michael Brecker Quindectet: Wide Angles
2003 Chick Corea: Rendezvous In New York
2003 Aaron Neville: Nature Boy: The Standards Album
2003 Steve Tyrell: This Guy's In Love
2003 Leni Stern: Finally The Rain Has Come
2004 Elvin Jones Jazz Machine: The Truth: Heard Live At The Blue Note
2004 Herbie Hancock: Herbie Hancock Special with Bobby McFerrin And Michael Brecker [DVD]
2004 Eliane Elias: Dreamer
2004 Andy Narell: The Passage - Music For Steel Orchestra
2004 Saxophone Summit: Gathering Of Spirits
2004 Harald Haerter: Catscan
2004 Will & Rainbow: Harmony
2004 Claus Ogerman: A Man And His Music
2004 David Garfield: Giving Back
2004 John Abercrombie Quartet: Live At The Village Vanguard Volume 3 [DVD]
2004 Soul Generation: Stop, Look And Listen
2005 Jason Miles: Miles To Miles: In The Spirit Of Miles Davis
2005 Eldar: Eldar
2005 Randy Brecker / Michael Brecker: Some Skunk Funk [DVD]
2005 Beatlejazz: With A Little Help From Our Friends
2005 Two Siberians: Out Of Nowhere
2005 Musica Caliente: Barrabas
2005 Chick Corea: Rendezvous In New York (10-DVD)
2005 Mica Paris: If You Could Love Me
2005 Randy Brecker, Michael Brecker: Some Skunk Funk
2005 Man Doki: Soulmates
2006 Michael Brecker Band: Michael Brecker Band In Japan [DVD]: Select Live Under The Sky
2006 Dizzy Gillespie All-Stars: Just Swing Baby
2006 Garland Jeffreys: I'm Alive
2006 Juliette Greco: Le Temps D'Une Chanson
2006 Chris Minh Doky: The Nomad Diaries
2007 Carmen Cuesta-Loeb: You Still Don't Know Me
2007 Michael Brecker: Pilgrimage

2007 Steps Ahead: Copenhagen Live [DVD]
2007 Steve Khan: Borrowed Time
2007 Harald Haerter: Catscan II
2007 Blue Oyster Cult: Discover
2007 Gary Haase: String Theory
2009 Herbie Hancock & The New Standard All Stars: One Night In Japan [DVD]
2010 Arif Mardin: All My Friends Are Here
2010 The Brecker Brothers: Live In Tokyo, U-Port Hall, 1995 [DVD]
2011 The J.B.s and Fred Wesley: The Lost Album Featuring Watermelo Man
2011 Michael Brecker Quindectet: Angle of Repose / Live in Japan [DVD]

Albums on which both Randy and Michael Brecker appear (excluding albums of previously released material)
1969: Paul Sylvan; Good Paul Sylvan
1969: Randy Brecker; Score
1970: Dreams; Dreams
1971: Air; Air
1971: Dreams; Imagine My Surprise
1971: Prairie Madness; Prairie Madness
1971: Hal Galper; Wild Bird
1972: Mike Mainieri and Friends; White Elephant Vol 2
1972: Hal Galper; The Guerilla Band
1972: Mike Mainieri and Friends; White Elephant Vol 1
1972: James Taylor; One Man Dog
1972: Gary Burton; In The Public Interest
1972: Horace Silver; In Pursuit Of The 27th Man
1972: Todd Rundgren; Something/Anything?
1972: James Brown; Get On The Good Foot
1973: Todd Rundgren; A Wizard, A True Star
1973: Crowbar; Crowbar
1973: Borderline; Sweet Dreams And Quiet Desires / The Second Album
1973: Michael Wendroff; Michael Wendroff
1973: The Fabulous Rhinestones; Free Wheelin'
1973: Mike Gibbs & Gary Burton; The Public Interest
1973: Lou Reed; Berlin
1973: Mark Murphy; Bridging A Gap
1973: Mark James; Mark James
1974: Hubert Laws; Chicago Theme
1974: Average White Band; AWB
1974: Johnny Winter; John Dawson Winter III
1974: Borderline; The Second Album
1974: Aerosmith; Get Your Wings
1974: Gato Barbieri; Chapter Three: Viva Emiliano Zapata
1974: B. J. Thomas; Longhorn And London Bridges
1974: Billy Cobham; Crosswinds
1974: Todd Rundgren; Todd
1974: Arif Mardin; Journey
1974: Rachel Faro; Refugees
1974: Luiz Bonfa; Manhattan Strut
1974: James Taylor; Walking Man
1974: Billy Cobham; Total Eclipse
1975: Black Heat; Keep On Runnin'
1975: George Benson; Good King Bad
1975: Mark Murphy; Mark Murphy Sings
1975: Esther Phillips; What A Diff'rence A Day Makes
1975: Steve Satten; Whatcha Gonna Do For Me?
1975: Luther Allison; Night Life
1975: Stark & McBrien; Big Star
1975: Ruth Copeland; Take Me To Baltimore
1975: George Benson; Pacific Fire
1975: Billy Cobham; Shabazz (Recorded Live In Europe)
1975: David Sanborn; Taking Off
1975: The Brecker Brothers; The Brecker Brothers
1975: The Manhattan Transfer; The Manhattan Transfer
1975: Billy Cobham; A Funky Thide Of Sings
1975: Don Sebesky; The Rape Of El Morro
1975: Esther Phillips; Esther Phillips And Joe Beck
1975: Bruce Springsteen; Born To Run
1975: Ron Carter; Anything Goes
1975: Parliament; Mothership Connection
1975: Russel Morris; Russel Morris
1975: Bazuka; Bazuka
1976: The Eleventh House featuring Larry Coryell; Aspects
1976: Ben Sidran; Free In America
1976: Patti Austin; End Of A Rainbow
1976: Esther Phillips; Capricon Princess
1976: Esther Phillips; For All We Know
1976: John Tropea; John Tropea
1976: Manhattan Transfer; Coming Out
1976: Roy Buchanan; A Street Called Straight
1976: Martee Lebous; The Lady Wants To Be A Star
1976: Gerry Brown & John Lee; Still Can't Say Enough

269

1976: Elton John; Blue Moves
1976: Jaco Pastorius; Jaco Pastorius
1976: Weldon Irvine; Sinbad
1976: Ringo Starr; Ringo's Rotogravure
1976: Jun Fukamachi; Spiral Steps
1976: The Brecker Brothers Band; Back To Back
1976: Blue Oyster Cult; Agents Of Fortune
1976: George Benson; Cast Your Fate To The Wind
1976: Laura Nyro; Smile
1976: Average White Band; Soul Searching
1976: Diana Marcovitz; Joie De Vivre!
1976: Parliament; The Clones Of Dr. Frunkenstein
1976: Bootsy Collins; Stretchin' Out In Bootsy's Rubber Band
1976: Rosie; Better Late Than Never
1976: Bette Midler; Songs For The New Depression
1976: Jack Wilkins; You Can't Live Without It
1977: Hal Galper; Reach Out!
1977: Domenic Troiano; Burnin' At The Stake
1977: Jun Fukamachi; Jun Fukamachi Live At The Triangle Theatre
1977: Eric Gale; Ginseng Woman
1977: Charles Earland; Revelation
1977: Malcolm Tomlinson; Coming Outta Nowhere
1977: Bob James; Heads
1977: Fred Wesley; A Blow For Me, A Toot To You
1977: Wild Cherry; Electrified Funk
1977: Andy Pratt; Shiver In The Night
1977: Garland Jeffreys; Ghost Writer
1977: William Eaton; Struggle Buggy
1977: Steve Khan; Tightrope
1977: The Brecker Brothers; Don't Stop The Music
1977: Bootsy's Rubber Band; Ahh...The Name Is Bootsy, Baby!
1977: Joe Farrell; La Catedral Y El Toro
1977: Billy Cobham; Inner Conflicts
1977: Tornader; Hit It Again
1977: Jun Fukamachi; The Sea Of Dirac
1977: Jun Fukamachi; Jun Fukamachi
1977: J. Geils Band; Monkey Island

1977: Kiki Dee; Kiki Dee
1977: John Tropea; Short Trip To Space
1977: Hank Crawford; Tico Rico
1977: Coal Kitchen; Thirsty Or Not...Choose Your Flavor
1977: Odyssey; Odyssey
1977: Phoebe Snow; Never Letting Go
1977: Jimmy McGriff; Red Beans
1977: Ringo Starr; Ringo The 4th
1977: Jun Fukamachi; Triangle Session
1977: Zbigniew Seifert; Zbigniew Seifert
1977: Idris Muhammad; Turn This Mutha Out
1977: Peter Bliss; Peter Bliss
1977: Average White Band; Benny & Us
1977: Harold Vick; After The Dance
1978: Rupert Holmes; Pursuit Of Happiness
1978: Frank Zappa; Zappa In New York
1978: Jon Faddis; Good And Plenty
1978: Various Artists; The Wiz [Original Soundtrack]
1978: Alessi Brothers; All For A Reason
1978: Chaka Khan; Chaka
1978: Garland Jeffreys; One-Eyed Jack
1978: Bill Chinnock; Badlands
1978: Various Artists; Starmania: l'Opera Rock de Michel Berger et Luc Plamondon
1978: Hal Galper; Speak with A Single Voice
1978: Wild Cherry; I Love My Music
1978: Tina Turner; Love Explosion
1978: Paul Mauriat Plus; Overseas Call
1978: Melanie; Phonogenic Not Just Another Pretty Face
1978: Carly Simon; Boys In The Trees
1978: Robert Palmer; Double Fun
1978: Marilyn McCoo & Billy Davis Jr; Marilyn & Billy
1978: Flora Purim; Everyday Everynight
1978: Hal Galper; The Hal Galper Quintet Live: Redux '78
1978: Hal Galper Quintet; Children Of The Night
1978: The Average White Band; Warmer Communications
1978: Ralph MacDonald; The Path
1978: Scarlet Rivera; Scarlet Fever
1978: Chris Hinze Combination; Bamboo Magic

1978: Jack Wilkins; Merge
1978: John Tropea; To Touch You Again
1978: Richard Tee; Strokin'
1978: The Brecker Brothers; Heavy Metal Bebop
1978: David Spinozza; Spinozza
1978: David Sanborn; Heart To Heart
1978: Steve Khan; The Blue Man
1978: Ben Sidran; Live At Montreaux
1978: Kate Taylor; Kate Taylor
1978: Jun Fukamachi; Jun Fukamachi & The New York All Stars Live
1979: Bad News Travels Fast; Ordinary Man
1979: Wilbert Longmire; Champagne
1979: Ralph MacDonald; Counterpoint
1979: Niteflyte; Niteflyte
1979: Saint & Stephanie; Saint & Stephanie
1979: Carly Simon; Spy
1979: Yusef Lateef; In A Temple Garden
1979: Bad News Travels Fast; Look Out
1979: David Matthews; Digital Love
1979: Charles Mingus; Me Myself An Eye
1979: Charles Earland; Coming To You Live
1979: Alec R. Costandinos & The Syncophonic Orchestra; Winds Of Change: A Musical Fantasy
1979: Kleeer; Winners
1979: Spyro Gyra; Morning Dance
1979: Mongo Santamaria; Red Hot
1979: Herbie Mann; Yellow Fever
1979: Bob James; Lucky Seven
1979: Desmond Child And Rouge; Desmond Child And Rouge
1979: The Average White Band; Feel No Fret
1979: Candi Staton; Chance
1979: John Mayall; Bottom Line
1979: Richard T. Bear; Red Hot & Blue
1979: Original Soundtrack; The Warriors
1979: Narada Michael Walden; Awakening - The Dance Of Life
1979: Bette Midler; Thighs And Whispers
1979: Warren Bernhardt, Michael Brecker, Randy Brecker, Mike Mainieri; Blue Montreux
1979: Steve Khan; Arrows
1979: The Writers; All In Fun

1979: Warren Bernhardt, Michael Brecker, Randy Brecker, Mike Mainieri; Blue Montreux II
1979: The Tony Williams Lifetime; The Joy Of Flying
1979: Casiopea; Casiopea
1980: Jun Fukamachi; On The Move
1980: Chaka Khan; Naughty
1980: Spyro Gyra; Carnaval
1980: The Brecker Brothers; DÄtente
1980: Charles Mingus; Something Like A Bird
1980: Manu Dibango; Gone Clear
1980: George Clinton and the P-Funk All-Stars; Plush Funk
1980: Yoshiaki Masuo; Song Is You And Me
1980: Parliament; Trombipulation
1980: Patti Austin; Body Language
1980: Stone Alliance; Heads Up
1980: Paul Simon; One Trick Pony
1980: J. D. Drews; J. D. Drews
1980: Ray Gomez; Volume
1980: The Spinners; Love Trippin'
1981: The Brecker Brothers; Straphangin'
1981: Chic; Take It Off
1981: Manu Dibango; Ambassador
1981: Chaka Khan; What Cha' Gonna Do For Me
1981: Diana Ross; Why Do Fools Fall In Love
1981: Garland Jeffreys; Escape Artist
1981: Herbie Mann; Mellow
1981: George Benson; GB
1981: Mike Mainieri; Wanderlust
1981: Carly Simon; Torch
1981: Masaru Imada; Carnival
1982: Peter Erskine; Peter Erskine
1982: Donald Fagen; The Nightfly
1982: Barry Finnerty; New York City
1982: David Matthews; Grand Cross
1982: Mark Gray; Boogie Hotel
1982: Michael Franks; Objects Of Desire
1982: Ron Carter; El Noche Sol
1982: Luther Vandross; Forever, For Always, For Love
1983: Gil Evans & Orchestra; Live in Lugano 1983 [DVD]
1983: Bob Mintzer and the Horn Man Band; Papa Lips

1983: Bob James; The Genie
1983: George Benson; In Your Eyes
1984: Frank Sinatra with Quincy Jones and Orchestra; L.A. Is My Lady
1984: Diana Ross; Swept Away
1984: Mark Gray & Super Friends; The Silencer
1984: Martha and the Muffins; Mystery Walk
1984: Barry Gibb; Now Voyager
1984: Steely Dan; Gaucho
1984: Lou Reed; New Sensations
1985: Don Grolnick; Hearts And Numbers
1985: Dire Straits; Brothers In Arms
1985: James Taylor; That's Why I'm Here
1985: Michael W. Smith; Big Picture
1985: Dolby's Cube; May The Cube Be With You
1985: James Brown; The CD Of JB: Sex Machine & Other Soul Classics
1985: Randy Brecker, Eliane Elias; Amanda
1985: Patti Austin; Gettin' Away with Murder
1985: Taeko Ohnuki; Copine
1985: Teruo Nakamura; Super Friends
1985: Bob Mintzer Big Band; Incredible Journey
1986: Ornella Vanoni; Ornella E...
1986: Grover Washington Jr; House Full Of Love: Music from The Cosby Show
1986: Eric Clapton; August
1986: Bob James; Obsession
1986: Cameo; Word Up!
1986: Original Soundtrack; A House Full Of Love: Music From The Cosby Show
1986: Chaka Khan; Destiny
1986: Michael W. Smith; The Big Picture
1986: Rare Silk; New Weave
1987: Michael Franks; The Camera Never Lies
1987: Hiram Bullock; Give It What U Got
1988: Hue And Cry; Remote
1988: Peter Erskine; Motion Poet
1988: Jorge Dalto; Listen Up!
!988: Dire Straits; Money For Nothing
1988: Eliane Elias; So Far So Close
1988: Cameo; Machismo
1988: The SOS All-Stars; New York Rendezvous

1989: Don Grolnick; Weaver Of Dreams
1989: Vince Mendoza; Vince Mendoza
1989: Third World; Serious Business
1989: Richie Beirach; Some Other Time - A Tribute To Chet Baker
1990: Paul Simon; The Rhythm Of The Saints
1990: Bob James; Grand Piano Canyon
1990: Randy Brecker; Toe To Toe
1990: Michael Colina; Rituals
1990: Claus Ogerman; Claus Ogerman Featuring Michael Brecker
1991: James Taylor; New Moon Shine
1991: L. J. Reynolds; L. J. Reynolds
1992: Sandy Bull; Vehicles
1992: Various Artists; After The Dance
1992: Garland Jeffreys; Matador & More
1992: The Brecker Brothers; The Return of The Brecker Brothers: Live in Spain 1992 [DVD]
1992: The Brecker Brothers; Return Of The Brecker Brothers
1992: Jenni Muldaur; Jenni Muldaur
1992: Toshinobu Kubota; Neptune
1992: John Simon; Out On The Street
1993: Beatnik Rebel; Science: Featuring Tony Verderosa
1993: Various Artists; World Of Contemporary Jazz Groups
1993: Leslie Mandoki; People
1993: Jay Leonhart & Friends; Live At Fat Tuesday's: May 13-16, 1993
1993: Laura Nyro; Walk The Dog & Light The Light
1994: The Brecker Brothers; Out Of The Loop
1994: Sergio Salvatore; Tune Up
1994: Urbanator; Urbanator
1994: Aerosmith; Box Of Fire
1994: Jonathan Butler; Head To Head
1994: The Brecker Brothers; The Brecker Brothers - Live
1994: BFD; BFD
1994: Kenneth Sivertsen; Remembering North
1994: Julie Eigenberg; Love Is Starting Now
1994: Marc Beacco; Scampi Fritti
1995: Toko Furuuchi; Strength
1995: Doky Brothers; Doky Brothers

1995: Various Artists; Jazz To The World
1995: Michael Franks; Abandoned Garden
1995: Alan Pasqua; Dedications
1996: Hue And Cry; JazzNotJazz
1996: Leslie Mandoki; People In Room No.8
1996: Bernard Purdie; Bernard Purdie's Soul To Jazz
1996: Smappies; Rhythmsticks
1996: Caecilie Norby; My Corner Of The Sky
1996: Nils Landgren Funk Unit; Paint It Blue
1996: Michal Urbaniak; Urbanator II
1996: Lenny White; Renderers Of Spirit
1997: Yoko Ono; A Story
1997: Joe Chindamo; Reflected Journey
1997: Horace Silver; A Prescription For The Blues
1997: Various Artists; Jazz Fusion Vol. 2
1997: Leslie Mandoki; The Jazz Cuts
1997: Various Artists; Vanguard Collector's Edition
1997: Various Artists; The Art Of Jazz Saxophone: Impressions
1998: Mark Murphy; Jazz Standards
1998: Sanne Salomonsen; In A New York Minute
1998: Eijiro Nakagawa; Peace
1998: Chris Minh Doky; Minh
1999: Mark Murphy; Songbook
1999: Michael Franks; Barefoot On The Beach
1999: Gary LeMel; Moonlighting
1999: Michel Berger; Voyou
1999: Mark Murphy; Mark Murphy Sings Nat King Cole And More
2000: Various Artists; Jazz Sampler, Vol. 1
2000: Don Grolnick Group; The London Concert
2000: Various Artists; Celebrating The Music Of Weather Report
2000: James Brown; James Brown's Funky People Pt. 3
2001: Randy Brecker; Hangin' In The City
2001: Randy Waldman; UnReel
2001: Laura Nyro; Angel In The Dark
2001: Jack Wilkins; Reunion
2001: Dean Brown; Here
2002: Will & Rainbow; Over Crystal Green
2002: Billy Cobham; Drum 'n' Voice, Vol. 1
2002: Mike Pope; The Lay Of The Land
2002: Randy Brecker; 34th N Lex
2002: Dennis Chambers; Outbreak
2003: Aaron Neville; Nature Boy: The Standards Album
2004: GRP All-Star Big Band; Rediscovery On GRP
2004: David Garfield; Giving Back
2004: Soul Generation; Stop, Look And Listen
2004: Claus Ogerman; A Man And His Music
2005: Jason Miles; Miles To Miles: In The Spirit Of Miles Davis
2005: Mica Paris; If You Could Love Me
2005: Beatlejazz; With A Little Help From Our Friends
2005: Man Doki; Soulmates
2005: Randy Brecker, Michael Brecker; Some Skunk Funk
2005: Randy Brecker / Michael Brecker; Some Skunk Funk [DVD]
2006: Garland Jeffreys; I'm Alive
2006: Chris Minh Doky; The Nomad Diaries
2007: Gary Haase; String Theory
2007: Blue Oyster Cult; Discover
2010: Arif Mardin; All My Friends Are Here
2010: The Brecker Brothers; Live In Tokyo, U-Port Hall, 1995 [DVD]
2011: The J.B.s and Fred Wesley; The Lost Album Featuring Watermelo Man

Single Releases by The Brecker Brothers

The Brecker Brothers, 1975, Vinyl 7-inch, 45 rpm, Arista, Arista 14, Sneakin' Up Behind You, 2.56, Sponge, 4.00, USA

The Brecker Brothers, 1975, Vinyl 7-inch, 45 rpm demo, Arista, Arista 14, Sneakin' Up Behind You (long version), 4.50, Sneakin' Up Behind You (short version), 2.56

The Brecker Brothers, 1975, Vinyl 7-inch, 45 rpm demo, Arista, Arista 14, Sneakin' Up Behind You (short version), 2.56, Sneakin' Up Behind You (long version), 4.50

The Brecker Brothers, 1975, Vinyl 7-inch, 45 rpm, Arista, AS-0122, Sneakin' Up Behind You (short version), 2.56, Sponge, 4.00, UK

The Brecker Brothers, 1975, Vinyl 7-inch, 45 rpm, Arista, J006-97.519, Sneakin' Up Behind You (short version), 2.56, Some Skunk Funk, Spain

The Brecker Brothers, 1976, Vinyl 7-inch, 45 rpm, Arista, AS 0182, If You Wanna Boogie…Forget It, Slick Stuff, USA

The Brecker Brothers, 1976, Vinyl 7-inch, 45 rpm demo, Arista, AS 0182, If You Wanna Boogie…Forget It (mono), 3.10, If You Wanna Boogie…Forget It (stereo), 3.10, USA

The Brecker Brothers, 1976, Vinyl 7-inch, 45 rpm demo 3 track, Arista, Arista 57, If You Wanna Boogie…Forget It, 3.10, Sneakin' Up Behind You, 2.56, Keep It Steady

The Brecker Brothers, 1977, Vinyl 7-inch, 45 rpm, Arista, Arista 117, Fingerlickin' Good, 3.29, Don't Stop The Music, 3.29, UK

The Brecker Brothers, 1977, Vinyl 7-inch, 45 rpm, Arista, AS 0253, Don't Stop The Music, 3.29, Fingerlickin' Good, 3.29, USA

The Brecker Brothers, 1977, Vinyl 12, 33 rpm promo disco special, Arista, ALD-02, Don't Stop The Music, 6.33, Fingerlickin' Good, 3.58, USA

The Brecker Brothers, 1977, Vinyl 7-inch, 45 rpm, Arista, 10 C 006-99209, Don't Stop The Music - Que No Pare La Musica, 6.33, Fingerlickin' Good, 3.58, Spain

The Brecker Brothers, 1978, Vinyl 7-inch, 45 rpm, Arista, Arist 211, East River, 4.20, Petals, 3.32, UK

The Brecker Brothers, 1978, Vinyl 7-inch, 45 rpm, Arista, AS 0365, East River, 3.31, Funky Sea, Funky Dew, 3.51, USA

The Brecker Brothers, 1978, Vinyl 7-inch, 45 rpm, Arista, 5C 006-62079, East River (La-Di-Da), 3.31, Some Skunk Funk, Netherlands

The Brecker Brothers, 1978, Vinyl 7-inch, 45 rpm, Arista, 2C 008-62116, East River, 4.20, Petals, 3.32, France

The Brecker Brothers, 1980, Vinyl 7-inch, 45 rpm, Arista, AS 0533, You Ga (Ta Give It), 3.37, Dream Theme, Produced by George Duke

The Brecker Brothers, 1980, Vinyl 7-inch, 45 rpm, Arista, AS 0558, Not Tonight, 3.32, Squish, 5.51, Produced by George Duke, USA

The Brecker Brothers, 1980, Vinyl 7-inch, 45 rpm promo, Arista, AS 0558, Not Tonight (stereo), 3.32, Not Tonight (mono), 3.32, USA

The Brecker Brothers, 1992, Maxi CD, GRP, GRP 9993-2, Big Idea (long wave version), 5.49, Big Idea (radio wave mix),

4.44, Big Idea (shortwave version), 4.21, Give The Drummer Some!, On The Backside, 6.32, Germany

The Brecker Brothers, 1992, Vinyl 12-inch, 33 rpm promo disco special, GRP, GRP8P-4016, Big Idea (long wave version), 5.49, Big Idea (radio wave mix), 4.44, Big Idea (shortwave version), 4.21, Give The Drummer Some!, On The Backside, 6.32, USA

The Brecker Brothers, 1992, Vinyl 12-inch, 33 rpm, MCA, MCST 1720, Big Idea (long wave version), 5.49, Big Idea (radio wave mix), 4.44, Big Idea (shortwave version), 4.21, On The Backside, 6.32, UK

The Brecker Brothers, 1992, Vinyl 12-inch, 33 rpm, GRP, GRP 40161, Big Idea (Smoothell Mix), 5.44, Big Idea (Tunnel of Hell Club mix), 6.53, Netherlands

The Brecker Brothers, 1992, CD Single, MCA, MCSTD 1720, Big Idea (shortwave version), 4.21, Big Idea (long wave version), 5.47, Big Idea (radio wave mix), 4.43, On The Backside, 6.32, UK

The Brecker Brothers, 1994, Maxi CD, GRP, GRZ-5158, African Skies, Secret Heart, Slang

Index

1
15 Miles to Provo, 29, 227

3
3 Views of a Secret, 234
34th N Lex, 7, 164, 171, 172, 189, 211, 220, 256, 267, 273

6
65th Birthday Celebration
    Live At The Blue Note In New York City, 254

7
75, 6, 157, 209
75th, 155
7th Avenue South (jazz club), 5, 60, 61, 87, 88, 91, 135

8
8.30, 76, 239, 241
80/81, 262
8th Avenue March, 241

9
9 1/2 Weeks, 264
900 Shares Of The Blues, 248

A
A Blow For Me, A Toot To You, 249, 260, 270
A Certain Beauty, 258
A Change Of Heart, 264
A Collection, 91, 208
A Creature of Many Faces, 57, 212, 215, 216
A Funky Thide of Sings, 5, 45, 46, 47, 56, 230, 248, 259, 269
A Funky Waltz, 77, 215, 232
A Gathering Of Spirits, 246
A Great Night In Harlem, 256
A House Full Of Love
    Music From The Cosby Show, 251, 264, 272
A Hundred Years From Today, 239
A Long Time Ago, 240
A Love Supreme, 145, 243
A Love Supreme - Acknowledgement, 243
A Lullaby Of Itsugo Village, 244
A Man And His Music, 256, 267, 273
A Manhattan Affair, 257
A New Kind Of Blue, 256
A New Regalia, 241
A Prescription For The Blues, 254, 266, 273
A Rio Affair, 252
A Secret Place, 248
A Street Called Straight, 248, 260, 269
A Time Of New Beginnings, 258
A Touch Of Light, 160

A Touch Of Love, 264
A Tribute To Curtis Mayfield, 253
A Tribute to Miles, 157
A Weaver of Dreams, 242
A Wizard, A True Star, 247, 259, 269
Abandoned Garden, 254, 266, 273
Abercrombie, John, 28, 30, 35, 43, 44, 46, 47, 48, 192, 227, 229, 241, 263, 264, 267
Abersold, Jamey (writer), 7, 150, 181, 209
About Love, 88, 262
Above And Below, 168, 214, 216, 217, 220
Accidentally On Purpose, 252
Acid Jazz, 254
Acogny, Georges, 263
Acoustic, 252, 257
Act Natural, 239
Adam Smasher, 39, 228
Adams, Greg, 54
Adams, Park, 232
Adderley, Julian (Cannonball), 13, 15, 23
Adderley, Nathaniel, 124
Adina, 185, 222
Adnet, Maucha, 137, 219, 257
Affairs, 254
Africa, 116, 187
African Skies, 132, 140, 162, 205, 211, 215, 217, 224, 275
After All, 31, 176, 253, 260
After All Is Said And Done, 253
After Love, 136, 138, 219
After Ours, 254
After The Dance, 249, 253, 261, 265, 270, 272
After Thought, 240
After You, 239
Against The Grain, 261
Agents Of Fortune, 248, 260, 270
Agony Of Defeet, 234
Ahh...The Name Is Bootsy, Baby!, 249, 260, 270
Aiaiai, 179, 221
Air, 241, 247, 259, 269
Air Dancing, 241
Airbop, 257
Akai (instrument manufacturer), 95, 107, 201
Akkerman, Jan, 261
Al Jarreau, 56, 114, 137, 265
Alexander The Great, 246
Alexander, Glenn, 252
Ali, Jerome, 233
Ali, Jimmy, 233
Alias, Charles Don, 36, 37, 79, 81, 82, 85, 120, 121, 122, 123, 135, 139, 141, 182, 192, 214, 215, 220, 223, 224, 228, 230, 234, 235, 236, 237, 243, 244
All 4 Love, 165, 220
All Blues, 243, 253
All For A Reason, 249, 261, 270
All I Want For Christmas, 255
All In Fun, 262, 271
All My Friends Are Here, 258, 268, 273
All Of Me, 150
All Or Nothing at All, 221
All Over The Place, 258
All the Tea in China, 100, 240
All There Is, 126, 214

276

Allen, Sanford, 215
All-In All-Out, 250
Allison, Luther, 248, 259, 269
Allison, Mose, 253, 254
Alsop, Lamar, 215
Altered Things, 253
Amadie, Jimmy, 257
Amanda, 6, 101, 102, 103, 188, 196, 218, 251, 264, 272
Amandamada, 102, 103, 218
Amandla, 120, 149
Ambassador, 251, 263, 271
Amber Road, 222, 246
Ambrosetti, Franco, 15, 263
America / Brasil, 254
America The Beautiful, 159, 245, 247
American Dreams, 7, 158, 159, 209, 245, 267
Amerika, 84, 234, 235, 237
Amesbury, Bill, 248
An Innocent Man, 263
Anagram, 174, 211, 225
And Another Thing..., 254
And Then She Wept, 171, 215, 217, 221, 222
Anderson, Jay, 119, 122, 224, 226, 243, 253
Andre, Wayne, 85, 236, 237, 238
Andrews, Jeff, 112, 223, 226
Andy Sheppard, 252
Angel In The Dark, 256, 267, 273
Angel Of Repose, 225
Angie, 261
Angle of Repose, 162, 225, 268
Angle of Repose / Live in Japan [DVD], 268
Animal Fat, 227
Another Hand, 114, 125
Another Jones, 231
Another Standard, 254
Another World, 265
Anthology, 253, 256
Anxiety, 43
Any Love, 252
Anything Goes, 248, 259, 269
Arc, 146, 147, 224, 253
Arc of the Pendulum, 147, 224
Aretha, 52, 256
Arista Records (record label), 5, 51, 52, 53, 54, 59, 68, 71, 75, 78, 101, 102, 138, 186, 189, 212, 213, 214, 215, 217, 230, 232, 274
Armageddon, 76
Arnold, Patrick, 256
Around The City, 257
ARP Odyssey (instrument), 248, 249, 250, 261, 270
Arriale, Lynne, 258
Arrows, 58, 139, 224, 250, 262, 271
Art Blakey's Jazz Messengers, 38
Art Of The Big Band, 242, 252
As I Am, 148, 224
As We Speak, 70
Ashby, Jay, 245
Asia, 15
Aspects, 230, 248, 260, 269
At Basin Street, 257
At Home, 110, 112, 114, 123, 211, 223, 264
At Montreux, 163
At The Point V. One, 266
At The Sound Of The Bell, 260
Atakoglu, Fahir, 258
Atlantic Records (record label), 42, 49, 123, 230

Auld Lang Syne, 228
Austin, Patti, 213, 215, 248, 250, 251, 260, 261, 262, 263, 264, 269, 271, 272
Avant-garde (music genre), 21, 32, 54
Avatar, 258
Avenida, 252
Awakening - The Dance Of Life, 250, 262, 271
AWB, 49, 56, 60, 247, 259, 269
Ayler, Albert, 21

B

Baby Grand, 261
Baby Plays Around, 256
Back Burner, 245
Back In The High Life, 251
Back In The Pool, 265
Back On The Case, 252
Back To Back, 5, 62, 71, 213, 248, 260, 270
Back To The Front, 263
Backer Steve (record producer), 5, 51, 53, 54, 62, 64, 187
Badlands, 249, 261, 270
Badrena, Manolo, 72, 214, 215, 217, 218, 235
Baffled, 70, 214, 215, 216, 217
Bailey, Philip, 255
Bailey, Victor, 117, 118, 120, 121, 167, 168, 169, 219, 220, 223, 240, 264
Baird, Robert (writer), 86, 87, 208
Baker, Chet, 25, 61, 252, 258, 260, 264, 272
Baker, LaVern, 253
Baker, Peter (Ginger), 120
Ball, Roger, 49, 257
Ballons
    Live At The Blue Note, 258
Baltimore MD, 117, 136, 150, 248, 260, 269
Bamboo Magic, 249, 261, 270
Bandits, 44, 229
Bangalore, 27, 218
Baptista, Cyro, 103, 218
Barbieri, Gato, 247, 248, 259, 269
Barcelona Spain, 128, 216
Barcus Berry (pick-up), 35
Bardaro, Gianni, 258
Barefoot On The Beach, 255, 267, 273
Bargeron, Dave, 82, 85, 219, 234, 236, 237, 238, 239, 240, 241, 242
Barlow, Tom (writer), 47, 207
Barnes, Katreese, 220
Barnes, Sidney, 229
Barnet, Charles, 257
Barney, Tom, 235, 238
Baron, Joey, 114, 218
Barrabas, 267
Barrett, Darren, 244
Bartz, Gary, 151
Basie, William Allen, 41
Basile, John, 266
Bathsheba, 72, 214, 215, 216
Battle Royal, 34, 227, 228
Bazuka, 248, 259, 269
Be Happy, 244, 260
Be Happy For Me, 260
Beacco, Marc, 253, 265, 272
Bear, Richard T., 250, 262, 271

Beard, James Arthur, 112, 113, 117, 118, 119, 120, 121, 122, 170, 171, 172, 211, 219, 221, 222, 223, 241, 265
Beatles, The (band), 16, 20, 59
Beatnik Rebel Science, 254
Beau Rivage, 140, 224
Beauty And Harmony, 265
Bebop (music style), 71, 121, 150, 163
Bebop United, 245, 257
Beck, Jeff, 73
Beck, Joe, 18, 227, 228, 247, 248, 259, 261, 269
Beckenstein, Jay, 244
Beethoven, 248
Before The Daylight, 264
Behind Closed Doors, Vol. 1, 255
Beirach, Richie, 252, 264, 272
Beirut, 15, 98, 101, 240
Belden, Bob, 162
Belden, Bob (writer record producer), 162
Belgrade Serbia, 241
Belle, Regina, 118, 219, 264
Belote, Doug, 258
Bennett, Tony, 114
Benny & Us, 249, 261, 270
Benson, George, 41, 59, 179, 192, 238, 248, 249, 251, 252, 253, 259, 260, 263, 269, 270, 271, 272
Berg, Bob, 7, 114, 115, 116, 124, 149, 150, 166, 167, 188, 191, 218, 219, 243, 244, 245, 252, 254, 255
Berger, Michel, 250, 255, 261, 266, 270, 273
Bergeron, Chuck, 254, 255
Berklee Music College, 25, 104, 110, 123, 124, 136, 142, 159, 161, 177, 182
Berlin Germany, 155, 247, 259, 269
Berlin, Irving (composer), 155
Bernhardt, Warren, 6, 18, 33, 75, 76, 77, 94, 96, 97, 215, 227, 228, 232, 235, 239, 240, 250, 262, 271
Bernstein, Peter, 145
Berrios, Steve, 122, 224, 243
Bette Midler, 191, 248, 250, 260, 262, 270, 271
Better Get Hit In Your Soul
  A Tribute To The Music Of Charles Mingus, 258
Better Late Than Never, 248, 260, 270
Bey, Andy, 226
Beyond the Limit, 241
BFD, 253, 265, 272
Big Band Renaissance, 254
Big Band Trane, 243, 254
Big Band, DR, 7, 181, 211, 221, 258
Big Band, Igor Butman, 257
Big Band, The Norbotten, 258
Big Band, Tolvan, 264
Big Band, WDR, 170, 171, 211, 221, 222
Big Boss Band, 252
Big Brother, 51
Big City, 253
Big City Magic, 253
Big Fun, 168, 220, 256
Big Idea, 125, 127, 214, 217, 274, 275
Big Neighbourhood, 258
Big Picture, 251, 263, 264, 272
Big Star, 248, 259, 269
Bill Evans, 7, 113, 117, 136, 137, 151, 161, 164, 167, 193, 209, 210, 220, 254, 256, 257
Billard, Beverly, 65, 215

Billard, Doug, 215
Billboard (magazine), 22, 43
Billy Cobham, 5, 14, 24, 28, 30, 32, 40, 41, 42, 43, 44, 45, 47, 48, 52, 117, 120, 123, 136, 160, 189, 207, 226, 227, 229, 230, 238, 247, 248, 249, 252, 255, 256, 259, 261, 267, 269, 270, 273
Bird Food, 245
Birdfingers, 39, 228, 256
Birdland, 184
Birdland (jazz club), 184
Birds Of A Feather, 256
Birds of Fire, 42
Birdsong, Edwin, 24
Bishop, Walter, 249
Bittersuite In The Ozone, 248
Bittersweet, 159, 245
Black Heat, 248, 259, 269
Black Night, 37, 228
Black Orpheus, 258
Black Sand, 256
Black, Brown And Beautiful, 247
Blackbird, 81, 234, 246
Blade, Brian, 156, 159, 160, 245
Blake, Alex, 45, 229, 230
Blakey, Arthur, 38, 195
Blam!!, 262
Blenzig, Charles, 265
Bley, Carla, 105, 158, 251
Bley, Paul, 105
Bliss, Peter, 249, 261, 270
Blixt, Karen, 257
Block, Daniel, 232
Blood Sweat & Tears, 5, 21, 22, 25, 27, 28, 29, 33, 34, 40, 51, 52, 58, 123, 189
Bloom, Steve (writer), 29, 207
Blow! Jazz Trumpet And Saxophone Virtuosos, 256
Blue Goo, 151, 219, 245
Blue in Green, 243
Blue Matter, 117
Blue Montreux, 6, 75, 77, 138, 215, 232, 250, 262, 271
Blue Moon, 223
Blue Moves, 248, 260, 270
Blue Note Records, 4, 18, 24, 25, 38, 41, 104, 182, 185, 204, 209, 218, 225, 226, 228, 242, 244, 251, 254, 255, 258, 267
Blue Rain, 180, 221
Blues, 21, 33, 52, 58, 60, 122, 143, 145, 185, 208, 222, 224, 233, 237, 242, 243, 244, 248, 252, 253, 254, 255, 257, 266, 273
Blues & Politics, 255
Blues & Soul (magazine), 60, 208
Blues for Pop, 242
Blues On The Other Side, 33
Body and Soul, 244
  Everything Happens To Me, 242
Body Language, 234, 250, 262, 271
Bofill, Angela, 261
Bohanon, George, 238
Bolin, Tommy, 42
Bollenback, Paul, 150, 151, 219, 245, 257
Bona, Richard, 124, 152, 220, 266, 267
Bond, James, 181, 244
Bonfa, Luiz, 247, 259, 269
Bonsanti, Dan, 234
Boogie Hotel, 251, 263, 271
Bookends, 246

Born Again, 253
Born To Dance, 261
Born To Run, 248, 259, 269
Borrowed Time, 268
Bosco, Joao, 178
Bossa Nova (music style), 256
Boston MA, 25, 75, 123, 145, 159, 161
Both / And, 246, 257
Both Sides Now, 171
Both Sides of the Coin, 93, 237, 238
Botti, Chris, 214, 266
Bottom Line, 250, 262, 271
Boulez, 241
Boussaguet, Pierre, 223
Boutte, Reginald, 229
Box Of Fire, 253, 265, 272
Box Of Photographs, 257
Boys In The Trees, 250, 261, 270
Bozzio, Terry, 61, 67, 68, 213, 215, 231
Brackeen, Joanne, 161, 260
Braden, Don, 254
Brailey, Jerome, 230
Brain Wave, 226
Brake, Brian, 235
Bralower, Jimmy, 223
Bramblett, Randall, 259
Brand New, 40
Brashear, Oscar, 238
Brass Nation, 255
Brastilava Jazz Days, 264
Brazil, 92, 94, 101, 136, 137, 179, 187, 256
Brazilian Affair, 242
Brazilian Jazz - The music And lyrics Of Claudia Villela, 266
Break Time, 231
Breakwater, 249
Brecker, Jessica, 173
Brecker, Robert (Bob), 15, 16
Brecker, Susan, 176, 210
Brecker, Tecosky (Ticky), 15, 16
Brexterity, 163, 225
Brickell, Edie, 265
Bridging A Gap, 247, 259, 269
Bright Size Life, 203
Brignola, Nick, 252
Broadbent, Alan, 159
Broadway, 18, 228, 256, 263
Broadway Joe, 228
Broadway My Way, 256
Bromberg, Brian, 258
Bronne, Ariana, 215
Bronner, Till, 266
Brooklyn NYC, 19, 41, 45, 51, 59, 105, 114, 120, 145, 160, 262
Brothers In Arms, 251, 264, 272
Brown, Alfred, 215
Brown, Clifford, 12, 15
Brown, Dean, 123, 130, 132, 135, 183, 214, 216, 220, 222, 256, 267, 273
Brown, Elmer, 85, 236, 237
Brown, Garnett, 43, 45, 229
Brown, Gerry, 230
Brown, James, 50, 54, 247, 251, 255, 259, 269, 272, 273
Brown, Josh, 215
Brown, Ray, 238
Brown, Sam, 227, 228

Browne Sugar, 262
Browne, Baron, 215
Browne, Tom, 262
Brubeck, Darius, 259
Brubeck, Dave, 41, 265
Bruford, Bill, 193, 200, 209
Bubbles, Brazil & Bossa Nova, 256
Buchanan, Roy, 248, 260, 269
Buchtel, Forrest, 236, 237
Bud Powell, 145
Buds, 77, 138, 215, 219, 232
Bull, Sandy, 253, 265, 272
Bullet Train, 91, 233
Bullock, Hiram, 65, 66, 69, 70, 86, 98, 153, 167, 168, 169, 213, 214, 215, 217, 220, 239, 240, 252, 256, 264, 272
Bump, 62, 213, 215, 217
Burgan, Janet, 254
Burno, Duane, 245
Burton, Gary, 20, 33, 106, 110, 247, 259, 264, 269
But Not For Me, 242
Butler, Jonathan, 253, 265, 272
Butman, Igor, 257
Butterfield, Paul, 52, 58
Buzz, 235
By Myself
    The Songs Of Judy Garland, 257
By The Company You Keep, 266
Bye Bye Blackbird, 246
Bye George, 143, 224

C

Cabin Fever, 141, 211, 224
Caecilie Norby, 253, 254, 257, 266, 273
Café Au Go-Go (jazz club), 22
Cahn, Danny, 233
Cajun, 99, 101, 240, 250
Cajun Sunrise, 250
Calazans, Paulo, 221
Calderazzo, Joey, 110, 112, 119, 121, 122, 139, 141, 143, 203, 223, 224, 226, 265
Calello, Charles, 262
Calico, 31, 227
Caliente!, 248
California, 171
Call, 37, 228, 242, 249, 254, 255, 261, 265, 270
Calliope, 193
Camby Bolongo, 249
Camouflage, 239, 240, 251
Campagnola, Jim, 222
Can You Feel It, 248
Candi Staton, 250, 260, 262, 271
Candles, 77, 215, 232
Cannonball Adderley, 15, 23
Cantaloupe Island, 241
Cape Verdean Blues, 243
Cape Wilderness, 244
Capitol Records (record label), 24, 25
Capricon Princess, 248, 260, 269
Cara, Irene, 215
Cardinal Rule, 175, 225
Cardona, Milton, 122, 224, 243
Cardoso, Teco, 177, 221
Carey, Mariah, 162
Carla, 105, 158, 235, 238, 251
Carlton, Gordon, 233

279

Carlton, Larry, 263
Carlwell, Carl, 69, 215
Carlwell, Sue Ann, 215
Carnaval, 87, 250, 262, 271
Carnegie Hall NYC (music venue), 173, 253
Carnegie Hall Salutes The Jazz Masters
   Verve At 50, 253
Carnival, 251, 263, 271
Caro, Joe, 153, 220
Carol Grimes, 261
Carroll, Jim, 251
Carter, Chuggy, 235
Carter, Clifford, 239
Carter, Ron, 43, 103, 104, 109, 218, 248, 251, 259, 263, 269, 271
Casablanca Records (record label), 50, 164, 229, 230, 231, 233
Casino de Montreux (concert hall), 263
Casino Lights - Live At Montreux, 263
Casiopea, 250, 262, 271
Cast Of Characters
   The Rupert Holmes Songbook, 256
Cast Your Fate To The Wind, 248, 260, 270
Castillo, Emilio, 54
Catalano, Frank, 255, 256
Catalano, Mike, 252, 257
Catching The Sun, 250
Cathcarte, Carter, 235
Catscan, 267, 268
Catscan II, 268
Catta, 243
Cavaliere, Felix, 247, 259
Celebrating The Music Of Weather Report, 255, 267, 273
Celebration, 254, 257
Centering, 235
Central Park, 228
Chaka Khan, 87, 161, 162, 249, 250, 251, 261, 262, 263, 264, 270, 271, 272
Chambers, Dennis, 7, 117, 118, 123, 126, 127, 128, 129, 130, 149, 162, 202, 214, 216, 217, 219, 243, 244, 245, 255, 256, 267, 273
Chambers, Joe, 232
Champagne, 250, 262, 271
Chancler, Ndugu Leon, 238
Change, 36, 227, 250, 251, 262, 264, 271
Chapter Three
   Viva Emiliano Zapata, 247, 259, 269
Charles Blenzig, 265
Charles Mingus
   Epitaph [DVD], 252
Cheltenham, 16, 23
Cherry, Don, 260
Chesky 20th Anniversary, 257
Chicago IL, 16, 51, 105, 150, 247, 259, 269
Chicago Theme, 247, 259, 269
Chick Corea, 11, 58, 72, 102, 119, 160, 161, 262, 267
Chick Corea Elektric Band (band), 72, 102, 119, 160
Chicken, 234, 235, 236, 237
Child Is Father To The Man, 247
Child of Wisdom, 31, 227
Children Of Productions, 231
Children of the Night, 245, 249, 261, 270
Childsplay, 257
Chime This, 111, 223, 226
Chimenti, Bryan, 229

China Moon, 244
China Road, 244
China Town, 244
Chindamo, Joe, 255, 266, 273
Chinnock, Bill, 249, 261, 270
Chong, David Lee, 233
Christopher Columbus, 242
Chromatic Fantasy, 81, 234
Ciccu, Bianca, 252
City Connection, 250
City Streets, 264
Cityscape, 235, 263
Civilized Man, 251
Clapton, Eric Patrick, 49, 251, 252, 264, 272
Clarendon Hills, 167
Clark, John, 238, 241
Clark, Robin, 213, 215
Clarke, Stanley, 244
Classical music (music genre), 45, 111, 145, 180, 193, 196
Claus Ogerman, 235, 252, 256, 260, 263, 265, 267, 272, 273
Claus Ogerman Featuring Michael Brecker, 252, 265, 272
Clayton-Thomas, David, 22, 261
Cleaves, Jessica, 233
Clinton, George, 5, 49, 229, 230, 233, 250, 262, 271
Close View, 245
Cloud Motion, 78, 215, 232
Club 1600 (music venue), 255
Coast To Coast, 250, 255, 265
Cobham, Billy, 5, 14, 24, 28, 30, 32, 40, 41, 42, 43, 44, 45, 47, 48, 52, 117, 120, 123, 136, 160, 189, 207, 226, 227, 229, 230, 238, 247, 248, 249, 252, 255, 256, 259, 261, 267, 269, 270, 273
Cocker, Joe, 251
Cole Porter In Concert
   Just One Of Those Live Things, 253
Cole, Nat King, 41, 255, 267, 273
Cole, Natalie, 117, 266
Cole, Richard, 255, 257, 258
Coleman, George, 226, 232
Coleman, Ornette, 19, 35, 105, 159
Coletivo, 257
Colina, Michael, 252, 264, 265, 272
Collection, 54, 75, 91, 208, 209, 210, 215, 216
Collette, Buddy, 238
Collins, Glenn, 230
Collins, Judy, 248
Collins, William, 49, 229, 230
Colombier, Michel, 262
Colomby, Bobby, 21, 22, 78, 230
Color Me, 256
Color Visions, 248
Colors Of Jazz
   For Sunday Morning, 252
   For Tropical Nights, 252
   From Dusk Till Dawn, 252
Colors Of Latin Jazz
   Shades Of Jobim, 256
Colton, Kenny, 233
Coltrane, John, 12, 16, 19, 20, 23, 28, 105, 107, 110, 111, 139, 145, 155, 156, 176, 196, 199, 209
Columbia Records, 22, 41, 51, 52, 53, 88, 149
Come Dream With Me, 267
Come On, Come Over, 78, 230

280

Coming Around Again, 264
Coming Out, 248, 249, 260, 261, 269, 270
Coming Outta Nowhere, 249, 261, 270
Coming To You Live, 250, 262, 271
Common Ground, 129, 216, 217, 254
Compared To That, 258
Compositions Coast To Coast, 255
Concord Records 30th Anniversary, 256
Condor (electrical device), 35, 40
Conquistador, 249
Continental Talk, 258
Continuum, 230, 234, 235, 236, 237, 253, 258
Cook, Richard (author), 94, 187, 193, 208, 209
Cook, Richard (writer), 94, 208
Cool Blue, 265
Cool Day in Hell, 162, 225
Cool Eddie, 169, 220
Cool Jamz, 266
Cooper, Gary, 229, 230
Copeland, Ruth, 248, 260, 269
Copenhagen Denmark, 11, 181, 207, 208, 222, 238, 268
Copenhagen Live [DVD], 238, 268
Copenhagen Sights, 238
Copine, 251, 263, 272
Copland, 243, 246, 254, 257, 266, 267
Copland, Marc, 243, 246, 254, 257, 266, 267
Coppola, Tom, 262
Corea, Chick, 11, 58, 72, 102, 119, 160, 161, 262, 267
Coryell, Julian, 266
Coryell, Larry, 5, 16, 18, 19, 20, 26, 39, 52, 58, 75, 77, 189, 207, 215, 218, 228, 230, 232, 247, 248, 256, 260, 261, 269
Cosby, Bill, 252
Costandinos, Alec R., 250, 262, 271
Coster, Tom, 266
Cowan, Benny, 233
Cowboys and Indians, 240
Coyote, 233
Cozmopolitan, 262, 263
Cranshaw, Robert, 38, 226, 228
Crawford, Hank, 248, 249, 250, 251, 253, 261, 270
Cream (band), 120
Creeper, 168
Crenshaw, Robert, 238
Crescent, 44, 229
Crescent Sun, 44, 229
Crisis, 80, 234
Crisol (band), 156
Cropper, Steve, 227
Cross Currents, 137, 252
Crossing The Bridge, 255
Crossing The Line, 257
Crossroads, 252
Crosswinds, 5, 43, 44, 47, 229, 247, 259, 269
Crowbar, 247, 259, 269
Crunk, Jaiman, 258
Crush It, 234
Cruz, Mario, 236, 237
Cruz, Rafael, 63, 213, 215, 217
Cry Me A River, 181, 221
Crystal Green, 256, 261, 267, 273
CTI Records
   Acid Jazz Grooves, 254
   The Birth Of Groove, 255

Cuber, Ronnie, 19, 33, 61, 165, 167, 191, 192, 207, 210, 220, 227, 228, 231, 232, 238, 245, 251
Cubicle, 249
Cuesta-Loeb, Carmen, 267
Curry, Lige, 233
Curtis, 'King', 23, 199
Cuscuna, Michael (record producer), 27, 207
Cusson, Michael, 265

D

D Trane, 157, 158, 245
D. B. B., 212, 215
da Costa, Paulinho, 69, 214, 215, 235
da Silva, Edson Aparecido, 219
Dalto, Jorge, 252, 264, 272
Daltrey, Roger, 263
Daniels, Eddie, 15
Danziger, Zach, 220
Dark Light, 231
Darqui, Alex, 230
Dave Grusin Presents GRP All-Star Big Band Live!, 253
David Clayton-Thomas, 22, 261
Davis, Billy, 249, 261, 270
Davis, Clive (Columbia executive), 5, 51, 52, 53, 54
Davis, Irene, 215
Davis, Mel, 49
Davis, Michael, 22, 29, 207, 232, 255, 256
Davis, Michael Eugene, 242, 243
Davis, Miles, 4, 12, 15, 25, 26, 29, 32, 35, 37, 38, 41, 51, 67, 70, 71, 72, 74, 86, 104, 106, 109, 114, 120, 122, 123, 127, 130, 131, 139, 141, 145, 149, 150, 151, 155, 156, 157, 161, 167, 173, 174, 181, 193, 198, 207, 208, 214, 220, 223, 227, 248, 253, 254, 256, 262, 265, 266, 267, 273
Davis, Raymond, 50, 229, 230, 233
Davis, Tony, 233
Dawn, 137, 219, 234, 252
Day Dream, 262
Daydream, 255
de Winkel, Torsten, 264
Deal, Bill, 255
Dedication, 257
Dedications, 254, 266, 273
Dee, Kiki, 249, 260, 270
Deep In The Night, 266
DeFrancesco, Joey, 7, 149, 150, 219, 244, 245, 255
DeJohnette, Jack, 105, 108, 111, 112, 139, 155, 173, 223, 224, 225, 234, 244
Del Gatto, Lew, 62, 66, 213, 215, 255
Delano, Peter, 265
Deliverance, 265
Delta City Blues, 143, 224
Denmark, 181, 222
Dennard, Kenwood, 86
Dennerlein, Barbara, 254
Denon Hi-Fi Check CD, 253
Denon Jazz Sampler, Vol. 3, 252
Departure, 258
Desire, 251, 263, 271
Desmond Child And Rouge, 250, 262, 271
Desmond, Trudy, 252
Destiny, 251, 259, 264, 272
Détente, 6, 68, 69, 213, 250, 262
Detroit, 49

Devil Lady, 29, 227
Devil Woman, 232
Dewey, 88
Dexterity, 163
di Meola, Al, 193
Dialogue, 262
Diana, 177, 191, 248, 251, 260, 262, 263, 270, 271, 272
Diane, 99, 179, 213, 215
Dibango, Manu, 250, 251, 262, 263, 271
Dig, 63, 213, 215
Dig a Little Deeper, 213, 215
Digital Big Band Bash!, 251
Digital Love, 250, 262, 271
Dimitriades, Peter, 215
Directions, 7, 155, 156, 160, 209, 211, 245, 267
Directions in Music, 155, 156, 211, 245, 267
Dirty Dogs, 150, 219, 245
Discover an American Original The Jazz Sampler, 255
Discovery, 263
Dixie Hop, 170, 220
Dixon, Darryl, 233
Dixon, Iain, 162, 225
DMX (instrument), 97
Do That Stuff, 231
Dockery, Wayne, 231
Doctor, Marcio, 170, 172, 211, 221, 222
Dodgion, Jerry, 218
Dogs in the Wine Shop, 224
Doky Brothers, 254, 266, 272
Doky, Christopher Minh, 152, 165, 181, 182, 220, 221, 222, 253, 255, 257, 266, 267, 273
Doky, Neils Lan, 223
Donato Deodato (EP), 247
Donato, Joao, 247, 249, 250
Donna Lee, 230, 236
Donny Osmond, 264
Double Clutch, 255
Double Dedication, 257
Double Fun, 250, 261, 270
Double, Double You, 263
Down 4 The Count, 152, 220
Down And Out, 226
Down Beat (magazine), 15, 32, 42, 46, 60, 68, 109, 207, 208
Dr. Funkenstein, 231
Dr. Slate, 148, 224
Dream, 27, 29, 37, 40, 70, 105, 158, 173, 214, 215, 216, 218, 227, 228, 241, 262, 267, 274
Dream Clock, 241
Dream Suite
  Asset Stop / Jane / Crunchy Grenola, 29, 227
Dream Theme, 70, 214, 215, 216, 274
Dreamer, 267
Dreamers Matinee, 262
Dreamland, 233
Dreams, 5, 28, 29, 30, 32, 33, 34, 35, 38, 40, 43, 52, 55, 59, 105, 134, 141, 155, 158, 159, 188, 189, 209, 225, 226, 227, 242, 245, 247, 251, 252, 255, 256, 259, 260, 262, 264, 267, 269, 272
Dreams Of Peace, 256
Dreamsong, 228
Drews, Jurgen D, 250, 262, 271
Drone, 37, 38, 97, 111
Drum machine, 113, 201

Dry Dreams, 251
Dudziak, Urszula, 263
Duke, David, 238
Duke, George, 43, 45, 48, 69, 99, 213, 214, 215, 217, 229, 274
Dunbar, Ronald, 233
Dunbar, Ted, 232
Dune, 249
Duo (In Two Parts), 238
Duprat, Ruria, 221
Dupree, Cornell, 44, 45, 192, 229, 253, 255
Duster, 20
Dylan, Bob, 16
Dynasty, 161, 189, 251, 252
Dyson, Ronnie, 250

E

Earland, Charles, 248, 249, 250, 260, 262, 270, 271
Earth Wind and Fire (band), 28, 56
East River, 67, 213, 215, 216, 217, 274
Easy Living, 242
Easy On, 227
Easy To Love, 243
eBop, 256
Echoes, 252
Echoes Of Ellington, Vol. 2, 252
Economou, Bobby, 230
Eder, Linda, 254, 255, 256, 257
Edith and the Kingpin, 233
Edwards, Debbie, 229, 230
Eeg, Sinne, 258
Egan, Mark, 102, 136, 137, 160, 168, 218
Eggers, David, 225
Ehrlich, Marty, 135, 242, 243
Eighty-One, 246
El Diablito, 252
El Moodo Grande, 253
El Nino, 224
El Noche Sol, 251, 263, 271
El Toro, 249, 261, 270
Eldar, 267
Electric, 4, 33, 51, 254, 259, 263
Electric keyboard (instrument), 176
Electric Lady, 254
Electric piano, 26, 35, 36, 37, 50, 78, 183
Electric Red, 4
Electric Spanking, 51, 263
Electrified Funk, 249, 260, 270
Electronic Wind Instrument (EWI), 6, 94, 95, 186, 187
Elegant People, 237
Elegy, 184, 222
Elegy For Mike, 184, 222
Elektra Records (record label), 53, 92, 233, 237, 239, 240
Elements, 136, 137, 168
Elements (band), 136, 137, 168
Eleven, 237, 256
Eleventh House (band), 5, 21, 39, 41, 43, 52, 58, 77, 189, 228, 230, 247, 248, 260, 269
Eliane Elias Sings Jobim, 266
Elias, Eliane, 11, 92, 101, 110, 124, 131, 136, 188, 214, 218, 237, 238, 241, 251, 252, 256, 257, 258, 264, 266, 267, 272
Ellington, Edward (Duke), 18, 99
Ellis, Don, 45

282

Emergency, 263
Emerick, Randy, 85, 234, 236, 237
Empty Skies, 254
Empty Streets, 241
Encounters, 258
End Of A Rainbow, 248, 260, 269
Englewood Cliffs NJ, 118, 225, 226
Enja 20th Anniversary Sampler, 253
Epilogue, 155
Epiphany, 267
Epitaph, 252
Equinox, 243
Erskine, Peter, 11, 59, 81, 82, 85, 88, 92, 95, 97, 99, 100, 101, 112, 113, 135, 161, 170, 208, 211, 221, 222, 223, 234, 235, 236, 237, 238, 239, 240, 241, 242, 243, 251, 252, 253, 255, 263, 264, 271, 272
Erskoman, 241
Escalator Over The Hill, 158
Escape, 151, 152, 164, 168, 251, 263, 271
Escape Artist, 251, 263, 271
Escher Sketch (A Tale of Two Rhythms), 224
Esther Phillips And Joe Beck, 248, 259, 269
Et Cetera, 253
Ethiopia, 89, 90, 194, 214, 215, 216, 217, 233
Eubanks, Robin, 135, 164, 225, 243, 244, 253
Europe, 45, 71, 110, 137, 167, 229, 238, 248, 259, 269
Evans, Bill, 220
Evans, Gil, 110, 155, 161, 238, 251, 263, 271
Evans, Janice, 233
Evans, Miles, 161
Evans, Sue, 229
Evening Faces, 164, 225
Evening Star, 249
Everyday Everynight, 250, 261, 270
Everything Happens To Me, 242
Everything Is On The One, 231
Everything Must Go, 117
EVI (Electronic Valve Instrument), 94, 95, 120
Evocations, 131, 215
EWI (Electronic Wind Instrument), 6, 94, 95, 96, 98, 99, 101, 107, 108, 111, 112, 113, 116, 120, 121, 122, 124, 127, 129, 130, 132, 136, 176, 195, 196, 204, 208, 210
Exiles, 264
Exit Up Right, 241
Experiment In White, 251
Eye Contact, 267
Eyes Of The Elders, 256

F

Faces & Places, 258
Faddis, Jon, 227, 236, 237, 238, 249, 261, 270
Fagen, Donald, 32, 119, 251, 253, 263, 271
Faitelson, Dalia, 256
Faith, Christine, 215
Fall, 6, 37, 85, 228, 233, 251, 263, 271
Fame [Original Soundtrack], 250
Fannie Mae / Eleven, 237
Farber, Mitch, 58, 252
Faro, Rachel, 247, 259, 269
Farrell, Joe, 43, 44, 229, 249, 261, 270
Farrell, Larry, 243
Fast Emotion, 263
Fate For Breakfast, 262

Faulk, Ken, 234
Fawlty Tenors, 89, 233
Fazendo Hora, 179, 221
Feel It, 248
Feel Me, 250
Feel No Fret, 250, 262, 271
Feels So Good, 248
Feiten, Howard, 235
Feldman, Lawrence, 219, 237, 239, 240, 241, 242, 243
Feldman, Mark, 162, 225
Felix Cavaliere, 247, 259
Felten, Eric, 254
Fender Rhodes (instrument), 50, 70, 72, 126, 257, 266
Fender Rhodes (keyboard), 50, 72
Ferguson, Maynard, 249
Ferla, Joe (recording engineer), 211
Ferris, Glenn, 45, 48, 49, 229, 230
Ferrone, Steve, 87
Festival, 9, 15, 23, 47, 75, 85, 130, 161, 170, 173, 195, 203, 222, 223, 236, 237, 254, 257, 258, 263
Field Song, 228
Fielder, Jim, 22
Fig, Anton, 256
Figments, 256
Figueroa, Sammy, 63, 66, 72, 213, 214, 215, 217, 232
Figure Eight, 37, 228
Finally The Rain Has Come, 267
Finders, Matt, 241, 242
Findley, Charles B, 234
Finnerty, Barry, 67, 71, 73, 102, 213, 214, 215, 217, 218, 251, 263, 271
First, 2, 15, 17, 47, 105, 129, 183, 222, 266
First Tune Of The Set, 183, 222
First Wish, 266
Fisher, Bruce, 261
Fitzgerald, Ella, 41, 181
Five Bars, 134, 242, 243
Five Months from Midnight, 225
Flack, Roberta, 254
Flash Flood, 44, 229
Floating, 77, 215, 232
Flood, 44, 229
Florida, 30, 82, 234, 263
Flying, 239, 250, 252, 262, 265, 266, 271
Flying Cowboys, 252
Focused, 255
Fogelberg, Dan, 263, 264
Folegatti, Ronaldo, 257
Folk music (music genre), 16, 27, 87, 111
Follow Me, 265
Follow The Stars, 222, 246
Footloose, 263
Footprints, 243
For All We Know, 248, 260, 269
For Lovers Only, 264
For Our Children Too, 266
For Rent, 256
Ford, Ricky, 232
Ford, Ron, 233
Fore!, 28
Foregone Conclusion, 166, 181, 221
Forever In The Arms Of Love, 264
Forever Young, 218

283

Forever, For Always, For Love, 251, 263, 271
Forgone Conclusion, 220
Forgotten Love, 230, 231
Forgotten Song, 222, 246
Forman, Mitchel, 240
Formanek, Michael, 242
Fortune, 248, 260, 270
Foster, Alex, 86, 236, 237
Foster, Aloysius, 103, 104, 110, 116, 218, 231, 240, 261
Foster, Frank, 192, 238
Four Chords, 92, 235
Four Miles, 254
Four Shades, 256
Four Worlds, 139, 219
Fowler, Walt, 230
France, 71, 167, 233, 245, 274
Franklin, Aretha, 52, 256
Franklin, Mallia, 233
Frankly Speaking, 266
Franks, Michael, 250, 251, 252, 254, 255, 260, 263, 264, 266, 267, 271, 272, 273
Fratangelo, Lawrence, 233
Free In America, 248, 260, 269
Free Spirits (band), 20, 150
Freedom, 151, 219, 245
Freedom Jazz Dance, 151, 219, 245
Freefall, 172, 221, 222
Freeland, Russ, 234
Freeman, Michele, 261
Freetime, 263
Freeze Frame, 251
Friday Night at the Cadillac Club, 219, 245
Friday the 13th, 238
Fried, Rob, 257
Friedlander, Erik, 162, 225
Friedman, David, 213, 215, 228
Friedman, Jerry, 31, 65, 66, 215
Friends, 5, 32, 34, 227, 241, 247, 251, 253, 254, 255, 257, 258, 259, 260, 263, 265, 266, 267, 268, 269, 272, 273
Friendship, 265
Friesen, David, 265
Frink, Laurie, 238, 239, 240, 241, 242, 243
Frisaura, Lorraine, 260
Frisell, Bill, 114
From All Sides, 264
From Hollywood, 252
From The Ashes, 256
From The Street, 266
Fukamachi, Jun, 248, 249, 250, 260, 261, 262, 270, 271
Full Moon, 247
Fuller, Curtis, 195
Fulwood, Ramon, 50
Funk, 46, 51, 53, 56, 67, 126, 129, 136, 138, 167, 168, 169, 170, 171, 181, 185, 189, 194, 202, 211, 212, 213, 215, 216, 217, 220, 221, 222, 229, 230, 239, 240, 249, 250, 254, 255, 257, 260, 262, 266, 267, 270, 271, 273, 274
Funk Academy, 257
Funky Beta One, 246
Funky Sea, Funky Dew, 64, 67, 68, 213, 215, 216, 217, 274
Funky Snakefoot, 247
Furry Sings the Blues, 233
Furuuchi, Toko, 254, 265, 272

Fusion (music genre), 13, 20, 22, 25, 32, 33, 38, 39, 41, 42, 43, 44, 45, 47, 48, 51, 52, 54, 55, 58, 60, 69, 76, 78, 79, 81, 87, 89, 102, 103, 105, 111, 113, 115, 116, 117, 122, 124, 134, 138, 150, 151, 164, 165, 166, 168, 169, 172, 177, 179, 181, 182, 193, 196
Fusion with Attitude, 257
Future 2 Future, 155
Future Street, 261

G

Gadd, Steve, 11, 34, 63, 66, 69, 75, 88, 90, 92, 120, 173, 192, 213, 214, 215, 227, 232, 233, 235, 238
Gaffney, Henry, 261
Gale, Eric, 248, 249, 260, 270
Galper, Hal, 5, 25, 35, 36, 37, 61, 189, 198, 218, 227, 228, 231, 247, 249, 259, 260, 261, 269, 270
Gambale, Frank, 73, 118, 168, 194
Gambia Africa, 244
Gamin On Ya!, 231
Gardner, Rick, 230
Garfield, David, 256, 267, 273
Garfunkel, Art, 262, 264
Garibaldi, David, 55
Garrett, Kenny, 142
Gaskin, Victor, 36, 227, 228
Gate Of Dreams, 260
Gathering Of Spirits, 245, 246, 267
Gatto, Roberto, 264
Gaucho, 87, 251, 263, 272
Geils, J, 253
Generation X, 255
Geneva Switzerland, 223, 257
Genie, 242, 251, 263, 272
Genres
  avant-garde, 21, 32, 54
  classical, 45, 111, 145, 180, 193, 196
  disco, 24, 49, 60, 65, 69, 78, 274, 275
  folk, 16, 27, 87, 111
  fusion, 13, 20, 22, 25, 32, 33, 38, 39, 41, 42, 43, 44, 45, 47, 48, 51, 52, 54, 55, 58, 60, 69, 76, 78, 79, 81, 87, 89, 102, 103, 105, 111, 113, 115, 116, 117, 122, 124, 134, 138, 150, 151, 164, 165, 166, 168, 169, 172, 177, 179, 181, 182, 193, 196
  jazz-fusion, 11, 13, 20, 24, 25, 26, 27, 29, 32, 34, 38, 45, 55, 56, 58, 61, 63, 64, 67, 68, 73, 74, 76, 78, 79, 86, 87, 88, 91, 94, 96, 98, 103, 106, 109, 118, 119, 120, 121, 122, 123, 124, 125, 126, 128, 131, 133, 139, 160, 167, 168, 178, 185, 186, 187, 188, 189, 198
  mainstream, 27, 32, 37, 39, 54, 71, 87, 89, 90, 94, 105, 106, 109, 113, 116, 117, 122, 139, 140, 151, 156, 172, 180, 187, 188, 197, 198
  R&B, 18, 24, 29, 49, 53, 58, 61, 118, 129, 131, 142, 145, 169, 186, 187, 193, 199
  rock, 11, 18, 20, 21, 22, 23, 24, 25, 26, 27, 28, 30, 33, 35, 36, 38, 39, 40, 42, 44, 45, 47, 51, 52, 57, 63, 64, 67, 75, 76, 77, 81, 87, 99, 110, 119, 120, 122, 123, 127, 131, 138, 167, 168, 172, 184, 189, 195, 196, 197, 199
  soul, 49, 72, 74, 78, 98, 169, 196
Genuit, Klaus, 211

Genus, James, 123, 126, 128, 130, 135, 141, 143, 198, 199, 208, 214, 216, 217, 224, 243
Germany, 114, 275
Gerrits, Louis (discographer), 9, 130, 195, 208, 209, 210, 212
Gershman, Paul, 215
Get On The Good Foot, 247, 259, 269
Get Your Wings, 247, 259, 269
Getting There, 264
Getz, Stan, 28, 38, 110, 181
Ghost Writer, 249, 260, 270
Giant Box, 247
Giant Steps, 236, 237, 242
Gibb, Barry, 251, 263, 272
Gibbs, Michael, 230
Gibson (guitar), 257
Gibson, David, 257
Gillan, Ian, 256
Gillespie, John Birks 'Dizzy', 12, 15, 32, 137, 257, 267
Gillette, Mic, 54
Ginell, R. S. (writer), 21, 207
Ginseng Woman, 249, 260, 270
Giuffredi, Andrea, 257
Give And Take, 160, 266
Give It Up, 166, 220
Give It What U Got, 252, 264, 272
Give Up The Funk (Tear The Roof Off The Sucker), 229
Giving Back, 256, 267, 273
Glass Art, 253
Glenn Alexander, 252
Global Sound-Diamond, 256
Gloria, 182
Go Ahead John, 207
Go Go, 22
God Must Be a Boogie Man, 233
Go-Go, 22
Goines, Lincoln, 239, 240, 241, 242
Going Dutch, 256
Goins, Glen, 229, 230
Golden, Lotti, 247
Goldfinger, 181, 221
Goldings, Larry, 145, 155, 224
Goldstein, Gil, 136, 155, 160, 161, 173, 211, 219, 225, 245, 257
Gomez, Eddie, 11, 33, 75, 77, 88, 92, 93, 95, 97, 192, 215, 218, 232, 233, 235, 237, 238, 239, 252, 263, 264
Gomez, Raymond, 250, 262, 271
Gone Clear, 250, 262, 271
Gonzales, Andy, 243
Good And Plenty, 249, 261, 270
Good Gracious, 127, 214, 217
Good King Bad, 248, 259, 269
Good Paul Sylvan, 247, 259, 269
Good-bye Pork Pie Hat, 233
Goodman, Jerry, 41
Goodwin, Bill, 36, 227
Goose Bumps, 261
Gordon, Peter, 82, 161, 225, 230, 234, 236, 237, 238, 241
Gorelick, Kenneth, 142
Gorrie, Alan, 49
Gottlieb, Danny, 102, 218
Goualch, Pierre-Alain, 246
Grace Under Pressure, 252

Graceland, 116, 137, 251
Grammy (award), 7, 55, 114, 139, 154, 156, 158, 161, 166, 171, 173, 177, 211, 215, 219, 220, 221, 222, 225, 246
Grand Cross, 251, 263, 271
Grand Piano Canyon, 252, 265, 272
Grant, Gary, 238
Grant, Tom, 254
Gratitude 'A So Low', 228
Graves, Peter, 78, 234, 236, 237
Gray Area, 138, 219
Gray, Mark, 69, 70, 72, 214, 215, 217, 235, 251, 263, 271, 272
Grease Piece, 63, 213, 215
Greco, Juliette, 267
Greek Theater (music venue), 163
Green Dolphin Street, 223
Green, Bunky, 250
Green, Grant, 260
Green, Urbie, 238
Green, William, 238
Greene, Lonnie, 233
Gregory Is Here, 228
Griffith, Mark (writer), 207
Griffith, Richard, 233
Grolnick, Don, 6, 11, 30, 31, 52, 55, 57, 58, 59, 62, 63, 64, 69, 88, 92, 95, 105, 108, 111, 121, 122, 134, 135, 141, 142, 160, 162, 164, 175, 189, 192, 199, 209, 212, 213, 214, 215, 217, 223, 227, 233, 235, 237, 239, 240, 241, 242, 243, 251, 252, 253, 255, 263, 264, 266, 267, 272, 273
Groove Elation, 254
Groove Jammy, Vol. 2, 255
Groovewords, 258
Gross, Henry, 263
Grossman, Steve, 16
GRP All-Star Big Band, 253, 256, 273
Gruntz, George, 253
Grusin, David, 179, 253, 266
Guaruja, 103, 177, 218, 221
Guillery, Adrian, 33
Guitar synthesiser, 154, 175
Guitars On The Move, 263
Gunfighter, 228
Gunia, Alex, 252
Gunslinging Birds, 254
Gwizdala, Janek, 200, 258
Gypsy, 77, 215, 232, 260

H

Haas, Steve, 37, 228
Haase, Gary, 165, 166, 220, 257, 268, 273
Habanera, 235
Hackensack, New Jersey (studios), 25
Hadala, Bartosz, 258
Haden, Charlie, 7, 105, 108, 111, 154, 158, 209, 223, 224, 245, 267
Hadrians Wall, 231
Haerter, Harald, 267, 268
Hakim, Omar, 120, 224
Half Moon Lane, 175, 225
Half Past Late, 147, 224
Hall, Carole, 161, 247
Halligan, Dick, 22
Hamilton, Chico, 19

285

Hamm, Stuart, 168
Hammann, Joyce, 162, 225
Hammer, Jan, 15, 41, 42, 97, 265
Hampton, Lionel, 161, 238, 254
Hampton, Locksley Wellington, 232
Hampton, Michael, 229, 230
Hancock, Herbie, 4, 7, 13, 51, 55, 58, 60, 65, 69, 78, 80, 104, 109, 111, 114, 151, 154, 155, 160, 169, 173, 176, 209, 211, 223, 224, 225, 230, 234, 240, 241, 244, 245, 258, 262, 265, 266, 267, 268
Handcuffs, 229
Hands, 251
Hands Down, 251
Hanky Panky, 240
Happy Birthday, 84, 234, 244
Happy Song, 241
Hargrove, Roy, 7, 155, 156, 160, 209, 211, 245
Harlem NYC, 244, 247, 256
Harlem River Drive, 247
Harlequin, 179
Harlow, Andy, 248
Harpoon, 132, 133, 136, 204, 215, 216, 217
Harris, Allen, 261
Harris, Eddie, 148, 151
Harrison, George, 20
Hart, William, 36, 227, 231, 245
Hartman, Dan, 248
Harvey, Michael, 220
Haskins, Clarence, 229, 231
Haslip, Jimmy, 253
Hatcher, Larry, 233
Havana Candy, 261
Havana Cuba, 261
Have You Seen Me Lately?, 265
Hawkins, Coleman, 32
Hayashida, Kenji, 266
Hayden, Shirley, 233
Haynes, Roy, 115, 124
Hazel, Eddie, 50, 231
He Had A Hat, 257
Head Hunters, 55, 114
Head To Head, 253, 265, 272
Heads Up, 250, 253, 262, 271
Hear & Now, 260
Heart & Soul, 258
Heart And Soul
    The Hank Crawford Anthology, 253
Heart Of A Champion, 255
Heart Of Darkness, 134, 242, 243
Heart Of The Matter, 240
Heart Of The Night, 254
Heart To Heart, 249, 261, 271
Hearts And Numbers, 239, 251, 263, 272
Heather, 44, 229
Heavy Metal, 6, 61, 67, 75, 130, 208, 213, 249, 261, 271
Heavy Metal Bebop, 6, 61, 67, 75, 130, 213, 249, 261, 271
Heckstall, Larry, 233
Heirs To Jobim
    A Musical Tribute, 254
Hejira, 79, 233
Hello Big Man, 263
Helm, Levon, 16, 182
Henderson, Joseph, 103, 116, 162, 181, 198, 218
Henderson, Scott, 168

Hentoff, Nat (writer), 25, 207
Herbie Hancock Quartet, 240, 265
Herbie Hancock Special with Bobby McFerrin And Michael Brecker [DVD], 241, 267
Here And There
    The Uncollected B.B. King, 256
Here I Come, 249
Here In My Heart, 266
Here She Comes Now, 31, 227
Herington, Jon, 117, 118, 219, 223
Hero With A Thousand Faces, 241
Herring, Roy, 213, 215
Herwig, Conrad, 253, 258
Hey, Jerry, 55, 238
Hideaway, 70
High Crime, 56
High Gear, 261
High Life, 251
Hino, Terumasa, 230, 250, 262, 263
Hinze, Chris, 249, 260, 261, 266, 270
Hip Hop, 240
His Eyes, Her Eyes, 245
His Majesty The Baby, 242
Hit Factory (recording studio), 116
Hit It Again, 249, 260, 270
Hit Or Miss, 218
Hit The Rhodes, Jack, 257
Hitchcock, Kenneth, 232
Hodges, Johnny, 247
Hofseth, Bendik, 101
Holdsworth, Allan, 73, 194
Holiday, Billy, 32, 41
Holland, Dave, 139, 140, 161, 224, 242, 244
Holley, Major, 238
Holli Be Home, 29, 227
Holliday, Billie, 32, 41
Holliday, Jennifer, 251, 265
Holly Knight, 264
Hollywood, 86, 250, 252
Hollywood Bowl (music venue), 86
Hollywood CA, 86, 250, 252
Hollywood Party Tonight, 250
Holmes, Cecil, 247
Holmes, Nick, 34, 227, 228, 247
Holmes, Rodney, 135, 182, 184, 185, 214, 216, 222
Holmes, Rupert, 249, 256, 261, 270
Holy Forest, 246
Holzman, Adam, 173
Homage, 258
Home Again, 252, 260
Homeless, 264
Honey Man, 238
Hooker, John Lee, 55
Hoover, Nina, 233
Horn Man, 237, 251, 263, 271
Horn, Shirley, 179
Horne, Lena, 247, 263
Horne, Sheila, 233
Horta, Toninho, 252
Hot House, 266
Hotcakes, 259
Hourglass, 266
House Full Of Love
    Music from The Cosby Show, 251, 264, 272
House Of The Rising Sun, 260
Houseparty
    Anthology, 253

286

Houston, Whitney, 52, 56
How Do You Keep The Music Playing?, 238
Howard, Ed, 246
Hubbard, Frederick Dewayne, 195, 260
Hudson, Garth, 16
Hula Dula, 166, 220
Human Bites, 239
Hurdy Gurdy, 115, 219
Hush, 182
Hutchcroft, Kim, 238

I

I Am Three, 256
I Been Through This Before, 153, 220
I Can See Your Dreams, 155, 225
I Do, 71, 214, 215, 216, 235
I Got Rhythm, 112, 243
I Hear a Rhapsody, 238
I Heard It Through The Grapevine, 241
I Love My Music, 249, 261, 270
I Love To Dance, 250
I Loves You Porgy, 243, 246
I Talk to the Trees, 220
I Thought About You, 258
   A Tribute To Chet Baker, 258
I Want to be Happy, 242
Ide, Yasuaki, 265
Idiot Savant (band), 95
If Ever I Should Leave You, 243
If I Be Your Lady, 247
If I Should Lose You, 192, 239
If The Shoe Fits, 250
If You Could Love Me, 257, 267, 273
If You Wanna Boogie...Forget It, 213, 215
If You Would Be Mine, 70
Ile Aye, 221
Ilg, Dieter, 114, 218, 252
Illinois, 105, 232
Imaginary Time, 254
Imagine My Surprise, 5, 30, 31, 227, 247, 259, 269
Implosions, 252
Impressions, 156, 209, 211, 243, 245, 254, 256, 273
Impressions Of Miles Davis, 256
Imprints, 267
Improvisation, 94, 237, 241
Impulse! Records (record label), 54, 109, 139, 141, 208, 209, 223, 224
In A New York Minute, 255, 266, 273
In A Sentimental Mood, 240
In A Silent Way, 25
In A Temple Garden, 250, 262, 271
In Concert, 253
In Essence, 257
In France They Kiss on Main Street, 233
In Love, 251, 261, 262, 263, 267, 271
In Out And Around, 231, 261
In Pursuit Of The 27th Man, 228, 247, 259, 269
In The Door, 265
In The Eighties, 240
In The Idiom, 6, 103, 115, 116, 188, 208, 218, 251
In The Moonlight, 258
In The Night, 249, 254, 260, 266, 270
In The Pocket, 260
In the Presence and Absence of Each Other, 235
In The Public Interest, 247, 259, 269
In The Shadows, 252

In The V.I.P. Room, 257
In Walked Maya, 241
In Your Eyes, 251, 263, 272
Incandescence, 155, 225
Incidentally, 115, 219
Incredible Journey, 239, 251, 264, 272
India, 150, 246
Indian Summer, 254, 266
Indiana, 15, 16, 58, 120
Infant Wilderness, 244
Infinity, 211, 254, 257
Infinity Ltd., 257
Initial Thrill, 264
Inner Conflicts, 249, 261, 270
Inner Mission, 258
Inner Voyage, 267
Inside Out, 67, 130, 185, 213, 215, 216, 217, 222
Instinct, 254
Instructions Inside, 171
Interview, 207, 209, 216
Into the Sun, 7, 136, 138, 160, 209, 211, 219, 254
Intro, 234, 235, 236, 237, 243
Introducing The Eleventh House With Larry Coryell, 228, 247
Introduction / Triple Play, 231
Introduction to Naked Soul, 224
Introspection, 251
Invictus Records (record label), 50
Invitation, 6, 82, 85, 234, 235, 236, 237, 251
Invocation, 257
Ipanema Brazil, 137
Irvine, Weldon, 248, 260, 270
Is What It Is, 258, 265
Ish, 260
Islands, 93, 237, 238
ISM-Ejercicio, 40, 228
It Creeps Up on You, 219
It Is What It Is, 258
It Might Be You, 159, 245
Itoh, Kimiko, 264, 265
Itsbynne Reel, 111, 113, 223, 225, 226
Ivan Lins, 179
Ivers, Eileen, 255
Ivy, Archie, 229

J

J. D. Drews, 250, 262, 271
Jacaranda, 247
Jacknife, 72, 214, 215, 216, 217
Jackson Jr, Paul Milton, 240
Jackson, Michael, 55, 114, 177
Jacksonville FL, 159
Jaco Pastorius, 6, 14, 71, 78, 79, 80, 82, 85, 86, 101, 117, 123, 161, 189, 208, 230, 233, 234, 235, 236, 237, 248, 251, 255, 256, 257, 260, 262, 263, 265, 270
Jamal, Ahmad, 156
James Bond Theme, 244
James Taylor, 42, 59, 154, 224, 247, 251, 252, 259, 260, 263, 264, 265, 266, 267, 269, 272
James, Cheryl, 233
James, Mark, 247, 259, 269
James, Robert McElhiney, 123, 161, 238, 247, 248, 249, 250, 251, 252, 260, 261, 263, 264, 265, 270, 271, 272
James, Tommy, 262

Jamming!, 257
Janet Burgan, 254
Japan, 82, 85, 88, 90, 91, 92, 110, 212, 213, 225, 236, 237, 244, 255, 257, 258, 267, 268
Jarreau, Al, 56, 114, 137, 265
Jarrett, Keith, 58, 145, 159
Jason, Neil, 67, 68, 69, 213, 214, 215, 217
Jazz Central Station
    Global Jazz Poll Winners Vol. 1, 254
    Global Jazz Poll Winners Vol. 2, 255
Jazz club
    7th Avenue South, 5, 60, 61, 87, 88, 91, 135
    Birdland, 184
    Café Au Go-Go, 22
    Penthouse NYC, 19
    Village Gate, 25, 30, 35
    Village Vanguard, 251, 258, 267
Jazz Door (record label), 86, 135, 216, 217, 218, 225, 226, 234, 236, 240
Jazz Fusion Vol. 2, 254, 273
Jazz Grunge, 254, 255
Jazz Hot (magazine), 71, 208
Jazz Lounge Vol. 13, 258
Jazz Masters, 253
Jazz Messengers, 38
Jazz Profile, 254
    Mose Allison, 254
Jazz Sampler, Vol. 1, 255, 273
Jazz Standards, 255, 266, 273
Jazz Takes On Joni Mitchell, 255, 256
Jazz Times (magazine), 105, 208
Jazz To The World, 254, 273
Jazz Workshop Revisited, 23
Jazz-fusion (music genre), 11, 13, 20, 24, 25, 26, 27, 29, 32, 34, 38, 45, 55, 56, 58, 61, 63, 64, 67, 68, 73, 74, 76, 78, 79, 86, 87, 88, 91, 94, 96, 98, 103, 106, 109, 118, 119, 120, 121, 122, 123, 124, 125, 126, 128, 131, 133, 139, 160, 167, 168, 178, 185, 186, 187, 188, 189, 198
JazzNotJazz, 254, 266, 273
Jazzpana, 265
Jeffrey, Paul, 232
Jeffreys, Garland, 249, 251, 253, 257, 260, 261, 263, 265, 267, 270, 271, 272, 273
Jenni Muldaur, 253, 265, 272
Jeremy & The Satyrs, 33
Jeru Blue
    Tribute To Gerry Mulligan, 255
Jesus, 86
Jigsaw, 264
Jill Jones, 251
Jimmy Mulidore & His New York City Jazz Band, 258
Joao Donato, 247, 249, 250
Jobim, Antonio Carlos, 137
Jobson, Eddie, 231
Joel, Billy, 51, 263, 264
John and Mary, 81, 234
John Coltrane, 23, 155, 156, 157, 158, 243, 245, 254
John Dawson Winter III, 247, 259, 269
John McLaughlin, 4, 32, 41, 113, 117, 150, 168, 194, 207, 266
John Patitucci, 156, 160, 162, 164, 173, 225, 245, 264, 265, 266
John Tropea, 43, 235, 248, 249, 260, 261, 269, 270, 271

John, Elton, 55, 56, 248, 254, 260, 270
Johnson, Bashiri, 117, 123, 126, 214, 219
Johnson, David Earl, 229
Johnson, Howard, 230
Johnson, Marc, 114, 241
Johnson, Michael, 262
Johnson, Robert, 233
Joie De Vivre!, 248, 260, 270
Jones Street, 150, 219, 245
Jones, Darryl, 100, 101, 219, 240
Jones, Elvin, 145, 146, 147, 148, 149, 224, 244, 267
Jones, Hank, 145
Jones, Jill, 251
Jones, Quincy (record producer), 55, 177, 179, 238, 251, 261, 263, 272
Jones, Rickie Lee, 251, 252
Jones, Thad, 15, 145
Joni, 6, 15, 79, 171, 199, 233, 255, 256, 262
Joplin Janis, 51
Jordan, Stanley, 256
Jordan, Steve, 69, 75, 77, 130, 132, 133, 214, 215, 217, 232
Joseph, Jonathan, 136, 137, 139, 219
Joshua, 159, 246
Joshua Redman, 159
Journey, 33, 180, 188, 209, 221, 239, 247, 251, 255, 258, 259, 264, 266, 269, 272, 273
Journey Thru An Electric Tube, 33
Joy, 39, 228, 250, 262, 271
Joy Ride, 39, 228
Judith, 248
Juilliard School of Music New York, 114
Jukola, 266
Jun Fukamachi, 248, 249, 250, 260, 261, 262, 270, 271
Jun Fukamachi & The New York All Stars Live, 249, 261, 271
Jun Fukamachi Live At The Triangle Theatre, 249, 260, 270
Jungle Fever, 261
Junkanoo, 254
Just Be Ourselves, 31, 227
Just Between Us, 138, 219
Just One of Those Things, 241
Just Swing Baby, 267
Just The Two Of Us, 266

K

Kadleck, Tony, 243
Kamakyriad, 253
Kasai, Kimiko, 264, 267
Kate Taylor, 249, 261, 271
Katewalk, 255
Kathy, 228
Katz, Mike, 234
Katz, Steve, 21
Katz, Zev, 239
Kawasaki, Ryo, 266
Keep it Steady (Brecker Bump), 213, 215, 217
Keep The Fire, 261
Keep This Love Alive, 252
Kennedy, Tom, 239
Kenny Kirkland, 105, 223, 240
Kent, Jeff, 28, 30, 227
Kenton, Stan, 58
Kessler, Mary, 125, 214

288

Kessler, Maz (record producer), 125, 130, 131, 214
Khan, Chaka, 87, 161, 162, 249, 250, 251, 261, 262, 263, 264, 270, 271, 272
Khan, Steve, 57, 58, 62, 63, 75, 76, 77, 78, 192, 213, 215, 217, 230, 232, 249, 250, 260, 261, 262, 268, 270, 271
Khan, Taka, 229, 231
Kiki Dee, 249, 260, 270
Kikoski, David, 104, 114, 218, 220
Kilgore, Robbie (record producer), 125, 127, 130, 131, 132, 151, 184, 201, 202, 214, 240
Kind Of Blue, 256
King Crimson (band), 75
King Of Blues 1989, 252
King of the Lobby, 125, 214, 217
King, Benjamin Earl Nelson, 258
King, Carole, 31, 264
Kirkland, Kenny, 105, 223, 240
Kishino, Yoshiko, 266
Kiss & Tell, 255
Kissed by Nature, 256
Klocek, Adam, 180, 222, 246
Klugh, Earl, 264
Knepper, James, 232
Knight, Gladys, 88, 262
Knight, Holly, 264
Knopfler, Mark, 263
Koch Jazz (record label), 207, 218
Kohon, Harold, 215
Konitz, Lee, 232
Konrad, Cezary, 180, 221, 222, 246
Kooper, Al, 21, 207, 248, 253, 254
Kowloon Jang, 230
Kozlov, Boris, 225
Krall, Diana, 177
Kryptos, 266
Kubota, Toshinobu, 253, 265, 272
Kuhn, Joachim, 262
Kuhn, Rolf, 254, 255
Kumalo, Bakithi, 136, 137, 219
Kuru / Speak Like A Child, 230
Kyoto, 91, 233

L

L. J. Reynolds, 252, 265, 272
L.A. Is My Lady, 192, 238, 251, 263, 272
La Catedral Y El Toro, 249, 261, 270
LaBarbera, Pat, 257
Lacroix, Jerry, 247
Lady Put The Light Out, 261
Lahm, David, 255, 256
Laird, Rick, 41
Lakatos, Tony, 255
Lakes, 142
Lament, 242
Lampkin, Tyrone, 50, 234
Landgren, Nils, 254, 266, 273
Language, 234, 250, 262, 265, 271
Larry Carlton, 263
Larsen, Neil, 261, 264
Last Frontier, 45, 229
Last Train Home, 98
Last, James, 262
Laswell, Bill, 151
Late Night With You, 235

Lateef, Yusef, 250, 262, 271
Latin, 41, 72, 77, 91, 93, 115, 116, 121, 122, 138, 143, 147, 154, 166, 175, 179, 188, 238, 239, 248, 256, 258
Latin Dance, 238, 239
Latin Jazz Fantasy, 256
Lauper, Cyndi, 257
Laurent, Gautier, 246
LaVerne, Andy, 254
Laws, Hubert, 234, 247, 248, 251, 259, 269
Lazar, Rick Shadrach, 255
Lazy Day, 238, 239
Le Lis, 43
Lead Me On, 261
Leave That Boy Alone!, 262
Lebous, Martee, 248, 260, 269
Ledford, Mark, 118, 214, 219, 266
Lee, David, 233
Lee, John, 55, 230, 248, 260, 269
Lee, Keiko, 257
Lee, Will, 30, 52, 55, 59, 62, 63, 102, 123, 127, 152, 165, 170, 182, 183, 184, 185, 192, 206, 211, 212, 213, 214, 215, 217, 218, 220, 221, 222, 227, 235, 238, 239, 241, 244, 253
Lefty, 264
LeMel, Gary, 255, 267, 273
Lennon, John, 48, 69, 75, 259
Lennon, Julian, 263
Leonhart, Jay, 253, 265, 272
Lerman, Danny, 257
Let It Go, 165, 172, 220, 221, 222
Letters, 253
Letting Go, 249, 260, 261, 270
Leverkusener Jazztage Festival, 170
Leviev, Milcho, 45, 46, 229
Levin, Tony, 34, 75, 77, 78, 193, 200, 215, 227, 228, 232
Levitate, 57, 172, 212, 215, 221, 222
Levy, Jesse, 215
Lew Tabackin Quartet, 251
Lewis, Huey, 28, 55
Lewis, Huey and the News (band), 28, 55
Lewis, Jimmy, 226
Lewis, Mel, 15, 260
Lewis, Tracey, 234
Lewis, Victor, 246
Lewis, Webster, 248
Liberated Brother, 38, 228
Liberty City, 80, 83, 234, 235, 236, 237
Liberty Records (record label), 24
Lieberman, Lori, 261
Liebman, Dave, 110, 245
Lies, 252, 264, 272
Life Changes, 256
Life Colors, 265
Life Stories, 264
Lifetime (band), 250, 262, 271
Light at the End of the Tunnel, 230
Light My Fire, 258
Lights On Broadway, 263
Like A Child, 240
Like A Thief In The Night, 254
Like That, 261
Lincoln Center, 241
Lincoln Center (music venue), 241
Lindsay, Gary, 234
Linhart, Peter, 254

Lins, Ivan, 179
Lion, Alfred, 24
Lionel Hampton, 161, 238, 254
Lippert, Jan, 267
Lipsius, Fred, 22
Lipuma, Tommy (producer), 235
Listen, 126, 252, 255, 256, 264, 267, 272, 273
Listen Up!, 252, 255, 264, 272
Little Big Horn, 263
Little Help From My Friends, 241
Little Miss P, 218
Live, 6, 7, 11, 61, 67, 68, 75, 87, 100, 114, 123, 128, 135, 137, 138, 149, 167, 177, 188, 207, 208, 209, 210, 216, 217, 218, 220, 225, 226, 229, 231, 235, 236, 237, 238, 240, 244, 246, 248, 249, 250, 251, 252, 253, 254, 255, 256, 257, 258, 259, 260, 261, 262, 263, 264, 265, 267, 268, 269, 270, 271, 272, 273
Live & Let Live - Love For Japan, 258
Live And Outrageous [DVD], 236, 257
Live At Basin Street East, 257
Live At Montreaux, 249, 261, 271
Live At Sweet Basil, 6, 114, 138, 208, 218, 252
Live At The Aurex Jazz Festival, 236, 257
Live At The Blue Note, 244, 251, 254, 255, 258, 267
Live At The Blue Note (N.Y.C.), 255
Live At The Bottom Line, 262
Live At The Green Mill, 256
Live At The Theatre Boulogne-Billancourt, Paris, 252
Live At The Town Hall, New York City, 255
Live At The Village Vanguard, 251, 258, 267
Live At The Village Vanguard 1978, 258
Live At The Village Vanguard Volume 3 [DVD], 267
Live In Europe, 229, 248, 259, 269
Live In Japan [DVD], 257
Live In Japan And Canada 1982 [DVD], 236, 257
Live in Lugano 1983 [DVD], 238, 251, 263, 271
Live In Montreal [DVD], 235, 257
Live In Montreux, 261
Live In Time, 254
Live In Tokyo, 216, 240, 258, 264, 268, 273
Live In Tokyo 1986, 240, 264
Live In Tokyo, U-Port Hall, 1995 [DVD], 258, 268, 273
Live On Broadway, 263
Live With Randy Brecker, 246, 258
Live!, 250, 253
Live! Coast To Coast, 250
Living In The Crest Of A Wave, 168
Lloyd, Ian, 261
Local Hero (Original Sound Track), 263
Locke, Joe, 220
Locker, Richard, 215, 220
Loeb, Chuck, 97, 98, 240, 241, 242, 256, 265, 266
Loggins, Kenny, 261
London UK, 47, 125, 134, 141, 182, 210, 243, 247, 255, 259, 267, 269, 273
Long Way Around, 234
Longhorn And London Bridges, 247, 259, 269
Longmire, Wilbert, 250, 262, 271
Longo, Mike, 248, 253, 254
Look, 227, 250, 256, 261, 267, 271, 273
Look In His Eyes, 227
Look Out, 250, 261, 271
Lookovsky, Harry, 215
Loose Threads, 175, 225

Lorber, Jeff, 257, 258
Los Angeles CA, 13, 17, 24, 45, 58, 142, 159, 204
Lost 4 Words, 119, 219
Lost In The Stars
 The Music Of Kurt Weill, 252
Lotti Golden, 247
Loud Jazz, 117
Louisiana, 101
Lovano, Joseph, 145, 242, 245
Love Explosion, 249, 261, 270
Love Is, 246, 249, 253, 263, 265, 272
Love Is Starting Now, 253, 265, 272
Love Island, 249
Love Like Ours, 159, 245
Love Play, 78, 215, 232, 260
Love Remembers, 253
Love Vibrations, 226
Love X 3, 253
Lovely Lady, 63, 213, 215
Lover Man, 89, 233, 243
Loving You, 231
Low-Lee-Tah, 39, 228
Loxodrome, 93, 237, 238
Lubahn, Doug, 28, 30, 227
Lucky Seven, 250, 261, 271
Lullaby, 244
Lumia, Guy, 215
Lunarputians, 44, 229
Lunatic Taxi, 266
Lundy, Carmen, 255
Lush Life, 104
Lyle Mays, 79, 91, 132, 233, 252
Lynn, Cheryl, 261

M

Mabern, Harold, 145
Maca, 221
MacDonald, Donald, 18, 33, 227, 228
MacDonald, Ralph, 49, 63, 192, 212, 213, 215, 217, 238, 249, 250, 261, 262, 266, 270, 271
MacDougal Street, 241
Macero, Teo (record producer), 256
Machado, Sizao, 221
Machismo, 252, 264, 272
Machu Picchu, 244
Mack The Knife, 13, 238
Mack, Jimmy, 261
MacPherson, Charles, 11
Mad Hope, 257
Madame Toulouse, 142, 224
Madness, 247, 259, 269
Maelen, Jimmy, 250
Magazine St., 258
Magic, 69, 76, 109, 180, 215, 221, 232, 247, 248, 249, 253, 257, 261, 262, 270
Magic Carpet, 76, 215, 232
Magic Land, 257
Magic Seven, 180, 221
Magic Theater, 248
Magic Windows, 69, 109, 262
Magnetic, 6, 98, 99, 100, 117, 125, 240, 264
Magnetic Love, 99, 100, 240
Mahavishnu, 32, 40, 41, 42, 43, 45, 47, 48, 52, 58, 73, 86, 168
Mahavishnu Orchestra (band), 32, 40, 41, 42, 45, 47, 48, 58, 73, 86

290

Mahogany, Kevin, 266
Mainieri, Michael, 5, 6, 11, 18, 32, 33, 34, 59, 61, 74, 75, 76, 77, 78, 87, 88, 96, 101, 117, 173, 208, 215, 227, 228, 232, 233, 235, 237, 238, 239, 240, 243, 244, 247, 250, 259, 260, 262, 269, 271
Mainstream (music genre), 27, 32, 37, 39, 54, 71, 87, 89, 90, 94, 105, 106, 109, 113, 116, 117, 122, 139, 140, 151, 156, 172, 180, 187, 188, 197, 198
Majal II, David, 234
Make Room For Me, 258
Malabe, Frank, 235, 238, 239, 240, 241, 242
Malach, Robert, 239, 240, 241, 243
Malasia (Malaysia), 221
Malone, Russell, 231
Malone, Tom, 230, 235
Malta, Yoshiaki, 232
Man, Slim, 255
Manchester, Melissa, 52, 263
Manchester, Sue, 227, 228
Mandel, Mike, 39, 228, 230
Mandoki, Leslie, 253, 254, 265, 266, 272, 273
Mango Theory, 266
Manhattan NYC, 17, 114, 139, 141, 145, 176, 206, 247, 248, 249, 254, 256, 257, 259, 260, 269
Manhattan School of Music, 114
Manhattan Strut, 247, 259, 269
Manhattan Transfer (band), 248, 249, 259, 260, 269
Manhattan Vibes, 256
Manilow, Barry, 52
Mann, Bob, 30, 36, 212, 215, 217, 227, 228
Mann, Herbert Jay, 250, 254, 262, 263, 271
Mantilla, Ray, 232
Mantooth, Frank, 254
Manuel, Richard, 16
Marc Copland And, 267
Marchica, Ray, 241
Marcondes, Caito, 221
Marcus Miller, 69, 71, 74, 120, 131, 214, 215, 217, 235, 238, 239
Mardin, Arif, 49, 247, 258, 259, 268, 269, 273
Mariah Carey, 162
Marilyn & Billy, 249, 261, 270
Marini, Lou, 58, 66, 213, 215, 231
Marinucci, Bruno, 258
Mark James, 247, 259, 269
Mark Murphy Sings Nat King Cole And More, 255, 267, 273
Markowitz, Phil, 240, 242, 243, 245
Marsalis, Branford, 142, 203
Marsh, Hugh, 264
Martignon, Hector, 255
Martin, Arif (arranger), 191
Martin, Lois, 162, 225
Mason Sr, Harvey, 212, 215, 217
Master Plan, 264
Mastertouch, 264
Masuo, Yoshiaki, 250, 262, 271
Mating Call, 254
Matrix, 196
Matta, Nilson, 258
Matthews, David, 249, 250, 251, 262, 263, 271
Maupin, Bennie, 41, 226
Mauriat, Paul, 249, 261, 270
Maximoff, Richard, 215
Maxine, 261

May The Cube Be With You, 251, 263, 272
Maya, 241
Mayall, John, 250, 262, 271
Mayer, John, 182
Mays, Lyle, 79, 91, 132, 233, 252
Maz & Kilgore (record producers), 127, 132, 151, 184
McBee, Cecil, 245
McCandliss, Paul, 236, 237
McCann, Les, 182
McCartney, Paul, 69
McCoo, Marilyn, 249, 261, 270
McCoy, Corky, 105, 139, 140, 211, 224, 254
McCracken, Hugh, 227, 228, 235
McCreary, Lew, 238
McCullough, Ullanda, 215
McDonald, Ralph, 56, 69, 213, 214
McFarland, Gary, 247
McFerrin, Bobby, 32, 240, 241, 267
McGriff, Jimmy, 249, 261, 270
McGruder, Jeanette, 234
McIntosh, Robbie, 49
McIntyre, Onnie, 49
McKinney, Carlos, 244
McLaughlin, John, 4, 32, 41, 113, 117, 150, 168, 194, 207, 266
McWilliams, Paulette, 215
Me Leve, 178, 221
Me Myself An Eye, 232, 250, 261, 271
Medianoche, 141, 243, 266
Medicated Goo, 31, 227
Mehldau, Brad, 159, 173, 175, 225, 245
Mehmari, Andre, 221
Mel, 15, 49, 260
Mel Lewis And Friends, 260
Mellow, 250, 263, 271
Members Only, 264
Mendelson, Leslie, 258
Mendoza, Vince, 111, 159, 170, 211, 221, 222, 252, 264, 267, 272
Mental Images, 253
Meowbaby, 257
Mercury High
  The Story Of Ian Gillan, 256
Mercy Street, 244
Merge, 250, 261, 271
Merry Go Town, 183, 185, 222
Metheny, Pat, 4, 13, 27, 79, 88, 91, 105, 106, 107, 108, 118, 137, 139, 140, 145, 146, 147, 148, 154, 155, 159, 160, 161, 173, 176, 188, 199, 211, 223, 224, 225, 233, 244, 262
Metropole, 18, 19, 258
Metzke, Paul, 227, 228
Mexico City, 161
Mezgo, 264
Miami, 30, 59, 97, 136, 137, 150
Miami Vice (TV Series), 97
Michael Brecker Band In Japan [DVD]
  Select Live Under The Sky, 267
Michael Wendroff, 247, 259, 269
Michel Colombier, 262
Michele Freeman, 261
Midler, Bette, 191, 248, 250, 260, 262, 270, 271
Midnight, 140, 154, 168, 174, 181, 221, 224, 225, 266
Midnight Creeper, 168
Midnight In The Garden Of Good And Evil, 266

Midnight Mood, 154, 225
Midnight Voyage, 140, 224
Milagro, 265
Mile by Jazz Mile, 255
Miles, 4, 12, 15, 25, 26, 29, 32, 35, 37, 38, 41, 51, 67, 70, 71, 72, 74, 86, 104, 106, 109, 114, 120, 122, 123, 127, 130, 131, 139, 141, 145, 149, 150, 151, 155, 156, 157, 161, 167, 173, 174, 181, 193, 198, 207, 208, 214, 220, 223, 227, 248, 253, 254, 256, 262, 265, 266, 267, 273
Miles 2 Go, 266
Miles Ahead, 155, 157
Miles Away, 220
Miles Davis, 4, 12, 15, 25, 26, 32, 35, 37, 41, 51, 70, 71, 74, 86, 104, 106, 120, 122, 127, 130, 139, 141, 145, 149, 151, 155, 156, 157, 167, 173, 181, 193, 207, 208, 256, 267, 273
Miles Smiles, 151
Miles To Miles
    In The Spirit Of Miles Davis, 256, 267, 273
Miles, Barry (writer), 248
Miles, Jason, 120, 214, 223, 256, 262, 265, 266, 267, 273
Milkowski, Bill (writer), 79, 83, 84, 85, 103, 104, 167, 208, 209
Milky Way, 253
Miller, Judd, 120, 159, 204, 208, 223
Miller, Marcus, 69, 71, 74, 120, 131, 214, 215, 217, 235, 238, 239
Millikan, Bob, 239, 240, 241, 242, 243
Million To One, 254
Million, Steve, 254, 255
Millman, Sophie, 258
Milton, 122, 224, 243
Mind Games, 49, 259
Mine Is Yours, 240
Mingus, 11, 79, 145, 161, 189, 218, 232, 250, 251, 252, 253, 254, 255, 256, 258, 261, 262, 271
Mingus Big Band 93
    Nostalgia In Times Square, 253
Mingus, Charles, 145, 232, 250, 252, 258, 261, 262, 271
Minh, 152, 165, 166, 181, 182, 220, 221, 222, 253, 255, 257, 266, 267, 273
Minimoog (instrument), 50
Minnelli, Liza, 254
Minsk, 121, 224
Mintzer, Bob, 59, 81, 82, 83, 85, 117, 119, 162, 189, 219, 234, 235, 236, 237, 239, 240, 241, 242, 243, 251, 252, 254, 263, 264, 265, 271, 272
Mironov, Jeff, 102, 214, 215, 218, 239, 241
Mirror Of My Mind, 266
Miss You In New York, 266
Misstery, 157, 245
Mister Magic, 247
Mitchell, Joni, 6, 15, 79, 171, 199, 233, 255, 256, 262
Mixed Grill, 170, 220
Mixed Roots, 261
Moanin', 256
Mobo, 264
Mobo Splash, 264
Modal music, 26, 38, 93, 106, 107, 109, 126, 139, 141, 142, 143, 149, 170, 174, 203, 204
Mode (of music), 65, 91, 103, 108, 114, 136
Modern Drummer (magazine), 48
Modern Times, 6, 95, 96, 97, 100, 239, 263

Modus Operandy, 164, 225
Moffett, Charnett, 264
Molineaux, Othello, 137, 230, 234, 235, 236, 237, 253
Momento, 89, 233
Monet, Kash, 215
Money For Nothing, 252, 264, 272
Money in the Pocket, 154
Monheit, Jane, 267
Monkey, 227, 249, 260, 265, 266, 270
Monkey Island, 249, 260, 270
Monster, 69
Montgomery, John Leslie (Wes), 32, 140
Montgomery, Wes, 32, 140
Montreal Canada, 85, 235, 236, 257
Montreal Jazz Festival, 85, 236
Montreux Jazz Festival, 47, 75, 258, 263
Montreux Jazz Festival 2009 [DVD], 258
Montreux Jazz Festival -25th Anniversary, 263
Montreux Switzerland, 47, 75, 77, 138, 215, 232, 250, 258, 261, 262, 263, 271
Mood, 99, 101, 154, 225, 240
Moody Modes, 46, 230
Moogy II, 250
Moon Germs, 44, 45, 229
Mooncycle, Makeeba, 165, 220
Moonlight Serenade, 242
Moonlighting, 255, 267, 273
Moonstone, 252
Moontide, 116, 218, 219
Morales, Richie, 72, 214, 215, 217
Moran, George, 238
More Jazz Takes On Joni Mitchell, 256
More Pointing, 239
More To Love, 228
Moreira, Airto, 69, 192, 214, 215, 217
Morgan, Lee, 195
Moritat, 254
Morning, 27, 87, 148, 218, 223, 224, 244, 250, 252, 262, 263, 265, 271
Morning Dance, 87, 250, 262, 271
Morning Island, 262
Morning Song, 27, 218
Morning Sun, 223, 263
Morris, Russel, 248, 259, 269
Morton, Brian (writer), 156
Mosello, Joe, 241
Moses, Bob, 18, 20, 248
Moses, J. C., 231
Mossman, Michael Phillip, 243
Mosson, Cordell, 229, 231
Mothership Connection, 51, 229, 248, 259, 269
Mothership Connection (Star Child), 229
Motion Of Love, 257
Motion Poet, 241, 252, 264, 272
Mottola, Tony, 238
Mount Fuji Jazz Festival, 173
Mouzon, Alphonze, 39, 77, 228
Move, 231, 250, 262, 263, 271
Mr. Chips, 251
Mr. Fone Bone, 235, 240
Mr. Fonebone, 236, 238
Mr. Funk, 240
Mr. Max!, 252
Mr. Skinny, 118, 219
Mr. X, 266
Mraz, George, 15, 231, 232

Mtume, James, 230
Muchacha Bonita, 244
Muhammad, Idris, 226, 248, 249, 253, 260, 270
Muldrow, Sidney, 238
Muller, Johannes, 246
Mulligan, Gerry, 255, 263
Multiplication, 249
Murata, Yoichi, 257
Murder, 251, 263, 272
Murphey, Brett, 234
Murphy, Elliott, 260
Murphy, Mark, 247, 248, 255, 259, 266, 267, 269, 273
Music For Soulful Lovers, 247
Music For Two Brothers, 255
Music From Siesta, 120
Music On The Edge, 252
My Corner Of The Sky, 254, 266, 273
My Favorite Songs Vol. 1, 267
My Favourite Things, 243
My Lady, 13, 31, 192, 227, 238, 251, 263, 272
My One And Only Love, 223, 264
My Romance, 240, 265, 266
My Ship, 155, 157, 158, 225, 245
My Turn, 253
Mysterious Traveller, 95
Mystery Walk, 251, 263, 272

N

N.Y. Special, 217
N.Y.C., 255
Naima, 157, 245
Nakagawa, Eijiro, 255, 266, 273
Naked Soul, 140, 224
Nal Tarahara, 258
Nalecz-Niesiolowksi, Marcin, 221
Name Game, 27, 218
Nardis, 19
Narell, Andy, 267
Nascente, 154, 225
Natural Ingredients, 250
Nature Boy, 247, 256, 267, 273
    The Standards Album, 256, 267, 273
Naughty, 87, 250, 262, 271
Nearness Of You
    The Ballad Book, 224, 267
Neesh, 123
Neloms, Bob, 232
Nelson, Billy, 50
Nelson, Gail, 226
Nelson, Oliver, 247
Neptune, 253, 265, 272
Net Man, 264
Never Alone, 121, 164, 224, 225
Never Die Young, 264
Never Letting Go, 249, 260, 270
Neville, Aaron, 256, 267, 273
New Beginning, 258, 267
New Doo Review, 234
New Jersey, 25, 102, 145
New Moon Shine, 252, 265, 272
New Orleans LA, 80, 139, 159
New Rochelle, 110
New Sensations, 251, 263, 272
New Weave, 251, 264, 272

New York, 15, 16, 17, 18, 19, 20, 21, 24, 25, 29, 32, 33, 34, 41, 45, 49, 51, 52, 58, 59, 61, 67, 71, 74, 75, 85, 86, 87, 90, 92, 94, 101, 103, 106, 110, 114, 117, 124, 125, 137, 139, 141, 142, 145, 153, 154, 156, 159, 160, 161, 162, 164, 167, 182, 183, 185, 189, 191, 192, 193, 197, 201, 204, 207, 208, 210, 227, 231, 241, 244, 249, 251, 252, 254, 255, 256, 258, 261, 262, 263, 264, 266, 267, 270, 271, 272, 273
New York City, 15, 41, 110, 153, 161, 210, 251, 254, 255, 258, 263, 271
New York Connection, 261
New York Minute, 244, 255, 266, 273
New York Rendezvous, 252, 264, 272
New York Sessions, 256
New York Times (newspaper), 106, 208, 263
Newman, Joseph, 238
Next Exit, 253
Nguini, Vincent, 265
Nice To Have Met You, 250
Nichka, 92, 235
Nicholson, Stuart (writer), 33, 207
Night Flight, 62, 63, 213, 215
Night In Calisia, 222, 246
Night Jessamine, 163, 225
Night Life, 248, 259, 269
Night Lights, 260
Night Of The Thumpasorus Peoples, 229
Night Song, 243
Nightfall, 159, 245
Night-Glo, 251
Nightingale, Maxine, 261
Nightline, 262
Nightline New York, 262
Nighttown, 108, 134, 242, 253
Nightwind, 264
Nightwings, 235
Nippon Columbia (record company), 88
Niteflyte, 250, 261, 271
NL 4, 91, 235
No Lonely Nights, 159, 245
No Return, 256
No Scratch, 218
No Smoking, 260
No Words, 180, 221
Nobody Knows, 226
Nock, Mike, 231, 261
Nomad, 253, 255, 257, 267, 273
Nonsequence, 256
Noodling, 29
Norby, Caecilie, 253, 254, 257, 266, 273
North Sea Jazz Festival, 9, 130, 195
Northern Cross, 93, 237, 238
Norwegian Wood, 244
Nostalgia, 253
Nostalgic Journey, 7, 180, 188, 209, 221, 258
    Tykocin Jazz Suite, 7, 180, 188, 209, 221, 258
Not A Word, 241
Not Ethiopia, 89, 90, 194, 214, 215, 216, 217, 233
Not Tonight, 69, 214, 215, 274
Nothing Personal, 108, 223, 226, 242
Notre Dame Jazz Festival, 15, 23
Now & Then
    A Portrait, 258
Now Hear This, 247
Now Is The Time, 258
Now Voyager, 251, 263, 272

Now You Know, 97, 239
Nuance
　The Bennett Studio Sessions, 258
Nugent, John, 255
Nussbaum, Adam, 110, 111, 119, 120, 223, 226
NYC Records (record label), 34, 88, 91, 208, 227, 233, 235, 240
Nyro, Laura, 248, 253, 256, 260, 265, 267, 270, 272, 273

O

Oberheim (synthesiser), 97, 100, 196
Objects Of Desire, 251, 263, 271
Obsession, 251, 264, 272
Oceans Between Us, 261
October Road, 267
Odds or Evens, 129
Ode to the Doo Da Day, 224
Odyssey, 248, 249, 250, 261, 270
Off the Wall, 56
Ogerman, Claus, 235, 252, 256, 260, 263, 265, 267, 272, 273
Oh My Stars, 57, 212, 215
Oh!, 253
Ohmori, Akira, 232
OkonKole Y Trompa, 230
Okura, Meg, 225
Old Devil Moon, 255
Old Town, 97, 239
Oleo, 150, 219, 241, 245
Olson, Byron, 253
On Again, Off Again, 261
On Broadway, 263
On Green Dolphin Street, 223
On The Backside, 127, 214
On The Corner, 160, 261, 264
On The Mark, 264
On The Move, 250, 262, 263, 271
On The Rise, 184, 222
On The Town, 248
One Bird, One Stone, 242
One by One, 247
One Finger Snap, 173, 243
One Man Band, 240
One Man Dog, 247, 259, 269
One More Angel, 266
One Night, 244, 268
One Night In Japan [DVD], 244, 268
One People, 243
One Thing Led to Another, 220
One Trick Pony, 250, 262, 271
One Way Road To My Heart, 258
One-Eyed Jack, 249, 261, 270
Ono, Yoko, 48, 254, 263, 266, 373
Oops, 96, 100, 239, 240
Opera Philharmonic, Bialystok Podlasie, 221
Opus Pocus, 230
Or Come Fog, 134, 242, 243
Oran, 243
Orange Was The Color Of her Dress, Then Blue Silk, 238
Orchestra, Kalisz Philharmonic, 180, 222, 246
Orchestra, Pirineos Jazz, 257
Orchestra, The Syncophonic, 250, 262, 271
Ordinary Man, 250, 261, 271
Oriente, 178, 221

Orienthology, 222, 246
Origin, 161
Original Rays, 108, 223, 226
Original Soundtrack, 249, 250, 251, 261, 262, 263, 264, 266, 270, 271, 272
Orloff, Gene, 66
Ornella E..., 251, 264, 272
Osaka Japan, 237
Osby, Greg, 240, 241
Osmium, 50
Osmond, Donny, 264
Othos Puxados, 221
Out Of Nowhere, 267
Out Of The Loop, 163, 171, 184, 204, 205, 211, 214, 253, 265, 272
Out On The Street, 253, 265, 272
Outbreak, 162, 256, 267, 273
Outlet, 264
Outrance, 149, 224
Over Crystal Green, 256, 267, 273
Over the Hills, 246
Overseas Call, 249, 261, 270
Overture, 151, 220
Owen, Chuck, 258
Owens, Jimmy, 43
Ozone, Makoto, 258

P

Pacific Fire, 248, 259, 269
Pac-Man Blues (Fannie Mae), 237
Paint It Blue, 254, 266, 273
Palau de La Musica (music venue), 128
Palladium, 232
Palmer, Robert, 207, 250, 261, 270
Palmer, Robert (writer), 207, 250, 261, 270
Panama, 41, 45
Pandamandium, 102, 218
Panhandler, 46, 230
Panita, Pawel, 180, 221, 222, 246
Pannall, Stevie, 234
Pao, Eugene, 264, 266
Papa Lips, 237, 238, 241, 251, 263, 271
Para Nada (For Nothing), 102, 218
Paradox, 6, 88, 91, 235, 263
Parahyba, Joao, 221
Parcival, 260
Paris by Night, 253
Paris France, 233, 252, 253, 257, 267, 273
Paris, Mica, 257, 267, 273
Parker, Charlie (Bird), 12, 35, 36, 37, 89, 112 159, 163, 227, 242, 245, 247, 250, 259, 262, 269, 271
Parker, Chris, 52, 55, 62, 63, 66, 102, 212, 213, 215, 217, 218
Parker, Maceo, 49, 229, 230, 234
Parliament / Funkadelic (band), 5, 49, 50, 51, 117, 189, 229, 230, 233, 248, 250, 259, 260, 262, 263, 269, 270, 271
Parnello, Joe, 238
Parris, Gil, 257, 258
Part Time Kiss, 244
Parting Should Be Painless, 263
Pasqua, Alan, 254, 265, 266, 273
Passage, 267
Passionfruit, 251
Pastiche, 249

Pastora, Lee, 229
Pastoral (To Jaco), 152, 220
Pastorius, Jaco, 6, 14, 71, 78, 79, 80, 82, 85, 86,
   101, 117, 123, 161, 189, 208, 230, 233, 234,
   235, 236, 237, 248, 251, 255, 256, 257, 260,
   262, 263, 265, 270
Pat Metheny Group, 79, 91
Patch of Blue, 92, 235
Patitucci, John, 156, 160, 162, 164, 173, 225, 245,
   264, 265, 266
Paul Bollenback, 150, 151, 219, 245, 257
Paul Simon, 6, 31, 58, 116, 124, 132, 137, 176, 250,
   251, 252, 259, 260, 262, 265, 271, 272
Pavane, 251
Pavone, Nat, 227, 228
Pawlik, Wlodek, 180, 209, 221, 222, 246, 258
Payne, Michael, 234
Payne, Sonny, 41
Peace, 226, 227, 243, 246, 254, 255, 256, 266, 273
Peace Of Mind, 227
Peace Piece, 254
Peace Pieces
   The Music Of Bill Evans, 254
Pearson, Columbus Calvin, 18, 24, 26, 188, 189,
   218, 247
Pedro Brasil, 177, 221
Peek-A-Groove, 234
Peel, Jerry, 234, 238, 241
Peep, 224
Peg, 257
Pelton, Shawn, 214
Pendergrass, Teddy, 250
Pendulum, 146, 147, 224, 250, 258
Penn, Clarence, 165, 220
Pensando em Voce, 244
Penthouse (jazz club), 19
People Get Ready, 266
People In Room No.8, 254, 266, 273
Pepper, Jim, 20
Peranzetta, Gilson, 179, 221
Percussion solo, 236
Performance, 114, 139, 196, 211, 215, 219, 259
Perhaps, 34, 40, 56, 61, 66, 71, 94, 99, 136, 149,
   179, 196
Perla, Gene, 244
Permit Me To Introduce You To Yourself, 226
Persimmons, 91, 233, 242
Persistent Dreams, 252
Person, Houston, 226
Peskin, Joel C. (writer), 208
Petals, 66, 213, 215, 274
Peter Bliss, 249, 261, 270
Peter Delano, 265
Peter Erskine, 11, 59, 81, 82, 85, 88, 92, 95, 97, 99,
   100, 101, 112, 113, 135, 161, 170, 208, 211,
   221, 222, 223, 234, 235, 236, 237, 238, 239,
   240, 241, 242, 243, 251, 252, 253, 255, 263,
   264, 271, 272
Pezband, 249
P-Funk (Wants To Get Funked Up), 229
Phantom Navigator, 113
Pharaoh, 21
Philadelphia PA, 15, 23, 113, 115, 117, 257
Phillips (electronics company), 219, 245, 248, 259,
   260, 269
Phillips, Esther, 248, 259, 260, 269
Phoenix, J, 165, 220

Phonogenic Not Just Another Pretty Face, 249, 261,
   270
Piano Introduction To No Words, 221
Pick Up the Pieces, 49, 56
Pickett, Lenny, 54
Picture Perfect Morning, 265
Picture This, 117, 252
Pierson, Jon, 227, 228
Pilgrimage, 7, 107, 173, 176, 211, 225, 267
Pillow, Charles, 161, 225
Pipe Dream, 27, 218
Pirates, 251
Platos Retreat And Other Funky Delights, 249
Play Jaco
   A Tribute To Jaco Pastoruis, 256
Plush Funk, 51, 250, 262, 271
Point Of No Return, 256
Point Of Presence, 266
Point Of View, 37, 228
Pointing At The Moon, 239
Politics, 255
Polydor Records, 24
Pomeranz, David, 247
Poole, Carla, 235, 238
Pools, 92, 93, 237, 238, 239
Pope, Mike, 256, 267, 273
Porter, Cole, 134, 253
Portrait, 96, 100, 230, 236, 239, 240, 258
Portrait of Tracy, 230, 236
Posk, Anthony, 234
Potter, Chris, 137, 181
Poussez!, 250
Powell, Benny, 238
Powell, Bud, 145
Powell, Doc, 256
Power Of Soul, 248
Power Play, 264
Power Station, 213, 223, 224
Prairie Madness, 247, 259, 269
Pratt, Andy, 249, 260, 270
Prayer for Peace, 243
Prelude, 231
Present Tense, 266
Presley, Elvis, 75
Prestia, Francis Rocco, 55
Price, Tony, 238
Priceless Jazz, 217, 255
Priceless Jazz 25
   Brecker Brothers, 217
Priceless Jazz Sampler, 255
Priceless Jazz Sampler, Vol. 4, 255
Prime Time Workout, 263
Prince, 4, 157, 181, 207, 221, 248, 257
Prince, Roland, 248
Princess, 248, 260, 269
Prism, 159, 245
Private Eye, 42
Progressions
   100 Years Of Jazz Guitar, 257
Proof, 190
Psychedelic Years, 253
Pugh, Jim, 234, 241
Pullen, Don, 249
Pulp Fusion, Vol. 2
   Return To The Tough Side, 255
Punchline, 252
Punk Jazz, 83, 234, 235, 256

295

The Jaco Pastorius Anthology, 256
Purdie, Bernard, 218
Purim, Flora, 249, 250, 261, 270
Purple Haze, 1
Purpura, Craig, 232
Pursuit Of Happiness, 249, 261, 270
Push, 151
Pushing Against The Flow, 254
Pyramids, 230

Q

Quadrant 4, 43
Quarrel of The Roman Merchants, 222, 246
Quartet, 110, 115, 159, 240, 251, 265, 267
Quartet Live, 240, 265
Que Viva Mingus!, 255
Queen, Alvin, 223
Quiet, 122, 224, 247, 254, 259, 269
Quiet City, 122, 224

R

R. N. Bee, 222
Radio, 171, 181, 191, 262
Radio Dream, 262
Radio-active, 239
Rafalides, Christos, 256
Raimondi, Matthew, 215
Rainbow Theatre (music venue), 47, 248, 256, 260, 261, 267, 269, 273
Rainey, Chuck, 26, 218
Rainsville, 243
Randezvous, 266
Randroid, 126, 134, 151, 152, 170, 184, 185, 200
Randy In Brasil, 188, 211, 221, 257
Rankin, Kenny, 266
Raph, Alan, 235
Ratliff, Ben (writer), 196, 197, 210
Rattletrap, 168, 220
Ray Simpson, 253
RCA Victor 80th Anniversary, 255
Reach Out!, 231, 249, 260, 270
Really In For It, 184, 222
Rebento, 179, 221
Record Label, Blue Note, 4, 18, 24, 25, 38, 41, 104, 182, 185, 204, 209, 218, 225, 226, 228, 242, 244, 251, 254, 255, 258, 267
Record Label, Capitol Records, 24, 25
Record Label, CBS, 52
Record Label, Columbia, 22, 41, 51, 52, 53, 88, 149
Record Label, Jazz Door, 86, 135, 216, 217, 218, 225, 226, 234, 236, 240
Record Label, Koch Jazz, 207, 218
Record Label, Liberty Records, 24
Record Label, Polydor, 24
Record Label, Verve, 53, 104, 144, 209, 224, 225, 245, 253
Record Label, Warner Bros., 52, 80, 82, 85, 86, 208, 231, 234, 235, 236, 237, 243
Record Label, Warwick, 52
Record Plant (recording studio), 34
Recordame, 90, 233
Red Baron, 43, 48, 229
Red Beans, 249, 261, 270
Red Hot & Blue, 250, 262, 271
Redbone, Martha, 256

Rediscovery On GRP, 256, 273
Redman, Dewey, 88
Redman, Joshua, 159
Reed, Lou, 247, 251, 259, 263, 269, 272
Reedus, Tony, 266
Reeves, Dianne, 240
Reflected Journey, 255, 266, 273
Reflection, 258
Reflections, 230
Refugees, 247, 259, 269
Regrets, 239
Reichenbach, William Frank, 215, 234, 236, 237, 238
Reid, Rufus, 145
Reiman, Poul, 256
Rekooperation, 253
Remember, 103, 258
Remember The Sound Homage To Michael Brecker, 258
Remembering, 253, 258, 265, 272
Remembering North, 253, 265, 272
Remembering You, 258
Remote, 252, 264, 272
Renaissance Man, 148, 201, 224
Renderers Of Spirit, 254, 266, 273
Rendezvous, 252, 264, 267, 272
Rendezvous In New York, 267
Rendezvous In New York (10-DVD), 267
Renold, Fritz, 255
Representing The Mambo, 264
Reprise, 100, 236
Restless, 265
Return Of The Brecker Brothers, 130, 172, 201, 214, 253, 265, 272
Return to Forever (band), 58, 73, 86
Reunion, 124, 173, 181, 201, 205, 222, 240, 256, 258, 267, 273
Revelation, 249, 260, 270
Reverence, 267
Reza, 84, 234, 235, 236, 237
Reza / Giant Steps, 237
Rhodes electric piano (instrument), 50, 70, 72, 126, 257, 266
Rhodes, Rick, 266
Rhythm & Blues (music genre), 18, 24, 29, 49, 53, 58, 61, 118, 129, 131, 142, 145, 169, 186, 187, 193, 199
Rhythm Machine, 249
Rhythmstick, 252
Rhythmsticks, 244, 254, 266, 273
Ribeiro, Edu, 221
Ribeiro, Rubinho, 178, 221
Rich, Buddy, 32
Richmond, 114, 161, 232
Richmond, Danny, 232
Rideout, Rex, 255
Riel, Alex, 266
Ries, Tim, 254
Right Back, 228
Right On, 40
Right On Y'all, 228
Right Track (studios), 154, 224, 225
Riley, Doug, 66, 213, 215, 217
Riley, Jim, 240
Riley, John, 242, 243
Ringo The 4th, 249, 260, 270
Rio De Janeiro, Brazil, 116, 137, 138, 177, 252

296

Rise And Fall, 37, 228
Risenhoover, Max, 123, 125, 214
Ritenour, Lee, 179, 238
Rituals, 252, 265, 272
Rivera, Scarlet, 249, 261, 270
Rivers, Sam, 35, 207
Roadhouse Symphony, 251
Robert, George, 258
Roberta, 210, 254
Robertson, Robbie, 16
Robinson, John, 238
Robinson, Scott, 242
Rock (music genre), 11, 18, 20, 21, 22, 23, 24, 25, 26, 27, 28, 30, 33, 35, 36, 38, 39, 40, 42, 44, 45, 47, 51, 52, 57, 63, 64, 67, 75, 77, 81, 87, 99, 110, 119, 120, 122, 123, 127, 131, 138, 167, 168, 172, 184, 189, 195, 196, 197, 199
Rock Away, 251
Rockberger, Oli, 182, 183, 185, 222
Rockit, 151
Rocks, 57, 66, 76, 166, 212, 215, 216, 217, 220, 232
Rodby, Steve, 154, 224, 225
Rodrigo (composer), 230
Rogers, Adam, 136, 137, 139, 160, 163, 164, 165, 166, 182, 183, 184, 185, 219, 220, 222, 225
Rogers, Barry, 19, 28, 30, 31, 35, 66, 213, 215, 227, 228, 234, 242
Rogers, D. J., 69, 215
Rogers, Jerome, 234
Rojo Y Negro, 243
Roker, Mickey, 26, 218, 226, 228
Roland (instrument manufacturer), 154, 248
Rollins, Sonny, 150
Romance, 240, 258, 264, 265, 266
Romance With You, 264
Rome Italy, 167
Romeo & Juliet, 248
Roney, Antoine, 244
Roney, Wallace, 266
Roppongi, 127, 214
Rosand, Aaron, 215
Rosenberg, John, 240, 241
Rosenberg, Roger, 225, 237, 239, 241, 242, 243
Rosenblatt, Joel, 124
Rosie, 248, 260, 270
Ross, Diana, 191, 251, 262, 263, 271, 272
Ross, Lucius, 50
Ross, Margaret, 238
Rouge, 250, 262, 271
Round Midnight, 181, 221
Round the Horn, 246
Rovatti, Ada, 166, 181, 182, 200, 220, 222, 256, 257
Rubalcaba, Gonzalo, 267
Rubber Band, 248, 249, 260, 270
Rubin, Alan, 66, 213, 215, 235, 238
Run For Your Life, 243
Rundgren, Todd, 55, 247, 259, 269
Rush Hour, 250
Russel Morris, 248, 259, 269

S

Sabal-Lecco, Armand, 123, 124, 132, 214
Sadownick, Daniel, 162, 225
Safari, 96, 101, 239, 240

Saint & Stephanie, 250, 262, 271
Saints & Sinners, 247
Saisse, Philippe, 244
Salas, Oscar, 234
Salles, Felipe, 258
Salomonsen, Sanne, 255, 266, 273
Saltzman, Larry, 214
Salvatore, Sergio, 253, 265, 266, 272
Samba de Bamba, 218
Sambop, 178, 221
Sample, Joseph Leslie, 72
Samuels, Dave, 145, 231
San Francisco, 54
San Francisco CA, 54
Sanborn, David William, 27, 58, 59, 62, 63, 64, 65, 70, 74, 78, 92, 114, 125, 137, 138, 161, 164, 165, 168, 182, 184, 192, 199, 212, 213, 214, 215, 217, 219, 220, 222, 230, 248, 249, 253, 254, 256, 259, 261, 263, 264, 267, 269, 271
Sanchez, Antonio, 161, 225
Sanchis, Mauri, 258
Sanders, Pharoah, 105
Sandke, Randy, 16, 207, 265
Sandoval, Arturo, 244, 266
Sandy, 66, 215, 253, 265, 272
Santamaria, Mongo, 250, 262, 271
Satoh, Masahiko, 250
Satten, Steve, 248, 259, 269
Saturday Night Live (TV show), 75, 123
Saulsby, Manon, 234
Savannah the Serene, 229
Save The Water, 228
Sax In The City, 256
Say What You Mean, 265
Say You Love Me, 251
Scaggs, Boz, 51
Scale (of music), 77, 144
Scampi Fritti, 253, 265, 272
Scarlet Fever, 249, 261, 270
Scenes From My Life, 266
Schaefer, Paul, 213, 215
Schaffer, Jim (writer), 39, 207
Schalk, Wolfgang, 266
Scheer, August-Wilhelm, 246
Schlitz, Don, 262
Schoen, Jeff, 213, 215
Schoenberg, Loren, 252
School 66 (Summer Big Band Camp), 259
Schuller, Gunther (composer), 180
Schulz, Ricky (music executive), 105
Schuur, Diane, 179
Schwarzberg, Allen, 213, 215
Schwimmer, Peter, 240
Science
    Featuring Tony Verderosa, 253, 265, 272
Scissors Cut, 262
Scofield, John, 45, 47, 110, 114, 117, 145, 151, 162, 183, 202, 229, 230, 244, 252, 254
Score, 5, 23, 24, 26, 27, 35, 187, 188, 207, 218, 247, 259, 269
Scott, Shirley, 41
Scott, Tom, 234, 245, 252, 253, 257
Scratch, 218, 250
Scratch My Back, 250
Scriabin, 111, 223
Scrunch, 131, 215
Scylla, 163, 225

297

Sea Glass, 107, 223
Sea of Tranquillity, 229
Sea of Wilderness, 244
Searching for the Right Door, 43
Season Of Glass, 263
Seattle WA, 19, 114, 153, 220
Sebastian, Ricky, 256
Sebesky, Don, 247, 248, 259, 269
Second Album, 247, 259, 269
Second Coming, 247
Second Great Quintet, 106
Second Phase, 44, 229
Secret Dreams And Forbidden Fire, 264
Secret Heart, 131, 215, 275
Secret Story, 160
Secrets, 117, 118, 219
Seducao, 264
Seduction, 262
Seifert, Zbigniew, 249, 260, 270
Seiter, Chris, 239
Select Live Saxophone Workshop, 264
Self Portrait, 96, 100, 239, 240
Self, Jim, 238
Senang, 266
Seneri, Vince, 257
Sentimental, 99, 101, 240
September Boy, 246
Septet, 255
Seraphic Light, 257
Serenade, 242, 262
Serious Business, 252, 264, 272
Serve Or Suffer, 257
Sessions, Tim, 254
Seven A.M. Special, 151, 219, 245
Seven Days, 155, 225
Shabazz, 5, 47, 229, 248, 259, 269
Shabazz (Recorded Live In Europe), 229, 248, 259, 269
Shades, 247, 256
Shadow Of Urbano, 264
Shadow Waltz, 231
Shadows And Light, 6, 79, 233, 262
Shadows Of Forgotten Love, 231
Shanachie, 236
Shanghigh, 165, 171, 220, 221, 222
Sharing Your Love, 251
She Loves To Hear The Music, 261
She Moves On, 116
Shearing, George, 41, 202
Shenandoah, 105
Shepp, Archie, 21
Sheppard, Andy, 252
Sheppard, Bob, 225
Shider, Garry, 50, 229, 231, 234
Shider, Kevin, 234
Shider, Linda, 234
Shine, 134, 252, 262, 265, 272
Shine The Light Of Love, 262
Shiver In The Night, 249, 260, 270
Short Trip To Space, 249, 260, 270
Shorter, Wayne, 13, 31, 35, 79, 81, 113, 156, 159, 160, 182, 195, 230, 234
Sidran, Ben, 248, 249, 253, 260, 261, 262, 269, 271
Siegel, Janis, 251
Sigismonti, Henry, 238
Silberstein, James, 256
Silhouettes, 245

Silva, Dawn, 234
Silva, Robertinho, 221
Silveira, Ricardo, 177, 178, 221
Silver, Horace, 5, 22, 28, 38, 41, 52, 114, 115, 124, 189, 198, 226, 228, 247, 254, 259, 266, 269, 273
Silverado, 150, 219, 245
Simon, Calvin, 50, 231
Simon, Carly, 250, 251, 253, 259, 261, 262, 263, 264, 265, 270, 271
Simon, Harris, 261, 262
Simon, John, 247, 253, 265, 272
Simon, Paul, 6, 31, 58, 116, 124, 132, 137, 176, 250, 251, 252, 259, 260, 262, 265, 271, 272
Simpson, Ray, 253
Sinatra, Frank, 13, 41, 192, 238, 251, 263, 272
Sinbad, 248, 260, 270
Sipiagin, Alex, 161, 163, 225
Six Persimmons, 91, 233
Sketchbook, 265
Sketches, 253
Sketches Of Miles
    Arrangements For Chamber Players And Jazz Soloists, 253
Skin Dive, 263
Skintalk, 256
Sklar, Leland, 42
Sky Train, 248
Skylark, 144, 181, 221, 224
Skyline Studio (recording studio), 141, 242
Skyward Bound, 93, 237, 238
Slang, 131, 136, 163, 215, 216, 217, 275
Sleep Warm
    The Jazz Slumber Project, 254
Sleeping Gypsy, 260
Sleepless Nights, 262
Slick Stuff, 63, 213, 215, 274
Slings and Arrows, 139, 224
Slo Funk, 239
Slow Fruit, 257
Sly, 62
Small World, 28
Small, Carl, 234
Smappies II, 266
Smile, 248, 260, 270
Smith, Bob, 238, 239, 240, 241
Smith, Michael, 251, 263, 264, 272
Smith, Steve, 100, 101, 168, 220, 240
Snitzer, Andy, 214
Snow, Phoebe, 249, 251, 252, 260, 261, 270
So Damn Happy, 256
So Far So Close, 113, 252, 264, 272
So Near, So Far, 104
So What, 141, 156, 245
So What/ Impressions, 245
Softly As In A Morning Sunrise, 223
Softly Spoken, 243
Softly..., 266
SoHo Sole, 150, 219, 245
Solarization, 44, 229
Solid, 252, 263
Solid Ground, 252
Soloff, Lew, 227, 228, 235, 238, 241
Some Other Time - A Tribute To Chet Baker, 252, 264, 272
Some Skunk Funk, 7, 46, 53, 56, 67, 126, 129, 136, 138, 169, 170, 171, 181, 185, 189, 211, 212,

213, 215, 216, 217, 220, 221, 222, 230, 257, 267, 273, 274
Some Skunk Funk [DVD], 257, 267, 273
Someday My Prince Will Come, 157, 181, 221
Something I Said, 100, 240
Something Like A Bird, 250, 262, 271
Something Real, 252
Something/Anything?, 247, 259, 269
Sometimes I See, 155, 225
Song For Barry, 129, 136, 172, 214, 216, 217, 221, 222
Song For Micaela, 256
Song Is You And Me, 250, 262, 271
Song Of The Sun, 265
Song to Seth, 89, 233
Songbook, 255, 256, 257, 266, 273
Songman, 255
Songs For The New Depression, 248, 260, 270
Songs From The Night Before, 254
Sonny, 41, 150, 234, 242
Sonny, Little, 234
Sony Music Corporation, 54, 215, 226, 227
Sophie, 258
Sophisticated Lady, 236, 237, 254, 265
Sorcerer, 156, 241, 245
Sorcery, 46, 230
Sorriso Novo, 263
Sorrow Is Not Forever ... But Love Is, 263
Sotti, Fabrizio, 255
Sotto Voce, 159, 245
Soul (music genre), 49, 72, 74, 78, 98, 169, 196
Soul Blueprint, 258
Soul Bop, 167, 169, 220
Soul Eyes, 90, 233
Soul Intro / The Chicken, 234, 235, 236, 237
Soul Of A Man
 Al Kooper Live, 254
Soul Searching, 248, 260, 270
Soulbop Band Live, 7, 167, 188, 210, 220, 256
Soulmates, 257, 267, 273
Sound Off, 147, 224
Sounds ... And Stuff Like That!!, 261
Soundtrack, 249, 250, 251, 252, 261, 262, 263, 264, 266, 270, 271, 272
Source, 235, 251
South Africa, 116, 136, 137
Southampton UK, 134, 135
Sozinho (Alone), 214, 217
Space, 49, 249, 260, 270
Spain, 6, 128, 209, 216, 253, 265, 272, 274
Spanish Fever, 249
Spanish Moss, 229
Speak with A Single Voice, 249, 261, 270
Spectrum, 5, 42, 43, 47, 207, 240, 252
Spherical, 127, 129, 136, 214, 216, 217
Spidit, 231
Spinozza, David, 214, 215, 227, 228, 244, 249, 261, 271
Spiral Steps, 248, 260, 270
Spirit, 250, 254, 256, 266, 267, 273
Spirit Of Deodato, 250
Spirits, 20, 150, 243, 245, 246, 266, 367
Splash, 102, 196, 218, 264
Sponge, 53, 57, 67, 68, 171, 206, 212, 213, 215, 216, 217, 221, 222, 274
Spot That Man, 134, 242, 243
Spreadeagle, 73, 214, 215

Springsteen, Bruce, 51, 248, 259, 269
Spy, 250, 262, 271
Spyro Gyra (band), 55, 87, 97, 177, 250, 254, 262, 263, 271
Square Peg, Round Hole, 257
Squids, 65, 67, 68, 213, 215, 216
Squish, 70, 214, 215, 216, 217, 274
Stamm, Marvin, 49, 56, 238, 239, 240, 241, 242, 243
Standards, 253, 255, 256, 265, 266, 267, 273
Standards And Other Songs, 253
Standards My Way, 265
Standing Tall, 71
Stanley Clarke, 244
Star, 123, 223, 229, 247, 248, 249, 252, 253, 259, 260, 265, 269, 272
Star Child (Mothership Connection), 229
Star Climber, 252
Star Eyes, 223
Star People, 123
Star Wars (film), 249
Star Wars And Other Galactic Funk, 249
Stardust, 266
Starfish and the Moon, 137, 151
Starlight, 255
Starr, Ringo, 248, 249, 260, 270
Starring Charie Allen, 259
Start Here, 171
Starting Now, 253, 265, 272
Staton, Candi, 250, 260, 262, 271
Stay With Me, 118, 264
Steely Dan (band), 32, 87, 96, 117, 162, 251, 263, 272
Steig, Jeremy, 33
Stein, Mitch, 182, 184, 222
Steiner, Nyle (inventor), 94, 95
Steinway (instrument manufacturer), 141
Stellina, 183, 222
Step By Step, 233, 262
Stepdance, 252
Steps Ahead, 6, 11, 32, 59, 61, 77, 87, 92, 94, 95, 98, 99, 100, 101, 106, 107, 117, 123, 125, 168, 173, 189, 195, 196, 198, 207, 208, 237, 238, 239, 240, 263, 264, 268
Sterling, Don, 234
Stern, Leni, 267
Stern, Mike, 59, 86, 100, 101, 106, 107, 108, 111, 112, 113, 117, 123, 125, 126, 127, 128, 129, 137, 149, 151, 160, 173, 181, 182, 184, 185, 192, 214, 216, 217, 222, 223, 226, 240, 253, 258, 264, 265, 266, 267
Steve Turre, 242, 254
Stewart, William, 145, 147, 148, 224, 242
Stigers, Curtis, 256
Still Crazy After All These Years, 31, 176, 260
Still Life (Talking), 118
Still The One, 265
Stone Free, 238
Stop, Look And Listen, 256, 267, 273
Stormy Weather, 238
Straight No Chaser, 244
Straight To The Heart, 263
Strange Vibes, 228
Stratus, 43, 123, 160
Strauch, Oliver, 246, 258
Strayer, Kerry, 255
Streeange, 165, 220

299

Street Dreams, 252
Street Life, 71
Street Of Dreams, 262
Street Smart, 252
Streisand, Barbra, 56
String Theory, 257, 268, 273
Struggle Buggy, 249, 260, 270
Stryker, Dave, 253
Stuart, Hamish, 49, 87
Stubenhaus, Neil, 238
Stuff, 63, 88, 213, 215, 231, 261, 274
Stuff Like That, 261
Stump, Paul (writer), 28, 207
Sumler, Diane, 213, 215
Summer In Central Park, 228
Summerhill, 252
Summers, Andy, 256
Summit, 209, 221, 222, 245, 246, 257, 267
Sumo, 99, 101, 240
Sunshine Clean, 228
Sunshine On Your Back Porch
  A Celebration Of Gennett Records, 257
Super Friends, 251, 263, 272
Super Nova, 266
Supergroovalisticprosifunkstication, 229
Supernatural, 24
Suspone, 111, 223
Sussman, Richard, 219, 258
Sutton, Ann E., 228
Swallow, Steve, 20, 106, 110
Swan Feathers, 258
Swedish Jazz
  Live from The Swedish Jazz Celebration 2007, 257
Sweet Dreams, 247, 259, 269
Sweet Dreams And Quiet Desires / The Second Album, 247, 259, 269
Sweet Soul, 253
Sweethearts
  Oceanlight Records Multi-Artist Pop Hits CD, Vol. 1, 258
Swept Away, 251, 263, 272
Swing Swing Swing, 257
Swinging Hour In New York, 255
Swish, 262
Switzerland, 75
Sylvan, Paul, 247, 259, 269
Symphony-Bantu, 265
Syms, Sylvia, 261
Synthesiser, 39, 47, 69, 71, 72, 81, 94, 95, 96, 97, 98, 99, 103, 108, 112, 116, 120, 125, 140, 154, 159, 175, 177, 178, 196, 204
Syzygy, 107, 223, 225

T

Tabackin, Lew, 251, 254
Tabula Rasa, 66, 213, 215, 217
Tailgunner, 249
Tailor Made, 252
Takahashi, Mariko, 265
Take a Walk, 92, 235
Take It Off, 251, 263, 271
Take Me To Baltimore, 248, 260, 269
Take That, 266
Taking Off, 59, 248, 259, 269
Tales, 7, 132, 139, 211, 224, 266

Tales From The Hudson, 139, 211, 224, 266
Talking Book, 59
Talking to Myself, 112, 223
Tank, John, 232
Taurian Matador, 43, 48, 229
Tavaglione, Steve, 204
Taylor, Chris, 220
Taylor, David Earl, 66, 213, 215, 219, 234, 238, 239, 240, 241, 242, 243
Taylor, James, 42, 59, 154, 224, 247, 251, 252, 259, 260, 263, 264, 265, 266, 267, 269, 272
Taylor, Kate, 249, 261, 271
Taylor, Martin, 255
Teach Me Tonight, 238
Tease Me, 169, 220
Techno Pop, 240
Tee, 70, 88, 192, 214, 215, 216, 217, 233, 249, 250, 261, 271
Tee Bag, 88, 233
Tee, Richard, 88, 192, 249, 250, 261, 271
Teepe, Joris, 256
Television, 54, 253
Tenderness, 265
Tenority, 254
Tentets, 263
Tenth Pinn, 48, 229
Teo, 256
Terrason, Jacky, 266
Terry, Clark, 15, 16, 18
Texas, 20, 71, 161, 201, 210
Thank You, Gerry! Our Tribute To Gerry Mulligan, 255
Thanks A Million, 254
Tharp, Ammon, 255
That Other Mile, 259
The 12th Man, 246
The Ada Strut, 151, 219, 245
The Aleph, 91, 235
The Amulet, 253
The Art Of Jazz, 254, 256, 273
  Saxophone [Slimline], 256
The Art Of Jazz Saxophone
  Impressions, 254, 273
The Art Of Tea, 260
The Atlantic Family Live In Montreux, 261
The Avatar Sessions, 258
The Bear Walks, 264
The Belly Dancer, 226
The Best of Everything, 238
The Big Picture, 251, 264, 272
The Birthday Concert, 6, 82, 208, 234, 235, 265
The Blue Man, 58, 249, 261, 271
The Blues, 122, 145, 248, 254, 266, 273
The Body Acoustic, 257
The Boss, 262
The Bottom Line, 262
The Brecker Bros. Collection, 216
The Brecker Brothers - Live, 217, 253, 265, 272
The Brecker Brothers Band Reunion, 7, 181, 222, 258
The Bridge, 255, 264
The Call, 37, 255
The Camera Never Lies, 252, 264, 272
The Castle Rocks, 166, 220
The Cat And The Hat, 262
The CD Of JB
  Sex Machine & Other Soul Classics, 251, 272

300

The Charlie Calello Serenade, 262
The Chicken, 234, 236, 237
The Clones Of Dr. Frunkenstein, 230, 248, 260, 270
The Complete Arista Albums Collection, 54, 75, 215
The Complete Blue Note Recordings, 209
The Cost Of Living, 223, 226, 242, 267
The Dipshit, 183, 222
The Dry Cleaner from Des Moines, 233
The Dukes, 251
The Earth Wants You, 253
The Elders, 256
The Electric Spanking Of War Babies, 51, 263
The Eternal Triangle, 257
The Fisherman, 166, 220
The Florida Concert, 234, 263
The Foreign Affair, 255
The Forgotten, 255
The Four Sleepers, 239
The Funky Waltz, 39, 228
The Fusion Syndicate, 258
The Gadd Gang, 264
The Geneva Concert [DVD], 257
The Genie, 251, 263, 272
The Gentleman and Hizcaine, 223
The Gift, 231
The Glider, 118, 219
The Guerilla Band, 37, 228, 247, 259, 269
The Gusch, 252
The Gypsy, 77
The Happy Medium, 226
The Hawk, 16
The Herbie Hancock Quartet Live, 240, 265
The Hottest Man in Town, 139, 219
The Immigrant / Godfather, 221
The Impaler, 143, 224
The Infinite McCoys, 247
The Inner Mounting Flame, 42
The Innocent Age, 263
The Jazz Ballad Song Book, 7, 181, 189, 221, 258
The Jazz Cuts, 254, 266, 273
The JazzTimes Superband, 7, 149, 219, 244, 255
The Jeff Lorber Fusion, 258
The Jobim Songbook, 257
The Joy Of Flying, 250, 262, 271
The Lady And Her Music - Live On Broadway, 263
The Lady Wants To Be A Star, 248, 260, 269
The Language Of Life, 265
The Latin Side Of Herbie Hancock, 258
The Lay Of The Land, 256, 267, 273
The Lionel Hampton International Jazz Festival 1997 [DVD], 254
The London Concert, 6, 134, 141, 243, 255, 267, 273
The Lost Album Featuring Watermelo Man, 258, 268, 273
The Main Attraction, 260
The Man With The Horn, 123, 167
The Manhattan Transfer, 248, 249, 259, 269
The Marble Sea, 218
The Maryanne, 29, 227
The Mean Time, 173, 225
The Meaning of the Blues, 224
The More Things Change, 250
The Morning of This Night, 148, 224
The Music Inside, 266
The Mystery Man, 241
The Nearness of You, 154, 225

The New Phil Woods Album, 248
The New Standard, 244, 266, 268
The Night You Were Born, 244
The Nightfly, 251, 263, 271
The Nightwalker, 133, 215
The Nomad Diaries, 257, 267, 273
The Original Rhondels
   The Sound Of Virginia Beach, 255
The Other Side Of Something, 257
The Other Side Of Standards, 255
The Passage - Music For Steel Orchestra, 267
The Path, 249, 257, 261, 270
The Path To Delphi, 257
The Philadelphia Story, 257
The Pleasant Pheasant, 229
The Poet, 157, 158, 245
The Promise, 150, 266
The Public Interest, 247, 259, 269
The Rain, 250, 267
The Rape Of El Morro, 248, 259, 269
The Real Me, 264
The Return of The Brecker Brothers Live in Spain 1992 [DVD], 253, 265, 272
The Reunion, 240
The Rhythm Of The Saints, 6, 116, 124, 252, 265, 272
The Ring, 239
The Runner Up, 258
The Saxophone, 242, 254
The Scene, 22
The Sea Of Dirac, 249, 260, 270
The Search Is Over, 264
The Second Album, 247, 259, 269
The Second Third Man featuring Michael Brecker, 266
The Section, 259
The Show Has Begun, 226
The Sidewinder, 246
The Silencer, 251, 263, 272
The Sky, 254, 256, 266, 267, 273
The Slag, 184, 222
The Sleaze Factor, 115, 138, 219
The Song Is You, 245
The Sorcerer, 156, 241, 245
The Soulful Crooner, 247
The Source, 235
The Spin, 250, 262, 271
The Spinner, 250, 262, 271
The Spirit Within, 256
The Target, 223
The Thing, 231
The Truth
   Heard Live At The Blue Note, 244, 267
The Tunnel, 46, 241
The Two Of Us, 266
The Vamp, 26, 27, 218
The Village, 251, 258, 267
The Virgin and the Gypsy, 215, 232
The Voice Of The Saxophone, 254
The Warriors, 250, 262, 271
The Way I Feel, 241
The Way Up, 4
The Weasel Goes Out to Lunch, 27, 218
The Wiz [Original Soundtrack], 249, 261, 270
Theatre By The Sea, 200, 258
Theme for a Dream, 228
Then I Came 2 My Senses, 220

Theodore, Laura, 254
Thielemans, Toots, 110, 234, 236, 237
Thighs And Whispers, 250, 262, 271
Think (Alternate Take), 259
Think/Something, 259
Thinking of You, 230
Third Stream (music genre), 180
Third World, 252, 264, 272
Thirsty Or Not...Choose Your Flavor, 248, 260, 270
This Is All I Ask, 181, 221
This Is My Life, 253
This Is The Thing, 231
This Moment, 36, 227
This World Upside Down, 255
Thomas, Gary, 150
Thomas, Grady, 50, 229, 231
Thomas, Greg, 234
Thomas, Joe, 249, 260
Thomas, Leon, 247
Thomas, Robert, 234
Thornton, Fonzie, 215
Thornton, Steve, 130, 132, 214
Three Card Molly, 244
Three Little Words, 242
Three Pieces, 242
Three Quartets, 262
Three Shades of Blue, 247
Three Times In Love, 262
Three Views of a Secret, 80, 83
Three Worlds Of Drums, 232
Threesome, 72, 214, 215, 216, 217
Thrifty Man, 115, 219
Thriller, 56, 177
Through Any Window, 264
Through the Window, 246
Ticino, 266
Tico Rico, 249, 261, 270
Tiger In The Rain, 250
Tightrope, 58, 249, 260, 270
Tijuca, 138, 219
Timbuktu, 162, 211, 225
Time In Place, 264
Time Is Of The Essence, 224, 267
Time To Fly, 247
Timeagain, 256
Timeless, 231
Timeline, 147, 224
Times Like These, 264
Times Square, 253
Tin Pan Alley, 144
Ting Chang, 115, 219
Titania (Danish TV Company), 92
Titus, 230
To Chi Ka, 262
To Touch You Again, 249, 261, 271
Toan, Danny, 230
Todd, 55, 247, 259, 269
Toe To Toe, 6, 117, 118, 219, 252, 265, 272
Tofani, David, 234
Together, 101
Tokyo Freddie, 166, 220
Tokyo Japan, 6, 7, 88, 100, 127, 135, 150, 166, 173, 209, 216, 220, 225, 236, 237, 240, 258, 264, 268, 273
Tokyo Live, 150
Tomlinson, Malcolm, 249, 261, 270
Tonight At Noon

Three Or Four Shades Of Love, 256
Tonight Is The Night, 254
Tony Williams, 104, 109, 173, 174, 244, 250, 262, 266, 271
Tony Williams Lifetime (band), 250, 262, 271
Too Late, 256
Tooley, Ron, 230, 236, 237
Torano, Sandy, 66, 215
Toronto Canada, 156, 245
Total Eclipse, 5, 44, 45, 229, 247, 259, 269
Total Happiness (Music from The Bill Cosby Show, Vol. 2), 252
Touch, 90, 137, 160, 170, 233, 238, 249, 261, 264, 271
Touchdown, 250
Tough, 255
Tower of Power (band), 54
Trading Secrets, 117, 118, 219
Traffic, 31
Train Of Thought, 263
Trains, 98, 101, 240
Transatlantic Connection, 257
Transfer Station, 262
Travelogue, 171
Travels, 140, 159, 245, 250, 261, 271
Triangle, 249, 257, 260, 270
Triangle Session, 249, 260, 270
Tribute, 157, 239, 252, 253, 254, 255, 256, 257, 258, 264, 272
Tribute To The Brecker Brothers, 257
Tricycle, 246
Trifan, Danny, 39, 228
Trilogy 1
    Convocation, 227
Trilogy 2
    Wild Bird, 227
Trilogy 3
    Change Up, 227
Tring-A-Ling
    Joanne Brackeen Meets Michael Brecker, 260
Trio (An Improvisation), 237
Troiano, Domenic, 249, 261, 270
Trombipulation, 50, 51, 233, 234, 250, 262, 271
Tropea, John, 43, 235, 248, 249, 260, 261, 269, 270, 271
Trumpets Eleven, 256
Truth Is..., 255
Try Livin It, 169
Try Me, 29, 227
Tumbleweed, 174, 225
Tune of the Unknown Samba, 231
Tune Up, 253, 265, 272
Turn The Music Up!, 262
Turn This Mutha Out, 249, 260, 270
Turner, Tina, 249, 261, 270
Turre, Steve, 242, 254
Turrentine, Stanley, 41, 247
Tutu, 120
Twilight, 57, 212, 215
Twin Tenors, 242, 265
Twins, 6, 85, 86, 236, 237, 255
Twins I & II
    Live In Japan 1982, 237, 255
Two Against Nature, 117, 162
Two Blocks from The Edge, 224, 266
Two For The Road, 58
Two For The Show, 265

Two Ts, 242
Tykocin Poland, 180, 188, 209, 221, 258
Tyler, Bonnie, 264
Tyner, McCoy, 105, 139, 140, 211, 224, 254
Tyrell, Steve, 258, 267

U

Ultrablue, 257
Uncle Bob, 89, 90, 233
Uncovered Heart, 252
Under The Hat, 256
Underground, 137
Underwood, Keith, 219
Unfunky UFO, 229
United, 2, 49, 161, 245, 257
Universal Syncopations, 257
Universal Syncopations II, 257
University of Indiana, 16
UnReel, 256, 267, 273
Unriel, 266
Until The Real Thing Comes Along, 238
Uotila, Jukkis, 251, 252
Upfront, 253
U-Port Hall Tokyo (music venue), 7, 135, 209, 216, 258, 268, 273
Uptown Ed, 77, 215, 232
Urban Contours, 241, 252
Urbanator, 253, 265, 266, 272, 273
Urbanator II, 266, 273
Urbaniak, Michal, 266, 273

V

Valentin, David, 243, 244
Valli, Frankie, 261
Valotte, 263
Vamp, 65, 129, 132, 168, 169, 184, 194, 206
Van Gelder, Rudy (recording engineer), 25, 41, 226
Vandross, Luther, 63, 69, 161, 162, 213, 215, 251, 252, 263, 271
Vanoni, Ornella, 251, 264, 272
Varga, George (writer), 110, 208
Variations on Misery, 238
Vaughan, Sarah, 179
Vazquez, Papo, 266
Verdell, Jackie, 226
Verderosa, Tony, 253, 254, 265, 272
Vernon, Edward, 227
Verve Records (record label), 53, 104, 144, 209, 224, 225, 245, 253
Vicari, Frank, 227, 228
Vick, Harold, 249, 261, 270
Vienna Austria, 15
Village Dawn, 137, 219
Village Gate (jazz club), 25, 30, 35
Village Vanguard (jazz club), 251, 258, 267
Vince Mendoza, 111, 159, 170, 211, 221, 222, 252, 264, 267, 272
Vincent, Pamela, 229
Virginia, 161, 255
Vitous, Miroslav, 15, 95, 257
Vocoder (instrument), 69
Voices, 114, 267
Vollenweider, Andreas, 266
Voudouris, Roger, 262
Voyager, 244, 251, 263, 272

Voyou, 255, 266, 273

W

Waiting For Chet, 231
Waking & Dreaming, 260
Walden, Chris, 266
Walden, Narada Michael, 230, 250, 251, 262, 271
Waldman, Randy, 256, 266, 267, 273
Walk The Dog & Light The Light, 253, 265, 272
Walker, Patti, 234
Walking Away, 249
Walking Man, 247, 259, 269
Walrath, Jack, 232
Walsh, Ed, 238
Wanderlust, 250, 262, 271
Warmer Communications, 250, 261, 270
Warnaar, Brad, 234, 236, 237
Warner Bros. Records (record label), 52, 80, 82, 85, 86, 208, 231, 234, 235, 236, 237, 243
Warriors, 250, 262, 271
Warwick (record label), 52
Warwick, Dionne, 52
Washer, Bill, 235
Washington Jr, Grover, 196, 247, 248, 251, 264, 272
Washington, Dinah, 41
Washington, Jeanette, 234
Washington, Peter, 134, 243
Watanabe, Kazumi, 89, 233, 262, 264
Watanabe, Misato, 266
Watanabe, Sadao, 103, 218, 262
Watch The Time, 261
Water Babies, 243
Watrous, William, 238
Watts, Jeff, 224
Wave Music Volume 3, 255
Wayne Out, 152, 171, 220, 221, 222
We Want Miles, 123
Weather Report (band), 4, 11, 26, 58, 73, 79, 81, 82, 86, 89, 95, 97, 117, 168, 169, 184, 255, 267, 273
Weaver Of Dreams, 134, 141, 242, 252, 264, 272
Weckl, Dave, 102, 182, 185, 218, 222, 253, 264
Wednesday Night Prayer Meeting, 232
Weill, Kurt (composer), 252
Weird Blues, 242
Weiss, Jerry, 22
Welcome To My Dream, 228
Wendroff, Michael, 247, 259, 269
Werner, Kenny, 252, 258
Wesley, Fred, 50, 165, 220, 229, 230, 234, 249, 258, 260, 268, 270, 273
Wess, Frank, 192, 238
West Coast, 54
West Side Story, 266
Whalum, Kirk, 123
What Can a Miracle Do, 213, 215
What is the Answer, 219
What is This Thing Called Love, 242, 243
What It Is, 24, 258, 265, 266
What It Takes, 252
Whatcha Gonna Do For Me?, 248, 259, 269
Wheeler, Kenny, 263
When Can I Kiss You Again?, 175, 225
When It Was, 215
When the Wind Stops, 246

303

White Elephant, 5, 32, 33, 34, 227, 247, 259, 269
White, Chip, 257
White, Lenny, 66, 215, 217, 230, 254, 266, 273
White, Lillias, 235
White, Michael, 266
Whitman, Dave, 213, 215
Whitty, George, 7, 124, 126, 128, 130, 133, 135, 136, 139, 145, 148, 152, 153, 160, 163, 165, 182, 184, 185, 196, 201, 209, 210, 211, 214, 216, 217, 220, 222, 224
Who Knows, 247
Why Do Fools Fall in Love, 233, 251, 263, 271
Wide Angles, 7, 137, 160, 211, 225, 267
Wigged Out, 266
Wilcox, David, 252
Wild Bird, 5, 35, 36, 37, 227, 247, 259, 269
Wild Indian Summer, 254
Wild Unit 2, 265
Wilderness, 244, 266
Wilkins, Jack, 232, 248, 250, 256, 260, 261, 267, 270, 271, 273
Williams, 43, 45, 104, 110, 161, 173, 174, 181, 226, 229, 234, 238, 240, 244, 250, 262, 266, 271
Williams, Andre, 234
Williams, Anthony, 104, 109, 173, 174, 244, 250, 262, 266, 271
Williams, Charles Anthony, 240
Williams, John, 43, 226, 229
Williams, Lawrence Lowell, 238
Williams, Leroy, 230
Williamson, Bruce, 253
Willie T, 141, 224
Willis, Allee, 213, 215
Willis, Dan, 225
Willis, Gary, 149
Wilson, Ernestro, 234
Wilson, Steve, 161, 162, 225
Wind Song, 257
Windjammer, 260
Winds Of Change
    A Musical Fantasy, 250, 262, 271
Wings, 247, 259, 263, 269
Winners, 250, 254, 255, 262, 271
Winter III, John Dawson, 247, 259, 269
Winwood, Steve, 201, 251
Wipe Away The Evil, 226
Wisdom, 31, 227
Wise One, 244
With A Little Help From Our Friends, 257, 267, 273
Without A Song, 242
Without You, 266
Wolf, Thilo, 255
Wolff, Francis (record producer), 24, 226

Woman Of Truth And Future, 230
Wonder, Stevie, 52, 59, 60, 75
Wonderful Music, 262
Woods, Phil, 25, 245, 248
Woodstock, 58, 233
Wooten, Victor, 168
Word Of Mouth, 6, 61, 80, 81, 82, 83, 85, 86, 161, 234, 236, 237, 257, 262
Word Up!, 251, 264, 272
Work It!, 256
Working People, 244
World Of Contemporary Jazz Groups, 253, 272
Worrell, Bernie, 50, 51, 229, 231, 234
Wright, Deborah, 229
Wynne, Phillippe, 234

Y

Yamaha (instrument manufacturer), 95
Yang, 101, 123
Yellin, Peter, 238, 239, 240, 241, 242, 243
Yellow Fever, 250, 262, 271
Yellowjackets, 87, 117
Yes (band), 104, 117, 147, 199
Yin, 40, 101, 123, 228
Yin Yang, 101, 123
Yin-Yang, 230
Yonekura, Toshinori, 266
Yoshida, Minako, 263
Yoshida, Miwa, 265
You Ga (Ta Give It), 69, 214, 215, 274
You Gotta Take a Little Love, 41, 226, 247
You Left Something Behind, 70, 214, 215
Young and Fine, 89, 233
Young And Foolish, 159, 245
Young Hearts Run Free, 260
Young Lions & Old Tigers, 265
Young, George, 34, 192, 227, 228, 238
Your Eyes, 251, 263, 272

Z

Zappa In New York, 231, 270
Zappa, Frank, 61, 189, 202, 231, 270
Zarie, Brigitte, 258
Zawinul, 15, 26, 79, 82, 89, 137, 154
Zawinul, Josef, 15, 26, 79, 89, 137, 154
Zbigniew Seifert, 249, 260, 270
Zjaca, Ratko, 258
Zobler, Erik, 215
Zonjic, Alexander, 264
Zorn, John, 114